Second Edition
VIOLENCE
The Enduring Problem

Alex Alvarez
University of Delaware

Ronet Bachman
Northern Arizona University

SAGE

Los Angeles | London | New Delhi
Singapore | Washington DC

Los Angeles | London | New Delhi
Singapore | Washington DC

FOR INFORMATION:

SAGE Publications, Inc.
2455 Teller Road
Thousand Oaks, California 91320
E-mail: order@sagepub.com

SAGE Publications Ltd.
1 Oliver's Yard
55 City Road
London, EC1Y 1SP
United Kingdom

SAGE Publications India Pvt. Ltd.
B 1/I 1 Mohan Cooperative Industrial Area
Mathura Road, New Delhi 110 044
India

SAGE Publications Asia-Pacific Pte. Ltd.
3 Church Street
#10-04 Samsung Hub
Singapore 049483

Acquisitions Editor: Jerry Westby
Editorial Assistant: MaryAnn Vail
Production Editor: Brittany Bauhaus
Copy Editor: Karin Rathert
Typesetter: Hurix Systems Pvt.Ltd
Proofreader: Bonnie Moore
Indexer: Terri Corry
Cover Designer: Scott Van Atta
Marketing Manager: Terra Schultz

Copyright © 2014 by SAGE Publications, Inc.

Printed in the United States of America

Library of Congress Cataloging-in-Publication Data

Alvarez, Alex.
Violence : the enduring problem / Alex Alverez, Ronet Bachman. — Second edition.

pages cm
Includes bibliographical references and index.

ISBN 978-1-4833-0030-6 (pbk. : alk. paper) — ISBN 978-1-4833-1270-5 (web pdf) — ISBN 978-1-4833-2399-2 (epub)

1. Violence—United States. 2. Violent crimes—United States. 3. Violence. 4. Aggressiveness. 5. Genocide.

I. Bachman, Ronet. II. Title.
HN90.V5A58 2013
303.60973—dc23   2013031333

This book is printed on acid-free paper.

13 14 15 16 17 10 9 8 7 6 5 4 3 2 1

Contents

Preface

The Second Edition of *Violence: The Enduring Problem* refines our attempt to write a broad interdisciplinary book that analyzes the patterns and correlates of interpersonal and collective violence using the most contemporary research, theories, and cases. In this, we believe that we have succeeded in creating a book that should help you make better sense of the nature and dynamics of a variety of different, yet connected, forms of violence. Through the use of a wide range of recent and historical sources, we explore a number of different types of individual and collective violence that includes homicide, assault, rape, domestic violence, robberies, genocide, riots, lynching, and terrorism among others. We were compelled to write this book primarily because violence remains one of the most pressing issues facing our nation and our world. In fact, at the time of this writing, the mass killing at Newtown, CT occurred, followed by the bombing at the Boston Marathon as we were getting the manuscript ready for press. These and incidents like it instill fear and distrust. In fact, the fear of violence consistently ranks as one of the most important issues facing American society, according to many public opinion polls. Unfortunately, the social and political debates on violence are all too often based on polemics, misinformation, emotion, and stereotypes. It is our hope that this book provides more of an empirically based and rational counterpoint to the discourse on violence.

This book differs from many of the other books on violence in a number of important regards. Our approach is interdisciplinary, whereas many other texts tend to approach the issue from the viewpoint of a specific discipline. We firmly believe that studying violence from the perspective of only one discipline will result in an incomplete understanding of the phenomenon. Human behavior is rarely explained satisfactorily through reference to the set of explanations offered by any one academic discipline such as criminology, psychology, or sociology. Instead, the answers to how and why humans behave as they do must rely on multiple explanations from a range of perspectives. We recognize that behavior is influenced biologically, psychologically, socially, historically, and politically, and this interdisciplinary vision has been our approach in this volume.

Violence: The Enduring Problem is also unique in that one of the primary themes of this book is that all violence is connected. While violence is often seen as consisting of discrete acts that are independent and separate from each other, the guiding premise of this book is that all violence is connected by a web of actions and behaviors, ideas, perceptions, and justifications that are explored throughout the different chapters. While the individual dynamics of specific violent behavior may vary somewhat, there are a number of threads that tie all violence together. By focusing on both interpersonal and group forms of violence, we hope we have been able to illustrate a number of these themes and linkages. This brings up another important point: our book does not solely focus on individual acts of violence, but instead incorporates chapters on both individual and collective forms of violent behavior. Because most books on violence tend to focus on either one or the other, a distinctive contribution of this book is that we provide the reader with information and discussions about both categories of violence.

To assist the reader, we have scattered various tables, charts, photos, and other visual aids throughout the chapters to help make sense of the information being presented. Additionally, we have provided a number of "In Focus" boxes that let the reader explore a number of issues in greater detail than the main narratives of the chapters allow. Each chapter also ends with a listing of key terms and ideas, as well as some discussion exercises that can guide you in exploring some of the points raised in the chapters further. We hope you find these pedagogical tools interesting and helpful.

This book does not provide all the answers to the age-old problem of violence, and we are not so naïve as to believe that this volume will change the world. We do, however, hope that it contributes to a better understanding of how and why we human beings so often engage in destructive and harmful behavior. If this better understanding contributes in some small way to making our world a little safer through greater self-awareness, more restraint, and more rational and empirically grounded policies and actions, then our purpose will have been achieved.

Acknowledgments

I would like to first begin by thanking my coauthor and long-standing friend, Ronet Bachman. Not only is she an excellent scholar and teacher, but more importantly I have found her to simply be a wonderful human being. I feel very lucky to have her as my dear friend. I also have a number of great colleagues who have given me their friendship, insight, and advice over the years and I wish to recognize a few of them. Thanks to Mike Costelloe and Rob Schehr for the coffee and conversation. A very special thanks to my riding buddies, Adam Kroger, Chris Hull, and especially Mark Sogge. Your rides keep me sane!

To my wife and partner, Donna, I wish to extend my deep and eternal gratitude. I honestly believe that she has helped me to become a better person. She is an inspiration and a joy. Last, I wish to acknowledge the importance of my children to my work. Ingrid, Joseph, and Astrid, you inspire me to help make this world a bit better, and you challenge me to be truer to my beliefs and ideals.

—Alex Alvarez

Of course, I first want to thank my extraordinary coauthor and dear friend, Alex. He is a consummate scholar who brings humanism to all of his projects, including this book—his devotion to eradicating hate in the world is truly an inspiration.

My other kindred spirits have also been responsible for me staying sane when attempting to juggle far too many balls: Peggy Plass, Dianne Carmody, Barbara Wauchope, Gerri King, and Michelle Meloy. You are the greatest friends in the world! I also have great colleagues who I am honored to claim as friends, and who provide both personal counsel and sage professional advice. And special thanks to Erin Kerrison, graduate assistant extraordinaire, who has become a true collaborator and dear friend.

Of course, nothing would be meaningful without the love and support of my family. To my mother, Jan Vermilyea, who has remained a true prizefighter in the face of far too many health adversities. To my father, Ronald Bachman, for his critical eye in all matters of life. To my son, John, who brings me joy and love far beyond my wildest dreams. And finally, I want to thank my husband, Raymond Paternoster, who has been my island in the storm, my searchlight in the fog, and every other cliché you can think of. Nothing I do would be possible without his support on the home front, or meaningful without his love in my life.

—Ronet Bachman

Last but not least, this book could not have been written without a great deal of personal and professional support, for which we are both profoundly grateful. We first wish to thank Jerry Westby, our talented editor at Sage, for his hard work and support on our behalf. Special thanks also to MaryAnn Vail and Brittany Bauhaus for their assistance at various stages of this project and to Karin Rather, for her meticulous editorial assistance.

We also want to thank the reviewers for their helpful comments and suggestions. Their time and effort has helped make this a better book. Thank you. Reviewers for the 1st Edition include:

Derral Cheatwood, *University of Texas, San Antonio*
John Collins, *Montclair State University*
Randall Collins, *University of Pennsylvania*
John E. Conklin, *Tufts University*
Erin Conley, *University of Illinois, Chicago*
Sue Cote, *California State University, Sacramento*
Rhonda Dobbs, *University of Texas, Arlington*
Michelle Emerson, *Kennesaw State University*
Carol Gregory, *Kent State University*
Cheryl Holmes, *Indiana University, Bloomington*
Christos Kyrou, *American University*
Ellen C. Lemley, *Arkansas State University*
Cheng-Hsien Lin, *Texas A&M University, Kingsville*
Daniel Lockwood, *Savannah State University*
Kenneth Mentor, *The University of North Carolina at Pembroke*
Mark Schuering, *Quincy University*
Courtney Waid, *Florida A&M University*

Reviewers for the 2nd Edition include:
Minna Cirino, *Shenandoah University*
Sue Escobar, *California State University, Sacramento*
Erin Heil, *Southern Illinois University, Edwardsville*
Drew Humphries, *Rutgers University, Camden*
Christopher Mullins, *Southern Illinois University, Carbondale*
Tracy Tolbert, *California State University, Long Beach*
Courtney Waid-Lindberg, *North Dakota State University*

As American as Apple Pie

Violence and disorder constitute the primal problem of American history, the dark reverse of the coin of freedom and abundance.

—David T. Courtwright[1]

Violence has accompanied virtually every stage and aspect of our national existence.

—Richard Maxwell Brown[2]

Every society is adept at looking past its own forms of violence, and reserving its outrage for the violence of others.

—Inga Clendinnen[3]

• Late in November 1864, a large force of cavalry militia led by Colonel John Chivington left Denver, Colorado, and early on the morning of November 29 ended up on the banks of Sand Creek where a large party of American Indians, mostly Cheyenne, were camped. They were flying a flag of truce in the belief that they were under the protection of the Colorado authorities.[4] With no warning or call for surrender, Chivington's soldiers attacked and killed around 130 Indians, many of them women and children. No prisoners were taken and many of the victims were mutilated after death. Explaining his practice of killing everybody, including children, Chivington reportedly asserted that "his policy was to kill and scalp all little and big; that nits made lice."[5]

- April 23, 1899, was a Sunday afternoon, which allowed more than 2,000 white Southerners to gather for the lynching of Sam Hose near the town of Newman, Georgia. Sam, an African American, had killed his employer during an argument. According to many accounts, he had acted in self-defense since his boss had pulled a gun and threatened to shoot him, but the fact that he was an African American who had killed a white man made that justification irrelevant. On that fateful Sunday, Sam Hose was stripped, mutilated with knives, soaked in oil, and then burned alive while the crowd participated and watched. Reportedly, his only words were, "Oh, my God! Oh, Jesus" as he was burning. The onlookers fought over pieces of his burned body to take home as souvenirs.[6]

- On March 1, 1989, a 17-year-old girl living in Glen Ridge, New Jersey—a relatively affluent suburb—went to play basketball after school. To someone who didn't know her well, she might appear almost normal, an outgoing teenager who loved sports. In reality, however, she was mentally retarded and very susceptible to suggestion and manipulation. At the park, a large group of popular male high school athletes enticed the young woman into the basement of one of their homes where they brutally raped her. Thirteen star athletes were present, and four were later convicted of raping the young girl with sticks and a baseball bat.[7]

- In February of 2008, Barbara Sheehan shot her husband, Raymond Sheehan, 11 times with two guns. Barbara claimed in trial that it was in self-defense after Raymond had threatened her with a loaded semiautomatic pistol. Their children testified that Barbara had suffered years of abuse. Barbara claimed that Raymond, who was a former police sergeant, told her he would kill her and be able to cover it up because of his investigation skills. After a heated argument, Barbara described how she was trying to flee their home with a gun when Raymond tried to stop her with his gun. She then fired five times. After he fell to the ground and dropped his gun shouting, "I'm going to kill you," she picked up his pistol and fired 6 more times.[8]

- On April 16, 2007, Cho Seung-Hui killed 32 students, faculty, and staff and left about 30 others injured on the campus of Virginia Tech in Blacksburg, Virginia. Cho was armed with two legally purchased semiautomatic handguns and a vest full of ammunition. As the police were closing in on the scene, he killed himself. This shooting rampage was the deadliest in U.S. history. Cho was described as a loner who was bullied in high school and never spoke to anyone, not even in classes when he was called upon to do so. In a college English course, his writings were so violent and disturbing that they prompted a professor to contact the campus police and university counseling services.[9] He sent an anger-filled video to NBC News explaining his actions and blaming others for the perceived wrongs that drove him to the mass killing.[10]

- During the midnight movie premiere of a Batman film on a Friday night in July of 2012 in Aurora, Colorado, James Holmes, 24, walked into the theater through an exit door. He was dressed head to toe in "ballistic gear" and a gas mask. After releasing a smoke device in the aisles, he began to shoot, killing 12 and wounding another 58. In the previous 60 days, he had legally purchased four guns at local gun shops. Holmes was a former PhD student and an honors graduate in neuroscience from the University of California, Riverside.[11]

Are these incidents of violence related? Was the murder of Sam Hose over 100 years ago in any way related to the mass killings that occurred at Virginia Tech or at the movie theater in Aurora? While each of these incidents is separated by time, space, circumstance, number of participants, and lethality, they are all in fact linked and part of the same continuum of violent behavior. We often tend to see **violence** as consisting of discrete acts that are separate from each other, as if each violent incident had occurred in a vacuum. But that is not the case. All violence is connected by a web of actions and behaviors, ideas, perceptions, and justifications. While the individual dynamics of specific violent behavior may vary somewhat, violent acts share a number of essential characteristics that bind them together into what is sometimes called the **unity of human aggression**.[12]

One of the primary themes of this book is that all violence is connected. There are a number of commonalities that link the various types of violence we discuss in this book. We find, for example, that violence—regardless of the form it takes—is usually perpetrated for the same kinds of reasons. Whether it's the bully in the schoolyard, a member of a lynch mob, or a dictator engaged in genocide, these perpetrators rely on similar arguments justifying their violence. In other words, people perpetrate violence for the same kinds of reasons. The white Southerners who lynched Sam Hose saw themselves as defenders of their race and privileged way of life. By killing a white man, Hose was seen as challenging white supremacy in the South. This is essentially the same mentality exhibited by Colonel Chivington and others like him, who defined their killing of American Indians in much the same way. For them, American Indian resistance to the encroachment of the settlers was seen as a threat to European and Christian civilization.[13] They saw their violence as being justified and provoked, not as unfounded **aggression**. From this perspective, the American Indians, including the women and children, had brought about their own destruction. One witness to the Sand Creek massacre remembered Colonel Chivington speaking to his men just before going into action and saying, "Boys, I shall not tell you what you are to kill, but remember our slaughtered women and children."[14] Clearly, he defined the subsequent violence as defensive and justified and hoped to evoke the same kinds of sentiments among his men.

Cho Seung-Hui also saw his violence as justified. He had been bullied in high school and remained an angry loner in college. In the video he left, he stated, "You had a hundred billion chances and ways to have avoided today, but you decided to spill my blood. You forced me into a corner and gave me only one option. The decision was yours."[15] This kind of violence is referred to as a form of "**righteous slaughter**" by the sociologist Jack Katz, who points out that the perpetrators of violence often undergo a process in which perceived humiliation is transformed into rage that can culminate in violence.[16] Frequently they perceive that their violence is in defense of some important value or principle. In none of the examples described at the beginning of the chapter were the victims defined as being innocent. Rather, they were perceived as having brought the violence upon themselves; in the eyes of the offenders, the violence they inflicted was entirely appropriate and justified. These perceptions create a potent rationale for harming others. Even some residents in Glen Ridge blamed the young, mentally retarded woman for her own rape. Many victim-blaming comments made it into the media, including "She teased them into it," "She asked for it," and

"She was always flirting."[17] In fact, some scholars have suggested that a great deal of violence—especially among street criminals—stems from a desire for retaliation in which offenders feel that their victim had wronged them in some way and that their violence was a righteous form of payback.[18] This commonality of motivation and perception is not the only thread that connects violence. We also find that violence commonly overlaps.

Think about your own behavior. You generally act in similar ways in different contexts. If you are kind to people in your own family, for example, you are generally going to be kind to strangers. Similarly, violence in one sphere of life often affects violence in another sphere. Individuals who are violent in one setting are more likely to be violent in others. In fact, the single best predictor for violent behavior is a history of previous violence.[19] Of course, this does not mean that an individual who engages in violence is destined for a life of violence; it simply means that those who engage in violence are more likely to do so in the future compared with those without a violent history. This shouldn't come as a surprise. People who engage in violence have already overcome normative boundaries against aggression and are more or less experienced in its perpetration. Essentially, their threshold for using violence has been lowered, which means that once someone starts using violence, it becomes easier to continue using it. The rape conviction of boxer Mike Tyson in 1992 would be an example of this. Boxers are trained in violence and Mike Tyson was certainly no exception. Speaking about an upcoming fight, Tyson once said, "My main objective is to be professional but to kill him. I want to rip out his heart and feed it to him. I want to kill people. I want to rip their stomachs out and eat their children."[20] While this might simply be hyperbole designed to sell tickets, Tyson's behavior out of the ring indicates there is more than a hint of truth to his statement. Tyson has had numerous encounters with the law, mostly involving violent behavior, such as domestic violence and assault as well as rape. Clearly he is an individual whose violence is not confined to socially accepted venues, such as the boxing ring.

Another example of people engaging in violence in multiple spheres of their lives is illustrated by the Pentagon's acknowledgment of the serious problem the military has been having with domestic violence among members of its armed forces. For example, at North Carolina's Fort Bragg military base, four army wives were murdered by their husbands or ex-husbands, with a total of 10 such fatalities occurring there since 2002. Including nonfatal incidents, there were 832 victims of intimate partner assault between 2002 and 2004 at Fort Bragg alone, according to U.S. Army figures. More recently, the military reported that 16 domestic violence fatalities were reported in 2010, a substantial increase from previous years. Child maltreatment cases were also reported to have increased during the same year. One possible cause for this ongoing problem in the military, according to various experts, may relate to the continuing stress and impact of repeated deployment to combat areas.[21] The violence some soldiers experience in war zones, in other words, may travel home with them and impact their relationships in their private lives.

Violence overlaps in other ways as well. Some suggest that the more a society legitimates violence in certain situations (e.g., war, capital punishment, and justifiable homicide), the more illegitimate violence (e.g., robbery and murder) there will

❖ **Photo 1.1** Mike Tyson was arrested after a brawl in New York.

be. This is sometimes referred to as **spillover theory**, which suggests that the values and justifications for violence in socially approved settings "spill over" into other settings and result in illegitimate forms of violence. One example of this spillover concerns the death penalty. Some have argued that, instead of decreasing rates of murder, capital punishment may actually serve to increase it. They point to the fact that the states that sentence the greatest number of people to death also tend to have the highest rates of homicide. One proponent of this argument—termed the **brutalization hypothesis**[22]—is the criminologist William Bowers, who argues, "The lesson of the execution, then, may be to devalue life by the example of human sacrifice. Executions demonstrate that it is correct and appropriate to kill those who have gravely offended us."[23] His brutalization argument suggests that the death penalty desensitizes society to killing and devalues human life and therefore increases tolerance toward lethal behavior, which in turn results in increases in the criminal homicide rate.

War—another example of legitimate violence—has also been found to increase rates of illegitimate violence, not just by soldiers returning from the battlefield and engaging in domestic violence but in the larger society as well. Some scholars have argued that a nation's involvement in war tends to legitimate the use of lethal force to resolve conflict within that nation's population.[24] When a nation or state goes to war, diplomacy is replaced by violence, which is perceived as rational and justified, at least by the leaders of that nation. It isn't unreasonable, then, for citizens of that society also to be more likely to choose force when confronted with conflict.[25] One of the largest studies to examine the effects of war on postwar homicide across nations was conducted by Dane Archer and Rosemary Gartner, who compared national homicide rates for men and women before and after small and large wars, including the two world wars. They also controlled for a number of factors in their comparison, including the number of combat deaths in war, whether the nations were victorious or defeated, and whether the nation's postwar economies were improved or worsened. Archer and Gartner found that most combatant nations experienced substantial postwar increases in their rates of homicide and concluded that "the one model that appears to be fully consistent with the evidence is the legitimation of violence model, which suggests that the presence of authorized or sanctioned killing during war has a residual effect on the level of homicide in peacetime society."[26] Put another way, "It is organized violence on top which creates individual violence on the bottom."[27]

A final example of the spillover thesis is something with which many of us are familiar—being spanked as a child. While most who experience this type of punishment grow up relatively unscathed, research suggests that children who are spanked are more likely to be aggressive as adults compared with children who were not spanked. Murray Straus, in his book *Beating the Devil Out of Them,* argues that the physical discipline of children legitimates other forms of violence in interpersonal confrontations based on his assertion that physical punishment is inescapably an act of violence.[28] Straus contends that the lesson learned by children who are spanked or otherwise physically punished is that violence is an acceptable means to an end. As such, physical responses to conflict may well spill over to other relationships, such as with an intimate partner or spouse.[29]

We also know that certain qualities or characteristics of violence seem to transcend time and place. We find, for example, that age and gender patterns are very consistent across different societies and in different eras. Young men tend to be responsible for most forms of violence regardless of the time period or the country.[30] Similarities also exist in terms of the motivations and justifications used by those who engage in violence, as we have discussed earlier in this chapter. We hope this discussion helps illustrate our belief that all violence is connected. Violence, in its many forms, is fundamentally linked through various shared qualities that we have briefly reviewed here. This is not to say, however, that all violence is identical. Collective violence, for example, is not simply interpersonal violence with a large number of perpetrators and/ or victims. The social and collective elements of group violence differentiate it from interpersonal violence in a number of ways. Yet both types still share a number of other important commonalities. In many ways, therefore, it can be said that acts of violence are simultaneously unique and comparable. So far, we have looked at several examples of violence, but we have not yet defined exactly what we mean by the term "violence." In the next section, you will see that coming up with a concrete definition of violence is not always such an easy task.

Defining Violence

Defining violence is a trickier job than you might expect given our apparent familiarity with the concept. Violence is one of those words that everyone knows, but few have grappled with in any detail. Despite this familiarity, we are usually fairly vague about its meaning, and our perceptions can vary tremendously depending upon any number of factors. While at first glance the concept seems clear enough, the more closely we examine violence, the more elusive it becomes. So before proceeding, we need to discuss some of the complexities and issues raised by attempts to define violence.

The first thing we need to understand is that violence encompasses many different kinds of behaviors in many different kinds of situations. Recognizing all of them as being categorically part of the same phenomenon can be difficult, especially if the violence is not always evident in the act. Pulling the trigger of a gun, for example, or pressing a button that launches a missile may not be violent actions in and of themselves, but the consequences of these actions unquestionably *are* violent. Do we perceive and define them the same way as hitting a person or stabbing someone—acts in which the violence involves human contact and the consequences are therefore more immediate and close? How about instilling so much terror and instability into someone's life that they flee their home with their children to an unknown land or refugee camp where food and safe drinking water aren't available on a regular basis but loss and insecurity are guaranteed? What if the perpetrator of this act was someone you pledged to "love and cherish until death do you part?" So which of these acts do we consider to be violence? All of them? Or only some of them?

We must also recognize that everyone perceives and understands violence in their own way, based on their individual history and the context of their life. Many people only use the term in reference to physical acts of aggression and harm, while others include emotional or psychological acts as well. For some, violence refers solely to human-perpetrated acts, while others include destructive natural forces, such as tornadoes, storms, earthquakes, and hurricanes. Accidental acts of harm are also not always defined as violence. If someone was injured by another person who intentionally hit them, most of us would clearly see this as an act of violence. Yet if the same injury occurred unintentionally—say, as the result of a collision on a basketball court or a soccer field—many of us would not define it as violence.

The perceived legitimacy of aggressive acts also affects whether or not they are defined as violence. Some individuals only use the word to refer to illegal or illegitimate acts of aggression. Other words are often used to describe aggressive acts that are socially approved. As an illustration, take two incidents that are behaviorally similar:

1. Scenario 1. During an attempted robbery, an offender shoots the store clerk because he perceives the clerk to be reaching down under the counter for a gun; the store clerk dies.
2. Scenario 2. After pulling over a driver for speeding, a police officer shoots the driver whom he perceives to be reaching into his coat for a gun; the driver dies.

The behavior in both scenarios is similar, yet the label given to each would almost certainly be very different. The first would undoubtedly be labeled as an act of felony murder, which in some states is the most likely kind of case to receive the death penalty. The second would most likely be ruled as the legitimate use of deadly force with no criminal label whatsoever attached. While the physical behavior is the same, the legal and social acceptability are very different, and this influences which words are used to describe each act.

Keep in mind that violence is a loaded word; it is a word rich in meaning that usually evokes powerful emotions. When people think of violence, they generally attach very negative connotations to it. This makes defining violence even harder because there are numerous acts that many of us do not perceive as violent, since they are perceived and defined as being acceptable and may even be encouraged. Commenting on this issue, the legal scholar Lawrence Friedman writes, "In part, violence is a matter of definition, or at least of perspective. . . . Every society defines a sphere of legitimate private violence."[31] In other words, the legitimacy or illegitimacy of any particular act lies not in any intrinsic quality of the act itself but rather in its definition. As we noted at the beginning of the chapter, evidence indicates that many perpetrators of violence see themselves as being justified in their actions and often define their acts as a legitimate response to some behavioral or ethical breach on the part of their victim. In this sense, the offender perceives his or her violence as a form of social control,[32] and this perception of the crime as a form of self-help serves to legitimize the act not only to the offender but perhaps to others as well.[33] Violent people often feel they are acting legitimately and morally to protect something they value or to exact the appropriate penalty from someone who has wronged them. Regardless of the context, violent offenders often provide justifications for their offenses. Like Cho Seung-Hui who claimed he was provoked to go on a shooting rampage at Virginia Tech, men who have been convicted of felony assault against their intimate partners also often justify their violence including such statements as "she disrespected me and deserved it," or "a man has a right to control a woman."[34]

We hope you can now see that, depending upon who is doing what to whom and the reasons why, we either accept or condemn acts of violence. Our understanding is therefore highly situational and contingent. This means that the context is extremely important in helping shape our understanding of and reaction to violent acts and actors. The context of violence is shaped in large part by several factors, including the following:

- The victim
- The offender
- The specific nature of the violence
- The location of the violence
- The rationale for the violence[35]

Let's start with the victim. If the victim is someone with whom we can identify or someone we know and can relate to, we are more likely to condemn the violence. Many factors, including gender, race/ethnicity, religion, sexual orientation, and nationality, play a role here. If the victim is someone who is like us, we are more likely to sympathize with them and see the situation through their eyes. On the other hand, the greater the social distance between us and the victim, the less likely that we will empathize with them. This judgment, however, does not occur independently of the perpetrator. If we know and can identify more easily with the perpetrator compared to the victim, we will be more willing to find ways to rationalize and even accept their violence. Figure 1.1 illustrates these relationships. Essentially, it is easier for us to rationalize, condone, and accept behavior from people who are like us, and it is easier for us to condemn and judge those who are different from us.

In the same vein, the type of violence affects how we perceive and define specific acts. Minor acts of violence are generally easier to accept than more severe forms. It is much easier to dismiss or minimize a push or a slap than a punch or a kick. The heinousness of an act of violence is also influenced by the brutality involved and the number of victims. Acts of violence involving gratuitous cruelty or torture are much less likely to be deemed acceptable. Location has also been an important variable. Historically, if violence was perpetrated in the home, it was generally conceded to be much more acceptable than if carried out in a public place or work setting. What happened behind closed doors was once considered to be private and no one's business. This was especially true if the victim was a wife or child and the perpetrator the

❖ **Figure 1.1**   Social Distance

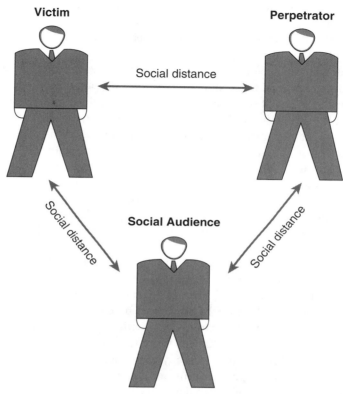

husband or father. In public, however, the violence was more easily condemned. The justification expressed for the violence is also important since it helps the social audience understand the rationale for the aggressive behavior. If we agree and/or understand the motivation, then it becomes easier to accept and even commend specific acts of violence.

In sum, it is important to recognize that our individual perceptions and definitions of violence revolve around a number of variables that help shape our understanding of the act and is testimony to the difficulty we have in defining it. In other words, our relationship with violence is complex and at times contradictory. Sometimes we condemn and punish those who inflict violence, and sometimes we celebrate and reward those who perpetrate it. We read or hear about a shooting somewhere, and we are appalled. The idea of moviegoers being ambushed by an armed gunman at a midnight screening of a Batman movie is horrific. The events at Virginia Tech, along with the massacre at Sandy Hook elementary school and the execution-style murders of the Amish schoolgirls in Pennsylvania, for example, have seared themselves into our collective awareness as horrible tragedies. Yet when Navy Seals killed Osama bin Laden, many applauded his death. When police officers shoot and kill someone they perceive as dangerous, such as when London police officers shot and killed a young Brazilian man they suspected of being a suicide bomber after the bombings there in July 2005, many rationalized the killing as an understandable act in a time of terror. Yet when drug dealers kill each other in pursuit of illegal profits, we almost universally revile it. In short, we judge acts of violence selectively. Some call forth our interest and compassion and demand an emotional response, while others barely stir any interest. Some receive our approval, while others earn our condemnation. We can see this differentiation at work in one study looking at attitudes toward different types of violence. Leslie Kennedy and David Forde examined the attitudes of a sample of Canadians to determine levels of support for the same act of violence in different situations. Their findings are summarized in Table 1.1 and reveal that the same violent behavior receives widely disparate levels of support and approval depending upon the situation in which it occurred. These results are consistent with earlier research in the United States.[36]

By now it is likely you will agree that defining violence is a difficult task, in large part because our understanding of its nature is so subjective and varied. We think it is helpful at this point to go over some definitions that have been proposed by those who study violence. Table 1.2 provides a list of some of the more popular definitions. We also include definitions of aggression, since both terms are often used interchangeably—even within the scholarly community.[37] We should note, however, that some researchers make distinctions between violence and aggression. For example, Bartol and Bartol contend that all violence is aggressive, but not all aggression is violent.[38] For them, violence only refers to aggressive physical behavior, while aggression can also refer to behavior that is psychologically harmful. Moreover, aggression is more often used in connection with a person's psychological affect, demeanor, and mindset, while violence is more specifically intended to encompass the harmful physical behavior itself. In many ways, aggression may precede and accompany violence. For the purposes of this book, however, the terms "violence" and "aggression" are so similar in their everyday usage that we will not make this type of distinction.

Reviewing Table 1.2, we find a range of definitions that differ and overlap in some important ways. First, all definitions agree that violence and aggression are harmful. Where they differ, however, is in conceptualizing what kinds of harm qualify as violence. Some of the definitions include inflicting psychological or emotional harm as violence, while others do not. But the bottom line is that, whether perpetrated for noble reasons or for petty and selfish ones, violence is about injuring, damaging, destroying, and killing. It is invariably destructive. This is not to say that violence cannot be perpetrated for constructive reasons but rather that the act of violence is *always* destructive. It is therefore important to differentiate between the intent or purpose of the act and the act itself. The behavior and the intent of the behavior are separate. The purpose of the violence may be positive or negative or perhaps even a mixture of both. But the violence itself always remains the same: injurious and damaging. Second, these definitions help us understand that violence can take a number of forms. The most common difference is that between physical and emotional or psychological violence, although not everyone agrees that nonphysical forms of aggression (e.g., verbal) can be considered violence.

There are many other ways that violence can be classified and categorized. One distinction that is sometimes drawn is between **expressive** and **instrumental** acts of violence. Instrumental acts of violence are those in which violence is a means to an end. An assault during an armed robbery, for example, would fit into this category.

Table 1.1   Attitudes Toward Violent Situations

Situation in Which One Man (Assailant) Punches an Adult Stranger	Percent of Respondents Who Approve of the Violence
If adult stranger was in a protest march showing opposition to the other man's (assailant's) views	9
If adult stranger was drunk and bumped into the man (assailant) and his wife on the street	8
If adult stranger had hit the man's (assailant's) child after the child accidentally damaged the stranger's car	26
If adult stranger was beating up a woman and the man (assailant) saw it	56
If adult stranger had broken into the man's (assailant's) house	47
Situation in Which Police Officer Strikes an Adult Male Citizen	**Percent of Respondents Who Approve of the Violence**
If the male citizen had used vulgar and obscene language against the officer	12
If the male citizen was being questioned as a suspect in a murder case	8
If the male citizen was attempting to escape from custody	67
If the male citizen was attacking the police officer with his fists	88

SOURCE: Revised from Leslie W. Kennedy and David R. Forde, *When Push Comes to Shove: A Routine Conflict Approach to Violence* (Albany: State University of New York Press, 1999).

The violence is committed to help accomplish the robbery, but it is not an end in itself. Expressive acts of violence, on the other hand, are those in which the motivations are expressive of some emotional state, such as anger or jealousy. In these cases, the violence serves to fulfill some internal or intrinsic desire. As the name implies, the violence is "expressing" something.

Another way of categorizing violence is provided by Peter Iadicola and Anson Shupe, who suggest that there are three main interconnected types of violence, which they label interpersonal, institutional, and structural. **Interpersonal violence** consists of the assaults, rapes, robberies, and murders, which often come to mind when thinking about violence. **Institutional violence**, on the other hand, concerns the violent behaviors that are perpetrated in organizational settings. For example, Iadicola and Shupe consider family violence a form of institutional violence because it happens within the context of the family. Also included are corporate and workplace violence, military violence, religious violence, and state-perpetrated violence, all of which occur within the context of established social institutions. **Structural violence** is all about discriminatory social arrangements that can also be construed as violence. Including structural arrangements in their definition allows Iadicola and Shupe to

Table 1.2	Definitions of Violence
Author	**Definition of Violence**
Webster's New Collegiate Dictionary	"Exertion of physical force so as to injure or abuse . . . intense, turbulent, or furious and often destructive action or force"[1]
The National Panel on the Understanding and Control of Violent Behavior	"Behaviors by individuals that intentionally threaten, attempt, or inflict physical harm on others"[2]
Newman	"A series of events, the course of which or the outcomes of which, cause injury or damage to persons or property"[3]
Iadicola and Shupe	"Violence is any action or structural arrangement that results in physical or nonphysical harm to one or more persons"[4]
Weiner, Zahn, and Sagi	"The threat, attempt, or use of physical force by one or more persons that results in physical or nonphysical harm to one or more persons"[5]
Bartol and Bartol	"Destructive physical aggression intentionally directed at harming other persons or things"[6]
Author	**Definition of Aggression**
Bartol and Bartol	"Behavior perpetrated or attempted with the intention of harming another individual physically or psychologically (as opposed to socially) or to destroy an object"[7]
Berkowitz	"Any form of behavior that is intended to injure someone physically or psychologically"[8]

NOTES:

1. *Webster's New Collegiate Dictionary* (Springfield, MA: G. & C. Merriam and Company).
2. Albert J. Reiss and Jeffrey A. Roth, eds., *Understanding and Preventing Violence* (Washington, DC: National Academy Press, 1993), 2.
3. Graeme Newman, "Popular Culture and Violence: Decoding the Violence of Popular Movies," in *Popular Culture, Crime, and Justice*, eds. Frankie Bailey and Donna Hale (Belmont, CA: West/Wadsworth, 1998), 40–56.
4. Peter Iadicola and Anson Shupe, *Violence, Inequality, and Human Freedom* (Lanham, MD: Rowman & Littlefield, 2003), 23.
5. Neil Alan Weiner, Margaret A. Zahn, and Rita J. Sagi, *Violence: Patterns, Causes, Public Policy* (San Diego, CA: Harcourt Brace Jovanovich, 1990), xiii.
6. Curt R. Bartol and Anne M. Bartol, *Criminal Behavior: A Psychosocial Approach* (Upper Saddle River, NJ: Pearson Prentice Hall, 2005), 241.
7. Curt R. Bartol and Anne M. Bartol, *Criminal Behavior: A Psychosocial Approach* (Upper Saddle River, NJ: Pearson Prentice Hall, 2005), 241.
8. Leonard Berkowitz, *Aggression: Its Causes, Consequences, and Control* (New York: McGraw-Hill, 1993), 3.

examine societal inequalities as violence in light of the negative effects that certain living conditions may have on a group. For example, they write, "Violence may be action that denies a minority group's access to education, health care, housing, an adequate diet, and other necessities of survival and human development."[39] While our book does not address structural violence per se, we do underscore the inequalities related to both the collective and individual violence that we examine. In addition, the violence we examine encompasses both interpersonal and institutional types of behavior.

At this point in your reading, you must be expecting us to tell you which definition we subscribe to in this book. Rather than disappoint you, we can suggest that the definition which most closely aligns with our approach in this book is the one presented by Iadicola and Shupe, who define violence as follows: "Violence is any action or structural arrangement that results in physical or nonphysical harm to one or more persons."[40] That being said, we also want to acknowledge that most of the definitions presented in Table 1.2 would serve our purposes equally well. While there are many ways to define violence, most of the attempts discussed above share a number of qualities, and the types of violence we have chosen to discuss in this book fall within these broad conceptualizations. Therefore, settling on a single definition to guide our discussion is not as crucial as it might otherwise be. In addition to defining violence, another important issue that must also be addressed relates to how we measure violence, and as you might imagine, attempting to measure the extent of violence in U.S. society is also a complex issue.

Measuring Violence

It is not our intention in this discussion to exhaustively review all of the sources of information on violence, nor do we provide a summation of all of the strengths and weaknesses of each method of collecting data. There are far too many data sets on violence, each encompassing different specific collection methodologies and populations, and each with its own unique set of strengths and weaknesses. Instead, we simply want to provide a brief introduction to a few of the main sources of data on violence and to discuss some of the primary pitfalls and shortcomings commonly found in attempts to accurately identify the scope and magnitude of violent behavior. Additionally, throughout the book in individual chapters, more specific estimates and measurement issues related to separate forms of interpersonal violence, such as murder, rape, and intimate partner violence, will be covered in more detail. The present discussion, on the other hand, should give you a more general sense of the more common ways in which information on violence is gathered, and some of the important and relevant concerns attached to them. While it might seem mundane and somewhat technical, we should remember that measurement is an important issue. The accuracy of our insights and explanations about violence is largely dependent on the quality of the information that we are able to gather. Moreover, resources and strategies aimed at preventing violence and helping violent crime victims are also based on these estimates. Bad information can and does result in poor choices being made by policy makers, politicians, activists, and other concerned citizens. Depending on who is gathering the data and what methods they employ to get that information, the results can vary widely. When most students are asked about how statistics on violence are gathered, they tend to think first and foremost about police reports. You will soon see, however, that relying on reports of crime to police is somewhat problematic. That being noted, we can say that estimates of interpersonal violence are usually based on reports to the police and surveys of the general population.[41]

Reports to Law Enforcement Officials

The most widely used source of statistical information about violent crime in the United States is the **Uniform Crime Reporting Program** (UCR), compiled by the Federal Bureau of Investigation (FBI). The UCR has collected information about criminal incidents of violence reported to the police since 1930; the reports are based on the voluntary participation of state, county, and city law enforcement agencies across the United States.

For the crime of homicide, information about both the victim and the offender (e.g., the gender and race of both, the relationship between the victim and offender, the weapon used) is obtained in a separate reporting program called the **Supplementary Homicide Reports** (SHR). Unfortunately, such detailed information is not collected for other crimes in the UCR. To remedy this problem, in 1988 the FBI implemented a change in its collection of crime information to include more characteristics of the incident; appropriately, this is called the **National Incident Based Reporting System** (NIBRS). NIBRS data is more specific than the UCR and includes many more offenses that local agencies have to report information on. It includes detailed information on crime incidents, including the characteristics of the victim, such as age, gender, race, ethnicity, and resident status. In all, NIBRS categorizes each incident and arrest in one of 22 basic crime categories that span 46 separate offenses. A total of 53 data elements about the victim, property, and offender are collected under NIBRS.[42] As you can imagine, it takes a great deal of time and money to make this change and fill out this paperwork at the local police department level. Because of this time and expense, only over half of all states currently use the NIBRS format for collecting information about reported crimes.

Both the UCR and the NIBRS data collection methods are problematic when estimating incidence rates of violence. It's not hard to imagine why. If victimizations are not reported to police, they are never counted in either data collection effort in the first place and, based on comparisons with national survey data, it is estimated that only about 40% to 50% of crimes become known to police. This is particularly problematic for certain types of violence, such as rape and violence that occurs between intimates, such as spouses and boy/girlfriends. We know that a large percentage of these victimizations are never reported to police. In sum, there is a great deal of evidence that documents the large gap between the true extent of victimization and offending and the amount of crime known to police. The major sources of this gap, according to Clayton Mosher, Terance Miethe, and Dretha Phillips, are the following: the inability of police to observe all criminal activity, the reluctance of crime victims and witnesses to report crime to the police, and variation in the recording of "known" crime incidents because of police discretion.[43]

Because of this weakness in police reports, random sample surveys of the population are often used as the social science tool of choice for uncovering more accurate information about violent victimization. However, as can be imagined, surveys employing diverse methodologies and different definitions of violence have resulted in tremendously diverse estimates. Taking violence against women as an example, survey estimates of how many women experience violence from an intimate partner annually range from 9.3 per 1,000 women to 116 per 1,000 women.[44] This is a huge range. Further, the methodological differences across survey methodologies often preclude direct comparisons across studies.

Since we discuss surveys used to measure various types of violence within the chapters of this book, at this point we will describe only two more general surveys. The first was designed to more accurately measure crime victimization and is sponsored by the Bureau of Justice Statistics (BJS) of the U.S. Department of Justice. It is called the **National Crime Victimization Survey** (NCVS). Instead of focusing on victimizations, the second survey we will discuss was designed to measure the offending behavior of adolescents and is called the **National Youth Survey** (NYS).

The National Crime Victimization Survey annually interviews over 100,000 individuals aged 12 or older and is the second largest ongoing survey sponsored by the U.S. government. It measures both violent and property crime victimizations. But asking respondents to recall incidents of victimization is a tricky business. How would you word questions to uncover incidents of violent victimization? After several changes and redesigns, the NCVS currently uses the screening questions listed in Table 1.3.

As you can see from Table 1.3, the screening questions rely on very behavior-specific wording instead of asking directly about victimizations using crime jargon such as "have you ever been robbed?"[45] This is important. A great deal of research has demonstrated that asking questions using behavior-based wording instead of legally based phrases uncovers a significantly greater number of victimizations, particularly when victims may not self-identify themselves as crime victims. As you might imagine, asking people about their experiences in this way uncovers many more victimizations than those reported only to police.

Who are the most likely offenders of violent crime? Relying on police reports to estimate who is most likely to perpetrate acts of violence involves the same problems as using these data to estimate who is most likely to be victimized. Are offenders who are arrested for violent offending actually representative of all offenders? The quick answer is no. Not surprisingly, early self-report surveys of offending behavior in the 1940s revealed that a relatively large number of committed offenses were undetected by the police. Although police report data at the time indicated offenders were more likely to be minorities from low socioeconomic backgrounds, self-report data revealed that a great number of offenses were being reported by people from relatively privileged backgrounds. As you might guess, these offenses rarely came to the attention of the police, and when they did, they rarely resulted in an arrest.[46] Based on these early studies, researchers interested in offending behavior—like those interested in victimization—began to rely on survey methodology instead of police reports. That trend continues to this day.

Table 1.3   Screening Questions Used by the NCVS to Uncover Violent
             Victimizations

---

1. Other than any incidents already mentioned, has anyone attacked or threatened you
    in any of these ways?
    a. With any weapon, for instance, a gun or knife
    b. With anything like a baseball bat, frying pan, scissors, or a stick
    c. By something thrown, such as a rock or bottle
    d. Include any grabbing, punching, or choking
    e. Any rape, attempted rape or other type of sexual attack
    f. Any face-to-face threats
    g. Any attack or threat or use of force by anyone at all? **Please mention it even if
        you are not certain it was a crime.**

2. Incidents involving forced or unwanted sexual acts are often difficult to talk about.
    Have you been forced or coerced to engage in unwanted sexual activity by:
    a. Someone you didn't know before
    b. A casual acquaintance
    c. Someone you know well?

If respondents reply affirmative to one of these latter questions, interviewers next ask
"*Do you mean forced or coerced sexual intercourse?*" to determine whether the incident
should be recorded as rape or as another type of sexual attack.

3. People often don't think of incidents committed by someone they know. Did you
    have something stolen from you OR were you attacked or threatened by:
    a. Someone at work or school
    b. A neighbor or friend
    c. A relative or family member
    d. Any other person you've met or known?

SOURCE: NCVS, Bureau of Justice Statistics

One of the most thorough contemporary surveys of offending behavior is the National Youth Survey, which was first collected in 1976 from a national probability sample of 11- to 17-year-olds. These youth were interviewed many times during the following years, with the last interview data collected in 1995, although there are similar surveys that have taken its place.[47] Table 1.4 displays some of the questions used to measure the violent offending behavior in the NYS. As you can see, here too researchers have used behavior-specific wording instead of relying on the use of crime categories and labels.

We hope this brief description of how we measure violence has given you a better sense of how information on violence is gathered and what are their corresponding weaknesses. Keep in mind that we will be talking about measurement issues regarding particular types of violence more extensively throughout the book. For now, though, we want to provide you with a general overview of the scope of violence in the United States and look at how this compares with violence in other times and places.

Table 1.4	Screening Questions Used by the NYS to Uncover Self-Reported Offending

(Introduction) This section deals with our own behavior. I'd like to remind you that all your answers are confidential. I'll read a series of behaviors to you. Please give me your best estimate of the exact number of times you've done each thing during the last year from Christmas a year ago to the Christmas just past.

    a. Carried a hidden weapon other than a plain pocket knife
    b. Attacked someone with the idea of seriously hurting or killing him or her
    c. Been involved in gang fights
    d. Tried to take something from someone with the use of force or with the threat of force.

NOTES:

1. Response options were (a) once a month, (b) once every 2 to 3 weeks, (c) once a week, (d) 2 to 3 times a week, (e) once a day, and (f) 2 to 3 times a day.

Violence and U.S. Society

When we turn on the evening news, read the local newspaper, or get on the Internet, we can't get away from the fact that violence, in its many forms, is a common companion in our lives. We live in a violent world. Whether we acknowledge it or not, the problem of violence pervades our lives and often defines who we are as individuals, communities, and nations. This is as true for the United States as it is for any other place around the world. We experience it in our homes, at work, and in public places. In fact, many of us experience violence directly as victims. In 2011 alone, according to the National Crime Victimization Survey, 5.8 million Americans over the age of 12 were victims of violent crimes.[48] When you consider that this type of victimization occurs every single day and that the effects of this victimization often last years, if not a lifetime, you begin to realize the impact that this violence has on our society.

Figure 1.2 illustrates rates of total nonfatal violence, which includes rape and sexual assaults, robbery, aggravated assaults, and simple assaults as well as a separate trend line for serious nonfatal violence, which excludes simple assaults. As you can see, violence peaked in the early 1990s and has generally been declining since that time. However, when homicide rates are examined (Figure 1.3), we learn that the decline in violence was not consistent across subgroups of the population. While homicide victimization rates declined for both white and black males, it remained virtually constant for white females and appears to have actually risen back to the high rates observed in the early 1980s for black females. As we will note again and again throughout this text, context matters! How do we compare to other countries?

Figure 1.4 reveals that, although the United States generally has very high rates of murder, we are not necessarily alone. However, if you look closely, we are in the company of countries such as Iraq and Brazil; rates of murder for other Western industrialized countries such as Sweden and Germany are less than half those of the United States. Rates of victimization are just the tip of the iceberg regarding our experiences with

❖ **Figure 1.2** Violent Crime Rates, 1993–2010, NCVS

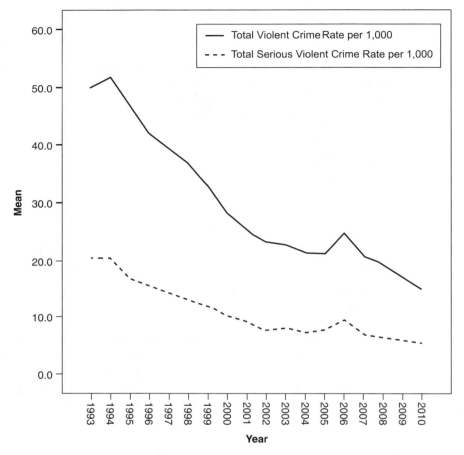

violence. In addition to direct victimization, we also often experience it vicariously. We thrill to see violence in sports and enjoy violent video and computer games. We flock to movies that are saturated with graphic acts of explicit and realistic violence. In fact, the average child will view 200,000 acts of violence and 16,000 murders by the time they are 18 years old.[49] Our airwaves are full of violent images, and research suggests that this trend is becoming more prevalent. In fact, there is evidence that media violence has become more plentiful, graphic, sexual, and sadistic.[50] Can we watch these images and not be affected by them? The evidence strongly suggests that we can't.[51]

We also worry about violence constantly and change our behavior in response to perceived threats of violence. We avoid certain parts of town, add security features to our homes, and vote for "get tough" laws in order to protect ourselves from violent offenders. During the first decade of the 21st century, Americans were fighting in Iraq and Afghanistan and news reports were full of fallen soldiers, car bombings, torture of prisoners, and beheadings of hostages. In short, whether domestically or internationally,

❖ **Figure 1.3** Homicide Rates for White and Black Males and Females, 1980–2008

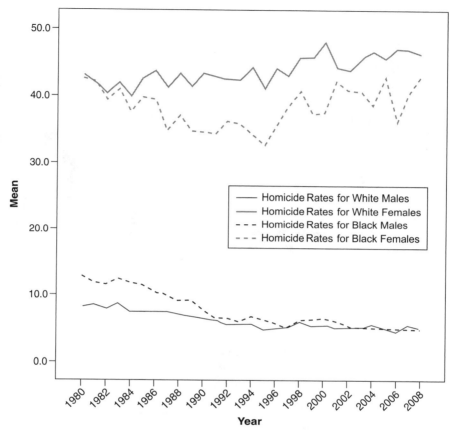

violence is part and parcel of U.S. life. In fact, Iadicola and Shupe assert that violence is the "overarching problem of our age" and suggest that every social problem is influenced by the problem of violence.[52] James Gilligan, a medical doctor who directed the Center for the Study of Violence at Harvard Medical School, put it this way:

> The more I learn about other people's lives, the more I realize that I have yet to hear the history of any family in which there has not been at least one family member who has been overtaken by fatal or life threatening violence, as the perpetrator or the victim—whether the violence takes the form of suicide or homicide, death in combat, death from a drunken or reckless driver, or any other of the many nonnatural forms of death.[53]

So it's safe to say that violence is not foreign to us, but rather is something with which we rub shoulders constantly. We know violence through our own lived experiences and the experiences of our family, friends, and neighbors as well as through the media images we view and the games we play.

❖ **Figure 1.4** Murder Rates per 100,000 by Country, 2004

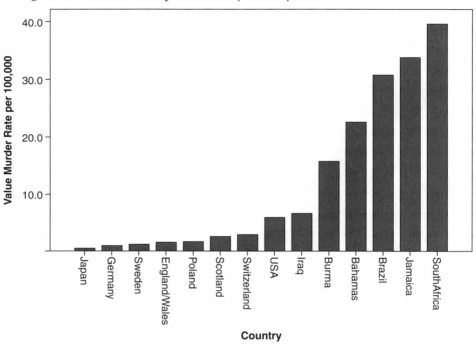

SOURCE: Adapted from The Guardian, Data Blog, *Global Homicide: Murder Rates Around the World,* http://www.guardian.co.uk/news/datablog/2009/oct/13/homicide-rates-country-murder-data.

At a deeper level, this means that our identities as citizens, parents, children, spouses, lovers, friends, teammates, and colleagues are often shaped by violence, at least in part. Who we are as individuals and as human beings is shaped by the culture within which we live. How we define ourselves, the ways in which we relate to others, and our notions of what we stand for and what we believe in are all determined in large part by the influences and experiences of our lives—or, as the great English poet Alfred Lord Tennyson once wrote, "I am a part of all that I have met."[54] In a similar vein, although a bit less poetically, the sociologists Peter Berger and Thomas Luckmann suggest, "Identity is a phenomenon that emerges from the dialectic between individual and society."[55] In short, our life experiences shape who we are. Therefore, if violence is a part of our reality, then it plays a role in molding us as human beings and influences how we understand the world around us. To acknowledge this is to understand that violence is part of who we are and central to knowing ourselves and the lives we lead.

Because of this prevalence and its impact on our lives, some have suggested that Americans have created and embraced a culture of violence. Culture is a nebulous concept that includes values, beliefs, and rules for behavior. Culture also dictates what is expected, what is valued, and what is prohibited.[56] Essentially, then, this argument contends that our history and experiences have resulted in a system of values and beliefs that, to a greater extent than in some other cultures, condones, tolerates, and even expects a violent response to various and specific situations.[57] Other scholars have further developed this theme by arguing that, instead of a culture of violence in the United States, there are **subcultures of violence** specific to particular regions or groups. First articulated by the criminologists Wolfgang and Ferracuti, this viewpoint suggests that members of some groups are more likely to rely on violence. As they suggest

> Quick resort to physical combat as a measure of daring, courage, or defense of status appears to be a cultural expectation . . . When such a cultural response is elicited from an individual engaged in social interplay with others who harbor the same response mechanism, physical assaults, altercations, and violent domestic quarrels that result in homicide are likely to be relatively common.[58]

This argument has been applied to various subcultural groups such as Southerners, young African American males, and others.[59] The South historically has had much higher rates of violence than other regions of the country, and many have suggested that it is a consequence of Southern notions of honor that demand a violent response to certain provocations. Southern culture, in other words, is more violence prone than other regional cultures. Violence, then, is something that appears to be embedded in our values and attitudes, which is why some have suggested that violence is "as American as apple pie."[60]

Yet, for something that is so much a part of our lives, we remain remarkably ill informed about what violence really is, how and why it is perpetrated, and what its consequences truly are. James Gilligan makes this point when he asserts that "human violence is much more complicated, ambiguous and, most of all, tragic, than is commonly realized or acknowledged."[61] Much of what we think we know owes as much to myth and stereotype as it does to fact. This shouldn't be a big surprise since so much of what we think we know is based on what we see on popular television shows and in movies. In fact, up to 95% of Americans cite the mass media as their main source of information on crime and violence.[62] Unfortunately, these images have been shown to be misleading, incomplete, and erroneous.[63] For example, on October 12, 1998, a 22-year-old gang member named Omar Sevilla, also known as "Sugar Bear," was shot to death as he walked to a drug and alcohol treatment center. On the same day, a German tourist named Horst Fietze was shot and killed while walking with his wife only a few blocks away from the site of the "Sugar Bear" murder.[64] While Sevilla's death went almost completely unnoticed in the press, Fietze's killing received a great deal of media attention. Such selective reporting is not unusual. One study of newspaper reporting on murder found that it was the atypical homicide that was reported on most frequently, while the routine type of killing was sometimes not even considered

❖ **Photo 1.2**   Referee trying to stop a hockey fight

worthy of any coverage.[65] More specifically, around 5% of homicides received the vast majority of all media attention. What kinds of killings constituted this 5%? Assassinations, mass murders, gangland killings, and particularly gruesome and sensationalistic murders received all the press coverage. Yet these types of murders are far and away the least common types of criminal homicide. To the average reader, however, who thinks that the newspaper reporting is complete, it may come to represent the typical homicide that they perceive to be most common.

The same is true for other forms of violent crime as well. During the mid-1990s, for example, a spate of news stories appeared about the problem of workplace violence that portrayed the United States as suffering "the epidemic of workplace violence."[66] These reports were often full of scary statistics and language that fed into and increased fears about the dangers of the workplace. Yet, as Barry Glassner points out, the rate of workplace violence is only around 1 in 114,000, which is hardly an epidemic.[67] Glassner also shows that, even though the term "going postal" entered popular culture as an expression of extreme workplace behavior, postal workers are actually two and a half times less likely to be killed at work than the average U.S. worker.[68] This misrepresentation doesn't mean that our places of employment are absolutely 100% safe, but most are certainly safer than the news reports suggest. Similar kinds of media-generated "crime epidemics" have been studied in regard to serial murder, child abuse, and various other types of violent offending.[69] Clearly, there is a need to develop a more accurate understanding of the nature and prevalence of violence, and that is the intent of this book.

Organization of the Book

The organization of this book is the result of an imperfect compromise on a number of different levels. First, of necessity we are not able to examine all of the varied types of violence that exist. While some readers might disagree with our choices, we have had to pick and choose which types to include and which types to exclude, and we feel that our choices provide a broad-based understanding of the varied ways in which violence is often manifested. Second, we recognize that we have not always been able to devote the amount of attention and space to various issues, perspectives, and theories. Many of the individual topics contained in this book have had entire volumes written about them, and it is simply beyond the scope of this book to address all of the relevant issues in the level of detail and depth that some may desire. Third and last, dividing this book into chapters on different types of violence regrettably contributes to the mistaken notion that the kinds of violence discussed in this book are discrete and separate events. However, for the sake of clarity and to conceptually assist the reader, we have chosen to structure the book around chapters that review specific types of violence in detail. The first chapters focus on interpersonal acts of violence, while the later chapters cover collective types of violence. The specific chapters are arranged as follows:

Chapter 2—Explaining Violence: This chapter provides a review of the various biological, psychological, and sociological theories that have explanatory power for violent behavior. Human behavior is complex and is subject to a variety of influences that are captured in the different perspectives we review in this chapter.

Chapter 3—Aiding and Abetting Violence: This chapter comprises a discussion of a number of elements that often are contributors to or correlates of violent behavior. Firearms, drugs, and alcohol are the most obvious of these, but this chapter also explores a number of other correlates, such as certain kinds of group dynamics that contribute to violent acts.

Chapter 4—Assault and Homicide: Since a large percentage of homicides occur as the result of conflict situations, such as fights or arguments, this chapter discusses homicide as the most lethal outcome on a continuum of assaultive violence. The chapter provides a broad discussion of the epidemiology of murder and assault in the United States as well as a contextual discussion of the "assault event" and delineates the interactions that are most likely to lead to homicide. The chapter concludes with a discussion of capital punishment, which is the most severe mechanism of social control for some types of homicide.

Chapter 5—Violence in the Home: This chapter provides a discussion of intimate partner violence, child abuse and neglect, and elder abuse. In addition to noting that all forms of violence occur in the home—including murder, rape, and assault—the chapter also talks about the crime of stalking, which often co-occurs with other intimate partner violence. The chapter concludes by discussing the various policies aimed at preventing violence in the family, including the efficacy of mandatory arrest policies and batterer treatment programs.

Chapter 6—Stranger Danger: This chapter provides a discussion of the stranger-perpetrated assault and homicide and looks at how it differs from similar violence perpetrated by known offenders. In addition, since robbery is more likely to be perpetrated by strangers than known offenders, it also provides an in-depth analysis of robbery in the United States. The chapter relies on official statistics to present the epidemiological overview but also offers insights into the motivations of robbery offenders from qualitative research that has been conducted with robbers themselves.

Chapter 7—Rape and Sexual Assault: This chapter reviews the major trends and patterns of rape and sexual assault. Additionally, it explores what is known about the type of individuals who perpetrate this form of violence and their rationales for doing so. Lastly, this chapter addresses rape in two contexts that rarely receive attention: rape perpetrated in U.S. prisons and rape perpetrated as a means of ethnic cleansing and genocide.

Chapter 8—Mob Violence: This chapter explores a number of examples of group violence that are largely spontaneous and involve informal and short-lived social groupings. Riots, lynchings, and vigilantism comprise the three primary types of mob violence reviewed in this chapter, with a number of different case studies reviewed within each category.

Chapter 9—Terrorism: Since the terrorist attacks of September 11, 2001, Americans have become very aware of and concerned about this particular type of group violence. This chapter begins with a discussion of the difficulties in defining terrorism, followed by a review of the different typologies of terrorist groups based on their motivations. Specific examples of terrorist groups and their acts are also discussed in terms of how they fit in with the typologies and motivations discussed earlier.

Chapter 10—Genocide: Genocide is a term that is increasingly familiar to many, given its apparent prevalence. This chapter provides an overview of the concept, including a number of well-known case studies from recent history, a discussion of the reasons why it is perpetrated, and a summary of its impact on the development and application of international human rights law.

Chapter 11—Toward Violence Prevention: The concluding chapter presents a brief review of some of the costs of violence in order to highlight the need for more effective means of preventing and/or reducing the frequency and severity of violence. A major focus of this chapter stresses the utility of relying on more of a public health approach to the enduring problem of violence that confronts our communities, our society, and our world.

Key Terms

aggression

brutalization hypothesis

expressive violence

institutional violence

instrumental violence

interpersonal violence

National Crime
  Victimization Survey

National Incident Based
  Reporting System

National Youth Survey

righteous slaughter

spillover theory

structural violence

subcultures of violence

Supplementary
  Homicide Reports

Uniform Crime
  Reporting Program

unity of human aggres-
  sion

violence

Discussion Questions

1. Go to the Federal Bureau of Investigation (FBI) website, www.fbi.gov/ucr/ 05cius/about/aboutucr.html, and find a link to its Uniform Crime Reporting (UCR) Program. Here you will find a historical discussion of the program and how the FBI is now implementing a new program called the National Incident Based Reporting System (NIBRS). What advances does the new NIBRS reporting system have compared with the older UCR program? Will the new system address problems of underreporting in general? Will it still be necessary to have other measures of victimization, like the National Crime Victimization Survey (NCVS)? Why or why not?

2. Spend a few evenings watching the news on a local television network. Monitor how the network covers incidents of violence, both locally and nationally. In your opinion, do you think it has captured the reality of violence in your area or in the nation? What types of violence are most likely to be portrayed? What types of victims and offenders are most likely to be represented?

3. Without looking back at the definitions of violence presented in this chapter, come up with your own definition of interpersonal violence. What elements must a definition have to be useful? Now try your hand at defining genocide. What elements do you believe are necessary to label a case of mass killing as genocide? Now list the ways in which you would measure two types of violence. Be specific. If you are going to use a survey, what types of questions would you ask respondents?

2

Explaining Violence

The origins of conflict have little to do with reason; they are rooted in the very nature of our species and the universe which we inhabit.

—Anthony Stevens[1]

It is unfair to blame man too fiercely for being pugnacious; he learned the habit from Nature.

—Christopher Morley[2]

Human beings have a marked hereditary predisposition to aggressive behavior.

—E. O. Wilson[3]

Research findings, policy choices for the control of violence, and public values are inevitably intertwined. Policy advocates can be expected to selectively publicize findings that support their positions and the methodological flaws in studies that produce contradictory findings.

—National Research Council[4]

As we were putting the final touches on this new edition, two brothers, Tamerlan (age 26) and Dzhokhar (age 19) Tsarnaev placed bombs at the finish line of the Boston Marathon, on April 15, 2013, killing three and wounding over 200. Within days law enforcement officials released images of two suspects that appear to have goaded the two brothers into action. First, they shot and killed a campus security officer at MIT, after which they carjacked a man and forced him to take out money at an ATM before he was able to escape and call 911. This led to a dramatic car chase with police and a shoot-out that left Tamerlan dead and Dzhokhar on the run. Boston was shut down while law enforcement agents swept the area before finally locating the severely wounded Dzhokhar hiding in a boat parked in a driveway. The boys were of Chechen heritage but had been living in the United States for several years. Chechnya is a predominantly Muslim republic in Russia and has been mired in separatist battles for independence since the early 1990s, and many speculate that the elder brother became influenced by radicals there. What motivated them to target the Boston Marathon? Headlines have been splashed across the media daily speculating about their motives, including, "Boston Suspects—Confused Identities and Conflicting Loyalties." This article stated, "As law enforcement and counterterrorism officials try to understand why Mr. Tsarnaev, 19, and his brother, Tamerlan, 26, would attack the Boston Marathon, they will have to consider a cryptic mix of national identity, ideology, religion, and personality."[5] Notice that this statement includes many factors that may have compelled the brothers to their tragic decision. On the other hand, it appears that the elder brother, a former golden globe boxer, had suffered a number of personal setbacks that left him increasingly angry and upset that his life was not working out as he had hoped and which soured him on his adoptive country.[6] Was this the cause of the terror attack? Was Tamerlan simply an embittered man whose inability to succeed in achieving the American dream helped turn him into a religious radical willing to use violence against innocent civilians? As more details emerge over time, light will be shed on the motivations of the two brothers, but it is likely that many questions will also remain unanswered.

When we hear about a mass shooting or see a brutal beating on the news or scores of people being confronted by gunfire from their own government, the first question usually asked is "how could someone do that?" Especially when it is particularly brutal or heinous, we often have a hard time grasping how and why individuals could do such horrible things. How can a man assault his wife over and over again, leaving her bruised and battered, both physically and mentally? How can a mother drown her children? What possesses a young man to take a gun to school and kill as many children as he can? How can a government massacre thousands of its own citizens? Unfortunately, the answers are neither straightforward nor easy. In fact, there is no single answer to these questions. Someone who engages in violence usually does so for many reasons, and even when there is a specific trigger, the behavior is also influenced by a number of other factors including biology, psychology, history, socialization, and culture. Someone who is insulted in a bar, for example, and lashes out at their antagonist is responding primarily to the slur, but their rejoinder is also dictated by their temperament, their conditioning, their life experiences, and a host of other factors. There is no one single cause that brings about violence in any given situation. Instead, we need to understand that behavior is typically the result of numerous elements that interact and influence our actions in many complex ways. This dynamic is even more complicated when it involves conflictual and stressful situations.

Both our history and contemporary existence are filled with violence. There is no time period in human history or any region of the world that has been free of conflict and violence. However, violence is still difficult to predict. Given the same situation, different people may not react the same way, and moreover, the same individuals may not act the same way twice in similar situations. For example, in times of war some soldiers will have a great deal of difficulty carrying out their duties, while others seem to relish engaging in violent behavior, a reality that the Abu Ghraib prison abuses seem to indicate. A night of partying at a bar may often end in a violent brawl for some, while others always seem to end up at Denny's for a different kind of grand slam. The bottom line is that there are many factors related to behavior and none of them individually are good predictors of violence. Many people live their entire lives without engaging in violent behavior, even though they are exposed to the same stresses, experiences, and influences that result in violence for others. Not every argument ends in a fight, not all marriages involve battering, not all men rape, not all nations go to war, and most crowds don't erupt into riots.

Evolution and history have conspired with biology to give humans the ability to engage in violent behavior, yet that potential is dramatically affected by temperament and personality as well as by the cultural, social, and political environments within which people find themselves. In order to explain violence, therefore, we must look at a number of influences and understand that they interact and affect human behavior in a multitude of ways and can vary tremendously from individual to individual and from situation to situation. Some of these influences are conscious while others operate at a subconscious level. In short, all human behavior is affected by a multiplicity of causes and motivations, and violence is no exception to this general rule. Because of this, no single theory alone can explain violence. We must look at a variety of theories, each of which can help us understand a portion of the puzzle that is human violence. These theories can be categorized into several broad categories that include **etho-logical** or **biological**/neurochemical theories, psychological theories, and sociological theories. Keep in mind, however, that these categories are not necessarily mutually exclusive; many theories overlap into more than one grouping. Many psychological perspectives, for example, also include sociological components and vice versa, and with these comments in mind we will begin our discussion with biology.

Ethological and Biological Explanations of Violence

A starting point to the problem of explaining the causes of human violence can be made with evolution and how it has impacted our abilities and propensities for violence. While much about our origins is unknown or disputed, what we do know is that we have evolved to inhabit a world in which violent behavior has often proved necessary for survival because it allows for a range of responses to the problem of staying alive. Of course, the lives of other animals that inhabit our planet are also characterized by a great deal of violence. We can see this when we examine the types of aggression in which animals routinely engage, as illustrated by Table 2.1.

Table 2.1   Typology of Animal Aggression

- Predatory aggression is intended to kill and eat prey.
- Male-on-male aggression is played out between males of the same species and has supremacy as its goal.
- Fear-based aggression is violence in response to a perceived threat where there is no escape.
- Maternal aggression revolves around females protecting their young.
- Irritable aggression derives from pain, frustration, or some sort of deprivation.
- Sex-based aggression is sometimes perpetrated by males who use violence or the threat of it for mating purposes.
- Instrumental aggression refers to aggression generated by experimentation on animals.
- Territorial aggression concerns the defense of land that animals or groups have defined as their own.

SOURCE: Adapted from K. E. Moyer, *The Psychobiology of Aggression* (New York: Harper & Row, 1976).

Looking at the listed motivations for aggressive behavior exhibited by animals in Table 2.1, it is easy to relate most of these to human aggression and violence. **Intermale aggression**, for example, is something that we can easily recognize among young men who sometimes struggle and compete for status by being the toughest and strongest. **Territorial aggression**, on the other hand, concerns animals that fight to control a piece of land they have marked or defined as their own. Is this so different from what people often do? Think about street gangs that use violence to protect their turf, or remember some of the territorial wars and border conflicts between nations. The recent exchanging of missiles between Israelis and Palestinians at the time of this writing is but one example, but examples abound. India and Pakistan have been fighting a limited conflict for over 20 years, because each nation disputes part of its shared border in the high Himalayas. The irony is that the mountainous terrain is so elevated, isolated, and remote that it is virtually uninhabitable, and more soldiers have died from high altitude sickness, avalanches, and falling into crevasses in the glaciers than from enemy action. Territorial aggression, even within the human species, is not always completely rational or useful.

One specific type of violence that was once believed to separate human beings from other animals is murder, since it was assumed that we were the only animals that killed within our own species.[7] While many animals kill, it usually involves animals outside of their species—the most common example is the predator/prey scenario in which certain animal species hunt and kill other animals for food. Certainly, animals sometimes kill others of their kind, but this was considered a rarity and usually accidental. When males of the same species fight for dominance or reproductive rights, the violence typically ends when one or the other submits. A lethal outcome is not usually the norm. However, more contemporary research is discovering that many species do frequently engage in violence against each other, and the outcomes are, in fact, often deadly.[8] We can certainly see this if we examine our closest relatives, apes—which include chimpanzees, bonobos, gorillas, and orangutans.

Genetically, humans are closest to chimpanzees. Research has shown that humans and chimps share between 96% and 99% of the same DNA makeup, which means that, genetically, humans are more closely related to chimpanzees than chimps are to gorillas.[9] Chimpanzee violence, therefore, can reveal much about the evolutionary roots of human violence. The image many people have of peaceful chimpanzees was largely shaped by the pioneering work of Jane Goodall, who spent many years studying and writing about the chimpanzees of Tanzania.[10]

Far from being peaceful, except in extremely unusual circumstances, we now know that chimpanzees routinely engage in murder, assassination, rape, raiding, and even what can be considered war.[11] Researchers have documented various instances in which groups of chimpanzees have attacked and killed males from rival groups. Sometimes it is an opportunistic attack on members of competitor groups that encroach on their range, while other times they have been observed stalking, ambushing, and killing chimpanzees in raids that take place on rival territory. Chimpanzees are territorial and, like many animals, defend their land vigorously from intruders and trespassers. They patrol the boundaries of their range and will attack chimpanzees not from their own group. In many ways, as we noted above, this mirrors the behavior of nations and gangs—both of which engage in the same kinds of territorial defense. Chimpanzees also engage in raids intended to kill all of the rival males of another group and incorporate the surviving females into their own community.[12] Can we characterize this as warfare or perhaps even as genocide? As you will see, many of the characteristics certainly appear to be the same.

Similarly, male-on-female chimpanzee violence appears to be very similar to human male-on-female violence. In fact, Wrangham and Peterson suggest that it may best be described as battering since, as they have observed,

> Chimpanzee battering and human battering are similar in three respects. First, they are both cases of predominantly male against female violence. Second, they are both instances of relationship violence; male chimpanzees batter females who are members of their community, ordinarily known to them for many years, often in contexts with nothing material, such as food or support for an ally, at stake. Third, like human battering, the battering of a female chimpanzee may take place during or be triggered by a number of superficial contexts, but the underlying issue looks to be domination or control.[13]

An important point to note is that chimpanzee violence generally and battering in particular is largely perpetrated by males. Female chimpanzees tend to be much less aggressive and violent than male chimps. Again, we see the same pattern when we examine human violence. One of the most consistent patterns of human violence is that it is largely perpetrated by males. Around the world and in most situations, most violent victims and offenders are men. Often, this violence revolves around issues of **status** and **dominance**. Male chimpanzees compete for status against other males within the same group, and much of their daily behavior revolves around this rivalry. It's interesting to note that once a male has achieved high status, his tendency to rely on violence falls dramatically. Much of the violence, in other words, is intended to help him attain higher rank and to preserve that position. A lower-ranked male who doesn't act submissively to a higher-ranked male, for example, risks a violent reprisal from the higher-ranked male.[14] How different is this from a young man who assaults someone over some perceived slight or act of disrespect? As you will see in Chapter 4, many murders occur because an individual feels disrespected or insulted by what someone else has said or done.[15] Wrangham and Peterson specifically suggest that pride is at the root of the quest for status and prestige. It's hard to dispute this when we acknowledge that perceived insults, challenges to status, and showing a lack of respect are all factors in a lot of violent behavior for both chimpanzees and human beings. In many ways, perhaps we have not traveled that far from our ancestral origins. Without overdoing these comparisons, we can certainly suggest that human and chimpanzee violence share many of the same origins and characteristics. This is important to recognize, since it illustrates that violence—or at least the capacity for violence—is part of our evolutionary heritage and is a quality we still share with our closest animal relatives. In short, the potential for violence resides within all of us. This ethological argument, as it is known, is summed up by Jeffrey Goldstein, who writes, "Our animal ancestors were instinctively violent beings, and since we have evolved from them, we too must be the bearers of destructive impulses in our genetic makeup."[16]

To suggest that we are predisposed to violence because of our evolutionary heritage, however, is not to say that we are doomed to violence. Not all people engage in violence, even though everybody is potentially capable of it. Many factors affect how and why individuals engage in aggressive behavior, including individual temperament, gender, emotion, biological predisposition and/or trauma, the presence or absence of weapons, alcohol, drugs, and the cultural, political, and situational contexts that people experience. It is therefore a mistake to classify people as either violent or peaceful. Humans are both. Some individuals engage in more frequent violence and/or more severe forms than others, but the bottom line is that everyone is capable of it. That being said, we can next look at some of the specific ways in which biology and chemistry have been linked with violent behavior.

It must be noted that explaining violence in biological terms has historically been fraught with controversy. This is largely because early research on biology and crime was based on faulty science that suggested the causes of crime lay with defective individuals. From this perspective, social and environmental factors were largely irrelevant. Early scientific studies focused on body types, skull shapes, bad genes, and atavistic (e.g., primitive) attributes to suggest that criminals were born, not made.[17] In the late 1700s and early 1800s, for example, Franz Joseph Gall suggested that criminals and violent offenders could be identified by looking at the shape of the skull, which was believed to reflect the personalities of the individual.[18] They subscribed to the belief that the spatial dimensions of the skull were dictated by the underlying development of the brain. Since specific parts of the brain were linked with specific functions, they hoped to identify the part of the brain that controlled crime and aggression by studying skull shapes. Advocates of this perspective, known as **phrenology**, took diligent measurement of prisoners' skulls in order to determine the specific type of skull shapes that would reveal criminality. This school of thought remained quite popular until the early 20th century in the United States. Similarly, the Italian physician Cesare Lombroso suggested in the late 1800s that criminals were born because

> . . . germs of an ancestral past lie dormant in our heredity. In some unfortunate individuals, the past comes to life again. These people are innately driven to act as a normal ape or savage would, but such behavior is deemed criminal in our civilized society.[19]

❖ Photo 2.1   Chimpanzee mother with baby attacks male

In essence, Lombroso was arguing that violent criminals were evolutionary throwbacks or **atavisms,** and the problem of crime rested upon the shoulders of individuals who were born to be violent and criminal. They could be identified, he concluded, through a number of distinguishing characteristics that included the following: a small head with a large facial area; a sloping forehead; large, protruding ears; bushy eyebrows that met over the nose; abnormally large teeth; and tattoos. Looking around a typical office setting or college classroom, one wonders how many workers or students might share some of these characteristics. In fact, later research challenging these notions concluded that these characteristics were as common in the general population as they were among offenders. As far-fetched as this work now seems, we can't underestimate its influence over the years for those looking to identify criminals through their appearance and demeanor. These notions clearly have implications for policies aimed at reducing crime and violence; if people are born that way, some may argue, why can't we just lock them up and throw away the key? See the problem?

As you can see, the implications of these theories are profound and disturbing. At different times, they have been used to justify racism, discrimination, oppression, slavery, and even genocide. If the causes of crime can be traced to born criminals, then we don't have to examine problematic social issues such as poverty, inequality, racism, and/or discrimination. Instead, our attention is focused on identifying, controlling, and punishing those who are supposedly born to be violent and/or criminal. Keep in mind that this kind of criminological research helped form the basis of the **Eugenics movement**, which tried to improve the human race through selective breeding practices, forced sterilization programs, and similar kinds of policies. These ideas also formed the philosophical justification for many discriminatory laws, beliefs, and policies.[20]

Because of their political and social misuses, many social scientists and others have an almost instinctive mistrust of biological studies of criminality. But science has come a long way from the early days of measuring body types and skull shapes and we now know a great deal more about how the human body functions. Ignoring the biological factors that influence behavior ultimately condemns us to an incomplete understanding of the causes of human violence. It also helps create a false dichotomy by suggesting that the causes of human behavior are either biological or social. The truth lies somewhere in between. Violence is indeed influenced by innate biological factors, but social, cultural, and political circumstances also affect violent behavior. One neuroscientist who studies violence summarizes it this way:

> Violence cannot be linked to one gene, one brain region, one actor; it cannot be viewed in isolation, and it cannot be detached from history. The product of both nature and nurture, aggressive behavior is an ongoing and collaborative effort between the world

of genes and proteins inside the neuron and the constantly changing and occasionally hostile world on the outside.[21]

So what does modern biology tell us about violence? What are the biological factors that affect the likelihood of a particular person engaging in violence? Recent research in this area has tended to focus on either brain injuries or on substances produced in the body, such as neurotransmitters and hormones. These two areas suggest that violence is at least partially the result of somebody's brain not working correctly because of head trauma or because the body is producing to much or too little of some substance that also affects behavior. It is to these schools of thought that we now turn the discussion.

Serotonin

In the brain, data messages are transmitted between nerve cells via a synapse, which is essentially a small gap between the nerve cells or neurons. **Serotonin** is a substance that helps relay those messages over the gap and allows them to proceed. Without serotonin, data messages don't make it across the gap or, if they do, they tend to be incomplete and garbled. Behaviorally, deficiencies in serotonin have been linked to a wide variety of disorders, such as depression, suicide, and anxiety. Importantly, they have also been linked with impulsive acts of aggression. People with low levels of serotonin appear to be more likely to engage in violence because their ability to control their aggressive impulses is diminished. Serotonin acts as an impulse inhibitor, and lower levels of this neurotransmitter hamper a person's ability to stop and think.[22] We need to understand, however, that while this may help explain certain types of impulsive violence that are essentially overreactions to some sort of provocation, serotonin levels do not help us to understand how other, more calculated forms of violence are perpetrated. At the risk of sounding redundant, we also need to remember that low levels of serotonin are not sufficient, in and of itself, to produce violence. Serotonin deficiency is just one of many possible contributing factors that help explain the puzzle of violence.

Testosterone

Another substance produced in the body that has received a tremendous amount of attention for its possible connection to violence is the hormone **testosterone**. Given that most violence is perpetrated by males, some have suggested that male aggression is linked with levels of testosterone. Proponents of this argument contend that individuals with higher levels of testosterone are more likely to be aggressive. Supporting evidence of this comes from animal studies showing that aggressive and violent animals become meek and mild when castrated and resume their violent behavior when given shots of testosterone.[23] On the other hand, while these studies appear to show a strong relationship between testosterone and aggression, research on humans reveals a much more complicated relationship between testosterone and violence. While some research has shown that the most violent offenders have higher levels of testosterone than nonviolent offenders, other investigators have failed to replicate these results.

Additionally, whereas some research has supported this finding in both adult[24] and juvenile populations,[25] other studies have not. For example, one Canadian project found no statistical difference in testosterone levels between men charged with violent crimes and those charged with nonviolent property offenses.[26] Other contrary evidence comes from the use of testosterone to treat a variety of medical conditions, including some sexual dysfunctions. Studies have shown that men who are given testosterone for these problems do not become more aggressive.[27] To further muddy the waters, evidence also shows that participation in sports affects men's testosterone levels. Winning tends to increase levels, while the losers are apt to have a decrease. Similar decreases and increases have also been measured in military personnel during basic training.[28] This suggests that winning in competitive situations increases testosterone levels in men, while losing depresses levels. What does this mean?

While the contradictory research does not allow a definitive answer, it does seem to imply that, in many ways, testosterone is more about status and dominance than about violence. This is illustrated by a study looking at status among prison inmates that found prisoners with low status also had low levels of testosterone. On the other hand, both nonviolent, high-status inmates and violent, high-status inmates had very similar high levels of the hormone.[29] As you can see, the empirical evidence about the relationship between testosterone and violence is extremely inconclusive, but what does appear clear is that when men compete for status, prestige, and dominance, their testosterone levels rise and fall according to their fortunes, regardless of whether or not they use violence in that struggle.

Brain Injuries

Other biological research on violence rather than focusing on hormones and neurotransmitters, has examined brain function by looking at things such as lesions in the brain caused by injuries, tumors, and other kinds of trauma to the head. This avenue of research was spurred by the University of Texas Tower shooter, Charles J. Whitman, who in 1966 killed 14 people and wounded 32 others before himself being gunned down by police.[30] His autopsy revealed that had a glioblastoma tumor growing in his brain. A commission formed to find out why Whitman perpetrated this crime concluded that the tumor could have contributed to his decisions to commit this mass murder. Although not everyone agrees with this assessment, it nevertheless helped spark interest in brain lesions and trauma to help explain some violent offending.

Antisocial and violent individuals have been subjected to magnetic resonance imaging (MRI), which relies on magnetic fields to view the tissue of the brain, and positron emission tomography (PET), a nuclear imaging technique that creates 3-D images of the brain. These studies have revealed that violent offenders, especially impulsively aggressive individuals, often have **brain dysfunctions** that are believed to have played a role in predisposing some of them to violent behavior.[31] One study using electroencephalographic (EEG) brain scans found that those who showed a long-term pattern of violent behavior were three times more likely (65%) to have abnormalities in the EEG readings than those who were rarely violent.[32] In a similar vein, a study of Danish men, English schoolboys, and California death row inmates concluded that brain trauma was an important element in producing violent behavior.[33] The difficulty with this kind of research, however, is deciding whether the lesions caused violent behavior or whether violence caused the lesions. It's not unreasonable to expect that someone prone to violence is also more likely to sustain head injuries as the result of violent encounters. Unfortunately, it is almost impossible to establish the appropriate time-order between these two variables. It's the old chicken versus the egg question as to which came first.

The biological theories we have just reviewed tend to focus on the physical functioning of the brain as it is affected by injury or various substances and chemicals. In contrast, psychological perspectives—while focusing on the same region of the body—tend to study the mind. If the brain is the machine, the mind is the product. Psychological perspectives therefore seek to understand violent behavior in terms of personality, character, and mental disorder. One of the most well-known psychological theories of violence involves what is commonly known as **psychopathy** or **sociopathy** but is more correctly termed **antisocial personality disorder**.[34]

Antisocial Personality Disorder

Most people are at least superficially familiar with this personality type, because it is a term that is used often in popular culture. This type of individual is characterized as being very narcissistic, reckless, and emotionally shallow (see Table 2.2). Importantly, they are also unable to empathize or feel compassion for others. For these individuals, the suffering of others does not touch them emotionally, so they have no compunction about hurting others. In many ways, it comes down to the issue of empathy. The ability to feel the pain of others, to put yourself in their place, to share their feelings is a crucial element in developing a moral sense of your actions. Research shows that morality develops best when young people are shown how their actions affect others, but individuals with this disorder show an impaired ability to empathize. Simply put, they can't process the pain and fear of others.[35] In addition to this, they also have a reduced ability to process fear, which means that the punishments and negative consequences that often prevent the majority of us from doing things we want don't really act as a deterrent to these individuals. Punishment doesn't scare them. These factors are combined with a tendency for them to be extremely self-centered, seeing others as a means to an end. As such, they do not hesitate to employ violence to fulfill their selfish goals. They act out of pure self-interest, without reference to a moral or ethical compass.[36] In fact, historically, this kind of disorder was originally defined as a kind of "moral insanity."[37] This doesn't mean, however, that they are crazy. These individuals are fairly well grounded in reality and understand right from wrong, they just don't appear to care.[38] People with this disorder are consequently marked by high incidence of instrumental forms of violence, which makes sense since instrumental violence is a means to an end.[39] They use aggression because it helps them get their way or acquire something they want. The fact that their violence harms and injures others is irrelevant to them. While many kinds of disorders are marked by reactive aggression or violence as a response to some threat or frustration, those with psychopathy tend to have higher levels of instrumental aggression.[40]

Table 2.2 Characteristics of Antisocial Personality Disorder
Inferred Personality Traits   • Glibness, superficial charm   • Grandiose sense of self-worth/narcissism   • Pathological lying   • Cunning, manipulative behavior   • Lack of remorse or guilt   • Shallow affect   • Callousness/lack of empathy   • Failure to accept responsibility for actions/blames others
Explicit Lifestyle Traits   • Constant need for stimulation/easily bored   • Parasitic lifestyle   • Poor behavioral controls/impulsive   • Early onset behavioral problems   • Lack of realistic, long-term goals   • Irresponsibility   • Juvenile delinquency
Other Traits   • Promiscuous sexual behavior   • Multiple short-term marital relationships   • Criminal versatility and skills

SOURCE: Table 2.2 Adapted from Eric W. Hickey, *Serial Murderers and Their Victims*, 2nd ed. (Belmont, CA: Wadsworth, 1997).

This type of personality disorder is most commonly associated with serial killers, although not all serial killers suffer from this disorder and, importantly, not everyone with this disorder is a serial killer. In fact, most of us have some antisocial tendencies, although not to the same degree as individuals diagnosed with antisocial personality disorder.[41] Furthermore, the National Institute of Mental Health estimates that only around 3% of the U.S. population can be categorized as having this problem.[42] The infrequency of this disorder, compared with the levels of violence in this country, indicates that most violent offenders do not fit into this classification, even though we often popularly describe violent individuals as being psychopaths or sociopaths. Importantly, it appears as if these individuals may represent a small but distinct class among violent criminals.[43] One study of violent incarcerated felons, for example, found that out of the sample of 321 felons, only 36 were diagnosed with psychopathy; these offenders had more arrests for more types of offenses, including more violent offenses, and they appeared to be proud of their violent behavior.[44] But again, this group represents a small percentage of all violent offenders. We know that a small minority of violent offenders tend to commit most crimes.[45] Among this group, those with psychopathy tend to be career criminals with more offenses and greater amounts of violence.[46] This serves to feed into the image of criminals as psychopaths. A fairly recent example of this tendency is the argument made by a number of criminologists who suggested that our society was home to a new breed of violent offender known as "**superpredators**." First popularized by the criminologist John DiIulio, this argument suggested that

> America is now home to thickening ranks of juvenile "superpredators"—radically impulsive, brutally remorseless youngsters, including ever more preteenage boys, who murder, assault, rape, rob, burglarize, deal deadly drugs, join gun toting gangs, and create serious communal disorders. They do not fear the stigma of arrest, the pains of imprisonment, or the pangs of conscience. They perceive hardly any relationship between doing right (or wrong) now and being rewarded (or punished) for it later. To these mean-street youngsters, the words "right" and "wrong" have no fixed moral meaning.[47]

Essentially, the description of these superpredators portrays young offenders as sociopaths. In reality, this dire vision of the future has not been fulfilled by rates of violent crime. In fact, rates of violent crime today are significantly lower than they were in the early 1990s. Unfortunately, this image of the ultraviolent delinquent remains a fixture of the popular imagination.

We can't turn from this image of the malevolent psychopath or teen superpredator without at least considering the ideas of Roy Baumeister and W. Keith Campbell, who suggest that, for some people, violence has an intrinsic appeal.[48] While recognizing that violence can occur for instrumental or ideological reasons, it can also result from individuals being bored and looking for the excitement, kicks, and thrills often found in risk-taking behavior, such as violence. Some of these individuals, in other words, may actually find violent behavior enjoyable. Specifically, Baumeister and Campbell identify three reasons why violence can be gratifying. The first is **sadism,** in which people derive pleasure from harming others. The second involves the gratification that can result from performing high-risk and potentially destructive behaviors and getting away with it. The third rationale suggests that individuals can find satisfaction from harming someone whom they perceive has threatened or somehow damaged their positive self-image.[49] In many ways, these ideas parallel the work of Jack Katz, who also emphasized the attractions of illegal behavior in his work on the seduction of criminality.[50] Katz's argument is that violence and criminality can have an intrinsic appeal for some individuals because it can be fun, exciting, and empowering. Other psychological perspectives pay more attention to the external forces that trigger aggression and violence rather than specific personality disorders. One such example is the **frustration-aggression hypothesis**.

Frustration-Aggression Hypothesis

The frustration-aggression hypothesis contends that violence is one possible response for individuals who feel, as the name implies, frustrated and thwarted in achieving something. It can be broken down into three main components: a person is blocked from achieving something they want; this results in them becoming frustrated and upset; and this frustration may lead them to respond violently.[51] In this scenario, violence is one of many possible responses. The violence may be instrumental in the sense that it is used as a way to remove some obstacle to achieving a goal, or it may be expressive as a way of venting that frustration or letting off some steam. Research indicates that certain factors increase the likelihood of a violent outcome, such as when a person perceives their frustration as being intentionally caused by someone else, when they perceive the hindrance as being unfair, and when an aggressive stimulus, such as a weapon or even aggressive music, is present.[52] The final psychological perspective that we will examine goes even further in weaving in external influences to help explain violence. While medical researchers were the first to discover the negative influence of stress on illness and mortality, social researchers soon discovered that **stress** was also related to behavioral outcomes, including violence.

Stress and Violence

As portions of this book illustrate, certain minority groups, who are often marginalized and overrepresented in measures of poverty, are overrepresented both among the perpetrators and victims of violent crime. This pattern tends to be fairly consistent across the board. Table 2.3 reports rates of total violent victimizations as well as robbery and total assault victimizations by race and ethnicity for 2011. As you can see, American Indian or Alaskan Natives have rates that are over 3 times those of whites, while African Americans have rates that are also higher than whites. This is true for both robbery and assault victimizations.

These patterns are largely because of the overrepresentation of minority communities among the ranks of the poor, where they not only suffer from **economic deprivation** but also from discrimination and racism. In other words, many minority

Table 2.3 Violent Victimizations per 1,000 Persons Age 12 and Older (Excluding Homicides) by Race/Ethnicity (National Crime Victimization Survey, 2010)

	Total Violent	Robbery	Total Assaults
Race/Ethnicity			
White*	13.6	1.4	11.6
Black*	20.8	3.6	16.1
Hispanic	15.6	2.7	12.0
American Indian or Alaskan Native*	42.4	4.3	37.9
Asian or Pacific Islander*	6.3	1.1	4.5
Two or more races*	52.6	8.0	43.5

* Excludes persons of Hispanic origin
SOURCE: Adapted from Table 9, Criminal Victimization, 2010, Bureau of Justice Statistics, U.S. Department of Justice.[53]

populations live in more impoverished and more difficult life situations, and these situations are largely responsible for their higher levels of violent crime. While cultural adaptations among poor minority groups may explain some of the violence,[54] much of it is also because of the circumstances of their lives. African American couples living in nonpoor neighborhoods are three times less likely than African American couples living in poor neighborhoods to suffer from intimate partner violence.[55] The same is true for homicide, with research indicating that poor African Americans experience much higher homicide rates than middle- and upper-class African Americans.[56] In short, violence is not distributed equally across society but instead occurs more frequently among some groups and in some locations compared with others. One possible explanation for this pattern relates to the effects of chronic stress on individuals and groups.

Human beings are tremendously adaptable creatures, and our bodies have many ways of responding to difficult and/or threatening situations. Our cardiovascular and immune systems, for example, respond to stressors in ways that help us cope and deal with life. In truth, all our physiological and neurological systems are affected by stress. Linsky, Bachman, and Straus summarize it this way:

> When the organism is faced with external threats, survival mechanisms prepare it for flight or fight. There is an emergency discharge of adrenaline, a quickening of the pulse, an increase in blood pressure, stimulation of the central nervous system, temporary suspension of digestion, a quickening of blood clotting, and a rise in the blood sugar. These physiological responses prepare the organism for heightened physical activity, such as aggression or flight.[57]

This flexibility allows human beings to survive in a sometimes dangerous, complex, and often changing world. Yet prolonged stress has many adverse affects on the body and mind because it puts a tremendous strain on the various systems and organs. Our bodies can handle stress in the short term, but in the long run our bodies' abilities to react wears out. Consequently our reactions get out of sync to stimuli or, as Debra Niehoff points out

> Forced to operate at a capacity for which they were never designed, the reciprocal processes that regulate neurotransmission and neuroendocrine function during stress overshoot, break down, or oscillate frenetically . . . Depression, impulsive Type H aggression, PTSD and antisocial personality disorder are very different expressions of a common failure to assign the correct emotional valence to memories, thoughts, or external events; as a result, stimulus and response are mismatched.[58]

In other words, prolonged stress compromises our ability to respond to events. How does this relate to patterns of violence? As we indicated above, we know that many forms of violence are concentrated among the ranks of the poor, and we also know that low-income neighborhoods and communities suffer from a disproportionate amount of social problems that often include high rates of drug and alcohol abuse, gang violence, street crime, and the like. Individuals in these communities also suffer the daily strains and indignities of living with few resources within a society which largely ignores their plight. People struggle to get by, to survive, and to make ends meet. They also have to be on their guard and react to potentially dangerous situations. In short, the poor tend to lead stressful lives that over time decrease their ability to cope. Violence, at least in part, may be a result of a declining ability to cope with stressful life situations. Debra Niehoff says it well when she points out that

> This is why bad neighborhoods, bad homes, and bad relationships breed violence—not because of a deterioration in moral character but because of a steady deterioration in the ability to cope. As stress wears away at the nervous system, risk assessment grows less and less accurate. Minor insults are seen as major threats. Benign details take on a new emotional urgency. Empathy takes a back seat to relief from the numbing discomfort of a stress-deadened nervous system.[59]

In many ways, then, violence is sometimes part of a developmental process rather than an absolute imperative. Human beings are outfitted with a nervous system that is capable of responding aggressively when we feel threatened, and the ways we respond to situations and experiences can then have a lasting effect on our neurobiological processes.[60] Being exposed to stressful situations results in certain responses, which in turn affect our subsequent reactions. The notion of the "vicious circle" is a cliché, but it is true nonetheless.

While there are a variety of other biological and psychological explanations of violence, these explanations all illustrate important ideas about how individuals come to engage in violent behavior. The weakness of these explanations, however, is that they cannot adequately explain patterns of violence. These theories are by their very nature individualistic in orientation and not that helpful in explaining differences in patterns of violence between different regions, countries, or populations. Why does one community or neighborhood have so much more violence than another? It's certainly not likely that everyone with low levels of serotonin or with brain lesions lives in some communities but not in others. Logically, we would expect these individual kinds of problems to be distributed randomly throughout society. Because of their focus on individual aberrations and pathologies, most biological and psychological theories are unable to address this question. We therefore need to look at the social units of society for further explanation and examine such things as the family, peer groups, neighborhoods, and the communities within which people live in order to further explain the origins of violence.

Sociological Explanations of Violence

Sociological explanations of violence tend to focus largely on structural and cultural life situations that affect the behavior of individuals and groups. Some sociological theories focus on large macro-units like society itself, while others focus on smaller units like the family. But, in general, they address themselves to determining what environmental conditions or situations help bring about violent behavior. So, while biological and psychological theories focus on internal pushes toward behavior, sociological theories tend to examine the external influences on behavior.

Economic Deprivation

One factor that has often been linked with violence is poverty—often referred to as economic deprivation. This, of course, is related to the stress literature we noted above since one element of stress would certainly be the inability to provide for your family. However, sociologists have articulated the manifestations of poverty in greater detail. Since the early part of the 20th century, criminologists have noted that poor neighborhoods, communities, and groups tend to have much higher rates of violence compared with those that are better off economically. Obviously, not all poverty is strongly connected with violence. Most poor people never engage in crime, much less violent crime. This reality has led a number of scholars to assert that it is not absolute poverty that is associated with criminality and violence, but rather inequality—sometimes referred to as **relative deprivation**. In other words, being poor and living within a relatively affluent community is a much more negative experience than being poor and living within a poor community. This can be generalized to the societal level as well; people who are poor in societies where some are extremely wealthy suffer greater compared to those who live in societies where the majority are similarly poor. The greater the gap between the haves and have-nots, it is believed, the greater the likelihood of negative outcomes, such as crime and violence.

A great deal of research has found that the most powerful predictor of homicide rates between cities, states, counties, and census tracts is income inequality between rich and poor.[61] One study examined research on this topic going back to 1967 and found that income inequality was strongly connected with violent crime throughout this time period, especially homicides and assaults.[62] So what is the connection between inequality and violent behavior? Williams and Flewelling articulate it this way:

> It is reasonable to assume that when people live under conditions of extreme scarcity, the struggle for survival is intensified. Such conditions are often accompanied by a host of agitating psychological manifestations, ranging from a deep sense of powerlessness and brutalization to anger, anxiety, and alienation. Such manifestations can provoke physical aggression in conflict situations.[63]

James Gilligan suggests that the linkage between poverty and violence is caused by one specific factor: **shame**. Based on his research, and experience working with prison inmates, Gilligan contends that

> It is difficult not to feel inferior if one is poor when others are rich, especially in a society that equates self-worth with net worth; and it is difficult not to feel rejected and worthless if one cannot get or hold a job while others continue to be employed. Of course, most people who lose jobs or income do not commit murders as a result; but there are always some men who are just barely maintaining their self-esteem at minimally tolerable levels even when they do have jobs and incomes. And when large numbers of them lose those sources of self-esteem, the number who explode into homicidal rage increases as measurably, regularly, and predictably as any epidemic.[64]

Similar to the frustration and aggression hypothesis but focusing more on the societal factors than the psychological manifestations, several sociologists have articulated what have been called **strain theories** of crime and violence.

Strain Theories

Strain theories generally contend that blocked or frustrated needs and desires may result in criminality and violence. One of the first theories to make this argument was developed by Robert K. Merton, who pointed out that people living in impoverished circumstances are placed under strain because their access to conventional and legitimate means of success is severely limited.[65] While the goals of success and material wealth are distributed throughout society, the means of accomplishing these goals are not. Merton believed that a state of "**anomie**" would result when individuals lived under conditions where legitimate means were not available to achieve societal goals. In our capitalist and money-oriented society, material wealth is equated with success. Yet the pathways to achieving these ambitions, such as getting a good education and getting a well-paying job with good benefits and opportunities for promotions, are hard to come by if you are poor. According to Merton, individuals may choose from a variety of adaptations that include: conformity to the goals even if the means are not readily available; retreatism, which involves a rejection of the goals and the means through drug or alcohol abuse; rebellion, which may involve an attempt to replace the accepted goals and means with new or revolutionary ones; and ritualism, signifying an acceptance of the status quo. Importantly for our purposes, an individual may choose to innovate or come up with creative ways of acquiring the things they value. For example, some may decide to deal drugs or hold up liquor stores in order to get the money to buy the things they want. Obviously, these choices come with increased risk of violent confrontation.

Steven Messner and Richard Rosenfeld have more recently developed what they call an **institutional-anomie theory of crime** that links crime to the existing social structure. Specifically, they suggest that the high rates of crime and violence found in U.S. society can, in part, be explained with reference to the notion of the "American Dream," which suggests that economic success can be achieved by anyone who works hard, plays by the rules, and is willing to engage in competition with others for jobs, income, and status. For Messner and Rosenfeld, anomie is the "deregulation of both the goals that people are encouraged to aspire to, and the means that are regarded as acceptable in the pursuit of these goals."[66] They contend that the economic goals of profit and material gain in U.S. society have no clear stopping points; no matter how much money you accumulate, there is always more that could be attained. The more you have, the more you want, and it is this that increases the unregulated and anomic quality of U.S. life. Messner and Rosenfeld importantly note that other institutions, such as the family and schools, provide alternative goals to profit and gain. However, when the roles of these other institutions are devalued in comparison to the economic institution, they lose their ability to temper and constrain the anomic tendencies inherent in a capitalist society like the United States. The result, Messner and Rosenfeld contend, is that our culture pressures people to strive relentlessly for success—primarily monetary success—and the fact that some consequently turn to crime and violence, they believe, should not be seen as surprising.

In his **general strain theory**, Robert Agnew refined anomie theory to include strains other than economic conditions.[67] For Agnew, the strains people experience revolve around much more than just differences between goals and the ability to achieve them. Specifically, he argues that strain can come from three main sources, which include the following situations: An individual is stopped from achieving a goal; something they possess or value is removed and/or threatened; and something negative or unwanted is imposed. When somebody experiences one of these three situations, and when that occurrence is accompanied by difficulty in coping and a sense of anger, then violence may result as that person lashes out to resolve the situation through force and aggression.

While there are other variations of these kinds of theories, they all share a basic contention that structural inequalities affect individual behavior. In contrast, another school of thought focuses more attention on the cultural and group adaptations to these disadvantaged conditions. These perspectives suggest that much violence stems from the values and beliefs adopted by certain groups.

Cultural Adaptations

Elijah Anderson suggests that some poor young African American men develop what he labels a "**code of the street**," which involves a strong sense of personal honor combined with a corresponding emphasis on guarding against personal affronts and insults.[68] These young men take respect very seriously and are more likely to respond violently to what is perceived as disrespectful. Anderson writes,

> Central to the issue of manhood is the widespread belief that one of the most effective ways of gaining respect is to manifest nerve. A man shows nerve by taking another person's possessions, messing with someone's woman, throwing the first punch, "getting in someone's face," or pulling a trigger. Its proper display helps check others who would violate one's person, and it also helps build a reputation that works to prevent future challenges . . . True nerve expresses a lack of fear of death. Many feel that it is acceptable to risk dying over issues of respect. In fact, among the hard-core street-oriented, the clear risk of violent death may be preferable to being dissed.[69]

In many ways, it is an oppositional subculture to the mainstream that places a premium on being treated right and deferentially. It is, according to Anderson, a cultural adaptation in the face of overwhelming alienation and racism and a way of asserting personal power in a society in which many feel powerless. In one sense, we can understand this cultural perspective as an extension of the literature on strain and frustration. Other sociological perspectives examine smaller social units such as peer groups and families in order to understand their influence on deviant behavior, including violence. The most general of these, **social learning theory**, combines various sociological and psychological insights in trying to make sense of the puzzle of human behavior.

Social Learning Theory

As the name implies, social learning theory contends that violence is learned in the same way that anything else is learned. We learn from the things we experience, the things we see, and the people with whom we associate. We learn from our surroundings, experiences, acquaintances, friends, and family. Research has shown that individuals learn to

❖ Photo 2.2   Gang member initiation

respond aggressively and violently when they are rewarded for it, when they observe it, when they are victimized by it, and when people don't develop strong positive connections with others.[70] Social learning theory specifically asserts that people learn through conditioning, reinforcement, and imitation and modeling. For example, people learn to expect either rewards or punishments for certain behaviors, such as a schoolyard bully who may come to expect respect from fellow students. Bullies may also learn to anticipate more tangible rewards, such as lunch money or favors, or

perhaps humiliating others makes them feel powerful for a moment. People learn not only from direct experience but also by watching what happens to others and modeling behavior based on those observations. This latter is especially true for children, who find out how to behave by watching their parents and others. Research indicates, for example, that children learn aggression when they view it, are positively reinforced for engaging in it, and/or experience it at the hands of others such as parents and siblings.[71]

One sociological variant of social learning theory, known as **differential association theory**, asserts that if you associate with individuals and groups who use violence and who have attitudes supporting and justifying violence, then you are more likely to engage in violent behavior yourself. Revolutionary in impact when it was first developed by Edwin Sutherland in the 1940s, this theory was one of the first to suggest that criminality and violence were not aberrations but were simply learned behaviors like all other behaviors.[72] What this theory explicitly recognizes is that friends, family, and acquaintances teach not only the techniques of criminality but also the motivations and attitudes supporting that behavior. Sutherland contends that crime happens when an individual comes to have a preponderance of attitudes supporting certain behaviors versus attitudes prohibiting that behavior. In regards to violence, people learn not only the methods of violence but the attitudes, rationalizations, justifications, and vocabulary as well.[73]

Youth gangs are a good example of differential association in action. Gangs are very good at inculcating violent attitudes among their membership. New members often undergo a ritualized beating by older members known as "**jumping in**" that is intended to prove the toughness of the new member but also symbolizes the centrality of violence to the life of the gang.[74] Within these groups, violence is often the preferred means of protecting each other, territory or turf, and reputation and status. Here's how one LA gang member framed it to a new recruit:

> You got potential, 'cause you eager to learn. Bangin' ain't no part-time thang, it's full-time, it's a career. It's bein' down when ain't nobody else down with you. It's gettin' caught and not tellin'. Killin' and not caring, and dyin' without fear. It's love for your set and hate for the enemy. You hear what I'm sayin'?[75]

Obviously, the ability to accept and mete out violence was fundamental to how this person defined being a gang member. New members into the gang are quickly socialized into this particular worldview that includes not only the "hows" of gang life, but the "whys" as well. Subsequently, the criminologists Robert Burgess and Ronald Akers revised some of Sutherland's ideas by suggesting that we not only learn from people with whom we associate but also from those we watch and with whom we identify. In other words, we can learn and imitate violent behaviors and attitudes from individuals and groups we have never even met. Perhaps the most obvious example of how this kind of learning works is the mass media.

Social Learning, Media, and Violence

The evidence connecting media images of violence and actual violent behavior is by now beyond doubt. Media violence and images affect those who view them.[76] Grossman and DeGaetano put it this way:

> Scientific evidence overwhelmingly supports media violence as a major, significant factor contributing to real-life violence in our society . . . Since 1950 there has been a total of more than 3,500 research studies conducted in America on the effects of media violence on the population. One random analysis of almost 1,000 studies found that all save only 18 (12 were funded by the television industry) demonstrate there is a tangible correlation between violent entertainment and violent behavior.[77]

A recent review of the effects of playing violent video games also confirms that exposure to video game violence increases the risk of aggressive behavior both in the short term and for players later in life, both for girls and boys, and for children growing up both in Eastern and Western cultures.[78] Let us be clear. Increasing the risk of aggression does not mean "causes" aggression. Media violence doesn't cause violence per se; instead, it teaches us how to interpret and understand situations. Script theory tells us that we often learn to associate certain roles and behaviors with certain social situations.[79] A script can be described as a mental or cognitive program that helps us define situations in understandable and meaningful ways. Scripts guide our behavior, help us solve social problems, and are typically linked with specific roles and plans of action.[80] Television and movies are ubiquitous and powerful sources for many of our attitudes and values, and watching violent media images provides us with the vocabulary of motives and situations that serves to increase the likelihood that we will also engage in violence. In other words, it helps teach us how to interpret and react to conflictual situations and thus helps to make a violent reaction more likely. For example, research shows that when individuals are repeatedly exposed to violent media, ambiguous events are more likely to be perceived as being hostile. Importantly, exposure to graphic violent images also desensitizes people to violent situations and events. Humans are adaptable and, given time, are capable of getting used to many things. Violence is no exception. The more someone is exposed to violence—either directly through experience or indirectly through images—the more inured one becomes to it. It becomes less extreme and traumatic. Violent television shows and movies can therefore serve to lower our threshold of acceptance and consequently increase the chances that we may resort to aggressive behavior. Obviously, there are a number of other factors that also affect the relationship between media and violence, including the maturity and stability of the person viewing, the type and frequency of the violence, as well as the context and consequences of the violence.[81] The bottom line, however, is that violence can be learned, at least in part, by watching violence in the media and by playing violent video games.[82]

The Cycle of Violence

Further support for the idea that violence is learned comes from the literature on domestic violence. One of the most consistent findings is that those who witness or experience violence and abuse as children are more likely to perpetrate it as adults. Often known as the **intergenerational transmission of violence theory** or the **cycle of violence** theory, this perspective points out that parents are often the strongest role models that children have, and when children see their father hitting their mother, for example, or experience one of their parents hitting or otherwise physically disciplining or abusing them, they cannot help but learn that this is how parents interact with each other and with their kids. Violence is thus understood to be a normal and acceptable part of family life. As a result, children who grow up in such environments are more likely to engage in similar acts of violence when they themselves are adults.[83] This is not to say that they are condemned to repeat this cycle. In fact, Cathy Spitz Widom and her colleagues found that most children exposed to violence in their families do not go on to perpetrate it.[84] But it does make it somewhat more likely. In short, the evidence strongly suggests that violence is, at least in part, a learned behavior. Other criminological perspectives focus more specifically on the effects that parenting and other social attachments have on an individual's ability to control their behavior through self-control.

Self-Control and Violence

Michael Gottfredson and Travis Hirschi articulated their **general theory of crime** based on the notion that individual criminality is the result of low self-control. While the concept of self-control may at first appear to be psychological, Gottfredson and Hirschi point out that low self-control is a product of early socialization and *not* a trait innate within individuals. They state

> The major "cause" of low self-control thus appears to be ineffective child-rearing . . . The minimum conditions necessary for adequate child-rearing . . . in order to teach the child self-control, someone must (1) monitor the child's behavior; (2) recognize deviant behavior when it occurs; and (3) punish such behavior. This seems simple and obvious. All that is required to activate the system is affection for or investment in the child.[85]

As you can see, the last condition denoting punishment for bad behavior recognizes the importance of the learning process discussed above. People who lack self-control, according to Gottfredson and Hirschi, tend to be impulsive, insensitive, physical (as opposed to mental), prone to risk-taking, short-sighted, and nonverbal. They contend that individuals generally develop levels of self-control by the age of 8 and, once developed, the trait remains consistent throughout one's life regardless of any changes in life circumstances. This last contention that self-control is not amenable to change once in place is where other theorists strongly disagree, however.

Informal Social Control

In their book, *Crime in the Making: Pathways and Turning Points Through Life*, Robert Sampson and John Laub strongly oppose the idea that life circumstances have no effect on changing behavior.[86] They contend that criminality is because of both structural factors, such as poverty, and from weak **informal social controls**, such as the family. As the result of these influences, Sampson and Laub believe that individuals develop poor social bonds with peers and have low attachments to conventional activities, such as school. Individuals with these low attachments have a more difficult time developing good relationships and getting good grades and good jobs. However, significant life events and changes can be "turning points" in their lives. For example, individuals may be on a certain trajectory that involves delinquency and violence, but as the result of a turning point, such as getting into a good relationship or landing a good job, individuals' paths can change. People can and do stop offending. The fact is that most offending behavior, including violent offending, does decrease as one ages. For example, people between the ages of 18 and 24 have the highest rate of homicide offending, and rates of offending decline significantly as age increases. Scholars like Sampson and Laub believe that this decrease in the probability of offending is because most people do in fact develop significant attachments later in life that provide the necessary social attachments to conventional society that deter them from engaging in crime.

In sum, it is safe to say that no single category of theory can adequately explain why people engage in violent behavior. When an individual assaults, murders, rapes, or otherwise acts violently, there is no one single motivating cause for that deed. Instead, we have to recognize that there were many things that influenced that act, including the biological and chemical makeup of the offender, their upbringing, their state of mind, temperament and character, their experiences, friends and family, as well as a host of other historical and situational factors. While the previously discussed theories do not represent a complete overview of all the theoretical arguments that have been proposed, they do provide a fairly representative summary of some of the major schools of thought. Additionally, in later chapters, theories that specifically address some of the unique dynamics of specific forms of violence, including routine activities theory and feminist theory, will be reviewed. At this point, however, it might be useful to transfer our attention to reviewing some of the perspectives that are important in helping us understand the nature of collective forms of violence that we discuss in the second half of this book.

Explaining Collective Violence

The motivations for participation in collective and group violence are often separate and distinct from the factors related to one-on-one acts of violence. A murderer who kills another person in a fight, for example, is usually acting out of different impulses than a soldier who kills the enemy during a war. This isn't to say that there is no overlap between the causes of individual and collective violence. Young men who join a violent gang, for example, may do so for many of the individualistic reasons outlined in the previous section, and these may interact with some of the group dynamics that we will explore in this section. It is therefore important to examine some of the ways groups facilitate violence. What characteristics do groups have that make it easier and/or more likely for members to act violently?

We began this chapter by pointing out that we are a violent species. We also need to note that we are social animals. Humans have evolved to live and work in groups. Groups play a powerful role in our lives and have a tremendous influence on our actions, beliefs, and perceptions. In fact, groups are so powerful that they can even cause a person to doubt their own senses or knowingly lie in order to conform to the group. One famous experiment that illustrates this was conducted by Solomon Asch in 1952.[87] Asch set up a situation in which a small group of participants were asked to look at some cards upon which were a series of lines of varying lengths. Each individual was then asked to select the longest line in front of the others. Unknown to one of the individuals, all of the others had been instructed to select a shorter line and say that it was the longest. Amazingly, about a third of all the experimental subjects gave what they knew to be the wrong line number half the time, while another 10% also answered incorrectly but less often. Replicated many times, this study illustrates the power of the group to influence our behavior and attitudes. Why are we so predisposed to groups? What is it about them that so affects us and makes us defer our will to that of the group? While there is no single answer to these questions, there are a number of qualities that groups possess which help us understand why we are so vulnerable to the influence of groups.

First, groups tend to possess legitimacy and authority. When a group of individuals come together as an organization, a gang, or a crowd, we tend to ascribe certain qualities to that collection of people, including a certain amount of legitimacy. Stated differently, groups have an authority that individuals within the group alone do not have. The mere fact that the group is composed of a number of people means that we automatically tend to defer to the whole. We live in a world in which we are taught to function within groups, organizations, and institutions. We learn to accept and defer to the judgments of collectives, whether in the boardroom or in the classroom. Team sports teach many of us the value of cooperation and teamwork. All of us belong to many different groups, some of which provide practical benefits, such as allowing us to make a living, while others simply provide us with a sense of belonging and place. It shouldn't be a surprise, therefore, that groups can dictate a great deal of our behavior, even if we don't necessarily agree with it.

The authority we ascribe to groups can compel fairly extreme behavior, as the British scientist and novelist C. P. Snow observed when he wrote, "When you think of the long and gloomy history of man, you will find more hideous crimes have been committed in the name of obedience than have ever been committed in the name of rebellion."[88] The work of Stanley Milgram, a student of Solomon Asch, certainly illustrates this point. In this famous series of experiments, Milgram was interested in finding out how far people would go on the orders of someone in authority.[89] He therefore designed experiments in which volunteers who replied to newspaper ads were paid to take part in a study that was ostensibly about the effects of electric shocks on learning. The volunteers didn't realize that they themselves were the subjects of the experiment. Seated at a machine, they were told to administer shocks of increasing voltage when the other supposed volunteer answered a question incorrectly. In reality, the machine did not administer any electric shock; the "learner" was actually a part of the experiment. These supposed victims were instructed to purposely answer questions incorrectly and then to yell in pain, plead, beg, and even hit their head against a wall at the higher dosages of electricity. Most experts assumed that only a few sick or pathological individuals would administer the higher voltage clearly marked "danger: severe shock."[90] Instead, Milgram found that most volunteers were willing to administer even potentially dangerous amounts of electric shocks to people who were obviously suffering if they were explicitly told to do so by someone in authority, in this case the experimenter. Importantly, most of the volunteers evidenced clear discomfort, tension, and unhappiness in following their instructions. Transcripts of the experiment document the extreme duress the subjects experienced, including statements such as, "I can't stand it. I'm not going to kill that man in there. You hear him hollering?"[91] In other words, the subjects didn't want to administer the shocks, but they felt compelled to. Groups command the same sort of power to compel individuals to comply. Perhaps this is why Freud wanted us not to "underestimate the power of the need to obey."[92]

In order to explain this respect for authority, Albert Bandura suggests the **theory of moral disengagement**. According to this argument, individuals learn (remember that Bandura is a social learning theorist) not to act in ways that go against their own personal standards of morality because that brings about self-condemnation and self-criticism.[93] But humans are very resourceful and have developed ways of selectively disengaging their moral prohibitions against negative or destructive behavior in order to avoid seeing themselves as bad people. Harmful behavior, for example, can be reconstructed as being moral or justified, in which case the behavior is redefined as a positive act. This can involve relying on various euphemisms to help shape perceptions of the act as being more innocent or making advantageous comparisons. Bandura uses the example of terrorists who see their "behavior as acts of selfless martyrdom by comparing them with widespread cruelties inflicted on the people with whom they identify."[94] Since moral control is strongest when an individual perceives personal responsibility for the harm caused, displacing or diffusing responsibility can also act as tools of moral disengagement. The larger and more hierarchical the group, the easier it is to avoid taking personal accountability and the easier it is to participate in harmful and violent acts. Bandura also points out that the consequences of bad behavior can be minimized or distorted, which also allows disengagement of moral prohibitions.

The last method of disengagement is **dehumanization**. It is easier to remove ethical restrictions against violence when we perceive the victims to be less than us or perhaps even less than human. During examples of genocide, for example, the perpetrators often label the victim groups as being cockroaches, insects, vermin, and similarly denigrating terms, thus making the violence against that group easier and more acceptable.[95] The more social distance between the perpetrator and the victim, the easier it is to inflict violence upon them. What Bandura was suggesting, therefore, is that the authority of the group calls into play certain practices of moral disengagement so that individuals are able to act in ways that are not outwardly consistent with their moral values but which are demanded or encouraged by membership in a collective. Morality, it seems, is often applied selectively. The authority of collectives is also aided in its ability to influence behavior by a number of other factors, the most important of which is **deindividuation**.

Deindividuation

Deindividuation, a phenomenon that facilitates violence in a group setting, is actually based on the classic work of Gustave Le Bon, who studied crowds in the late 1800s.[96] Le Bon suggested that

> The psychological mechanisms of anonymity, suggestibility and contagion transform an assembly into a "psychological crowd." In the crowd the collective mind takes possession of the individual. As a consequence, a crowd member is reduced to an inferior form of evolution: irrational, fickle, and suggestible. The individual submerged in the crowd loses self-control and becomes a mindless puppet, possibly controlled by the crowd's leader, and capable of performing any act, however atrocious or heroic.[97]

Sigmund Freud expanded the work of Le Bon and suggested that, in groups, individuals display certain behavioral characteristics that include (1) the lessening of a conscious individual personality, (2) a convergence of thoughts and emotions in a common direction, (3) emotions and unconscious drives displacing reason and rationality, and (4) the propensity to immediately carry out intentions as they develop.[98] Essentially, then, deindividuation refers to the long-noted phenomenon of individuals who lose their sense of self and individuality when in a group. This loss of a personal identity means that individuals are more capable of acting outside of the boundaries of their normal behavior. There is freedom in a crowd—the freedom to do things that otherwise would be unthinkable. Think of the members of a lynch mob or riot who in their normal, everyday life may be fairly nonviolent and peaceful yet in the grip of the mob's fury allow themselves to be swept along and embrace the violent actions of the group. According to research, the process of deindividuation is aided by a number of circumstances that include anonymity, loss of individual responsibility, arousal, sensory overload, new or unstructured situations, and drugs and/or alcohol.[99] In the present day, this perspective has been used to explain the violent and destructive behavior of hooliganism, violent crowds, lynch mobs, and even genocide.[100]

Another factor that facilitates participation in group violence is **conformity to peer pressure**, which is especially strong among members of military and paramilitary groups. This, of course, is related to social learning theory, which recognizes the strong rewards that peer groups can provide to their individual members. A great deal of research indicates that, during war, men fight not for ideology, nationalism, or even hate—although these factors can still be present—but rather for their fellow soldiers. This is captured in the powerful work of Christopher Browning, who studied the actions of the German Reserve Police Battalion 101 in Poland during World War II.[101] Composed of a cross-section of Germans from a variety of professions, the battalion was ordered to participate in the mass shootings of Polish Jews rounded up in a variety of Polish villages. Even though one of their commanding officers excused soldiers from the duty if they felt they couldn't do it, most did in fact participate, even though they found the task to be horrific and disgusting. Browning argued that most of the men—around 80% to 90% of them—participated because they didn't want to let their buddies down. They felt that they had a collective obligation and to shirk their duty would be to shift their share of that responsibility on to the shoulders of their fellows. Importantly, those few who did not participate went out of their way to seek the goodwill of their comrades and avoid any possible reproach.

This pressure to conform is heightened by the training that military personnel undergo. All soldiers and paramilitary forces go through some form of basic training or boot camp that is designed to socialize soldiers into becoming able and willing members of an organization fundamentally rooted in violence. This training is intentionally difficult and harsh, since it is designed to break the individual down both psychologically and physically and then rebuild them in a military mold—one that replaces individualism with group loyalty, pride, and obedience.[102] The rigors of the training ensure that members of the group become fiercely bonded to each other and, as a result, will support each other, even in the perpetration of atrocities. This pressure to conform to the expectations of a group, however, is not limited to military settings. All groups exert power and influence over their members, including gangs, work groups, and sports teams. Gang rapes in fraternities and among team athletes are examples of how these collectives can help facilitate violence.

Conclusions

This chapter has illustrated the diversity of motivations and structural conditions that impel individuals and groups into acts of violence. Human behavior, as we have discussed, is not easily categorized. Individuals often act within a context that brings victims and offenders together, and this context cannot be separated from the participants' historical, cultural, structural, psychological, or biological backgrounds. Although we could not discuss every theory on violence here, we tried to examine the most widely relied-upon explanations. We will refer back to these arguments throughout the text and also provide additional explanations when we examine specific types of violence, such as homicide, rape, and violence against women.

Key Terms

anomie

antisocial personality disorder

atavisms

brain dysfunctions

code of the street

conformity to peer pressure

cycle of violence

dehumanization

deindividuation

differential association theory

dominance

economic deprivation

ethological and biological explanations of violence

Eugenics movement

frustration-aggression hypothesis

general strain theory

general theory of crime

informal social controls

institutional-anomie theory of crime

intergenerational transmission of violence theory

intermale aggression

jumping in

phrenology

psychopathy

relative deprivation

sadism

serotonin

shame

social learning theory

sociopathy

status

strain theories

stress and violence

superpredators

territorial aggression

testosterone

theory of moral disengagement

Discussion Questions

1. The main assumption of the Eugenics movement is that the human race can be improved through various forms of intervention, including sterilization. The modern Eugenics movement was first formulated by Sir Francis Galton. In the United States, the movement was exposed for being behind many horrific policies, including mass sterilizations of subgroups of people such as those with mental deficiencies. The horrors being perpetrated by Nazi Germany were also soon connected to the philosophy of the Eugenics movement. Some contend that even talking about the biological factors that may be related to violence is flirting with disaster because of atrocities committed in the past, which were based on such notions of biological determinism. What risks do we have as a society when we investigate the connections between neurochemical or other physiological conditions and violence? Do the benefits outweigh the costs? What policies would be necessary to prevent the atrocities of the past from happening again?

2. Students often think that theory remains an abstract endeavor that is never applied to the real world. However, virtually all public policy is based on some theoretical perspective. Delineate at least three policies you are aware of that have been implemented to reduce some type of violence (e.g., youth violence, gun violence). From what you know about each policy, what theory or theories identified in this chapter could help explain the rationale for the policy? That is, what does the theory say about the causes of violence that would have led to such a policy?

3. The Criminal Justice Department at Florida State University has a website devoted to links to various sites that cover or in some way are related to major criminological theories (www.criminology.fsu.edu/crimtheory/theorylinks.htm). Select at least two theorists on the list and outline their theoretical contributions to the study of violence.

3

Aiding and Abetting Violence

All the focus on the small number of people with mental illness who are violent serves to make us feel safer by displacing and limiting the threat of violence to a small, well-defined group. But the sad and frightening truth is that the vast majority of homicides are carried out by outwardly normal people in the grip of all too ordinary human aggression to whom we provide nearly unfettered access to deadly force.

—Richard A. Friedman, MD[1]

Media-violence exposure is only one risk factor underlying aggression and violence. It may be the least expensive risk factor to modify—it costs little to choose nonviolent forms of entertainment.

—Craig Anderson[2]

Violence does not happen in a vacuum, although we often seem to imagine that it does. We talk about violence and describe it as something that just happens or which explodes out of nowhere. Yet this couldn't be further from the truth. Violence occurs in various kinds of settings and its perpetration is aided and abetted by a number of different social, political, economic, racial, ethnic, and interpersonal dynamics—many of which are discussed throughout this book. It is important to recognize that no single factor causes violence; rather, it is often the result of a convergence of situational and structural factors. The focus of this chapter is on examining several factors believed to be connected to the use of violence and aggression, including the availability of firearms, drugs and alcohol, and the media. It is important to note that these are correlates, not causes. Alcohol, for example, does not cause violence nor do guns. Yet both nonetheless play important roles in helping to make the perpetration of violent behavior more likely. In other words, they are facilitators or enablers rather than causes.

The issues surrounding these correlates are strongly debated among policy makers, not only in the United States but also in many countries around the world, with social policy decisions and public discourse frequently dictated by emotion and politics rather than scientific research. All too often this means that intelligent discussion of these issues is clouded and hampered by the confusion produced by these nonrational decision-making processes and the money that fuels them. For what it's worth, we hope that by the end of this chapter you will have a clearer picture of the empirical realities surrounding the gun control debate, our War on Drugs, and the media's connection to violence.

Guns and Violence

In Chapter 4 you will learn that the majority of all homicides in the United States are committed with a firearm, especially handguns. In fact, the jump in homicide rates witnessed in the late 1980s through to the mid-1990s was primarily attributable to an increase in **handgun homicides**. The rate of homicides committed with other types of weapons, including other guns, remained relatively stable during this time. Figure 3.1, which shows the rate of homicides by weapon type for 1980 through 2008, illustrates this well. Since 2000, the percentage of nonfatal-violence victimization involving a firearm has remained stable. However, the number of people in the United States still facing offenders armed with a firearm is staggering. In 2010, over 12,000 rape victims, over 140,000 robbery victims, and over 184,000 assault victims faced an offender who was armed with a firearm.[3]

Not everyone, however, is at equal risk. A person's vulnerability to gun violence varies according to certain demographic characteristics. According to the National Crime Victimization Survey, approximately one in three male violent crime victims face an armed offender compared with one in five female victims of violence. African American and American Indian victims of violence are more likely to face armed offenders compared with their Hispanic and white counterparts. The young are also more at risk of firearm violence, with those victims 20 years of age and younger being more likely to face an offender with a firearm compared with those 21 years of age or older.[4] Vulnerability to weapon violence is also related to household income, since individuals living in households making less than $7,500 are generally more likely to face offenders with weapons, in particular firearms.[5] It is clear, then, that poor and minority populations are particularly vulnerable to gun violence. However, it is important to remember that there is no group in the United States that is immune to gun violence, as the mass shootings that occur all too frequently can attest.

❖ **Figure 3.1   Homicides by Weapon Type, 1980–2008**

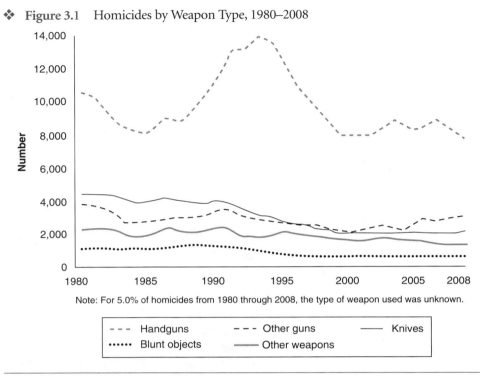

Note: For 5.0% of homicides from 1980 through 2008, the type of weapon used was unknown.

- - - Handguns   - - - Other guns   —— Knives
····· Blunt objects   —— Other weapons

SOURCE: Cooper and Smith, 2010. Homicide Trends in the United States, 1980–2008. Bureau of Justice Statistics, U.S. Department of Justice (2011).

Obviously, the availability of guns increases the likelihood that a violent interaction will result in death. The comparison between the Newton, Connecticut, mass school shooting and a similar attempt at a mass killing in China provides a powerful illustration of this reality. On December 14, 2012, a 36-year-old man wielding a knife entered a grade school in Henan Province, China, and stabbed over 20 students, but none of the wounds resulted in death.[6] Compare this to the Sandy Hook Elementary School shooting on the very same day, where a young man armed with a semiautomatic rifle sprayed children with bullets, hitting some of them as many as 11 times. Of course, we know the heart-wrenching outcome of this incident; 20 first graders and seven adults were killed before the gunman shot himself.[7]

Clearly, when a conflict escalates to an assault, the weapons used in the incident matter. Several countries have rates of assault and robbery that are similar to those of the United States, but their rates of murder are significantly lower. This has led scholars such as Franklin Zimring and Gordon Hawkins to contend that the distinctive feature of the United States is not so much the violence but the deadliness of the violence.[8] It is guns that make the context of these victimizations so different and more frequently lethal. All firearms are deadly weapons. Research indicates that when guns are used in a conflict or felony situation, the likelihood of someone being killed increases dramatically. In fact, when a conflict arises in the home, the availability of a gun rather than a knife increases the likelihood of death by three times.[9] Knives are also deadly weapons, but the difference is that they are not as easily used to kill someone as a gun is. To use a knife, an attacker needs to be within arm's reach of his or her victim, who can fight back, whereas a gun allows someone to use it from a distance, even if it's only a few feet. Knife wounds are also more likely to be survivable compared to gunshot wounds.[10]

The increased firepower offered by **semiautomatic weapons** is also cause for concern. In fact, the production of handguns has increasingly moved away from revolvers to semiautomatic weapons, which can fire more rounds and which now account for 80% of all handguns produced.[11] Semiautomatic weapons allow offenders to inflict multiple wounds, and obviously the more wounds a victim sustains, the greater the likelihood of death. For example, in a recent study that examined all threats with firearms in a large metropolitan area, results indicated that threats escalated to attacks in the same proportion whether assailants were armed with semiautomatic pistols or with regular revolvers (about 68%). However, cases involving semiautomatic weapons were more likely to involve multiple shots and multiple victims but not more likely to result in injury for those victims shot.[12]

Ammunition has also become more lethal. For example, certain bullets are designed to expand or mushroom after hitting the target. Others have hollowed-out tips that are filled with very soft lead that enlarges on impact, and still others are designed to tumble after they hit and can travel large distances within the body, bouncing off bones and slicing through organs, arteries and veins, and as much tissue as possible.

Unfortunately, all of this extreme firepower has not been made any more difficult to use. In fact, the triggers of most firearms are relatively easy to pull, requiring only a few pounds of pressure to fire. Aiming, of course, takes more effort. That is why people who are involved in gun altercations are more likely to be wounded than to die and why more people are actually missed than are wounded. Even with the high proportion of missed shots and nonfatal wounds, however, these weapons substantially raise the likelihood of a lethal outcome. In short, the availability of guns in general and semiautomatic handguns in particular is inextricably linked to the dangerousness of the violence played out on our streets and in our homes. So what factors are related to the high rate of gun violence in the United States?

Guns, Culture, and Violence

Bumper stickers alerting people that "This Vehicle Is Protected by a Colt 45" or "You Can Have My Gun When You Pry It From My Cold Dead Fingers" are not something you would see on automobiles in the majority of industrialized nations, yet messages like this are not uncommon on the streets of the United States. Other images of our gun culture abound in media portrayals of our past and our present. Think of the movie *Patriot,* in which noble colonists with guns in hand stand against the British Redcoats, or *3:10 to Yuma* and *Tombstone* that portray the wild West as a place where good guys engaged in gunfights against desperados These kinds of images place firearms at the center of our country's beginnings, from our fight for independence to our westward expansion. Michael Bellesiles puts it this way

Many if not most Americans seem resigned to, or find comfort in, the notion that this violence is immutable, the product of a deeply embedded historical experience rooted in the frontier heritage. Frequent Indian wars and regular gun-battles presumably inured Americans to the necessity of violence.[13]

In short, we have enshrined and mythologized guns and the role they played in our past. What is the result of our fascination with firearms? Well, compared with other industrialized nations, we are the most armed. We have more guns per capita than any other nation in the world. According to a Gallup poll in 1993, about 51% of Americans reported having a gun in their homes. By 2006, this percentage was down to 40%, but still one in four U.S. households reported having a gun—in fact, 30% reported personally owning a firearm,[14] and by 2011 this number has increased to 47%.[15] The average number of guns among private households that own guns is now up to 4.4, which constitutes a significant increase over the last 25 years. If we averaged the number of guns privately owned in the United States across all Americans, the average would be 1.7 guns per person.[16] Moreover, there has been an increase in the percentage of the sales of all handguns, which are usually not purchased for sport or hunting. Handguns now account for nearly half of all new gun sales.[17] This is significant since, as we pointed out earlier, a majority of all violent crimes committed with a firearm involve handguns.

How does the United States' availability and ownership of guns compare with other nations? The primary source of gun ownership data comes from surveys collected by the United Nations Office of Drugs and Crime (UNODC). In 2007, the most recent year for which data was available, the surveys showed that with less than 5% of the world's population, the United States has roughly 35% to 50% of the world's civilian-owned guns.[18] As you can see from Table 3.1, the United States ranks number one in terms of gun ownership of all industrialized nations and on average, owns about 88 firearms for every 100 people compared to the majority of industrialized nations with fewer than 20 and often fewer than 10 firearms per 100 people. In fact, England and Wales have a very low rate of gun ownership despite the fact that a provision similar to the United States' Second Amendment is contained with the English Bill of Rights (we will return to the Second Amendment in the next section).[19] As you will see in the following chapter, the most likely precipitating circumstance for murders and assaults is a conflict situation, such as an argument or fight. Clearly, if someone has a firearm at their disposal during such an altercation, the probability of harm and death is increased. But what does the empirical literature have to say about the relationship between guns and violence, especially in regards to the issue of self-protection?

Do increases in gun availability actually lead to more violence? A great deal of research demonstrates that they do. For example, one study examined statistics of gun ownership and gun-related violence and found that increases in gun density did increase the rate of robberies with guns and the rate of robbery homicides.[20] Not all accept the validity of this relationship, however. Some have argued that, instead of increasing rates of violence, guns allow citizens to protect themselves against predatory criminals. When asked, U.S. gun owners are about equally likely to report that they own their weapons for self-protective purposes as they are to report owning them for target shooting and hunting.[21] The **self-protection argument** suggests that when

Table 3.1	Rank of Percent of Population Owning Guns, and Average Number of Firearms per 100 Persons by Country for Industrialized Nations, 2007

Country	Rank of Percent Gun Ownership	Average Number of Guns per 100 People
United States	1	88.80
Switzerland	2	45.70
Finland	3	45.30
Sweden	4	31.60
Norway	5	31.30
France	6	31.20
Canada	7	30.80
Austria	8	30.40
Germany	9	30.30
Iceland	10	30.30
New Zealand	11	22.60
Greece	12	22.50
Belgium	13	17.20
Luxembourg	14	15.30
Australia	15	15.00
Turkey	16	12.50
Denmark	17	12.00
Italy	18	11.90
Spain	19	10.40
Russia	20	8.90
Ireland	21	8.60
Portugal	22	8.50
Israel	23	7.30
Ukraine	24	6.60
England and Wales	25	6.20
Hungary	26	5.50
Scotland	27	5.50
China	28	4.90
Taiwan	29	4.40
India	30	4.20
Netherlands	31	3.90
Poland	32	1.30
Japan	33	.60
Singapore	34	.50

SOURCE: Adapted from Data from The Guardian, DataBlog.

NOTE: Gun homicides and gun ownership listed by country.

private citizens have weapons in their homes or are able to carry concealed weapons, they are less likely to be successfully targeted by criminals.[22] Gary Kleck and Marc Gertz, for example, have found that a number of people who own guns have used them in self-protective ways: About 1.1% of persons owning guns had used them in a defensive way during the year preceding the interview in 1993. When respondents were asked about the preceding five years, the estimate increased to 3.4%. Generalizing this to population figures indicates that Americans use guns for self-protection as often as 2.1 million times a year. While this may seem like a large number, given the fact that there are over 200 million guns in private ownership in the United States, this means that only about 1% of them are used for self-defense in any given year.[23] On the other hand, other surveys have not found support for this finding. According to the National Crime Victimization Survey (NCVS), for example, there are only about 82,000 victimizations in which victims used a gun for self-protective purposes every year—about one-ninth of that reported by Kleck and Gertz.

Another methodological issue related to estimating the extent of **defensive gun use** is how often "self-protective behavior" is actually justifiable as such. For example, drug dealers often carry guns to protect themselves from robberies, but should this be classified as self-protection since the enterprise is illegal to begin with? Interviews with incarcerated felons confirm the use of guns for protection when engaging in illicit or illegal activity.[24] Should we view defensive gun use in these cases in the same way as for any other case? Is a homeowner who uses a gun to protect themselves from a burglar the same as a drug dealer defending themselves from armed robbers? These are tricky questions to answer, and the whole debate is made even more difficult by the fact that the controversy over how much guns provide protection versus increasing violence is as much an ideological debate as an empirical one. The same is true for the gun control debate, to which we now turn.

Gun Control Legislation

The role of guns in U.S. society and their regulation is a highly contested issue that is informed as much by politics, belief, and popular culture, as it is by research. Some of this debate also revolves around the **Second Amendment** to the Constitution, which states:

> A well regulated Militia, being necessary to the security of a free State, the right of the people to keep and bear Arms, shall not be infringed.

The term "**Militia**" in the amendment creates some confusion since it isn't clear if it means that only a select group of citizens who serve as soldiers have the right to bear arms or if it is an individual right. While there is controversy about what this amendment actually guarantees Americans, the Second Amendment is inextricably linked to our current gun culture and the debate on gun control.

Gun control legislation occurs at many levels, including the federal, state, and local, but except where noted, the laws discussed here represent federal efforts at gun control legislation. The majority of gun control measures to date have been generally focused in three main areas and have consisted of the following: regulations intended to reduce the supply and overall availability of guns; regulations designed to limit the availability of guns to high-risk groups, such as felons; and regulations calculated to affect how guns are used, including such things as antitheft measures and locks.[25]

Today, the debate about gun control sometimes intensifies after a significant tragedy, such as a school or workplace shooting. For example, after the Sandy Hook Elementary School shootings, President Obama declared he would make gun control a "central issue" during his second term. Of course, gun control is frequently debated after a mass shooting, but the debate rarely leads to action. However, many believe the massacre of 20 innocent first graders has significantly changed the landscape. President Obama stated, "This time, the words need to lead to action."[26] Only time will tell. Despite these sporadic bursts of heightened attention to gun control, controlling firearms actually has a long history in the United States. For example, in 1927 the U.S. Congress passed the first gun control measure, which prohibited the sale of handguns to private individuals through the mail. Unfortunately, like many attempts that followed, this bill had virtually no effect since manufacturers could still ship handguns to customers through private carriers.[27]

During Prohibition, Congress passed two more Bills, the **National Firearms Act of 1934** and the **Federal Firearms Act of 1938**, which were both intended to decrease gang-related violence and also to control the illegal distribution of alcohol. By taxing them heavily, legislators sought to decrease the use of guns, such as sawn-off shotguns and machine guns that were most often used by gangsters. Several decades later and in the wake of urban rioting and the assassinations of Martin Luther King Jr. and Robert F. Kennedy, Congress once again turned its attention to gun control by passing the **Gun Control Act of 1968**. According to James Jacobs, this act had at least five objectives:

1. To prohibit interstate firearms sales
2. To prohibit sales to an expanded list of "dangerous categories of people," including people who had previously been convicted of a felony, minors under 18 years of age, and anyone "adjudicated as a mental defective"
3. To add other "dangerous devices" to the list of prohibited weapons
4. To prohibit the importation of so-called "Saturday Night Specials"
5. To prohibit the importation of surplus military weapons[28]

In the 1980s, Congress changed tack and moved to increase the penalties for using a firearm during the commission of a crime instead of trying to limit guns. The **Armed Career Criminal Act of 1984** imposed a mandatory minimum 15-year prison term on a convicted felon who had three previous convictions for robbery or burglary and who possessed or received a firearm. This act was later amended several times to include sentencing enhancements (i.e., increases sentences on top of other sentences received) for those who used a gun and were convicted of violent offenses and drug offenses, those who used a gun loaded with armor-piercing ammunition during the commission of a violent crime, and those who transferred a firearm knowing that it would be used to commit a violent crime or for drug trafficking.[29] Additionally, the **Bureau of Alcohol, Tobacco, and Firearms** (ATF) was authorized to grant licenses to dealers and manufacturers and to enforce the other requirements of this gun control legislation.

Legislation does not happen in a vacuum. Lobbying groups respond to virtually all legislation, and the **National Rifle Association** (NRA) is no exception. In fact, the NRA is perhaps the most powerful lobbying organization in Washington, D.C. Claiming that any legislation aimed at controlling the possession of guns by citizens infringed upon their rights, the NRA and its congressional backers passed the **Firearms Owners' Protection Act of 1968** (FOPA). Among other things, this law prohibited the federal government from centralizing the records of firearms owners or firearms transactions and allowed federal firearms licensees to sell arms at temporary locations, such as gun shows.[30] This led to a sharp increase in the number of gun shows across the country, which are still not regulated by federal gun control legislation.

The next major gun control law that Congress passed was the **Brady Handgun Violence Prevention Act (Brady Bill) of 1993**, which mandated criminal history background checks on persons applying to purchase firearms from federally licensed firearm dealers. This bill was fueled in large part by the attempted assassination of President Ronald Reagan, which resulted in the wounding and paralysis of James Brady, President Reagan's assistant. Among other things, the act established the **National Instant Criminal Background Check System** (NICS) and required a background check by the FBI or a state point of contact on all persons applying to receive firearms from a registered firearms dealer. Theoretically, before anyone can obtain a gun through a dealer, they must wait five days after purchase so this check can be completed. This waiting period and subsequent check are to make sure high-risk applicants are prevented from obtaining a firearm. Such high-risk groups, as detailed by the law, include fugitives from justice, those dishonorably discharged from the U.S. armed forces, those convicted of a crime punishable by imprisonment for more than one year, those convicted in any court of domestic violence, those under restraining orders to protect intimate partners or children, those who have renounced U.S. citizenship, unlawful users of controlled substances or those addicted to controlled substances, and those adjudicated to be mentally defective or committed to a mental institution, to name just a few. However, recall the provision of the Firearms Owners' Protection Act that allowed firearms dealers to sell guns at gun shows. Neither the Brady Bill nor any other gun control regulation currently applies to those transactions conducted at gun shows or other sponsored events. Based on the number of gun sales stopped by the checks, many agree that it is a relatively useful tool to keep guns out of the hands of high-risk individuals. For example, since the inception of the Brady Bill, about 2% of all applications for firearm transfers have been rejected each year. While this may not seem like a lot of rejections, it translates into stopping about 1,228,000 high-risk individuals from obtaining a gun—at least through legal means. A felony conviction or indictment is typically the most common reason for rejection.[31]

In 1994, Congress again passed another gun control measure, the **Assault**

❖ Photo 3.1 Gun shows sell everything from assault rifles to all types of handguns and accessories.

Weapons Ban (AWB). Assault weapons are difficult to define but are generally considered to be semiautomatic rifles that look like military weapons, such as AK-47s and Uzis. The AWB banned 19 such weapons. This was a largely symbolic measure because these types of weapons are rarely used in crimes and are functionally equivalent to all other semiautomatic long guns that are still legal.

Based on public sentiment, many states have enacted their own form of gun control legislation. On average, the majority of Americans (56%), according to a recent Gallup poll, believe that the laws governing the sale of firearms should be stricter.[32] However, a majority sentiment is not always the most powerful predictor of policy. This brings us back to the NRA. As James Jacobs describes, "The NRA's core message is that (1) gun control proposals are a smoke screen for confiscation, (2) the Second Amendment constitutes an absolute bar to gun controls, and (3) no gun control has ever, or will ever, work."[33] Consequently, after the passage of the Brady Bill and the Assault Weapons Ban, the NRA poured millions of dollars into federal and state elections to remove politicians who had voted for their passage. Before the 2000 elections, the NRA spent nearly $20 million to support antigun control candidates. It was a very successful campaign. The climate in the Congress regarding gun control legislation has changed dramatically, as can be seen by a number of actions taken—and, importantly, not taken. In September 2004, for example, the new Congress let the 10-year federal ban on assault weapons expire, making the banned weapons once again legal to buy—although, as we noted earlier, this issue is largely symbolic.[34] In the present era, the national mood has clearly tended against gun control. The Gallup poll reports that a record low 26% of Americans favor a handgun ban, which differs significantly from the 60% that approved this measure in 1959, the year Gallup began surveying this topic.[35] At the same time, the poll notes that gun ownership is higher than it has been since the early 1990s. Of those surveyed, 47% report owning a gun, which represents an increase of 41% from the previous year.[36]

There are, however, indications that attitudes may be starting to change. Consider the following examples and the responses to them. On October 2, 2006, a man armed with a pistol and a shotgun with 600 rounds of ammunition shot 10 girls execution-style at the small Amish school, killing five of them and then killing himself. After the rash of shootings in the fall of 2006, the White House held a conference on school safety on October 10, where many topics were discussed, including metal detectors, school bullies, the value of religious beliefs, and good communication between parents and schools. There was not one mention by the panelists or from President Bush of guns or of gun control. Let's contrast this with two more recent shootings. On the morning of January 8, 2011, Gabrielle "Gabbie" Giffords, a member of the U.S. House of Representative was visiting her hometown of Tucson, Arizona, and was meeting with constituents from her home district.[37] The event was dubbed "Congress on Your Corner" and was being held in the parking lot of a Safeway grocery store. A table had been set up where congresswoman Giffords was meeting and talking with local residents when a man later identified as Jared Loughner produced a semiautomatic handgun and shot her in the head.[38] His weapon was a 9mm Glock that had a large capacity 33-round magazine that he then used to start shooting at the other people gathered around in the parking lot. Before he was finally tackled and disarmed, Loughner managed to kill five people and wound 13 others. One of those injured later died at the hospital. This shooting prompted renewed interest in the issue of mental illness and gun control, which only increased after the Sandy Hook shootings in December 2012. These horrific tragedies have prompted a contentious national debate on gun control that continues to unfold as we write these lines. Most recently, on April 17, 2013, the Senate rejected the Manchin-Toomey background check amendment in a 54-46 vote.[39] Intended to curb gun violence, this bill would have expanded background checks for any advertised sale of a firearm and was supported by an overwhelming majority of the American public. So the debate continues and, as noted above, we will see if they result in any lasting action.

Alcohol

If you have ever been to a party and observed people having too much to drink, you have probably also observed a fight or two. If this is true for you, you aren't alone. Many sources document the frequent connection between alcohol and violence. From colonial times, through our nation's westward expansion, to contemporary accounts, you will find many narratives describing the phenomenon of drinking and fighting. All too often, however, these popular fables have been used to demonize certain populations and justify discrimination and racism. Robert Nash Parker states that

> All through the late eighteenth and nineteenth centuries, and into the early twentieth century, alcohol consumption was linked to the violence of groups perceived as economic threats to the established groups that had preceded the newer groups to, or were less powerful in, the new world: Native Americans, African-American slaves (and even former slaves after the Civil War), and the more recent immigrant groups like the Irish and the Italians.[40]

From this perspective, alcohol was largely a problem of certain populations. Despite this selective reading of our history, there is a great deal of research that finds a widespread link between alcohol and violence. Marvin Wolfgang, who examined the characteristics of murder in Philadelphia in 1955, conducted one of the first empirical examinations of the link between alcohol and violence. He found that 55% of the offenders in his sample had been drinking alcohol prior to the murder.[41] During this same time period, approximately the same proportion of homicides were found to involve alcohol in Chicago.[42] Contemporary research suggests that the link is still the same—and not just for homicide. In fact, a report by the U.S. Department of Justice indicates that four out of 10 violent crimes involved alcohol,[43] while others have found rates of alcohol involvement in violence to be much higher.[44] Alcohol also has been strongly linked to particular types of violence, such as intimate partner violence. Furthermore, the relationship between alcohol and violence has been found in other countries as well, including Russia, Finland, Germany, Iceland, Canada, and France, to name just a few.[45] It has also been found that countries with higher consumption rates of alcohol also have higher rates of violence.[46]

None of these studies, however, establishes a causal relationship between alcohol and violence. To do so, researchers would need to conduct experiments in which individuals are randomly assigned to two groups: an experimental group to drink alcoholic beverages and a control group that would drink nonalcoholic beverages. After consumption, individuals from both groups would be observed to measure the magnitude of violent behavior. Most studies of this type have used what is called the "**Taylor Paradigm**" to measure aggression.[47] Aggression here is usually measured by the extent to which subjects give electric shocks to planted confederates (individuals pretending to be subjects themselves but who are really part of the experiment) for some incorrect answer on a given test or task. In experiments like this, the only factor that is different across groups is the ingestion of alcohol. As such, if the level of shocks or some other measure of aggression is higher for individuals in the experimental group compared with the control group, then we can believe that alcohol was the cause because it is the only thing that is different about the two groups. Generally, experimental studies of this nature find that intoxicated subjects give a greater number of higher shocks than their sober counterparts.[48] As you might imagine, one of the problems with this type of research is assuming that giving shocks in a laboratory setting is the same as starting a brawl after the bars close on a Saturday night, but nevertheless, it is safe to conclude that there is a very strong link between alcohol and violence.

While we have established that alcohol is related to violence, we still need to ask why. What is the nature of the connection or link between alcohol and violence? Not all alcohol use results in violence, and alcohol by itself does not directly cause violence. Instead, we have to examine some of the physiological and contextual elements that make alcohol-related violence more or less likely. Physiologically, alcohol affects individuals differently, but generally alcohol can dramatically affect the central nervous system: It is both a depressant and a stimulant. That is, it can tranquilize an individual, but in small amounts it can also act as a stimulant by triggering the release of a neurotransmitter called dopamine.[49] It also affects the part of the brain that controls inhibitions, generally serving to reduce them. If you haven't experienced this for yourself, interviews with college students provide illuminating insight into how this sometimes feels. For example, one college sophomore described, "When you put that alcohol in your system, an *S* grows on your chest like Superman. Liquor makes you get bigger than what you are. You feel like you can whip the world."[50] Other writers have termed this "liquid courage" and "testosterone by the glass."[51] So alcohol, depending in part on how much is consumed, can either rev someone up or calm them down. This is where the context comes into play.

The physiological effects of alcohol are mediated by the social context and social conditions within which it is used. For example, an interaction that has the potential for violence is influenced by a number of factors, including the perceptions of the actors involved and the actions of bystanders. At an aggregate level (e.g., cities), Robert Nash Parker found that the relationship between alcohol availability and homicide varied by the social context of the cities. For example, cities that had a combination of both high rates of alcohol availability (measured by the rate of liquor stores per 1,000 population) and an above average rate of poverty had significantly higher homicide rates than places that had only one or neither of these conditions. Parker also found that alcohol increased negative effects of other variables, such as the effects of low social bonds between residents and their home, school, and work. Importantly, Parker found that, despite these interaction effects, alcohol availability still had a direct relationship with rates of homicide. That is, cities with higher rates of alcohol availability also had higher rates of homicide.[52]

Cultural expectations also play an important role in determining the effects of alcohol. People generally respond to alcohol the way they believe they should or can. For example, a young man in a bar who believes that responding to an insult with a punch will be tolerated or even expected will be more likely to throw a left hook compared to the same inebriated young man who believes such action would not be tolerated and would be deemed unacceptable by his friends. Craig MacAndrew and Robert Edgerton documented the cultural responses to alcohol by historically investigating the learned responses to the substance by several subgroups. For example, they found that American Indians' first contact with alcohol did not result in drunken brawls and mayhem but rather in fear and passivity. Only after watching white settlers engage in drunken fights did they learn that alcohol *should* produce aggression and violence, and their behavior soon began to conform to this expectation.[53] Clearly, when cultural values tolerating violence are combined with the **disinhibiting** effects of alcohol, the likelihood that violence will result—particularly in conflict situations—is higher. Importantly, alcohol is not the only drug that helps facilitate violence.

Illicit Drugs

It is important to point out that it is somewhat difficult to talk about a general relationship between illicit drugs and violence because there are so many different kinds of illegal substances. As with alcohol, we do have self-report information from offenders on whether they were under the influence of drugs at the time of their offense. For example, in 2002 the percentage of convicted inmates reporting they were under the influence of particular types of drugs at the time of their offense was as shown in Table 3.2.[54] Recall from the earlier section that alcohol was involved in about 60% of violent offenses committed by a sample of prison inmates.[55] But the connection of illicit drugs to incidents of violence is not nearly the same as that of alcohol. In fact, urinalysis of arrested offenders indicates that only a small percentage of violent offenders are under the influence of illicit drugs at the time of their offense—generally less than 7%.[56]

There are three primary ways in which illicit drugs may be related to violence: violence that results from the **psychoactive effects of drugs**; violence that results from trying to support a drug addiction (e.g., robbery); violence resulting from the illegal selling of drugs. In regards to the psychoactive effects of illicit drugs, several studies have been conducted that have attempted to find a link between various drugs and violence; the results, however, have been inconsistent. In addition, all of these studies are correlational and not experimental, which means that no causal relationship has been established. Moreover, what we do know about the connection between illicit drugs and violence is often distorted by the media. Think about

Table 3.2	Percentage of Inmates Under the Influence of Drugs at Time of Offense
Drug	**Percentage Influenced**
Marijuana or hashish	13.6
Cocaine or crack	10.6
Heroin/opiates	4.1
Depressants	2.4
Stimulants	5.2
Hallucinogens	1.6
Inhalants	0.2

SOURCE: Adapted from *Drugs and Crime Facts*, Bureau of Justice Statistics, U.S. Department of Justice.

the media frenzy around marijuana in the 1930s, which is one of the first examples of how the media play a prominent role in creating attitudes toward a particular drug. Media reports linked marijuana with extreme violence and insanity, and this resulted in marijuana being dubbed the "killer weed." More recently, **crack cocaine** has received this same kind of attention. Crack cocaine, a version of its powder derivative, began hitting the streets of the United States during the 1980s. It was cheaper than powder cocaine and produced a more intense high, although one that was shorter lived. The first mention of crack cocaine in the U.S. media occurred on November 17, 1985, in the *Los Angeles Times*. Almost instantaneously, other newspapers began to herald the coming of a new drug scare. In less than a year, "the *New York Times,* the *Washington Post,* the *Los Angeles Times,* the wire services, *Time, Newsweek,* and *U.S. News & World Report* collectively wrote more than 1,000 stories in which crack had figured prominently."[57] The general themes of the media accounts claimed that crack was more addictive than powder cocaine and that people who used crack were more likely to become violent. In June 1986, Len Bias, a University of Maryland basketball player, suffered a heart attack that resulted from a cocaine overdose less than two days after the Boston Celtics drafted him. The media connected Len's death to the use of crack, even though later autopsy results revealed that he had ingested powder cocaine. This, of course, only served to fan the fires of the media frenzy.

In fact, the distribution and use of crack—particularly the turf battles over its sale (we will discuss this further below)—were creating chaos in inner-city neighborhoods, but its connection to violence because of its psychoactive impacts on the individual had very little empirical support. The empirical literature actually refutes the popular contention that crack cocaine leads to an increase in violence. For example, Jeffrey

Fagan and Ko-Lin Chin found that crack cocaine users in their sample were already involved in property and violent crime prior to their first ingestions of crack.[58] As such, the use of crack did not act as a catalyst for criminality in general or violent crime in particular. Other research supports this finding, including one study that examined whether inmates under the influence of crack at the time of their offense were more likely to have committed a violent offense than those under the influence of powder cocaine or alcohol. Results indicated that inmates under the influence of alcohol were about four times as likely to have committed a violent offense compared with either crack or powder cocaine users.[59] So it appears that crack cocaine does not generally make a person violent even though that was what the media reporting and popular images strongly suggested.

Another substance that has been linked to violent behavior is **phencyclidine**, otherwise known as PCP, angel dust, ozone, whack, or rocket fuel. This drug can be ingested in many forms and can result in feelings of invulnerability, paranoia, and extreme unease—all of which can lead to aggression. Others contend that because the drug releases stress hormones, it can also increase an individual's strength.[60] Except for a few case studies, however, there is no empirical evidence supporting the link between PCP and violence.

Other research has underscored that, similar to alcohol's relationship to violence, much depends on the social context in which drugs are consumed. For example, Henry Brownstein interviewed murderers who were under the influence of substances during their crimes and found the violence was more likely attributable to such things as saving face and maintaining an image than to the ingestion of drugs.[61] In short, there does not appear to be much evidence that supports the idea of drugs having a significant psychoactive role in producing violent behavior. This brings us to the next major pathway, which is violence that stems from attempts to maintain an **addiction**.

Dennis Donovan defines addiction as a

> progressive behavior pattern having biological, psychological, sociological, and behavioral components. What sets this behavior apart from others is the individual's overwhelmingly pathological involvement in or attachment to it, subjective compulsion to continue it, and reduced ability to exert personal control over it.[62]

Essentially, addiction turns a desire or craving for something into an urgent need. When someone is addicted to a drug, they must continue taking it in order to prevent their body from going into withdrawal. Symptoms of withdrawal can include cramping, nausea, chills and sweats, and in extreme cases, coma and even possibly death. In some cases, individuals will do almost anything to make the symptoms go away, including committing crime in order to support their habit. Some may sell drugs to support their habit, while others may turn to prostitution to get money. However, evidence suggests that most do not turn to violence. Of the small percentage of addicts who do turn to crime, offenses such as burglary, larceny theft, auto theft, fraud, and embezzlement are typically the kinds of crimes engaged in to obtain money or items that can be sold for money.[63] Of course, some addicts

❖ **Photo 3.2**   Drug dealer selling drugs

do commit violent crimes, but the media portrayal of the addicted crack or heroin addict randomly creating violent mayhem is far from the reality. However, the violence created by the illegal drug market, the last of three pathways, presents a more consistent picture for the drugs and violence connection.

The path that an illegal substance takes to the consumer depends on a number of factors, including its point of origin (e.g., Mexico, Colombia, Afghanistan, or your neighbor's hidden greenhouse) and its final destination. However, virtually all illegal drugs make a journey that involves a number of people, from the grower or manufacturer to the dealer on the street. The buying and selling of drugs on the street typically involves a complex routine and numerous people in order to prevent detection by police. As Barri Flowers explains, "These may include people who 'steer' buyers to sellers for money or drugs, others who may

serve as lookouts or guards for the drugs, and yet others who may deliver or collect money or drugs."[64] At all levels of this process, violence is not uncommon. In fact, while questions remain about the psychoactive and addiction linkages between illicit drugs and violence, very few scholars question the fact that the distribution and sale of these substances is directly related to violence. For example, when illicit drugs have been linked to homicide, the link is usually related to trafficking, not to the ingestion or addiction of drugs.[65] Like all illegal enterprises where the prospect of profit is large and legal options nonexistent, the only forms of protection and justice are those that the drug dealer can enforce themselves. As Hope Corman concludes, "Drug producers and sellers have no other recourse to settling disputes and force is a typical method in obtaining power."[66]

There are many sources of violence generated by the illegal drug business, not just the violence that erupts from rival gangs staking out their territory. Table 3.3 presents the situations that most often result in violence related to the distribution and sale of illicit drugs. Because those involved in the illegal drug trade generally do not have recourse to the criminal justice system, they usually depend on street justice. Moreover, because there is no form of insurance to recoup their losses in cases of theft and robbery, the incentives for self-protection and street justice are even higher. One way that we have often tried to reduce the impact of this form of violence is through various legislative initiatives designed to prohibit and control the distribution and usage of these substances.

Table 3.3 Sources of Violence in the Illegal Drug Business
• Guarding drug-producing crops during harvest season • Territorial disputes between rival drug dealers • Enforcing normative codes within dealing hierarchies • Robberies of drug dealers and the dealers' violent retaliation • Elimination of drug informers • Punishment for selling poor quality, adulterated, or phony drugs • Punishment for failing to pay debts • Punishment for stealing, tampering with, or not sharing drug supplies • Punishment for stealing, using without permission, or not sharing drug paraphernalia

Alcohol and Drug Control Legislation

The history of legislation to control the sale and use of alcohol and drugs in the United States is long and extensive, dating back to the 1830s when the first laws were penned to limit the availability of alcohol to American Indians—but in this section we will only concentrate on a few key pieces of legislation.

Although some states attempted to restrict a few substances, including alcohol, during the 19th century, most drugs—including morphine and cocaine—were legal in the United States until the early 20th century. The first significant federal legislation concerning drugs occurred in 1914 when Congress passed the **Harrison Act**, which served to make the nonmedical use of morphine and cocaine illegal. Suddenly, thousands of law-abiding middle-class citizens found themselves on the wrong side of the law. Significantly, while the original act allowed physicians to prescribe these drugs for addicts, a later Supreme Court decision prohibited such practices. Within a few years, an illegal drug distribution system became well established in the United States.[67]

During this same time period, several states had also outlawed the sale of alcohol; however it was not until the ratification of the Eighteenth Amendment in January 1919 that Prohibition became federal legislation. The first section of the Eighteenth Amendment of the Constitution states

> After one year from the ratification of this article the manufacture, sale, or transportation of intoxicating liquors within, the importation thereof into, or the exportation thereof from the United States and all territory subject to the jurisdiction thereof for beverage purposes is hereby prohibited.[68]

In October 1919, the **National Prohibition Act**, also known as the **Volstead Act**, gave federal agencies the power to enforce the **Eighteenth Amendment**. After alcohol became more difficult to obtain, marijuana markets began to appear across the country.[69] As we noted earlier, the response was a media campaign by the federal government demonizing the so-called "killer weed." The federal narcotics commissioner at the time, Harry Anslinger, was primarily responsible for the campaign;

he supplied information and placed advertisements in magazines, periodicals, and newspapers alleging that marijuana was connected to cases of extreme violence. There was little empirical evidence to support this connection, however. Nevertheless, by the mid-1930s the majority of states had passed antimarijuana legislation, and in 1937 Congress passed the **Marijuana Tax Act,** which levied a tax on anyone who sold marijuana. While the act itself did not penalize the use of marijuana, it did stipulate harsh penalties for not following the legal procedures set out by the bill, which included a fine of up to $2,000 and five years' imprisonment. Obviously, the potential costs of being in the marijuana business became so high, no pun intended, that most got out of the business.[70]

Similar to the street violence designed to control the illegal drug markets, prohibition created similar scenes as rival groups competed for control of the illegal distribution of alcohol. Think of the Saint Valentine's Day massacre in which members of Al Capone's organized crime group killed seven members of Bugsy Moran's gang by posing as police officers and pretending to arrest the rival bootleggers. After lining them up, they were executed.[71] Essentially, it was all about fighting over who would control the flow of alcohol into Chicago. In addition, the Great Depression and World War I left the U.S. government in a great deal of debt. One of the only ways the U.S. government can make money is through taxes, and the increasing violence on the streets combined with this need for revenue played a significant role in the ratification of the Twenty-First Amendment. The first section of the amendment is very brief. It simply states, "The eighteenth article of amendment to the Constitution of the United States is hereby repealed."[72] Other sections of the amendment essentially gave states the ability to control grain alcohol distribution in their own states. In fact, many states remained "dry" for several years—the last state to allow distribution was Mississippi, which did not allow alcohol to be sold until 1966. Today, the control of alcohol distribution in many states is offered to counties and local jurisdictions, and there are still a few "dry" counties scattered through the United States.

The next key piece of legislation at the federal level was the 1970 **Controlled Substance Act**. This was important because it consolidated all previous drug laws into one law designed to control prescription drugs *and* illicit drugs. This legislation created five categories or schedules used to classify drugs based on several criteria that included their accepted medical use and their potential for abuse and addiction. The Drug Enforcement Administration and the Department of Health and Human Services were given authority to amend the placement of drugs on a particular schedule.[73] Many contend that placement of certain drugs on a particular schedule is more often based on political pressure than on empirical reality. For example, **Schedule I** lists those drugs that have no accepted medical utility and a high potential for abuse, and **Schedule II** lists substances having a high abuse risk but also some accepted medical purpose. Marijuana, which has strong empirical support from the medical profession as an effective pain reliever, is still placed on Schedule I and grouped with such drugs as heroin. Cocaine, on the other hand, which has very limited medical use and a very high risk of being abused, is placed on Schedule II.

As you can see, the majority of these laws were aimed at reducing the supply of drugs, not necessarily reducing their demand. In fact, while federal efforts aimed at reducing demand do exist, these efforts have been miniscule compared with those aimed at reducing supply. A critical 1965 decision by the Supreme Court in *Robinson v. California,* however, served as an impetus for increased attention to treatment for drug addiction. The Court ruled that imprisonment for the misdemeanor crime of using a controlled substance violated the Eighth Amendment protection against cruel and unusual punishment because addiction was an illness. This led to an increase in treatment efforts by the federal government. The **Community Mental Health Centers Act of 1963** was the first to provide states and other jurisdictions with federal assistance for treatment programs. The amendments to this act passed in 1968 further served to bring narcotic addiction into the purview of mental illness.

Beginning with the Reagan presidency and continuing today, the attempts to combat illicit drug use have primarily emphasized law enforcement responses to reducing the supply of drugs. One of the key contemporary pieces of legislation has been the **Anti-Drug Abuse Act of 1988**, which called for mandatory minimum sentences for the possession and distribution of drugs by their type and weight. Many scholars have termed the era we are now in as the "**War on Drugs**." The primary strategy of this war has been to amplify the legal penalties for trafficking and possession of illicit drugs; consequently, our nation has taken many prisoners of war. In fact, because of our War on Drugs, we now have one of the largest prison populations on earth—2.2 million—and this number doesn't include those in jail or on probation or parole. Since 1995, our prison population has grown by nearly 80%, and drug-related offenses have been responsible for the majority of this growth.[74] While the percentage of drug-related offenders sent to prison has stopped increasing since 2000, they still remain the most frequent category of new inmates sent to federal prisons, compared to both violent and property crime offenders. Table 3.4 displays the number of sentenced prisoners under state jurisdiction by offense as of December 31, 2011, the most recent data available as of this writing. At the end of 2011, there were 96,400 prisoners sentenced for drug offenses in federal prisons, compared to 14,900 and 10,700 violent and property crime offenders sentenced under federal jurisdiction. While this disparity does not exist at the state level where violent offenders make up the majority of prisoners, it remains to be seen whether the federal government's War on Drugs that creates this disparity in federal prisons is working.

There are other negative consequences of the War on Drugs that especially affect minority subgroups within the U.S. population. For example, data indicate that African Americans are no more likely to use illicit drugs than are whites; however, they are overwhelmingly represented in drug-related arrest statistics. In fact, the National Criminal Justice Commission points out

> African Americans make up about 12% of the U.S. population and about 13% of all monthly drug users, but make up 35% of those arrested for drug possession, 55% of those convicted for drug related offenses, and 74% of those sentenced to prison for drug possession.[75]

In addition, some policies enacted by Congress are inherently racist in nature. Recall the Anti-Drug Abuse Act of 1988 that increased criminal penalties for the possession and trafficking of illegal substances. Crack cocaine received the harshest

Table 3.4	Estimated Number of Sentenced Prisoners Under Federal Jurisdiction by Offense, December 31, 2011
Category of Offense	**Number**
Violent Offenses	14,900
Property Offenses	10,700
Drug Offenses	96,400
Public Order	69,000

SOURCE: Adapted from E.A. Carson and W. Sabol, *Prisoners in 2011.* Bureau of Justice Statistics, U.S. Department of Justice, Table 11.

penalties compared with all other drugs. The act mandated that individuals caught with possession of 5 grams of crack were to receive an automatic mandatory minimum sentence of five years in prison, while there was no mandatory minimum prison sentence stipulated for the possession of powder cocaine. In addition, there is a "100 to one" quantity ratio used for sentencing traffickers of these drugs. Crack cocaine carried a mandatory minimum sentence of five years for first-time trafficking of 5 grams. In contrast, 500 grams of powder cocaine is needed to elicit the same penalty. Thus it took 100 times more powder cocaine to activate the same penalty that is applied to those trafficking crack. This disparity existed for nearly 30 years until Congress addressed the issue by passing the **Fair Sentencing Act of 2010,** which reduced the disparity to 18 to 1. While this act served to reduce the sentences of many offenders serving time for crack cocaine possession, the disparity still exists, although it is a step in the right direction for remedying an obvious inequity in sentencing drug offenders.[76]

Has our War on Drugs been effective in reducing the demand or consumption of illicit substances? Here, there is generally strong agreement that the demand for drugs appears to be as great as ever; there are new synthetic drugs hitting the streets on a regular basis. For example, a new type of heroin is becoming popular because it is no longer necessary to inject it—inhaling the new powder produces the same intense high. In addition to the illicit drug market, Americans are also getting creative and are using and abusing prescription drugs in ever greater numbers. Unfortunately, prescription drugs, while legally prescribed to treat medical conditions, can be just as addictive as street drugs and just as debilitating in their consequences. The National Institute of Drug Abuse reports that the most abused classes of prescription drugs include opioids (often prescribed to treat pain), central nervous system depressants (often prescribed to treat anxiety and sleep disorders), and stimulants (prescribed to treat narcolepsy, ADHD, and obesity).[77] Clearly, the War on Drugs has done very little to affect the consumption of illegal drugs. In fact, when asked by the Gallup Poll, more American teens believed that the issues of drugs, alcohol, and smoking were the most pressing problems they faced today compared with all other issues.[78]

The Media and Violence

Like most of us, you have probably been exposed to—and may even enjoy—watching violent television shows and movies or playing violent video games. While we don't have national averages on the amount of time spent watching violent television or movies or playing violent games, we do have numbers reflecting exposure to these forms of media generally, and the numbers are fairly disturbing. For example, it is estimated that U.S. children watch an average of three to four hours of television daily.[79] Older children and adolescents (8- to 18-year-olds) play video games, on average, between 1.2 and 7.5 hours per week. While boys tend to play video games more often than girls, both groups still play regularly. So we know kids spend a great deal of time in front of the television and playing video games. We don't know exactly how much of this time is being spent viewing violent images, but we do know that violent television and movies as well as violent video games are more popular than media with nonviolent content.[80] For example, one study found that 80% of the most popular video games currently on the market are violent in nature. Moreover, with new and more powerful graphics technologies, the cartoonish violence depicted in the early generation of video games is becoming ever more realistic and graphic. This also has important implications for evaluating the research on violent video games since studies from previous eras of games might lead to very different results. Earlier generations of video games that were once thought to be violent would be considered mild by today's standards.[81]

There are several different theoretical rationales explaining the possible connection this has to violent behavior. The most obvious is **social learning theory**, which contends that we learn aggression like any other behavior—by watching others and imitating their behavior. Theoretically, of course, children can learn from many sources, including their parents, peers, and media characters. A behavior is more likely to be acquired if, among other things, the viewer can identify with the model and the viewed behavior is rewarded in some way.[82] When someone imitates a behavior, the reinforcements or rewards they receive will also increase the likelihood that the behavior will be continued in the long term. Recent advancements in our understanding of this learning process suggest that children learn not only specific behaviors from models but can also learn more general and complex social scripts. As we discussed in Chapter 2, these scripts can be understood as a set of rules for how to interpret, understand, and deal with a variety of situations,

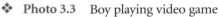

❖ Photo 3.3   Boy playing video game

including conflict.[83] Importantly, once these scripts are learned, they serve to guide future behavior. For example, children may not only learn the act of hitting, they also learn that hitting is an appropriate way to deal with frustration and conflict. In addition, from repeated observations, children also develop beliefs about what types of behavior are acceptable and will be tolerated.

There are other paths that link media violence and individual aggression. The arousal component of watching violence or playing a violent video game is also connected to aggressive behavior. Arousal increases the heart rate and other physiological conditions that can serve to strengthen an individual's response, including aggression. An aroused state appears to be particularly linked to aggression when someone is provoked.[84] **Emotional desensitization** is also related to the likelihood that watching violent media will increase aggressive behavior. Craig Anderson and his colleagues define emotional desensitization as the reduction in distress-related physiological reactivity to observations or thoughts of violence.[85] In other words, the first time you play a game like *Halo* or *Mass Effect* you may feel a bit squeamish; however, the more frequently you play, the less squeamish you become. In short, you become desensitized and more used to it. That's not always a bad thing since viewing violent media can be used to help children and adults come to grips with and deal with real fears and anxieties.[86] But barring these kinds of situations, becoming more used to violence serves only to make its use easier.

Does all of this consumption of violence increase an individual's likelihood of acting violently themselves? Well, when we ask our students whether they believe that being exposed to this violence increases their violent behavior, the overwhelming majority say no. However, we both have children, and remember watching them having light sabre duels after seeing one of the Star Wars movies or roughhousing after a Power Rangers episode. Of course, we can't conclude that being exposed to a violent movie causes violent behavior simply by observing our own kids.

How do we know that watching violent television or playing violent video games actually increases the likelihood of kids acting violently themselves? It would not be enough to simply ask kids how much time they spend playing violent video games and then observing their behavior for aggression or violence. If we observed a high frequency of violence in these kids, we wouldn't know whether playing the violent video games was actually responsible for violent behavior or if they were predisposed towards violence to begin with, and that is why they were attracted to violent games in the first place. However, there are a large number of studies that have done just this—they ask kids to report how often they watch or play games with violent content and then ask them and sometimes their parents and teachers about their aggressive behavior. These studies generally report a very strong correlation between exposure to violent media and aggressive behavior, but as we learned in our discussion about alcohol and violence, correlation does not mean causation.

An experimental design would also be needed to determine the causal effects of violent media exposure on violent behavior. For example, the typical experiment would take a group of children and randomly assign each of them to either an experimental or a control group. The experimental group would watch a violent show (or play a violent video game) and the control group would watch a nonviolent show (or play a nonviolent game). After the exposure, children from both groups would be observed playing and acts of aggression would be tallied; this is called a posttest. Sometimes a pretest may also be used in which the children would be observed for aggression before the exposure to the media. If the children who were exposed to the violent presentation acted more aggressively compared with the children in the control group, you could assume that it was attributable to the violent media exposure, because random assignment ensures that this is the only difference between the two groups of children. An illustration of this kind of research, conducted by Brad Bushman and his colleagues, is provided in Figure 3.2.

There are numerous studies using experimental designs that have found a direct relationship between exposure to television or film violence and the likelihood that children and adolescents will be physically violent toward each other. In fact, Anderson and his colleagues conclude that

> The evidence from these experiments is compelling. Brief exposure to violent dramatic presentations on TV or in films causes short-term increases in youths' aggressive thoughts, emotions, and behavior, including physically aggressive behavior serious enough to harm others.[87]

There have also been a few studies that have monitored the effects of violent media exposure on children over a protracted period of time to determine the long-term consequences of such exposure. Perhaps one of the most extensive was carried out by Rowell Huesmann and his colleagues, who began collecting data on a sample of children in first through fifth grades in the Chicago area beginning in 1972. The most recent data for this sample was taken in 1992 from more than 300 of the participants who were now in their early 20s. Among other things, results of this research indicate that, compared with those who had infrequently viewed violent television as children, both men and women who frequently viewed television violence during childhood were significantly more likely to engage in physical violence as adults. This included such violence as having "pushed, grabbed, or shoved their spouses," or "shoving, punching, beating or choking" someone who had made them angry.[88] In sum, there appears to be evidence that watching violent television or films in childhood is linked to both short-term violence and long-term violence into young adulthood.

What about video games? Policy makers and parents alike are increasingly concerned about video game play, not only because of their realistic nature but because children playing these games are active participants in the violence, not just passive observers. There have been several randomized experiments that have found that playing violent video games is related to increased aggressive behavior in the short term. There have also been a few studies that have followed kids over time to determine the long-term effects of violent video play. For example, one study followed a group of students annually from 9th through 12th grades asking them about the types of video games they played, the average number of hours they played, and about their own aggressive behavior (e.g., such things as "How often have you pushed or shoved someone in anger during the last school year?"). Researchers found that kids who played violent video games for longer periods of time were also more likely to be aggressive

❖ **Figure 3.2**   Bushman Experimental Design

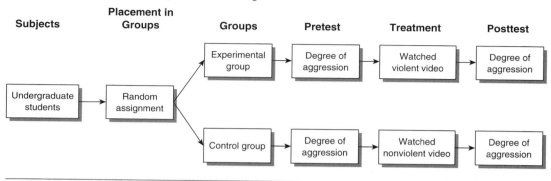

over the entire span of high school. In fact, this effect remained even after other important variables such as gender, peer deviance, parental control, and other demographic
factors were controlled.[89] Recent research has also investigated the effects of violent
media exposure to brain activity. For example, using magnetic resonance imaging to
monitor brain activity, a few studies have also found a relationship between playing
violent video games and neurobiological activity typically associated with aggression.
In one study, researchers observed the brain activity of male students playing a realistic
video game depicting first-person shooting and found brain activity patterns characteristic of aggressive thoughts.[90]

In sum, there is a substantial body of research indicating that being exposed to
violent media content increases aggressive and violent behavior both in the short term
and even into adulthood. It is important to note, however, that not all studies that
have examined the connection between media violence and aggression have found a
causal connection. In addition, the experiments that have found causal connections
between media violence and aggressive behavior are not without their critics. Some
contend that many of these experiments have provided controlled conditions that do
not simulate the same level of arousal without the violent content, and that it is therefore invalid to infer that the violent content is solely responsible for increased levels of
aggression—it may simply be an aroused state. Another criticism has been that some
laboratory experiments may have encouraged their subjects to act aggressively by
showing them violent films and then giving them the opportunity to engage in some
type of aggressive behavior. This condition, some contend, sets up a "demand factor"
whereby subjects feel compelled to do what they believe researchers expect them to do
(i.e., act aggressively).[91]

As we have already stated in this book, our position is that there are many factors related to violence—that is, there is no single causal factor. Violence happens in
a complex social environment, bringing together many factors that both increase and
decrease the chances of a violent event occurring. Being exposed to media violence is
simply one of those factors. Many policy makers have used a nutritional analogy when
talking about media "consumption." Like food consumption, it takes very little effort

to make good nutritional choices when selecting a media diet for children. A steady diet of violence, it seems to us, would inherently contribute to an unhealthy outcome, just as would a steady diet of sugar.

Conclusions

In this chapter, we have discussed three factors that are important for understanding the etiology of violence, particularly in the United States: the availability of firearms, alcohol and drug consumption and their prohibition, and media violence. None of these factors alone is a direct cause of the high rates of violence we observe in the United States. However, evidence suggests that they each serve to increase the likelihood that certain situations are more likely to culminate in violence. For example, a conflict situation precipitated by the need to protect one's reputation and/or self-image has an increased likelihood of turning violent if alcohol is present, and this situation is certainly more likely to turn lethal if a gun is available.

Some of the steps that can be taken to reduce the effects of these factors are fairly simple. For example, one study found that when parents watch and discuss the content of violent television with their children, the effects of the violence on children's behavior is reduced.[92] Of course, as we just mentioned above, limiting exposure to media violence is also an alternative.

There have also been several promising programs to reduce gun violence at the local level. One such program is the **Boston Gun Project**. This project is an inter-agency working group that includes members of several organizations: the Boston Police Department; the Bureau of Alcohol, Tobacco, and Firearms; the Massachusetts Department of Parole; the Boston school police; and a research team from Harvard University. All program participants communicate with one another to share intelligence on a regular basis in order to try to meet the project's goal of preventing violence in inner-city neighborhoods through heightened surveillance, rapid identification of violence and violent groups, and swift sanctions, such as arrest and conviction. The program is based on the assumption that general deterrence will work, that by increasing the costs associated with gun violence young people will be less likely to use guns to solve conflicts. Although there are no formal evaluations on the long-term affects of the program, the fact that Boston's youth homicide rates have fallen since the project's inception is promising.[93]

Key Terms

addiction

Anti-Drug Abuse Act of 1988

Armed Career Criminal Act of 1984

Assault Weapons Ban of 1994

Boston Gun Project

Brady Handgun Violence Prevention Act (Brady Bill) of 1993

Bureau of Alcohol, Tobacco, and Firearms

Community Mental Health Centers Act of 1963

Controlled Substance Act of 1970

crack cocaine

defensive gun use

disinhibitor

Eighteenth Amendment

emotional desensitization

Fair Sentencing Act of 2010

Federal Firearms Act of 1938

Firearms Owners' Protection Act of 1968

Gun Control Act of 1968

gun control legislation

handgun homicides

Harrison Act of 1914

Marijuana Tax Act of 1937

militia

National Firearms Act of 1934

National Instant Criminal Background Check System

National Prohibition Act or Volstead Act

National Rifle Association

phencyclidine or PCP

psychoactive effects of drugs

Schedule I drugs

Schedule II drugs

Second Amendment

self-protection argument

semiautomatic weapons

social learning theory

Taylor paradigm

War on Drugs

Discussion Questions

1. Since the authorization of the Brady Bill in 1994, which requires background checks for gun buyers making purchases at authorized gun dealers, the U.S. Congress has not implemented any new legislation to control the sale or distribution of guns in the United States. Many states, however, continue to implement their own legislation, some making gun ownership and gun carrying less restrictive, and others making gun ownership and carrying more restrictive. If you consider yourself against gun control, provide a debate with at least four points arguing *in favor* of gun control. If you consider yourself in favor of more gun control, provide a debate with at least four points arguing *against* gun control.

2. Many jurisdictions are attempting to deal with the burgeoning number of inmates sent to prison for drug-related offenses. One new avenue that has been implemented by many states is to create special courts called drug courts, which typically offer offenders treatment in lieu of prison. Conduct a descriptive analysis of the ways in which your local jurisdiction deals with drug-addicted offenders. Does the corrections department offer any special treatment program such as therapeutic communities? Is there a drug court in your local jurisdiction? If so, which types of offenders qualify to be adjudicated in the drug court? How are juvenile cases handled?

3. Go to the Bureau of Justice Statistics (BJS) website (www.ojp.usdoj.gov/bjs) and do a search using the terms "drugs and crime." From the list of options you are given, select "Drugs and Crime Facts." You will be given a list of publications and summary information about all sources of data that have any relevant information about the relationship between drugs and crime, including the extent to which drugs and alcohol are involved in criminal victimization and offending and the extent to which inmates under both state and federal correctional jurisdictions are in treatment for substance abuse treatment. Write a report on at least one topic presented in the document.

Assault and Murder

A Continuum of Violence

Every unpunished murder takes away something from the security of every man's life.

—Daniel Webster[1]

In many respects, homicide is a relatively simple and straightforward event. It requires merely motive, opportunity, and only a modicum of skill.

—Terance D. Miethe and Wendy C. Regoeczi[2]

A murder victim lies dead, and law enforcement searches for clues to apprehend a suspect. The friends and family react in horror, and they only have one question: why?

—Kim Egger[3]

On May 31, 2005, two Florida teens, Christopher Scamahorn, 14, and Jeffery Spurgeon, 18, confessed to beating a 53-year-old homeless man with their fists, feet, and sticks. The victim died from blunt force trauma to the head and body. The teens told the police that they attacked the man "for fun" and to "have something to do."[4] About six months later, on January 12, 2006, a security surveillance camera videotaped three teens attacking three other homeless men with bats. One of the victims, Norris Gaynor, was killed.

Did these teens intend to kill the homeless men? Or were they only interested in assaulting their victims? It appears as if these attacks were inspired, at least in part, by a series of videos known as "Bumfights" in which homeless men are paid and given alcohol to do demeaning things, including fighting each other. This suggests that killing was never the underlying motive. Regardless of intent, however, many scholars who study violent crime contend that the context and underlying factors related to assault and murder are very similar. Murder, in other words, is simply the most lethal form of assault—or as Leslie Kennedy and David Forde explain

> It makes more sense to see acts of violence on a continuum, where fatal actions represent an extremely harmful escalation of more mundane disagreements or coercive actions. The fact that one party ends up dead need not make us change our view of why these conflicts occur, although they clearly make our search for answers about how to curtail this escalation to violence much more urgent.[5]

Although there are many different factors that influence violent assaults, the majority of homicides appear to be sparked by relatively minor conflicts and disagreements. As we have already discussed in this book, what often separates nonlethal assaults from those that result in death is the availability of a firearm, and/or the availability of medical resources needed to treat injuries. In this chapter, we examine some of the general patterns and types of assault and homicide that tend to occur most frequently. Since other chapters discuss more specific forms of assaultive violence, such as violence that occurs within the home (Chapter 5), sexual assault and rape (Chapter 7), and violence between strangers (Chapter 6), we do not review them in any detail in this chapter. Instead, a large portion of this chapter focuses on the different types of homicide. We begin, as always, by examining a number of definitional issues.

Defining Assault and Homicide

Assault is a term that covers a wide range of actions and can vary from a simple threat of harm to a near-fatal attack. The National Crime Victimization Survey (NCVS) includes both aggravated and simple assault within its estimate of violent victimization. An **aggravated assault** is defined as "an attack or attempted attack with a weapon, regardless of whether or not an injury occurred and attack without a weapon when serious injury results." A **simple assault**, on the other hand, is an "attack without a weapon resulting either in no injury, minor injury (for example, bruises, black eyes, cuts, scratches, or swelling) or an undetermined injury requiring less than 2 days of hospitalization. Simple assaults also include cases of attempted assault without a weapon."[6]

The Federal Bureau of Investigation (FBI)'s Uniform Crime Reporting system collects detailed information on aggravated assaults only. For the FBI, an aggravated assault is defined as "an unlawful attack or threat of an attack by one person upon another for the purpose of inflicting severe or aggravated bodily injury." It is usually accompanied by the use of a weapon or by other means likely to produce death or great bodily harm.[7] When an aggravated assault and theft occur together, it becomes a robbery, which are discussed in Chapter 6. When an assault culminates in death, then it obviously becomes a homicide.

Homicide

Most of us use the terms "murder" and "homicide" interchangeably, but they are really distinct categories of killing. Homicide is a general term for the killing of another individual, whereas murder refers to the specific legal category of criminal homicide. In this chapter, however, we will use the terms interchangeably for ease of discussion. As with all crimes, the legal definitions of murder vary from state to state, but there are typically three types: excusable, justifiable, and murder. Figure 4.1 displays the different kinds included in most state statutes.

Justifiable homicides are killings judged to be legally acceptable because they occurred in defense of life or property. **Excusable homicides**, on the other hand, are accidental or unintentional killings that did not occur because of negligence or recklessness. **Criminal homicides**, the kind of killing we are most concerned with here, generally include two categories—murder and manslaughter—with various types subsumed under each. **First-degree murders** are generally committed with both premeditation and deliberation. **Premeditation** refers to the knowledge and intention to kill while **deliberation** implies that the killing was planned and thought about rather than committed on impulse. **Second-degree murders** are considered a little less serious because they do not involve premeditation and deliberation. Instead, they are more spontaneous in nature. Some states also have **felony murder** statutes for murders that occur during the commission of another felony, such as a robbery. And finally, **manslaughters** are criminal homicides in which the degree of responsibility is considered much less than murder, not only because premeditation and deliberation are absent but also because the offender did not act with malice. Most states also divide manslaughters into voluntary (e.g., someone killed while overwhelmed by emotion or passion) and involuntary (e.g., someone killed because of another individual's reckless behavior). If you are thinking that the distinction between these different degrees of homicide appears to be somewhat indistinct and arbitrary, you are absolutely correct. In many ways, the legal differences between first-degree murder and second-degree murder and manslaughter depend upon how the killing is interpreted by others. It is truly a subjective evaluation. Essentially, the various types of murder are differentiated based on the state of mind and intentions of the person perpetrating the violence, and it is hard for others to really know what is in somebody else's mind. Their intent can only be guessed or inferred from their actions and words, and that is a judgment call.

Estimates of Assault

In 2011, there were over one million aggravated assault and almost four million simple assault victimizations that occurred in the United States against individuals 12 years of age or older. Less than half (48%) of these were reported to the police.[8]

❖ Figure 4.1 Homicide Types

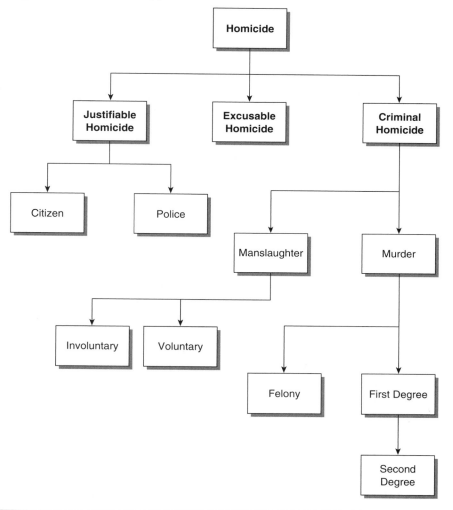

Many scholars contend that even this is an undercount of all assaults that actually occur—particularly of those that are hard to measure, such as assaults that occur in the home.

Generally, assaults make up the majority of nonlethal violent crime victimizations. For example, in 2011 the NCVS recorded 7,424,550 violent victimizations; of those, 87% were assaults. The majority of these assault victimizations were simple assaults.[9] Males have higher rates of assault compared with females, which is consistent with what we know about violence generally. The context of the assault, however, is very different across gender groups. As you can see from Table 4.1, females are much more

Table 4.1 The Percentage of Assault Victimizations Against Males and Females By Victim/Offender Relationship, NCVS 2010

Victim/Offender Relationship	Female Victims	Male Victims
Intimate Partner	23%	5.5%
Other Relative	7.5	8
Friend/Acquaintance	30.5	32.5
Stranger	32	41.5
Relationship not Identified	7.5	13
Total	100%	100%

SOURCE: Adapted from Table 5, *Criminal Victimization in the United States, 2010*, Bureau of Justice Statistics.

likely to be assaulted by people they know compared with males. American Indian or Alaskan Natives have rates of assault that are more than twice those of other race/ethnic groups, followed by African Americans, whites, and Hispanics.[10] The young are more likely to be the victims of assault, with assaults dropping off sharply for those over the age of 25 compared to younger age groups. For example, the average assault rate per 1,000 persons between the ages of 12 and 24 is about 22.8 compared to a rate of only 9.2 for those 25 years of age or older.

In the vast majority of all aggravated assaults, a weapon was used, regardless of the victim–offender relationship. However, strangers were more likely to be armed for both aggravated and simple assault victimizations with firearms compared with known offenders who were more likely to use knives.[11] For nonfatal violence in general, about 22% of victims were injured when their attackers were strangers compared to about 31% when the victims knew their attackers.[12] Thus, contrary to the stereotype that strangers pose the greatest threat to our safety, we are more likely to be harmed by people we know. In other words, while strangers are more likely to get involved in assaults, it is those perpetrated by people who know each other that are more likely to result in harm. As you can see from Figure 4.2, rates of both aggravated and simple assault peaked around 1994, but the peak was highest for rates of simple assault. Since that time, they have generally been declining, with simple assaults declining more precipitously than aggravated assaults. However, both simple and aggravated assault rates appear to have stabilized in recent years.

When Assaults Become Lethal—Homicide

In 2011, there were 12,664 people murdered in the United States; over 9,800 males and over 2,800 females. This translates into a rate of 4.8 per 100,000 U.S. inhabitants. From 1980, rates were declining until the late 1980s, at which time they

❖ Figure 4.2   Aggravated and Simple Assault Rates, 1993–2011

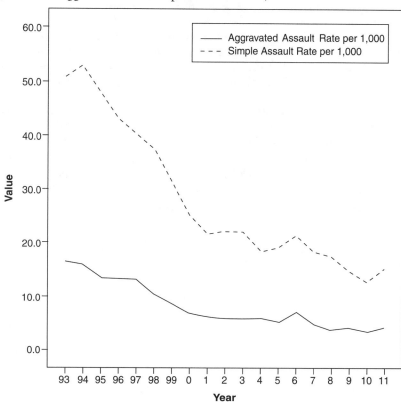

SOURCE: Data obtained from the Bureau of Justice Statistics, *Criminal Victimization in the United States, Statistical Tables*, NCJ 227669.

peaked for people between 14 and 34 years of age, with rates for those aged 18 to 24 reaching an extreme high near 24 per 100,000. Those in the age groups above age 35 generally declined during this entire time period while offending rates for those aged 14 and under remained relatively stable and low (Figure 4.3). When these rates are further disaggregated by race, we see that it is only young males who witnessed such high peaks of offending during this time, and this included both African American and white males.

The other factor that contributed to the high rates of murder witnessed in the 1990s was handguns. Figure 4.4 displays homicide rates from 1980 to 2008 by the weapon used to kill. The majority of homicides during this time were committed with firearms, which John Lofland termed "**facilitating hardware**" for lethal violence.[13] In fact, after reviewing thousands of homicide narratives from police reports, Terance Miethe and Wendy Regoeczi concluded that the dynamics of a conflict or dispute change dramatically once a firearm becomes involved. They state

The narrative accounts are filled with numerous instances of homicides that would have been difficult, if not impossible, to commit if it was not for the availability and use of a firearm. These situations are best represented by (1) drive-by shootings and (2) young males being "picked on" or "dissed" by groups of males, leaving the scene, and then returning with a gun. Within these particular situations, firearms provide a unique opportunity structure for homicide because they are highly lethal weapons, easily used to equalize strength differentials, and may be employed without direct physical contact with the victim.[14]

It is also important to note that this generally declining trend has not been present everywhere in the United States. Several cities in the United States have experienced significant increases in murder over the past few years. For example, in Chicago, homicides were up by 38% in 2012 compared to 2011, occurring primarily in the most impoverished neighborhoods. Philadelphia is another city that was witnessing an increased number of murders in 2012, while other cities like New York City and Los Angeles continued a downward or stable trend in lethal violence.[15]

❖ Figure 4.3   Homicide Victimization Rates by Age, 1980–2008

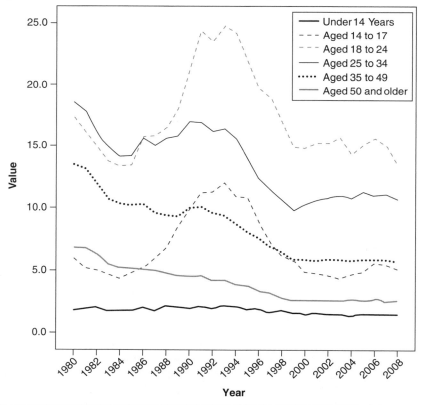

SOURCE: Cooper and Smith, *Homicide Trends in the United States, 1980–2008*, Bureau of Justice Statistics, NCJ 236018, 2011.

Clearly, the United States has very high rates of assaultive violence, and when a gun is available these conflicts often end in death. But are these rates high compared with other countries that are similar to us? This is a harder question to answer than you might think because it can be difficult to ensure that you are comparing the same things. Because definitions of assault vary tremendously, for example, this crime is fairly challenging to compare across nations. Although there are also differences for homicide rates, it is more comparable than assault rates because there is less variation in terms of what constitutes murder, at least in most industrialized and democratic nations. Table 4.2 displays rates of homicide for the United States along with several other nations similar in economic and political climate. As you can see, the United States has the distinction of being number one in terms of lethal violence; in fact, the United States has a rate that is almost two times higher than the next highest rates. Of course, there are other countries with even higher rates of murder, but

❖ **Figure 4.4** Homicide Victimization Rates by Weapon, 1980–2008

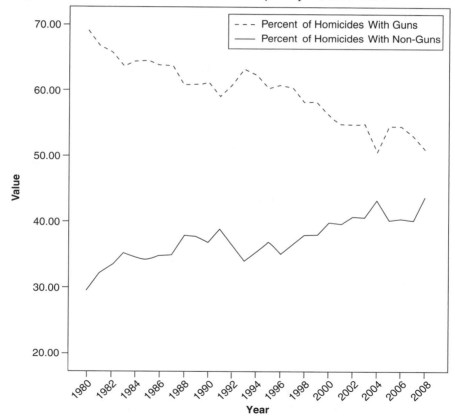

SOURCE: Cooper and Smith, *Homicide Trends in the United States, 1980–2008*, Bureau of Justice Statistics, NCJ 236018, 2011.

these countries are usually struggling with some type of political, economic, or social turmoil. Countries like Colombia, for example, have extremely high rates of murder (61.1), because of internal conflict against drug cartels and revolutionary movements intent on overthrowing the government.[16] Other countries in Central America such as Honduras, El Salvador, and Guatemala, experience extremely high rates of murder, which have also been fueled by drug trafficking and the corruption of public officials that usually follows in its path.[17]

In sum, compared with other industrialized and democratic nations, the United States has very high rates of assault and homicide. Although the decline in rates of assault and homicide has been leveling off over the past two years, the good news is that these rates are leveling out at rates nowhere near those observed in the early 1990s. At this point, it is important to note that all of these violent encounters don't just happen but are instead the outcome of certain kinds of violent encounters, and it is to these that we now turn.

Violent Interactions

You have probably heard the old saying that "life is a stage, and we are all actors." A theory called **symbolic interactionism** also contends that human behavior—including assaults and homicides—occurs in social situations, and that the meanings people attach to their behavior is an important element in understanding what takes place in a given circumstance. To others, a given interaction may appear to be the same; however, to those involved, their perception and interpretation of the meaning of the situation can vary dramatically and produce different reactions and behaviors. For example, one person may be pushed in a bar and perceive the push as an insult to his or her honor, while another person may interpret it as a simple accident and ignore it. The latter person will probably continue on their way without further incident while the first person may shove back, increasing the likelihood of a violent ending to the situation. This means that, like all social events, the outcome of the encounter depends on the perceptions and behaviors of the actors involved. Because of this, violent events tend to be evolutionary and sequential in nature, with a beginning and an end. In other words, violence is often patterned behavior.

As we saw in Chapter 2, theories that attempt to explain violence focus on several levels of explanation, from geographical units like states and cities down to the individual level. Other researchers, however, have focused exclusively on violent events as the units of analysis: the offender, the victim, and the circumstances surrounding the event. A basic assumption with these types of analyses is that violent events cannot be separated from the physical and social settings within which they occur. As Terance Miethe and Wendy Regoeczi assert, "As social events, crimes are said to be intricately linked to the routine activities of subsequent victims and offenders, the places in which these activities occur, the behavior of witnesses and bystanders, and the particular circumstances of the situation."[18] To distinguish between the primary precipitating circumstances of assaultive violence, researchers have classified homicide situations into what are termed instrumental and expressive events. Instrumental murders are those conducted for explicit, future goals such as acquiring money or property. Robbery

| Table 4.2 Homicide Victimization Rates for a Sample of Industrialized Nations, 2004–2005 ||
Country	Homicide Rate per 100,000
Luxembourg	.4
Japan	.5
Singapore	.5
Austria	.7
Norway	.8
Germany	1.0
Iceland	1.0
Denmark	1.1
Ireland	1.1
Italy	1.2
Spain	1.2
Sweden	1.2
Australia	1.3
Netherlands	1.4
Portugal	1.4
Canada	1.5
New Zealand	1.5
France	1.6
United Kingdom—England & Wales	1.6
Belgium	2.1
Israel	2.6
Finland	2.8
Switzerland	2.9
United States of America	5.9

SOURCE: The Guardian. DataBlog: Facts are Sacred, "Global Homicide: Murder Rates Around the World," Downloaded on January 8, 2013 from http://www.guardian.co.uk/news/datablog/2009/oct/13/homicide-rates-country-murder-data.

murders are usually classified as instrumental. In contrast, expressive murders are often unplanned acts of anger, rage, or frustration, typically precipitated by a conflict situation, such as an argument or fight.[19] Keep in mind, however, that these are not absolute separate categories. A robber, for example, may commit their violence to get money or valuables but also engage in these crimes because they get a kick out of them. In other words, any act of violence may contain both instrumental and expressive motives at the same time.

Other researchers have developed more detailed classifications to characterize the evolution of a social interaction from a conflict to an assault to murder. Based on his analysis of murder situations, David Luckenbill distinguished between six different developmental stages that characterize the most typical homicide transaction:

1. The eventual victim says or does something that is offensive to the eventual murderer. This phase marks the opening round of a series of interactions that Luckenbill terms a "**character contest**," in which at least one actor—but usually both—will attempt to establish or "save face."

2. The murderer interprets the previous interaction as offensive; in many cases, this interpretation is mediated by bystanders and witnesses who help interpret what happened.

3. A variety of response options are available to the eventual murderer, including walking away from the event; however, if retaliation is chosen, violence becomes almost inevitable. In some cases, this is when murder occurs.

4. Interaction between the parties escalates, and both perceive the situation as a confrontation to which the only appropriate response involves aggression and violence.

5. Violence is used to resolve the conflict. The offender may procure a weapon that is at hand, or briefly leave the scene to get one.

6. The final stage involves the murderer either fleeing, remaining, or being held by bystanders; the choice is determined by the social context, including the relationship between the victim and offender.[20]

It might seem that people kill over very slight insults or affronts; what Luckenbill's research indicates is that while the initial issue may be petty and ultimately meaningless, as the interaction continues, it becomes more about "face," social status, and certain ideas about what it means to be a man. Several researchers have found that a large percentage of homicides involve "character contests." In fact, the depiction of homicides involving the victim as an active participant as well as the offender was first introduced by Marvin Wolfgang in 1958. He coined the term "**victim precipitation**," which simply means that victims sometimes start the conflict that ends in their own death.[21] Kenneth Polk labels these types of events as confrontational homicides because they are characterized by altercations that typically evolve from verbal exchanges of insults into physical contests.[22] What all these terms convey is the fact that a homicide is often an event in which the victim is not always an innocent bystander but is often an active participant as well.

Most recently, Terance Miethe and Wendy Regoeczi analyzed narratives from homicide cases from four large cities in the United States and concluded that most homicides occur in situational contexts that have changed little over the past three decades. They found expressive homicides involving disputes and arguments to be more prevalent than instrumental homicides, with males being the primary perpetrators of both but particularly of instrumental homicides. Their research also suggests that **confrontational homicides** occur between a wider range of victims and perpetrators and situations than was often believed. They found that, while these "character contests" did most often involve males, they also often involved female offenders, occurred in both public and private settings, and were not restricted to minority group members. Often beginning with what many would call "trivial altercations," Miethe and Regoeczi found that alcohol was a common element in many of these conflicts and that the victim often provoked the offender in some way—the phenomenon mentioned above as "victim precipitation." This kind of scenario is particularly common for youth homicides, given that they very often revolve around honor contests and issues of respect. Others have termed these confrontations the "young male syndrome" because of the hypersensitivity of many young men about saving face.[23] James Gilligan, who has been studying violence and violent offenders for over three decades, contends that all violence is an attempt to achieve justice—or at least what the offender perceives to be justice. His perspective certainly highlights the importance of perception in understanding these interactions. Gilligan writes, "When individuals and groups feel their 'honor' is at stake, and an intolerable degree of humiliation or 'loss of face' would result from a failure to fight for that honor, they may act violently. The loss of self-esteem is experienced subjectively as the death of the self. People sacrifice anything to prevent the death and disintegration of their individual or group identity."[24]

Although both males and females were involved in all types of murder, Miethe and Regoeczi found that each gender group typically killed within different situational contexts. Male offenders generally killed in situations involving acquaintances of the same age, gender, and race in disputes that occurred in public at night. Beginning in the 1990s, they found that male offenders were increasingly younger and increasingly relying on guns as their weapon of choice. Females were disproportionately more likely to kill family members and intimates of the opposite gender in private locations. Compared with earlier decades, females in the 1990s began killing in a more diverse array of social situations and, similar to their male counterparts, were killing at increasingly younger ages.

In sum, research that examines assaults and homicides as social events illustrates the interactive pattern of escalating tension that sometimes culminates in murder. This is why Harries calls murder a process crime.[25] Death is not always inevitable. In fact, Blumstein estimates that, for every murder, there are 50 nonfatal assaults. The final act of an assault is contingent on the individual responses to the situation. At any point in the process, choices could be made that would de-escalate the conflict and end the interaction. Unfortunately, when interactions end lethally, it is often because both actors defined the situation as one in which violence was not only appropriate but preferred to a verbal or other nonviolent response. Not all murders, however, fit this interactional pattern. Some forms of felony murder, for example, in which a stranger commits a robbery and kills the victims, don't necessarily result from an escalating series of actions and reactions. Similarly, when we look at multiple murders, we often find a very different dynamic and sequence of events at play.

Multicide

Although the percentage of murders involving multiple victims has been increasing over the past three decades, these types of homicides still comprise only about 5% of all murders.[26] Despite the low frequency of these murders relative to lone-offender and victim incidents, they grab the largest proportion of media attention. These kinds of killings are generally referred to as **multicides**, which means they involve the killing of more than one person. There are three broad types of multicide: mass murder, spree murder, and serial murder. In this section, we will highlight the general characteristics of each, although we should point out that there is no real consensus on what constitutes each category. While we tend to be fairly familiar with the names of famous serial killers—like Ted Bundy and Jeffrey Dahmer—we don't always know what elements must be present to make someone a serial killer. Is serial murder when one person kills several people at a single moment in time or does it have to involve killings over a period of time? If so, how much time must pass between the murders? One day? One week? One year? Issues such as these make defining the categories somewhat problematic, and with this in mind we turn to the first category: mass murder.

Mass Murder

Mass murder is generally understood to have taken place when someone kills four or more victims in one location at one general point in time. The killings may stretch over a period of hours, but they are all part of the same emotional experience.[27] For example, Cho Seung-Hui began his deadly rampage at Virginia Tech by killing two students in a dormitory, followed two hours later by a series of attacks in a classroom building that left 30 more people dead. In other incidents, the murders may take place in different locations, but they are usually within the same general area and the same general time frame. For example, when 16-year-old Jeff Weise killed his grandfather and the older man's girlfriend in their home and then went to Red Lake High School and killed eight people, including himself, most still consider this an incident of mass murder because the killings occurred within a relatively small geographical area. One of the most infamous cases from U.S. history that illustrates this well concerns Charles J. Whitman and the University of Texas Tower in Austin on July 31 and August 1, 1966.[28] A student at the university, Whitman, a former Marine and Eagle Scout decided to commit mass murder. He first went to visit his mother in her apartment and after hitting her in the back of the head, strangled and then stabbed her to death before tucking her body in bed and covering it with the bedspread. From there he went home where his wife Kathy was sleeping after a long day at work and killed her in her sleep by stabbing her multiple times with a large hunting knife. He then gathered a variety of weapons, cleaned and prepared them for what was to come, and concealed them in a footlocker. Driving to the university he went to the tower and, disguised as a worker in coveralls, he took the elevator to the observation deck on the 28th floor where he attacked the receptionist and after shooting and killing three people who were coming up the stairs, barricaded himself on the observation deck where he began firing at whoever came within range. He killed 14 people and wounded another 32 before Austin police gained access to the observation deck and shot him.

Another common characteristic of these events is that mass murderers often take their own lives after their rampage, either killing themselves directly or in other cases, staging the situation in such a way that police officers are left with no choice but to kill the mass murderer—a scenario sometimes referred to as "suicide by cop."[29] Charles Whitman clearly fell into this latter category.

Mass Murder in the Workplace

One common setting where many mass murders take place is the workplace. In August 1986, Patrick Sherrill went to the Edmond, Oklahoma, post office where he worked and killed his supervisor and 14 employees before finally killing himself. This was one of a string of shootings in the mid-1980s and early 1990s that occurred at postal installations, and the term "going postal" soon entered our vocabulary. This is somewhat ironic since postal workers tend to be statistically safer from becoming victims of workplace violence than many other professions.[30] The term, however, resurfaced in January 2006 when a former female postal worker who had been put on medical leave for psychological problems shot and killed five people at a large mail-processing center in Goleta, California, and then shot herself. What made this incident so noteworthy is that it is believed to be the deadliest mass murder carried out by a woman. But this case is the exception to the rule, since the vast majority of mass murders are committed by men. So who are the men perpetrating this kind of violence?

The vast majority of mass killings are committed by white, middle-aged men.[31] Mass murderers are often frustrated and angry individuals who frequently have a history of written complaints against them and by them. They often feel that they have been wronged and suffer from a sense of injustice about their situation. For example, Doug Williams—who eventually went on a workplace killing rampage—was a known racist and often taunted and threatened African American employees at the Lockheed plant where he worked. In fact, many of his coworkers had predicted that he would one day do something terrible.[32] Another mass murderer, Matthew Beck, who killed four of his superiors at the Connecticut State Lottery, had filed a grievance contending that he was being assigned jobs outside of his work classification and that he deserved a raise. Just days before his killings, he told coworkers that he planned to sue the Lottery. Larry Hensel was given various warnings about his inappropriate comments and rants about religion and politics, and when layoffs were forced on the company by hard economic times, Hensel was let go. This job loss, combined with a deteriorating family situation, created a man who, in the subsequent words of his attorney, "was distraught, disgruntled, and unbalanced."[33] Shortly after losing his job, the former electronics technician showed up at his former workplace with a shotgun and a hit list and killed two individuals before leaving the scene on a mountain bike. He later showed up at a sheriff's department and turned himself in. Unfortunately, this is just one example from many.

Table 4.3 displays a few of the most deadly workplace shootings to happen in the United States since 2000. As you can see, another characteristic of mass murder in the workplace is the availability of high-powered and semiautomatic weaponry that greatly facilitates the lethal violence.

It is important to remember that, although mass murders are the most likely to make the headlines, there are hundreds of employees killed on the job every day.

In fact, since 1999 the Bureau of Labor Statistics estimates that in the United States there has been an average of 642 homicides in the workplace annually.[34] The majority of these homicides occurred in retail establishments and were the result of robberies. In fact, employees working in retail sales are much more likely to be killed on the job compared with law enforcement officers or taxi drivers. While these incidents capture our attention, there are many more assaults than homicides on the job. In fact, the Bureau of Justice Statistics estimates that almost two million assault victimizations occur to individuals on the job every year. Professions most likely to experience an assault on the job (other than retail employees) include law enforcement officers and taxi drivers.[35] Clearly, some jobs are more dangerous than others. In addition to mass murders in the workplace, school shootings have emerged as another setting in which mass killings sometimes take place.

Table 4.3	Selected Workplace Shootings Since 2000
December 26, 2000	Software engineer Michael McDermott, 42, killed seven coworkers at Edgewater Technology, an Internet consultant firm in Wakefield, Massachusetts. He was armed with an AK-47 assault rifle, a shotgun, and a semiautomatic handgun.
February 5, 2001	A former employee shot eight people, killing four, at the Navistar International Corporation, a diesel engine manufacturing plant in Chicago, Illinois, before killing himself.
July 8, 2003	Doug Williams shot and killed six people including himself at a Lockheed Martin plant near Meridian, Missouri. He was armed with a shotgun and a semiautomatic rifle.
August 27, 2003	After being fired, Salvador Tapia went to a Chicago auto parts company armed with a semiautomatic handgun, killing six former coworkers. He died in a shoot-out with police.
July 2, 2004	Elijah Brown killed five coworkers at a Kansas City, Kansas, meatpacking plant before killing himself.
January 31, 2006	Jennifer Sanmarco killed five former coworkers at a mail-processing plant in Goleta, California, before killing herself. She was armed with a 9mm semiautomatic pistol.
November 5, 2009	Nidal Malik Hassan, a U.S. Army officer stationed at Fort Hood, Texas, opened fire at the Soldier Readiness Center on the base while shouting "Allahu Akbar" or God is Great. He was shot and wounded by police officers and placed into custody.
August 3, 2010	At a disciplinary hearing at Hartford Distributors in Manchester, Connecticut, Omar Thorton pulled out a 9mm Ruger and killed eight, then killed himself.
September 29, 2012	Andrew Engeldinger lost his job at a factory in Minneapolis, Minnesota, and returned the next day with a 9mm Glock handgun, killing five and then killing himself.

Mass Murder at School

It is a sad reality that we can divide school shootings into college, high school, and secondary school settings and sadder still that they happen frequently enough to necessitate an update in this edition. On April 16, 2007, Cho Seung-Hui went on the deadliest school shooting in U.S. history. In fact, it is the most deadly mass shooting in any setting and resulted in 32 students, faculty, and staff killed before the shooter killed himself on the campus of Virginia Tech in Blacksburg, Virginia. The deadliest school shooting to occur at a high school occurred on April 20, 1999, in Littleton, Colorado, at Columbine High School, where Dylan Klebold and Eric Harris went on a shooting rampage that resulted in the death of 13 of their fellow students before they killed themselves. Like mass murderers who strike in other contexts, Cho, Klebold, and Harris all had a long history of rage and anger. This rage was depicted vividly on Harris's website where he described his hatred, "God, I can't wait until I can kill you people I'll just go to some downtown area in some big [expletive] city and blow up and shoot everything I can."[36] And the deadliest elementary school shooting occurred on December 14, 2012, when 20-year-old Adam Lanza killed his mother at her home, then went to Sandy Hook Elementary School and killed 20 first graders, 6 teachers and staff, and then shot himself using several semiautomatic weapons. Not much is known about Lanza's motive, but former classmates described him as intelligent but quiet and socially awkward.[37]

As noted earlier, another mass shooting took place on March 21, 2005, at Red Lake High School, located on an American Indian reservation in northern Minnesota. On that day, Jeff Weise killed his grandfather and his companion and, then went to the school where he killed a teacher, a security guard, five students, and finally himself, leaving a total of 15 people dead. Like the others, there were warning signs in Weise's life before the shooting. He was often the target of teasing and as a result kept mostly to himself. He often drew pictures of people dying, along with Nazi swastikas. Several postings were made to a neo-Nazi Internet site that were later attributed to him, including one that asserted, "It's hard being a Native American National Socialist, people are so misinformed, ignorant and close minded, it makes your life a living hell."[38]

As the evidence indicates, most mass murderers tend to be very angry people with a great deal of hostility toward those they believe to have wronged them in some way. Many believe that these acts of violence could be decreased if more social and personal support systems were available in society. James Fox and Jack Levin echo this sentiment when they state

> The real culprit in explaining mass murder can be found in society itself and in a trend that has affected almost everyone. During recent years, there has been an eclipse of community, a dwindling of the social relationships—family ties and neighborliness—that had protected former generations of Americans from succumbing to disaster . . . For too many Americans who suffer, their misery has no company.[39]

Lest we give a false impression, we need to point out that, like homicide in general, homicides in middle and high schools have been in decline during the past decade. It is also important to look at long-term trends, not just one incident. For example, in 2003 through 2004, there were 49 violent deaths at schools compared to only 13 in the 2008 through 2009 school year, and 11 in the 2009 through 2010 school year (Figure 4.5). Of course, the number of people killed in a mass shooting fluctuates greatly, and a mass killing like the Sandy Hook Elementary School that resulted in such a high number of deaths skews such trends. Moreover, it is important to place these homicides in the larger context of homicides against young people. Although mass shootings at schools receive a great deal of media attention, they account for a very small proportion of all murders against children and adolescents. For example, in 2008 through 2009, there were 1,562 murders against those aged 5 to 18 years old and only 17 of those occurred in schools.[40]

Violence in the schools can have many negative consequences, but it is also important to note that the decline in violence at schools seems to have affected students' fear levels. The percentage of students who reported that they were afraid of being attacked at school or on the way to and from school decreased from 12% in 1995 to only 6% in 2007.[41]

❖ **Figure 4.5**   Number of Homicides in School Against Those 5 to 18 Years of Age, 1992–2009

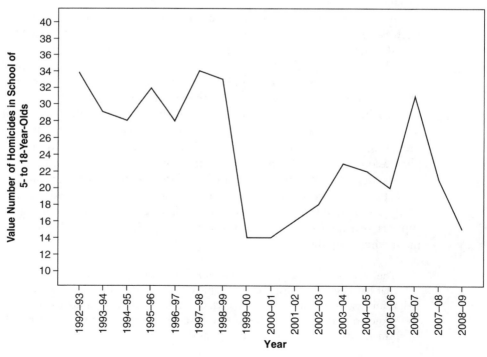

SOURCE: *Indicators of School Crime and Safety, 2011*, U.S. Department of Education and Bureau of Justice Statistics.

Serial Murder

In 1974, a series of ten murders occurred in the Wichita, Kansas, area in which the victims were strangled and/or tortured and then killed. It began in January of that year when the bodies of Julie and Joseph Otero were found strangled in their home, along with two of their children—Joseph Jr., who was suffocated with a plastic bag, and Josephine, who was found hanging by a rope tied to a water pipe. Semen was found around the victims' bodies. A few months later, in April, Kathryn Bright, a 21-year-old, was found stabbed to death in her home. It wasn't until March 1977 that the next connected murder occurred, when 24-year-old Shirley Vian was also found tied up and strangled in her home, followed in December by 35-year-old Nancy Fox, who was killed in a similar way. After another hiatus that lasted until April 1985, 53-year-old Marine Hedge was discovered after she had been strangled in her home and her body subsequently dumped in a ditch. This murder was followed in September 1986 by that of Vicki Wegerle, a 28-year-old who was strangled in her home. In January 1991, Delores "Dee" Davis was strangled and her body then dumped in a rural area near a river.[42] Who committed these terrible crimes, and why did they do it? It would take many years before the answer was finally known.

Soon after the first killings began in 1974, a *Wichita Eagle* newspaper reporter received an anonymous phone call telling him he could find a letter hidden in a mechanical engineering book at the city library. The letter claimed responsibility for the Otera killings and provided details about the incident that could only have been known by the killer. During the next few weeks, more letters arrived at the *Wichita Eagle* and all were signed "BTK," or "Bind, Torture, Kill." The killer was soon called the **BTK killer**. The killer made several contacts with police until 1979, when all contacts stopped for a few years. In April 1985, after the naked body of Marine Hedge was found in a ditch, police suspected that the BTK killer was at it again, but were unsure since the perpetrator had never removed bodies from the victims' homes before. In September 1986, Vicki Wegerle's husband returned home to find her body. Six years would pass before another body, that of Delores Davis, was found near a river. There was still no communication between BTK and the media or police. Then, in March 2004—over 30 years after the first murders—the *Wichita Eagle* again received a letter enclosing photographs of Vicki Wegerle's body. Other letters soon arrived with more personal items from the killer's victims. A computer disk was also sent to a Wichita television station that was subsequently tracked down to the killer's church. In April 2005, Dennis Rader—the BTK killer—was arrested and charged with 10 counts of first-degree murder for the crimes that had haunted Wichita for over 30 years.

Who was Dennis Rader? He graduated from Wichita State University with a degree in justice administration in 1979 and

❖ Photo 4.1 Serial killer Dennis Rader in court

worked as an ordinance enforcement officer. He lived with his wife and had two adult children. Rader was a Cub Scout leader and before his arrest was elected president of the church council at the Lutheran church where he was a member. Although many later described him as a bit "weird," others noted the many good works he performed, including helping elderly neighbors with their yard work.[43] In August 2005, Rader was sentenced to 10 consecutive life terms for his murders and will spend the rest of his life in a maximum-security prison near Wichita.[44]

Although they both have multiple victims, **serial murders,** such as those committed by the BTK killer, are very different from mass murders. John Douglas and Mark Olshaker define a serial murderer as one who kills on at least three occasions, with what can be called an emotional cooling-off period between the incidents. This cooling-off period can last days, weeks, months, or years. The important distinction is that each event is emotionally separate from the others.[45] A more comprehensive definition of serial murder was developed by Steven Egger, who identified a number of additional characteristics that typically characterize serial murders:

1. There is generally no prior relationship between the victim and the attacker.

2. Subsequent murders are at different times and have no apparent connection to the initial murder.

3. Subsequent murders are usually committed in a different geographical location.

4. The motive is usually not material gain but the murderer's desire to have power or dominance over his victims.

5. The victims may have symbolic value for the murderer or are perceived to have little status or prestige and, in most instances, are unable to defend themselves or alert others to their situation. Individuals who are particularly at risk are those whose situations make them powerless, such as prostitutes, homeless people, missing children, and single women.[46]

According to Egger,

Serial murderers increasingly captivate our attention; the bottom line is that the topic sells books and movies. In fact, Eric Hickey traced the number of films about serial murder and found that from the 1960s to the 1990s, the number of films on serial murder more than quadrupled.[47]

But how often does a serial murderer strike? How many of the several thousand intentional killings that occur in the United States are actually the result of a serial killer? Unfortunately, this number is a bit difficult to estimate. Do we count a bank robber who kills several people during the course of his or her life of crime as a serial killer? How about a mob contract killer who kills for money? For example, Louis Eppolito and Steven Caracappa—both former law enforcement officials—were sentenced to life in federal prison in 2006 for killing eight people for the Mob in New York City for up to $65,000 a hit.[48] Should they be considered serial murderers? Even if there was a consensus on what to include, there are still many other problems inherent in estimating numbers. In fact, neither the FBI nor the Centers for Disease Control and Prevention keep separate records for serial killings. The only agency that even attempts to count serial killings in the United States is the FBI's Behavioral Sciences Investigative Support Unit at the National Center for the Analysis of Violent Crime. They don't rely on official data, however, but instead use reports from newspapers and wire services. As you can imagine, these sources are less than ideal.

Why is it so hard to count serial murders? Much of the difficulty has to do with connecting murders that take place in different geographical locations. Identifying a murder as part of a serial case requires the killer to leave distinctive identifiers, sometimes called "signatures," at the crime scene, such as folding the victim's clothes or leaving a common object. Connecting killings across different jurisdictions is problematic for several reasons but primarily due to communication issues. Steven Egger uses the term "linkage blindness" to describe the poor communication about unsolved murders or missing persons across law enforcement jurisdictions.[49] It is also very expensive to conduct long-term investigations of several murders, particularly when they have occurred in different jurisdictions. For example, in King County, Washington, it cost millions of dollars to finally capture 54-year-old Gary Ridgway, who had become known as the Green River Killer. Ridgway killed 48 young women between the ages of 16 and 38 from 1982 to 1998 before his DNA evidence was finally linked to four of his victims. He pleaded guilty in November 2003 to 48 counts of aggravated murder in the first degree. At his sentencing hearing, Ridgway stated, "I wanted to kill as many women I thought were prostitutes as I possibly could."[50]

As you can see, the reality is that identifying a murder victim as part of a larger pattern can be very difficult. Every year, there are many murder victims who remain unidentified; they are left in shallow graves, in garbage dumps, in woods, and in roadside ditches—these, along with a proportion of the thousands of missing children and other individuals, may have been victims of serial killers. Determining how many, however, is virtually impossible. Despite these obstacles, several scholars have attempted to estimate the number of serial murderers active in the United States in a given year. Several leading researchers estimate the number to be around 35 active serial killers in a given year,[51] while others place the number much higher.[52]

Characteristics of Serial Murderers

One of the things you may have noticed in our discussion above is that, like mass murderers, serial killers tend to be male and white. There are notable exceptions to this, however. For example, Aileen Wuornos admitted to killing seven men but was only convicted of killing six because one body was never found. Another woman, Genene Jones, who was a licensed nurse, was convicted in 1984 of killing a young girl in her care with a lethal dose of a muscle relaxant along with other charges related to the injury of seven other children who had not died but who had also been injected with the drug. There was not enough evidence to convict her of the 47 other suspicious deaths of children that occurred on her watch at the Bexar County Medical Center Hospital. Insufficient evidence in the case was further compounded because hospital officials threw out most of her employment records after her first conviction because they were afraid of bad publicity and further embarrassment.[53]

There have also been nonwhite serial murderers, although they are the exception. For example, Wayne Williams, an African American man, was convicted of killing two young African American boys in Atlanta, Georgia in the late 1970s, but was suspected in the deaths of at least 20 other missing young African American boys. Despite these exceptions, the majority of serial killers who have been caught have been white, middle-aged males.

Another distinction for serial killers is their victims. Recall from our discussion of murder in general that victims and offenders most often know each other. In contrast, serial murderers tend to kill strangers. Targeting strangers may be a strategy designed to protect them from detection by authorities. Killing strangers may also serve to dehumanize the victims and thus make it easier to kill them. Serial killers also tend to target victims who are vulnerable, choosing particular subsets of the population. As noted above, the Green River Killer targeted prostitutes who, by the very nature of their profession, make themselves vulnerable. In fact, Gary Ridgway specifically asserted that

> Well, low-risk victims would be, ah, ah, prostitutes who eagerly get in your car for . . . for money, and they wouldn't be missed. Where the high risk victim would be like somebody at a college . . . They would be more of a . . . of a risk of . . . of, ah, people caring more about 'em, and friends asking questions . . . low risk prostitutes they're not . . . they're not as valued as much as a college person . . . or a business person.[54]

Moreover, Ridgway tried to stay away from more experienced prostitutes who he called "hardcore" and said, "There's a few of them that were just too tough to kill,"[55] preferring instead to target younger, less experienced, and therefore more vulnerable prostitutes. Other serial killers have targeted students, elderly people who live alone, hitchhikers, and the homeless. By targeting vulnerable populations, they can more easily isolate and dominate victims who are not able to protect or defend themselves. Prostitutes, for example, frequently get into vehicles with total strangers and often drive to secluded areas. These same behaviors, of course, make them extremely vulnerable to victimizations of many kinds, including serial killing.

There are two other factors common to serial killers. Although there are exceptions, most kill alone and most also have previous criminal records. For example, Ted Bundy had a history of shoplifting and juvenile car theft before he confessed to killing scores of women before he was put to death in the state of Florida. Despite these similarities among serial killers, Holmes and Holmes classify serial killers into six typologies, based on the explicit or implicit motives of the killer:

1. **Hedonistic lust killers** are distinguished by their effort to obtain sexual pleasure from killing. The lust killer derives direct sexual satisfaction from murdering his victims or by having sex with the corpse or by mutilating or cutting off sex organs.

2. **Thrill killers** also may derive sexual satisfaction from their murders, but they require a live victim for sexual satisfaction. They derive pleasure from torturing, dominating, terrorizing, and humiliating their victims.

3. **Comfort killers** murder for creature comforts, such as financial gain.

4. **Power/control killers** murder to obtain a sense of domination and total control over their victims. Although sex is sometimes involved, the pleasure is primarily derived from the complete control the killer has over his victim.

5. **Mission killers** are on a mission to rid the world of a group of people they perceive as unworthy or inferior in some way.

6. **Visionary killers** are rare because they suffer from some form of psychosis: They frequently perceive voices or images that command them to kill. Recall from Chapter 2, however, that only a small percentage of violent offenders have mental disorders such as this, which is true for serial killers as well.

As you can see, serial killers do not represent a homogeneous group. Despite this, we are still compelled to understand their behavior. When we read about someone like Ted Bundy or the BTK killer, it is hard not to ask, "How can someone do something so terrible?" We want to believe that anyone who is capable of such atrocities must have completely broken from reality and suffer from severe psychosis. But this is far from accurate. Although serial killers have different motives, scholars who study this kind of violence have determined some common factors that have been present in the lives of apprehended serial killers.

The first is that most killers, as their selection of victims underscores, are very aware of right and wrong and know how to avoid detection. James Fox and Jack Levin put it this way:

> They know right from wrong, know exactly what they are doing, and can control their desire to kill—but choose not to. They are more cruel than crazy. Their crimes may be sickening, but their minds are not necessarily sick . . . Indeed, those assailants who are deeply confused or disoriented are generally not capable of the level of planning and organization necessary to conceal their identity from the authorities and, therefore, do not amass a large number of victims.[56]

Although most do not suffer from psychosis, several serial killers have been diagnosed with a personality disorder, widely known as sociopathy or psychopathy but now labeled "antisocial personality disorder,"[57] which we discussed in Chapter 2. The characteristics of this disorder include insincerity, a lack of shame or remorse, an inability to love, extreme selfishness, and the lack of a conscience. Because they lack a conscience, the suffering of others does not affect them in the way that it affects most people who might empathize and sympathize with another person's pain. People suffering from this disorder are often perceived to be aggressive, charismatic, and intelligent, but they also suffer from chronic feelings of emptiness and isolation.[58] Because they often have a need to dominate and control, they are often drawn to careers believed to convey the power they crave, such as law enforcement. The BTK killer, for example, had a degree in criminal justice and worked in a division of law enforcement—albeit on the fringe. John Wayne Gacy, another serial killer, was fascinated with the idea of becoming a police officer and was described by his wife as a "police freak." Gacy also exhibited some of the other characteristics of this disorder: He was an outgoing, hard-working businessman who hosted street parties in his neighborhood, dressed as a clown to entertain children in the hospital, and belonged to several civic organizations. However, Gacy also tortured and killed 30 young men and boys, whose bodies were found under the floorboards in his house.[59] Like others with this disorder, Gacy was able to lead a relatively normal life on the outside, including having a job and a family. Of course, most of the people with this disorder are not violent, and even fewer become serial killers. So what other factors may be related to serial killing?

Another condition that is common in the histories of serial killers is suffering abuse and/or neglect as children. There are many mechanisms that may be related to previous abuse and neglect as a child and to adult offending. As we saw in Chapter 2, social learning theory would say these individuals learn through imitation and modeling that violence is a tool they can use in their relationships with others. Cathy Spatz Widom, who has studied the effects of childhood abuse, suggests that violent offending may arise in adolescence and adulthood because those victimized as children learn destructive coping mechanisms, including skills in manipulation and denial as well as violent behavior.[60] General strain theory would suggest childhood abuse acts as a form of negative stimulus that causes stress and strain; if this strain manifests as negative emotions such as anger and rage, violence would become increasingly likely as a result.

Other factors that frequently appear in the histories of serial killers include what has been termed the **homicidal triad**: bed-wetting past an appropriate age, cruelty to animals, and fire setting.[61] Any one of these behaviors alone may not be a factor, but according to John Douglas, many serial killers he studied displayed at least two of the three qualities in childhood. Of the three, cruelty to animals is the most analogous behavior to killing and as such may be a more significant warning sign. This behavior was notable in many contemporary serial killers, including Edmund Kemper, who buried the family cat alive in the yard and, after its death, decapitated it and put its head on a spindle. Another time, he sliced off the top of another cat's skull and then tortured it while it convulsed. Henry Lee Lucas reportedly tortured and killed animals and then had sex with their bodies; he later did this with his victims. David Berkowitz, the famous Son of Sam serial killer from New York, also reportedly tormented small animals when he was a child. These are just a few examples.[62]

Despite the similarities across the lives of serial killers, there is no one causal explanation for why they can perform the acts they do. As with all violence, there are undoubtedly myriad factors that somehow allow individuals to perform such acts without remorse, including biological and neuropsychological factors, environmental factors, such as observing and experiencing violence at the hands of others, and cultural factors, such as being bombarded by images that glamorize violence on a daily basis.

Spree Murder

Spree murder appears to be the least common of the three types of multicide. While spree murders involve multiple victims at multiple locations, the difference between a killing spree and a serial killing is that there is no emotional cooling-off period between the murders involved in a spree killing. Therefore, the killings tend to take place over a shorter period of time.

The most infamous case of spree murder in the United States occurred in the winter of 1958 in Nebraska, when Charles Starkweather and his girlfriend Caril Fugate went on a week-long killing spree. This spree killing has been the basis for several movies including Oliver Stone's 1994 *Natural Born Killers*. Starkweather killed a gas station attendant after he robbed the station, in an apparent attempt to get rid of the witness. Six weeks later, the Starkweather and Fugate killing spree began after an argument with Caril's mother. Returning to the Fugate house after the argument, Starkweather confronted both Caril's mother and stepfather with a .22 rifle and shot them both in the head. He used the butt of the rifle to kill Caril's two-and-a-half-year-old sister. The stepfather apparently showed signs of life and was then finished off with a knife. Caril and Charles moved the bodies out of the way and sat down to watch television. They apparently stayed in the house with the dead bodies for several days before killing a nearby farmer for his money and heading out on the road. They abandoned their car and were picked up by two high school students, who they also murdered. In Lincoln, Nebraska, they broke into a home, killing the husband and wife along with their maid. On the road again, they murdered a traveling salesman for his car but were discovered in the act. After a high-speed chase, both were apprehended and later convicted of first-degree murder.

A more recent spree killing occurred in the Washington, D.C., area and has become known as the Beltway sniper attacks.[63] The spree began on October 2, 2002, with a series of five fatal shootings in less than 15 hours in a suburban county in Maryland, north of Washington. The spree continued for the next three weeks and resulted in 10 people being murdered and three others receiving critical injuries. The victims were apparently selected at random and crossed all race/ethnicity and gender lines. The killings were performed in a sniper attack fashion with a high-powered rifle from relatively long distances and occurred at gas stations and parking lots within the suburban areas of Maryland, Virginia, and Washington, D.C. All the shootings occurred close to an interstate, which provided the killers with an easy escape route after the shootings occurred. Because there were no visual cues that a shooting had just happened, victims who slumped over at the gas pump or near their cars in a parking lot were frequently assumed to have had heart attacks until a closer inspection revealed gunshot wounds. Residents of the area were terrified, and many stayed hidden in their homes and did not allow their children to go to school. Bulletins describing the possible vehicle were distributed to all media, including television and radio. Unfortunately, these descriptions were initially off base, describing a white van. When the correct description of a blue sedan was released, it only took hours for two witnesses to spot the occupied car at a Maryland highway rest area. The Beltway sniper ordeal ended when John Allen Muhammad and Lee Boyd Malvo, his much younger accomplice, were arrested as they slept at the rest area in the car that had been their killing machine. The car was a former police car that had been rigged with a firing port in the trunk from where the shooter killed his victims. Both were convicted for their crimes and Muhammad was executed by lethal injection in November 2009, while Malvo continues to serve a life imprisonment term in Virginia.

As you can see, both of these murderous rampages illustrate the signs of a spree killing: they are relatively short-lived but violent killings that don't seem to have a lot of direction or planning. Their victims were innocents who just happened to be at the wrong place at the wrong time. The other common characteristic of spree killings—characterized in both those discussed—is that the rampage is usually stopped only when the killers are captured or killed.

Capital Punishment

We end this chapter with a discussion of capital punishment because it is the most extreme form of punishment that states and the federal government can hand down as a sanction for murder. At the end of 2012, the death penalty was authorized as punishment for capital murder in 35 states, by the federal government, and by the U.S. military. As with any legislation, however, the criteria that make a murder eligible for death vary by state. In some states, prosecutors can seek death for defendants in all first-degree murders, while other states mandate that at least one aggravating circumstance is present (e.g., killing more than one victim, killing during the commission of another felony).

Even though 35 states allow capital punishment, only a few use capital punishment on a regular basis. For example, in 2011, a total of 43 inmates were executed; only 13 states actually performed an execution, with Texas executing the most (13), six executions in Alabama, five in Ohio, and less than five in the other states with Idaho, Virginia, South Carolina, Delaware, and Missouri each only executing one.[64]

Nationally, the number of people sentenced to death and the number of people actually executed had been rising steadily since the Supreme Court reaffirmed the use of the death penalty in *Gregg v. Georgia* in 1976.[65] However, as can be seen from Figure 4.6, the number of people who have been executed has started to decline. This declining trend is also evident for the number of people sentenced to death nationally.[66] The reasons for these declines will be explored below. First, however, we will briefly discuss the theoretical rationales for capital punishment.

What justification can there be for an act of state-sponsored violence, such as capital punishment? Is it justified because it prevents additional acts of violence? Theoretically, violence prevented by capital punishment can occur two ways: someone who is thinking about committing a murder refrains from doing so because they fear the death penalty—a **general deterrence argument**; and someone who has committed murder is put to death and therefore is prevented from committing another murder in the future—an incapacitation argument. Both of these arguments are based on the utilitarian position that an act of violence committed by the state—the execution of someone—is justified because it produces a net good.

The general deterrence argument argues that people generally refrain from committing murder because they fear execution. Actually, the argument is not that the death penalty deters would-be murderers compared with no punishment at all, but that the death penalty inhibits some people from committing murder who would have killed someone if the punishment were life imprisonment or some other sentence rather than death. Is there evidence that there is a general deterrent

❖ Figure 4.6   Number of People Executed by Year

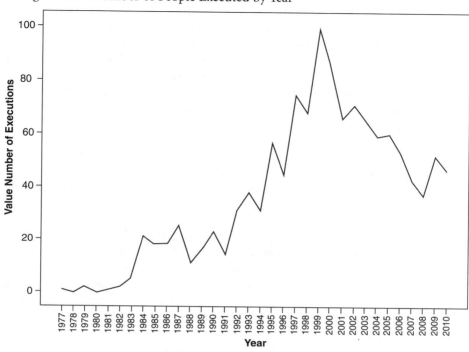

SOURCE: Snell, *Capital Punishment, 2010—Statistical Tables,* Bureau of Justice Statistics.

effect for capital punishment in the United States? Well, if the death penalty deters murder better than life imprisonment, then jurisdictions that punish murder with the death penalty should have lower homicide rates than comparable jurisdictions that punish murder with life imprisonment. The evidence, however, suggests that this is not the case.

The earliest data on this issue come from work by Thorsten Sellin, whose research strategy involved systematic comparisons of homicide rates between states that were similar in as many respects as possible but which differed on their policy of using the death penalty. He found that, within the same geographic region, those states that had the death penalty did not seem to have lower rates of homicide than states in the same geographic area that did not.[67] Peterson and Bailey updated this study covering the period of 1973 through 1984 by comparing sets of data in death penalty and life imprisonment states. They also found that, averaged over a 12-year time period, the annual homicide rate in death penalty states (8.5 homicides per 100,000 population) was actually higher than the rate in states without the death penalty (7.6 homicides per 100,000 population). Their analysis—like that of Sellin—provided no evidence of reduced homicide rates in death penalty states.

The problem with these simple comparisons, of course, is that we must assume that states with the death penalty are comparable to states with only life imprisonment penalties on other important social and economic factors. More recent research has been able to statistically control for other factors within states in addition to the punishment type in order to determine whether the death penalty is a more effective deterrent to murder than life imprisonment. Results of these studies are somewhat mixed.[68] However, after an extensive statistical review of the studies, Richard Berk concluded that "for the vast majority of states for the vast majority of years, there is no evidence for deterrence in these analyses."[69]

The **incapacitation** justification for capital punishment is that executing those who commit murder is the only effective way to keep them from ever killing again. In a sense, this argument can hardly be refuted. If you execute someone who committed murder, the chance that they will kill again is zero. The real issue, then, is not whether capital punishment is effective in incapacitating those who have committed murder, but whether it is the only way to incapacitate them. Can murderers effectively be prevented from killing again by incarcerating them for life without the possibility of parole or for long periods of time before releasing them?

One way to examine this question is to compare the recidivism rates of convicted murderers with the recidivism rates for other types of offenders. Evidence from a recent Bureau of Justice Statistics study of recidivism rates from fifteen states reported that, compared with homicide offenders, offenders in 19 other offense categories all had higher three-year recidivism rates and most rates were over twice as high. In fact, when the outcome measure was rearrest, homicide offenders had the lowest recidivism rate compared with all 21 other offense categories. Another interesting question examined by this report was whether homicide offenders exhibit a special tendency to commit new homicides when they return to the community. Based on the data presented in the report, the answer to this question appears to be "no" as well. Of the homicide offenders released in 1994, 1.2% were rearrested for a new homicide within three years of release. This was much lower than for other violent offenses: 8.5% of those released from prison for robbery were rearrested within three years of their release for committing a homicide. These data suggest that when homicide offenders are eventually released from prison, they do not exhibit comparatively high levels of future offending or future homicide.

The final justification for capital punishment is **retribution**. Retribution has nothing to do with public safety—it is a moral justification. The argument here is simply that murderers should be executed because they deserve to be. Because we cannot determine the validity of this argument on the basis of empirical data, there is rarely a middle ground for advocates and opponents of this argument. Taking a retribution argument literally would require all convicted murderers to be sentenced to death. This is not only inconsistent with constitutional law but ignores the extreme variation across murder contexts, even across first-degree murder contexts, such as those killings committed under the influence of drugs or alcohol, those committed under emotional duress in which the offender expresses a great deal of remorse, and so on. As an alternative to this literal interpretation of retribution, some have argued that life without the possibility of parole is a legitimate alternative to death and does not trivialize the moral harm of first-degree murder.[70]

At a societal level, even if we accept the premise of retribution, we have to ask ourselves: "At what cost?" Research has clearly demonstrated that the likelihood of receiving a death sentence is dependent not only on legally relevant factors, like the seriousness of the offense, but also on other factors, like the jurisdiction in which the offense took place and demographic characteristics of the victim and the offender, such as race. What this means is that whether you receive a death sentence is often a matter of where you live and who you killed, not just the fact that you committed murder. For example, after analyzing all homicides that were eligible to receive the death sentence (1,311 cases) in the state of Maryland for the years between 1978 and 1999, Raymond Paternoster and his colleagues found that black offenders who killed white victims were significantly more likely than other racial combinations to be sentenced to death. They also found that defendants who killed in particular jurisdictions in Maryland were much more likely to be sentenced to death compared with other jurisdictions. This was true even after controlling for legal factors like the heinousness of the offense.[71] This and other studies like it have called into question the fairness of capital punishment in the United States. Adding urgency to this belief is the number of innocent people who have been held on death row, sometimes to within days of their death, and then been exonerated by DNA or other evidence.

In the last 25 years, over 100 people in the United States awaiting execution on death row have been freed after it was discovered that they were innocent. These exonerations were usually obtained through aggressive investigations from outside advocates such as the Center for Wrongful Convictions at Northwestern University Law School.[72] In fact, releases from death row are becoming so common that they rarely even make the national news. Despite this inattention, their stories are sobering. For example, after spending almost 18 years—nearly one-third of his life—on death row, in 2002 Juan Roberto Melendez was proven innocent and released from a Florida prison. His years in prison were spent mostly in his cell, except when he was allowed to exercise for two hours on Mondays and Wednesdays and the three times a week he was allowed a five-minute shower—all of the time being shackled. When he was released, he kissed the ground because he had never seen the ground during his time in prison. Melendez said, "When I was released, I was given 100 dollars, a pair of pants, and a shirt. That's it. Nobody ever apologized."[73] Unfortunately, this is similar to the treatment received by many exonerated defendants.

This reality has led a few states to place a moratorium on executions until their state's trial and sentencing procedures are reviewed. For example, in 2000 Illinois Governor George Ryan, who was a conservative pro–death penalty governor, announced that there would be a moratorium on all executions in the state until he could be sure—with moral certainty—that no innocent man or woman was facing lethal injection. Governor Ryan stated, "We have now freed more people than we have put to death under our system—13 people have been exonerated and 12 have been put to death. There is a flaw in the system, without question, and it needs to be studied."[74] At present, several other states have a moratorium on executions while their states were being reviewed, with many reviewing challenges to the lethal injection process and others examining repealing the death penalty altogether.[75] In sum, not only does the United States have some of the highest rates of murder compared with all other Western and industrialized nations, we also are unique in our efforts to control this violence through the use of capital punishment. In fact, because of our use of capital punishment, our nation could not be a member of the European Union, which strongly opposes the use of capital punishment. As Raymond Paternoster states, "In using the death penalty the United States finds itself in the uncomfortable company of such repressive regimes as the People's Republic of China, Iran, Iraq, Korea, [and] Libya."[76]

Conclusions

We have seen that most violent interactions fall on a continuum, with many factors related to the outcome, including the perceptions of the situation both by the eventual victim and offender, the behavior of bystanders, and the availability of a firearm. Although national assault and murder rates in our country are at much lower levels than they were in the early 1990s, the decreasing trends we have seen over the past several years have now leveled off, and in some cities they are climbing back to these earlier peak levels. We have also seen that the rise in violence observed in the 1990s was primarily attributable to killings by young males armed with handguns. While rates of assault and murder are highest for young males in general and young minority group males in particular, we have seen that multicide, in the form of mass and serial killings, is more often committed by middle-aged white men.

Together with the data presented in Chapter 1, the information presented in this chapter has underscored the fact that our society has the unfortunate honor of being at the top of the rankings in rates of violence compared with other industrialized nations around the globe. Also, unlike most other industrialized and Western democracies, the United States relies on capital punishment in many of our states.

Key Terms

aggravated assault

BTK killer

character contest

comfort killers

confrontational homicide

criminal homicide

deliberation

excusable homicide

facilitating hardware

felony murder

first-degree murder

general deterrence argument

hedonistic lust killers

homicidal triad

incapacitation

justifiable homicide

manslaughter

mass murder

mission killers

multicide

power/control killers

premeditation

retribution

second-degree murder

serial murder

simple assault

spree murder

symbolic interactionism

thrill killers

victim precipitation

visionary killers

Discussion Questions

1. Go to the Federal Bureau of Investigation (FBI) website and find statistics on justifiable homicides under its Supplementary Homicide Report Section (www.fbi.gov/ucr/05cius/offenses/expanded_information/murder_homicide.html). Find tables for the most recent data on justifiable homicides committed by both law enforcement officials and by private citizens. How do these incidents compare?

2. First, find the capital punishment statutes in your state. You can find this easily on many search engines including the LexusNexis State Capital search engine. If your state does not allow capital punishment, find a neighboring or regional state that does. According to the state statute, which crimes are eligible for capital punishment and which factors within an offense make it death eligible (e.g., multiple victims, the killing of a police officer). Now go to the Bureau of Justice Statistics website (www .ojp.usdoj.gov/bjs) and find the most recent publication on capital punishment. Find the table listing the number of people under sentence of death by state. Now go to the Federal Bureau of Investigation website and find rates of murder by state under its Supplementary Homicide Report Section (www.fbi.gov/ucr/05cius/offenses/expanded_ information/ murder_homicide.html). Make a list of states by the rate of murder and the number of people under sentence of death. Do you see any relationship between these two variables?

3. What role do the media play in shaping our attitudes toward interpersonal violence? Do representations of homicide on evening news shows accurately reflect the true nature of lethal violence in the United States? Why or why not?

4. The National Criminal Justice Reference Service (NCJRS) is a clearinghouse sponsored by the U.S. Department of Justice (www.ncjrs.gov). Go to its spotlight on gangs (you can find this by doing a search for "spotlight on gangs" or simply "gangs") to find summary information about a number of facts including findings from the National Youth Gang Survey. You can also find information on innovative approaches that have been undertaken by jurisdictions to combat gangs and gang-related violence. For example, the city of Baltimore, Maryland, has implemented a successful approach to decrease the incidents of drug-related homicides (www.ncjrs .gov/html/bja/gang). Using this website as a resource, highlight the strategies that Baltimore has introduced. How have they measured the extent to which these new policies are actually working? What other indicators could they have used? What other factors may have been responsible for any decline in homicides that was observed in Baltimore?

5

Violence in the Home

Women are more at risk from violence at home than in the street. It is important to shine a spotlight on domestic violence globally and to treat it as a major public health issue. Challenging the social norms that condone and therefore perpetuate violence against women is a responsibility for us all.

—Dr. Lee Jong-Wook, Director General of the World Health Organization[1]

While I struggled at school to hide my family life, and I still performed quite well, it became increasingly difficult to live a double life, attending honors classes during the day and returning home from school as late as I could. At night, I slept with a twirling baton tucked under my bed, never knowing when I might have to wake up in the middle of the night and protect myself from my father's unpredictable and violent outbursts.

—Miko Rose, child abuse survivor[2]

Family violence is an umbrella term that includes a wide range of behaviors, including physical, sexual, financial, and verbal or other emotional abuse between a number of dyadic relationships: intimates (e.g., spouses and ex-spouses, boy/girl-friends and exes); parents and children; siblings; and the elderly and their caregivers, including their children. Entire texts have been written on each of these topics and it would be impossible to cover them all in detail within this single chapter. Our goal, therefore, in this chapter is to provide you with a better understanding of what we know about a few particular forms of violence within the home and how we know it.

Many of you may be confronted with family violence in your careers, whether you are working within the realm of criminal justice, the medical field, or in the social service sector. We therefore believe your understanding of this problem should go beyond sensational descriptions. Here we provide you with the knowledge to make educated decisions about situations to which you may be exposed in the future. We begin the chapter with a discussion of the violence that occurs between intimate partners.

Intimate Partner Violence

❖ Photo 5.1   Couple in a violent argument

IN FOCUS 5.1

The Story of Amy Jones

Amy Jones married her high school sweetheart, Christopher Rezos, in 1995 after they had dated for eight years. Although Christopher never hit Amy, he was always very critical of the things she did and attempted to control everything in her life. Even simple tasks, such as loading the dishwasher had to be done his way. The couple had two small sons, Michael, 3, and David, 7, and lived in southwestern Ohio when Amy began to realize that she no longer wanted to be married to Chris. They separated in 2004, and he moved into a hotel room. Amy met him at his hotel room one night in July 2004 to discuss the conditions of their divorce. When Chris asked her to give him full custody of their two sons, Amy told him no. The next thing she remembers is blood running down her face after he bludgeoned her over the head with a flashlight. She tried to fight back, but he continued to hit her over the head. The next thing she remembered was being dragged across the floor into the bathroom. Hotel security arrived just in time to save Amy from being drowned in the bathtub by Chris. Amy had several skull fractures and a broken vertebra. It took over one hundred staples to put her skull back together.

(Continued)

(Continued)

Chris was arrested and put into jail to await his trial. However, because he was a first-time offender, he was released on bail within three weeks. Despite an order of protection that prohibited Chris from seeing Amy, the violence did not stop. Just after his release, Amy was going to pick up her sons in their van when Chris grabbed her from the back seat where he had been hiding and shot her through the head. She remembers the gunshot and driving off the road; he then shot her a second time in the head before fleeing the scene. Miraculously, Amy survived.

While Chris was awaiting trial for his second attempted murder charge, he once again tried to kill her, this time by hiring a hit man from inside jail. Luckily, another inmate alerted the police about the attempt and Amy escaped becoming a victim for a third time. Christopher is now serving a 30-year prison term without the possibility of parole, but Amy will probably never feel completely safe again.

In Focus 5.1 illustrates that violence between intimate partners—even extreme violence—can occur in families that have all the outward appearances of normalcy. As the old saying goes, "appearances can be deceiving." The term "intimate" generally refers to spouses, ex-spouses, boy/girlfriends and exes. Other phrases that are sometimes used to describe this same type of violence include wife battering, wife abuse, intimate terrorism, and spousal violence. The Centers for Disease Control and Prevention have provided a very useful definition when describing **intimate partner violence (IPV):**

> the intentional use of physical force with the potential for causing death, disability, injury, or harm. Physical violence includes, but is not limited to, scratching; pushing; shoving; throwing; grabbing; biting; choking; shaking; slapping; punching; burning; use of a weapon; and use of restraints or one's body, size, or strength against another person.[3]

Intimate partner violence has been around forever, but it has only been in the past 30 years or so that it has finally been acknowledged as a social problem. As recently as the 1970s and into the 1980s, police rarely made arrests when they were called to the scene of an intimate partner assault because it was thought to be a "private matter" that wasn't the concern of the criminal justice system. The law, it seemed, didn't extend past the front door. Widespread beliefs about the nature of the family and of gender roles contributed to this lack of attention. Fortunately, attitudes and policies have changed—largely as a result of the activism of various victims' and women's rights groups. Today, violence that goes on behind closed doors between intimates is usually treated like any other type of violence, with arrest being the norm rather than the exception. Because intimate partner violence is usually more private and hidden than some other forms of violence, its detection and intervention remain somewhat problematic, as does our ability to measure its perpetration. So how much violence goes on between intimate partners?

Estimating Rates of Violence Against Women

Despite over 20 years of research, the amount of intimate partner violence against women and men is still frequently disputed. For many reasons—including the stigma often attached to intimate partner violence, the fear of perpetrators retaliating, and numerous other safety concerns—estimating how often it happens has always been difficult and cannot be discussed appropriately without briefly reviewing the methodologies used to collect the data. Scholars and activists typically rely on a few different sources of information on the nature and scope of intimate partner violence. Each of them, however, has significant shortcomings that affect the quality of the information gathered. One commonly used source of information on intimate partner violence, for example, is the Uniform Crime Reports (UCR) that, if you remember, are compiled by the FBI from police reports. Relying on police reports, however, is especially problematic for intimate partner violence. The primary reason is that a large percentage of these crimes are never reported to police. Surveys have shown that, at best, only about 50% of intimate partner assaults are reported to police, and at worst, fewer than one in four are ever conveyed.[4] Another problem with using police report data is that, except for the crime of homicide, the current UCR program does not include information on the victim–offender relationship within its reports. This means that it isn't even possible to determine the magnitude of violence perpetrated by specific offenders, such as intimates, within UCR data. One exception to this rule is the crime of homicide, which tends to be reported more reliably than other less serious forms of violent victimization. An offshoot of the UCR program, the Supplementary Homicide Reports (SHR) data are collected by the FBI and allow us to examine homicides between partners. In fact, this is one of the better sources that allow us to monitor trends of these killings, since it provides a consistent set of information over time. On the other hand, we shouldn't forget that intimate partner homicides represent only a fraction of all intimate partner violence.

Figure 5.1 displays the number of intimate partner homicides broken down by the specific victim and offender relationship. As you can see, the proportion of intimate homicides involving a spouse began decreasing over the past few decades, while the proportion of those involving a boyfriend or girlfriend began increasing. Whereas the difference between the two categories was once remarkably different, by 2008, the proportion of intimate partner homicides committed by a spouse compared to those committed by boy/girlfriends was virtually the same. The percentage of those committed by ex-spouses has remained relatively constant. When we examine intimate homicides by gender (Figure 5.2), we see that females are more likely to be the victims and the percentage of female victims has been increasing while the percentage of male victims has been in decline.

Why have there been fewer male victims of intimate partner homicides while the number of females killed by intimates has been increasing? One reason may be that there has been an increase in the services available for battered women that allow them to escape abusive relationships. Some research indicates that

❖ Figure 5.1   Homicides by Intimates, by Relationship of Victim to Offender, 1980–2008

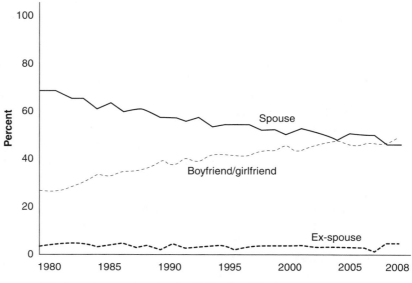

Note: Percentages are based on the 63.1% of homicides from 1980 through 2008 for which victim/offender relationships were known.

SOURCE: Cooper and Smith, *Homicide Trends in the United States, 1980–2008*, Bureau of Justice Statistics, 2011.

female-perpetrated intimate partner homicide is often a last-ditch response to being battered.[5] Typically, these women have been repeatedly victimized over time by their male partner and, trapped in an intolerable situation, escape by killing the man responsible for their abuse. Because this kind of killing is so often defensive in nature, scholars have investigated whether factors that facilitate a woman's escape from an abusive relationship are related to this decline. They have found that states and cities which provide more resources for abused women—such as shelters, hotlines, and legal services—also tend to have significantly lower rates of female-perpetrated partner homicide against male partners. Such services, it is believed, offer women protection and escape from abusive relationships and increase awareness that there are alternatives available to them.[6] This suggests that the more choices a woman has, the less likely it is that she will feel trapped into killing her abusive intimate and that is why the rate of male victimization has dropped. On the other hand, this argument isn't the only possible explanation for these patterns of victimization.

As we have seen, overall violence has been decreasing since the late 1980s. Unfortunately, rates of nonlethal violence against intimates have not declined nearly as much as total rates of violence, as revealed in Figure 5.3. Since 2005, the rate of

❖ Figure 5.2   Homicides of Intimates, by Sex of Victim, 1980–2008

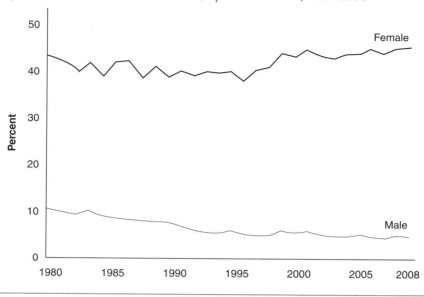

SOURCE: Cooper and Smith, *Homicide Trends in the United States, 1980–2008*, Bureau of Justice Statistics, 2011.

nonlethal violence against intimate partners, including rapes, robberies, and assaults, has not declined for females but has declined about 39% for males.[7]

Recall from Chapter 1 that both the UCR and the National Incident Based Reporting System (NIBRS) data collection methods rely exclusively on reports to the police. If victimizations are not reported, they are never counted in either of these two data collection programs. Because of this weakness, random sample surveys of the population are sometimes used as the tool of choice for uncovering incidents of violence within families. However, as can be imagined, surveys using diverse methodologies and different definitions of violence have resulted in tremendously dissimilar estimates. For example, estimates of how many women experience violence by an intimate partner annually range from 9.3 per 1,000 women to 116 per 1,000 women. Furthermore, the differences across survey methodologies often preclude direct comparison across studies. There have been only three large nationally representative surveys that have estimated the annual rates of IPV: the **National Family Violence Survey** (NFVS), the **National Crime Victimization Survey** (NCVS), and the **National Violence Against Women and Men Survey** (NVAWMS). Because of their procedural differences, each of these surveys has resulted in quite different estimates of IPV. While most researchers are familiar with the methodological differences between surveys, few policy makers take these into account when making generalizations about how often intimate partner violence takes place. This has unfortunately led to widespread confusion and controversy.

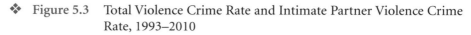

❖ **Figure 5.3** Total Violence Crime Rate and Intimate Partner Violence Crime Rate, 1993–2010

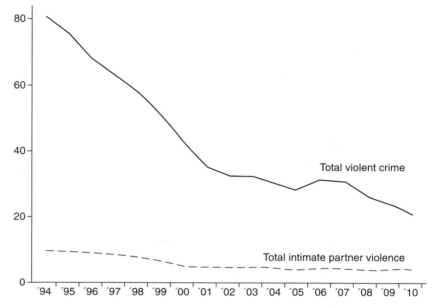

SOURCES: Catalono, *Intimate Partner Violence, 1993–2010,* Bureau of Justice Statistics, 2012.

Knowing more about the differences between the surveys may help in clarifying the situation somewhat, so in the next sections, we want to highlight these methodological differences.

The NFVS was the first national survey devoted exclusively to estimating incidents of IPV. Its sample included only married or cohabiting couples and measured violence using an instrument called the **Conflict Tactics Scale** (CTS).[8] The introduction to the CTS asks respondents to "think of situations in the past year when they had a disagreement or were angry with a specified family member (husband, child, etc.)" and to indicate how often they engaged in each of the acts included in the CTS. The list of acts covered in the Conflict Tactics Scale spans a range of behaviors, including reasoning, verbal aggression, and physical aggression or violence. Physical violence by the CTS index is often subdivided into two categories: minor violence and severe violence. These categories consist of the following acts:

Minor violence

    a. Threw something
    b. Pushed, grabbed, or shoved
    c. Slapped

Severe violence

    a. Kicked, bit, or hit with a fist
    b. Hit or tried to hit with something
    c. Beat up
    d. Choked
    e. Threatened with a knife or gun
    f. Used a knife or fired a gun

Estimates from the 1985 NFVS indicate that about 11.6% of couples had experienced some type of assault in the previous 12 months. Extrapolated to the total married population, this survey estimates that almost one out of eight husbands carried out one or more violent acts during the year of this study. Further, the rate of severe violence perpetrated by husbands indicates that about 1.8 million women were beaten by their partner that year. The NFVS also estimates that rates of violence perpetrated by wives against husbands are very similar to rates of violence perpetrated by husbands against wives. Herein lies one of the most frequent criticisms of the CTS methodology: that it measures acts of violence in isolation from the circumstances under which the acts were committed. As critics point out, for example, it ignores who initiates the violence, the relative size and strength of the persons involved, and the nature of the participants' relationship.[9] Murray Straus and Richard Gelles, the researchers who carried out the most recent NFVS, are quick to point out that the meanings behind these estimates are often misunderstood. They acknowledge that

> To understand the high rate of intrafamily violence by women, it is also important to realize that many of the assaults by women against their husbands are acts of retaliation or self-defense. One of the most fundamental reasons why women are violent within the family (but rarely outside the family) is that for a typical American woman, her home is the location where there is the most serious risk of assault.[10]

It should be noted here that a new version of the CTS called the CTS2 has been developed to address some of the methodological deficiencies of the original scale, but the new version still does not allow a researcher to account for the sequence of events that precipitated an act of violence. Thus acts of aggressive violence can still not be separated from those assaults that were used in self-defense.[11]

The National Crime Victimization Survey

The NCVS interviews all household members aged 12 or older, not just adults. To measure incidents of violence by intimate partners and family members, the NCVS asks the following questions after the general questions about acts of violence or theft:

> Other than any incidents already mentioned, has anyone attacked or threatened you in any of these ways:
>
>   a. With any weapon, for instance, a gun or knife
>   b. With anything like a baseball bat, frying pan, scissors, or a stick

    c. By something thrown, such as a rock or bottle
    d. Include any grabbing, punching, or choking
    e. Any rape, attempted rape or other type of sexual attack
    f. Any face to face threats
    g. Any attack or threat or use of force by anyone at all? Please mention it even if you are not certain it was a crime.

To further cue respondents about incidents of victimization not perpetrated by strangers, they are then asked the following:

People often don't think of incidents committed by someone they know. Did you have something stolen from you OR were you attacked or threatened by

    a. someone at work or school,
    b. a neighbor or friend,
    c. a relative or family member, or
    d. any other person you've met or known?

Estimates of intimate partner violence from the NCVS indicate that in 2010, the rate of intimate partner violence (IPV) against females was 5.9 per 1,000 compared to a rate of only 1.1 for males This translates into nearly one million females aged 12 and over being violently attacked by their intimate partners annually, which does not include homicides.[12] Rates of IPV affect all racial and ethnic populations, but some individuals within these groups are much more at risk. Women who are separated, for example, appear to be extremely vulnerable compared to females in other marital status relationships, including those who are divorced. Moreover, young adults appear more vulnerable to IPV compared to those over 50.[13] Also notice that, unlike the NFVS, the NCVS finds that females have much higher rates of intimate partner violence compared with males, which is consistent with the homicide data discussed previously.

The National Violence Against Women and Men Survey

Unlike crime surveys, the NVAWMS was a nationally representative survey that was introduced to respondents as a survey on personal safety. This context is important because, unlike the NCVS, it does not communicate to respondents that interviewers are interested in crimes. The NVAWMS measured physical assault by using a modified version of the Conflict Tactics Scale.[14] Respondents included women and men 18 years of age and older; they were asked about assaults which had occurred as children and as adults using the following screening questions:

Not counting any incidents you have already mentioned, after you became an adult did any other adult, male or female ever . . .

    a. Throw something at you that could hurt?
    b. Push, grab or shove you?
    c. Pull your hair?
    d. Slap or hit you?
    e. Kick or bite you?

f. Choke or attempt to drown you?
g. Hit you with some object?
h. Beat you up?
i. Threaten you with a gun?
j. Threaten you with a knife or other weapon?
k. Use a gun on you?
l. Use a knife or other weapon on you?

The NVAWMS obtained higher estimates than the NCVS but lower estimates than the NFVS: 1.3% of women and 0.9% of men reported being assaulted by their intimate partners every year. Importantly, this survey also examined how many women and men experienced violent attacks over the course of their adult lives. Over one in five women (22%) and 7.4% of men had been assaulted by an intimate partner in their lives.

The National Intimate Partner and Sexual Violence Survey

Yet another survey was conducted by the Centers for Disease Control and Prevention (CDC) known as The **National Intimate Partner and Sexual Violence Survey** (NISVS). Like the NVAWMS, the NISVS not only asked respondents about victimizations that happened to them in the past 12 months but also about victimizations they had experienced in their lifetimes. And like the NVAWMS, the survey also measured a representative sample of the adult men and women 18 years of age and older. In addition to questions about coercive control (e.g., tried to keep you from seeing or talking to your family or friends, kept track of you by demanding to know where you were and what you were doing), which are often behaviors that precede physical violence in relationships, the physical violence questions included those from above, with the addition of "slammed you against something," "burned you on purpose," and "hurt you by pulling your hair." However, unlike the NVAWMS, estimates of physical violence excluded threats of violence. Respondents were specifically asked about all intimate partners including same-sex couples.

Estimates from the NISVS reveal that about 4% of women and 4.7% of men had experienced a physical attack by an intimate partner in 2010. However, women were more likely than men to be victimized by severe acts of physical violence, which did not include slapping, pushing, or shoving.[15] As you can clearly see, the ways in which people are asked about their victimization experiences significantly impact the number of people estimated to have experienced violence. Unfortunately, policy makers and researchers alike rely on published estimates of violent victimization from one or more of the surveys without recognizing or understanding the limitations of each. When you ask, "How many men and women are assaulted by their intimate partners each year?" the answer you get depends on which survey you rely on. To facilitate comparisons across these survey methodologies, Table 5.1 displays the key differences in table form. Is it possible to compare incident rates across surveys? The simple answer is no. Because of the methodological differences between the different surveys, comparisons of their different estimates of intimate partner violence are not valid. How accurate can it really be to compare information from the NFVS, which interviewed only married and cohabiting couples, with estimates generated from

Table 5.1   Factors That May Contribute to the Different Rates of Intimate Partner Violence From Four Survey Methodologies

	National Crime Survey (NCVS)— Only survey done annually	National Violence Against Women and Men Survey (NVAWMS)	National Family Violence Survey: Conflict Tactics Scale (CTS)	National Intimate Partner and Sexual Violence Survey (NISVS)
Sample	Random sample of individuals age 12 and older. May result in lower estimates due to decreased risk of victimization for younger and elderly respondents.	Random sample of women and men 18 years of age and older.	Random sample of married or cohabiting heterosexual couples 18 years or older. May result in higher estimates.	Random sample of women and men 18 years of age and older.
Directly asks about violence perpetrated by current and former intimate partners?	No. Asks only about "friends" and/or "family members."	Yes.	Asks only about victimizations by current partner.	Yes
Behaviors included in screening questions about victimization?	Were you attacked or threatened with any weapon, with anything like a baseball bat, frying pan, scissors, or a stick, by something thrown such as a rock or bottle, any grabbing, punching, or choking, any rape or sexual attack, any face-to-face threats, any attack, or threat, or use of force?	Threw something at you that could hurt, pushed, grabbed, or shoved, pulled your hair, slapped or hit you, kicked or bit you, choked or attempted to drown you, hit you with some object, beat you up, threatened you with a gun, threatened you with a knife or other weapon, used a gun, knife, or other weapon.	Threw something at partner, pushed, grabbed, or shoved, slapped, kicked, bit, or hit with fist, hit or tried to hit with something, beat up, choked, threatened with a knife or gun, used a knife, or fired a gun.	Threw something at you that could hurt, pushed, grabbed, or shoved, pulled your hair, slapped or hit you, kicked or bit you, choked or attempted to drown you, hit you with some object, beat you up, hurt you by pulling your hair, slammed you against something, burned you, used a gun, knife, or other weapon.

the NCVS and NVAWMS that relied on national probability of samples of men and women in general, regardless of marital status? However, when the NCVS and the NVAWMS data are restricted to a similar context (i.e., adult victimizations involving lone offenders), research indicates that estimates of intimate partner violence still remain higher from the NVAWMS and the NISVS compared with the NCVS. This is undoubtedly due to the more specific screening questions used by the NVAWMS and also the specific questions about acts perpetrated by husbands, boyfriends, and former intimates.[16] In sum, when you are asked how many men and women experience intimate partner violence, your answer should be, "That depends on the methodology used to obtain the estimates." Regardless of which data set you rely on, however, the bottom line is that intimate partner violence is a significant problem. For all too many women, their partner poses more of a risk for serious harm and death than a stranger on the street. So why do intimates engage in such violent behavior against a loved one?

Risk Factors for Intimate Partner Violence

The theories discussed in Chapter 2 explaining violence in general can also be applied to violence between intimates, so we won't reiterate them here. There are, however, a few additional theoretical insights specific to intimate partner violence that can also be used to help us better understand this particular form of violence.

Power and Dominance

Issues of power, dominance, and control are fundamental to most feminist theories of violence against women. An important element of this perspective is the contention that intimate partner violence—both sexual and nonsexual—is an expression of a patriarchal social structure. **Patriarchy** refers to the inequity of power held by males over females. The term comes from the Greek word for patriarch or "father as ruler."[17] Accordingly, this theory proposes that the subjugation of women by men is built into the organization of society. From this viewpoint, violence perpetrated by men against their intimate partners is an act of social control in defense of traditional male prerogatives.[18] There is much research to support this point of view. For example, after studying violent couples for over two decades, R. Emerson Dobash and Russell Dobash concluded that the male batterers in these relationships did not believe their partners had the same rights as men to argue, negotiate, or even debate. In fact, verbal arguments were seen by these men as "a nuisance and a threat to his authority, and violence is often used to silence debate, to reassert male authority, and to deny women a voice in the affairs of daily life."[19]

This perspective is not without its detractors, however. For example, Janice Ristock, who studies violence within lesbian relationships, points out that dominance and power arguments—based as they are on a patriarchal and misogynistic view of society—are unable to explain the dynamics of IPV within same-sex relationships. Her point is not that feminist theories of power and patriarchy do not explain IPV but rather that intimate partner violence is not a unitary phenomenon.[20] Closely related to the feminist paradigm of patriarchy is the notion that culturally sanctioned beliefs about the rights and privileges of husbands have historically legitimized men's domination over their intimate partners, including the use of violence. Research has shown that men are generally more accepting of violence against women and that the most culturally traditional men (i.e., those who accept traditional sex-role orientations such as aggression and athleticism for males and submissiveness and femininity for females) are the most accepting of violence in intimate relationships.[21] Yet these structures, values, and attitudes are not the only possible explanations for IPV. Another school of thought focuses on the way in which attitudes toward violence may be passed down between generations.

The Cycle of Violence

The **intergenerational transmission of violence theory**, sometimes referred to as the **cycle of violence**, contends that those who experience and/or witness violence as a child are more likely to become violent in adulthood, compared with children who do not experience or witness violence. This contention is primarily based on the theoretical premises of social learning theory, which holds that violence is learned just like any other form of behavior. Despite the logic behind this assumption, and some research which supports this notion, other work suggests that its applicability is somewhat limited. To perform a valid test of the theory, you would have to follow children who were abused over their lifetimes and determine whether they had an increased risk of engaging in violence as adults compared with an equivalent sample of children who were not abused. As you can imagine, even with a lot of resources this would be hard to do. There have, however, been a few longitudinal studies that have done just this. Perhaps the longest and most recent ongoing study of this kind has been conducted by Cathy Widom and her colleagues. They have found that, although there is an increased risk of childhood abuse victims being arrested as adult offenders compared with kids who did not experience abuse, the vast majority of abused kids go on to become productive, law-abiding citizens.[22] In other words, while children who witness or experience violence when young may be at greater risk for replicating this behavior, they are not condemned or predestined to act violently in their own lives. Other explanations, however, appear to have greater power to predict and explain intimate partner violence. It appears, for example, as if economic inequality is also a significant contributor to this particular form of violence.

Poverty

Low income appears to be significantly related to IPV, since it appears most often among those in the lowest income categories and decreases as one moves up the income scale.[23] While intimate partner violence does appear among all social classes, it is substantially higher among the poor. There appear to be several reasons for this. Lack of economic opportunities, fewer resources, low educational levels, and the stress of being poor might all contribute to higher rates of violence between intimates.[24] This factor also appears to be related to the higher reported rates of intimate partner violence among minority populations. Some research indicates that when economic factors are taken out of the equation, race is no longer a significant factor. In other words, the higher rates of minority group intimate partner violence may have more to do with the fact that minority groups are overrepresented among the ranks of the poor than with anything else.[25] One study, for example, found that African Americans living in poor neighborhoods were three times more likely to suffer from IPV as opposed to African Americans living in middle- and upper-class neighborhoods.[26] Incidentally, the same pattern held true for whites and Latinos—albeit in slightly different percentages. In addition to economics, we can also point to the role of alcohol in facilitating IPV.

Alcohol Use

Research indicates that alcohol use is related to all forms of violence; however, some studies have shown it to also be a significant factor in IPV. In fact, it has been reported to be a factor in between 25% and 85% of assaults between intimates.[27] However, it is not just drinking, but men's binge drinking in particular that appears to significantly increase the risk of this form of violence.[28] That is, men who drink sporadically but who drink large quantities during each episode of drinking—hence the term "binge drinking"—are at particular risk of abusing. It is important to note, however, that drinking alcohol does not cause violence; rather, we need to remember that it is a correlate, as we discussed in Chapter 3. What this means is that the effects of alcohol are mediated by context and the individual. Drinking alcohol, in other words, doesn't cause someone to abuse and batter their significant other. There needs to be other kinds of issues and conflicts behind the violence. For some, alcohol may act as a disinhibitor for individuals already predisposed to violence—the alcohol simply removes their self-control and judgment, allowing them to lash out violently. For others, it may act as an excuse to engage in violence and not feel personally accountable, because they can blame the alcohol. Alcohol may also serve to magnify a sense of personal power and control. In each case, however, the alcohol facilitates the violence but doesn't cause it.

Societal Responses to Intimate Partner Violence

As we noted at the beginning of the chapter, the criminal justice system has only recently begun to treat intimate partner violence as a criminal matter appropriate for police and prosecutorial concern. In fact, as recently as 20 years ago, many jurisdictions viewed this violence as a private matter and a few even required victims of spousal assault to pay prosecutors a fee to adjudicate their batterer.[29] Beginning in the 1970s, however, significant lobbying efforts by victims' rights groups in general and women's rights groups in particular began to erode the antiquated notion that intimate partner violence against women should remain behind closed doors, and this resulted in new legislation.

In 1994, the U.S. Congress passed a landmark piece of legislation called the **Violence Against Women Act** (VAWA). In addition to establishing the Violence Against Women Office within the U.S. Department of Justice, it was intended to improve criminal justice and community-based responses to intimate partner violence, dating violence, sexual assault, and stalking. This act was reauthorized in 2000, again in January 2006,[30] and most recently in February 2013.[31] This legislation established the federal government in a leadership role in encouraging local governments, including

American Indian tribes, to improve their response to both female victims and to those who victimize them and provided the impetus for a number of important initiatives and practices that continue to dominate our response to this form of violence, such as the mandatory arrest policies, which have become so prevalent.

Mandatory Arrest

In 1981, the first large-scale experiment to test the deterrent effects of arrest on batterers, called the **Minneapolis Domestic Violence Experiment**, was conducted by Lawrence Sherman and Richard Berk.[32] The theoretical foundation of this experiment was based on the notion of deterrence—the belief that arrest would deter offenders from assaulting their partners in the future. The primary research question driving the study was, "Does arresting a man who has assaulted his partner decrease the probability that he will assault her in the future compared to other tactics typically used such as separating the parties?" The study required 51 patrol officers to randomly adopt one of three possible responses to situations in which there was probable cause to believe that domestic violence had occurred. They were instructed to (1) separate the perpetrator and victim for eight hours, (2) advise them of alternatives that might include trying to mediate disputes, or (3) arrest the abuser. Over a period of about 17 months, 330 cases were generated. The authors then evaluated the possible success of each of these different strategies for deterring offenders from repeating their abusive behavior. Recidivism was in turn measured both by official arrest statistics, such as arrest reports and, when occasionally available, through victim interviews. Official arrest statistics revealed that 10% of those arrested, 19% of those advised, and 24% of those removed repeated the violence against their partners. From these results, Sherman and Berk concluded that arrest provided the strongest deterrent to future violence and consequently should be the preferred police response. This pioneering experiment, supported by significant lobbying work by feminist and women's organizations, generated policy changes in how the criminal justice system treated perpetrators of intimate partner violence. Lawsuits brought against police departments for negligence and other civil claims were also instrumental in convincing law enforcement to treat violence against women by their partners as they would other crimes.[33] Today, virtually all states and the District of Columbia have **mandatory arrest** policies for felony domestic assaults and warrantless arrest for an unwitnessed domestic violence-related misdemeanor assault. Mandatory arrest policies require police to detain a perpetrator when there is probable cause that an assault or battery has occurred or if a restraining order is violated, regardless of a victim's consent or protestations.[34]

To test the validity of any experimental findings, an important principle of science is replication. Accordingly, in the late 1980s the National Institute of Justice (NIJ) funded replication experiments of the Minneapolis study in six cities. Interestingly, the published findings from these replications—which became known as the **Spouse Assault Replication Program** (SARP)—did not uniformly find that arrest was an effective deterrent in spouse assault cases. In fact, the results were equivocal at best: Findings ranged from arrest having no effect, to arrest having a slight deterrent effect and, alarmingly, to arrest actually increasing the probability of future violence. In an attempt to systematically compare results across experimental sites, Joel Garner and his colleagues examined the original SARP analyses in detail. While these researchers did find a modest effect for arrest in decreasing recidivism, they concluded that a minority of women were still repeatedly victimized by their intimate partners, regardless of arrest.[35]

The mixed finding regarding arrest and intimate partner violence recidivism has led some researchers to investigate other factors that may interact with the condition of arrest. For example, Raymond Paternoster and his colleagues examined whether the manner in which sanctions were imposed had an effect on intimate partner violence recidivism.[36] Their research was motivated by a body of social psychological literature on a concept called "**procedural justice**," which contends that conformity to group rules is as much or more because of fair procedures in delivering sanctions as it is to fair or favorable outcomes. A key proposition of procedural justice is that adhering to fair procedures will cement a persons' ties to the social order because it treats them with fairness and worth and certifies their full and valued membership in the group. In this view, being treated fairly by authorities, even while being sanctioned by them (i.e., arrested), influences a person's view of their own legitimacy and ultimately that person's obedience to group norms. In other words, how a person is treated is as important as the outcome. Informed by this literature, Paternoster found that when suspects arrested for intimate partner violence perceived that they were treated fairly by the police, they were significantly less likely to engage in IPV in the future compared with those who perceived themselves as being treated unfairly.

Others have called for research to examine whether **victim empowerment** impacts recidivism. Victim empowerment generally means that victims' rights and wishes are factored into the process of administering justice. One study examined the effects of victim empowerment in an experiment testing the effects of mandatory prosecution.[37] Mandatory prosecution requires government attorneys to bring criminal charges against batterers, regardless of the wishes of the victim. There is variability, however, in the extent to which victims are allowed to drop charges once they have been filed. As Mills explains, "A hard no-drop policy never takes the victim's preference to drop the charges against the batterer into consideration. A soft no-drop policy permits victims to drop the charges under certain limited circumstances."[38] Other studies have found that when victims were given the option to drop charges, they were at the lowest risk for being victimized again compared with victims who were not allowed to drop charges.[39]

Unintended Consequences of Mandatory Arrest Policies

Since mandatory arrest statutes have been implemented, several states have observed an increase in the number of incidents in which police arrested both the offender and the victim—dual arrests. For example, after mandatory arrest was adopted in a Minnesota county, 13% of the arrests in the first year were of the victims, rising to 25% the following year.[40] Data from the **Kenosha Domestic Abuse Intervention Project** indicate that, after a mandatory arrest law went into effect in Wisconsin, women experienced a 12-fold increase in arrests while the number of men arrested doubled during the same time period.[41] While some speculate that a portion of these arrests may be valid, others perceive more nefarious reasons for the increase in dual arrests. As Saunders reports,

> Advocates suspect that a "backlash" against new [mandatory arrest] policies has occurred among some officers because they resent limits placed on their discretion and have little sympathy for female victims to begin with . . . Consequently, they may arrest victims on trivial charges or for violence used in self-defense.[42]

To decrease the probability of dual arrests, some states have incorporated language such as "**primary aggressor**" or "predominant aggressor" within their statutes. This is intended to allow officers to distinguish between a person who is a victim largely using violence to defend themselves and the abuser. Other states have been more proactive. For example, Massachusetts law requires written justification for arresting both the offender and victim in order to reduce dual arrests.[43] Given the inconsistent and sometimes deleterious consequences of mandatory arrest policies for IPV victims, some have called for a moratorium on them. For example, one scholar stated

> I recommend that jurisdictions spend precious resources not on implementing mandatory policies but rather on developing programs that would provide tailored services to battered women. Toward this end, funds should be allocated to train law enforcement personnel to distinguish the fearful from those who can be empowered.[44]

Those who defend mandatory arrest and prosecution policies, however, have argued that victims of intimate partner violence are too helpless to make appropriate arrest or prosecution decisions and/or are too fearful to affirmatively decide to press charges. In sum, there is a great deal of ambiguity surrounding the question of how arrest may impact the probability of men assaulting their partners. The roles played by the police in both preventing violence and with its consequences are extremely complex. While the deterrent effect of mandatory arrest policies is far from clear, it is important to remember that laws serve other important societal functions, and we shouldn't minimize the importance of those. Laws can serve notice to a community that such violence will not be tolerated. Practically speaking, laws dictating police intervention can also give the victim access and information to a number of support services, such as shelters and other social service agencies, or make them aware of legal tools such as **civil protection orders**.

Civil Protection Orders

Today, all 50 states offer victims of IPV some form of civil protection or temporary restraining order. These are generally called civil protection orders (CPO), and while there is significant variability across states regarding the availability and the scope of the relief provided, a CPO generally offers victims a temporary judicial injunction that directs an assailant to stop battering, threatening, or harming the woman as well as other family members and/or children. To obtain a CPO, a victim is generally required to go through two steps. First, they need to obtain an order commonly referred to as an emergency order. These temporary orders usually expire after several weeks and are issued solely on the basis of a victim's petition. At the time an emergency order is granted, the judge typically sets a date for a hearing on the second order of protection, often referred to as the plenary or permanent order. The emergency order and notice of the plenary hearing must then be served on the respondent (assailant), who has an opportunity to attend the second hearing. If a permanent CPO is granted at the second hearing, it generally remains in effect for a period of six months to one year.[45]

In theory, the advantages of a CPO, either in lieu of criminal prosecution or while awaiting criminal prosecution include the following:

- It is a quick form of legal protection compared to a criminal hearing.
- It relies on a standard of proof based on the preponderance of evidence compared with guilt beyond reasonable doubt.
- It serves to protect victims who are awaiting criminal prosecution or divorce/custody hearings.
- It provides a form of early intervention in cases that do not yet fall within the purview of criminal statutes.[46]

If a batterer violates the CPO, the sanctions vary from being arrested and charged with civil contempt, to charges of criminal contempt, to a misdemeanor of violating the order, or a combination of the three.

But how effective are CPOs in protecting women? Unfortunately, only a few studies have investigated this question. Adelle Harrell and her colleagues conducted one of the most ambitious assessments of protection orders in Denver and Boulder, Colorado. They examined many factors, from a sample of 350 restraining order cases that included interviews with victims over a nine-month period after the order was filed as well as official records for protection order violations. Unusually, they also studied the perceptions of a sample of men named on the restraining orders about the consequences of the CPOs. It is important to note that the history of abuse and violence experienced by women seeking a temporary restraining order was extensive: 56% of the women reported that they had sustained a physical injury during the incident that led them to seek relief from a CPO.[47] Unfortunately, this study also revealed that the legal consequences for offenders who violated an order were not very consistent. For example, in the 290 incidents of victims reporting a violation to the police, only 59 arrests were made.

The primary recommendation offered by this study was that all parties involved—including victims, judges, and law enforcement officials—require education about what the order allows and prohibits. Victims need to understand how violations can be reported to the court, and police need further education regarding the correct response to violations of CPOs.[48] Other researchers have examined the barriers present in the system that prevent many victims from obtaining CPOs in the first place. After surveying a national sample of domestic violence organizations that help battered women obtain protection orders, researchers found that while the statutes themselves were generally protective of women's interests, there were serious problems implementing them. Along with specific implementation problems, a large proportion of service providers believed that women of color, women with few economic resources, and non-English speaking women were particularly vulnerable to the barriers blocking access to CPOs.

Instrumentally, one of the most serious access problems identified by respondents was the lack of knowledge regarding the availability of protection orders to begin with. Many victims simply don't know they exist or what purpose they serve. In addition, the majority of respondents believed that many women had trouble completing even the so-called "simplified forms" on their own. Here is how one service provider put it:

> Almost all petitioners who have first tried to fill out their own papers without our assistance give up because of the volume of papers, the length of instructions, and an inability to fully understand the instructions.[49]

Other barriers to CPOs were logistical and included the need to travel great distances to the courthouse, access to courts and judges during weekdays only, and the necessity to take time off from work and/or find babysitters for lengthy and often unpredictable amounts of time. Virtually all research has found that once a woman has been successful in obtaining an order, it is the legal enforcement of that order by police that remains the weakest link in the system. Scholars have found several problems inherent in the enforcement process. First, law enforcement officials are often slow in serving emergency orders and often refuse to arrest violators, even when the individual is clearly in violation of the order. Second, prosecutors are often reluctant to press charges against those who violate CPOs, and third and last, judges often impose minimal sentences even on repeat violators.[50]

So do civil protection orders shield victims of intimate partner violence? In sum, the few studies that have been conducted have found that, while protection orders were useful for preventing violence in some cases, they were less effective in preventing new incidents of violence from men who had long histories of violent behavior. To increase the efficacy of CPOs, service providers have recommended the creation of coalitions or task forces to facilitate communication among the involved parties to improve enforcement procedures for civil protection orders, including representatives from the local domestic violence program, the police department, the prosecutor's office, the judiciary, and perhaps local hospitals and private attorneys. Jurisdictions with such coordinated response systems usually have significantly fewer barriers to accessing the courts and obtaining these orders of protection. This leads us to the next innovation for fighting IPV.

Coordinated Community Responses to Domestic Violence

Coordinated community responses to violence against women across the domains of criminal justice, social services, and victim advocacy groups are increasingly being employed to both prevent and ameliorate the consequences of this violence. It should be noted that these coordinated responses are also being implemented to fight the other forms of family violence we discuss in the remaining sections of this chapter, including child and elder abuse. Unfortunately, there is extreme variability in how agencies coordinate their work across communities. Some include limited partnerships between domestic violence programs and specific criminal justice agencies, while others are comprehensive interventions run by nonprofit agencies. Moreover, these efforts have proven to be somewhat transitory in nature—depending, for example, on the availability of funds and political support.

While very little is known about the effectiveness of these initiatives, many communities have embraced them because of the assumption that organizing a few elements of the community's response around a common objective (e.g., to prevent violence against women) will produce better results than creating new practices or programs. Another innovative response concerns the creation of **fatality review teams** in many jurisdictions.[51] Pioneered by the criminologist Neil Websdale, these teams bring together a variety of members from various groups that have an interest in preventing intimate partner violence and can include law enforcement officers, judges, defense and prosecuting attorneys, victim advocates, mental health workers, county coroners, and survivors among others. These teams then systematically review intimate partner deaths in their community with an eye toward understanding how the killing happened and how the community might respond better in the future in order to better intervene and protect battered women. Today, teams operate in all but nine states and have been successful in changing policies, affecting legislation, and improving interagency communication and cooperation in a number of locations. Similarly to coordinated community response groups, however, the fatality review teams are volunteer driven and their ability to actually prevent domestic violence-related deaths is unknown.

Violence in Gay/Lesbian/Bisexual/Transgender (GLBT) Relationships

Although most states in the United States still do not legally recognize marriage outside of heterosexual relationships, there are hundreds of thousands of nontraditional families in this country comprising **same-sex unions**, both with and without children. Unfortunately, no national studies have been conducted that directly investigate how much violence exists in these types of relationships. The NVAWMS provides an indirect assessment of the magnitude, because it asks respondents whether they have ever lived with a same-sex partner as part of a couple. Rates of violence for those who answer in the affirmative are then compared with rates for those respondents who do not. Results suggest that there was more IPV between same-sex cohabitants than between opposite-sex cohabitants but that most of this violence was perpetrated by men. The NCVS is also able to indirectly measure violence between same-sex intimate partners since it asks victims whether their assailant was male or female. While a lack of official statistics exists, there is no lack of evidence that violence exists in GLBT couples from clinical and small self-selected samples.[52] Unfortunately, the options for those in abusive GLBT relationships are typically quite limited, since victims of violence in GLBT relationships do not have equal access to social services or to the criminal justice system in the same way as victims of heterosexual violence. Although the majority of states have gender-neutral domestic violence laws, evidence suggests that the police and courts do not always treat violence that occurs in GLBT couples in a professional and objective manner.[53] Fortunately, our definitions and laws regarding what constitutes a family continues to evolve, and we hope victims of violence in GLBT relationships will soon be afforded the same equal access to social, medical, and criminal justice services as hetero couples enjoy.

Stalking

Stalking first entered our society's consciousness after the murder of Rebecca Schaeffer in 1989. Twenty-one years old, Rebecca was an actress starring in a popular sitcom, *My Sister Sam*. A fast-food worker from Tucson, Arizona, named Robert Bardo became obsessed with the young actress and for over two years sent her numerous love letters. He eventually traveled to Los Angeles in the hope of tracking her down, paid a private detective to find her address, and went to Rebecca's apartment and shot her twice after she answered the door, killing her. When stalking turns deadly for celebrities, it makes media headlines. However, the crime of stalking is most often perpetrated by intimate or former intimate partners. We therefore want to spend a little time in this chapter reviewing what we know about stalking.

❖ **Photo 5.2** Accused killer Robert John Bardo in court

After Shaeffer's death, California implemented the first antistalking legislation in 1990. It was not until then that the legal term of *stalking* was coined. According to the model antistalking code for states developed by the NIJ, stalking is defined as

> A course of conduct directed at a specific person that involves repeated visual or physical proximity, nonconsensual communication, or verbal, written or implied threats, or a combination thereof, that would cause a reasonable person fear, with repeated meaning on two or more occasions.[54]

So how many people are stalked annually and how do we measure it? Does stalking involve unwanted repeated attempts at contact or only unwanted repeated attempts at contact that make someone feel fear? If we feel fear, how much fear is necessary for an act of stalking to be considered a crime? A "great deal of fear" or just "some fear?" The National Intimate Partner and Sexual Violence Survey (NISVS) used the following definition of stalking:

> Stalking victimization involves a pattern of harassing or threatening tactics used by a perpetrator that is both unwanted and causes fear or safety concerns in the victim….a person was considered a stalking victim if they experienced multiple stalking tactics or a single stalking tactic multiple times by the same perpetrator and felt very fearful, or believed that they or someone close to them would be harmed or killed as a result of the perpetrator's behavior.[55]

The tactics measured included unwanted phone calls, text messages or hang-ups, unwanted emails or messages through social media, unwanted mail or presents, unwanted following from a distance or through the use of devices such as GPS systems, showing up at the victim's home or workplace, leaving items for victim to find, or doing things that indicate the stalker had been in the victim's home or car. Research conducted by Cupach and Spitzberg has identified eight specific tactics commonly employed by stalkers which include:

- **Hyperintimacy** refers to excessive and repetitive attempts to win the target over. It is often disguised as friendship or courtship.
- **Mediated contact** concerns the stalker using technology to constantly stay in touch through facebook, texting, calling, and faxing.
- **Interactional contact** is when the stalker joins the same clubs or groups, shows up at the same places, and tries to engage with the person who is the obsession of the stalker.
- **Surveillance** refers to the stalker getting as much information as they can about the target's life, movement, and patterns of activity.
- **Invasion** is all about breaking into the victim's home and property.
- **Harassment and intimidation** are, as the title indicates, strategies in which the stalker attempts to irritate and inconvenience the target through their persistent interference in the victim's daily life.
- **Coercion and threat** refers to when a stalker's method of contact is violence and can include kidnappings and assaults.[56]

In 2010, the NISVS found that about 16% of women had been stalked at some point in their lifetimes and 4% had been stalked in the 12 months prior to the survey. The incidents for men was much lower, with about 5% of men experiencing stalking in their lifetimes and just over 1% experiencing it in the past 12 months. For lifetime reports of stalking, the majority of female victims (66%) were stalked by intimate partners, while the male victims were equally likely to be stalked by intimate partners and friend/acquaintances (41% and 40% respectively). The NCVS also conducted a special Supplemental Victimization Survey (SVS) in 2006 that measured stalking. It found that 2.2% of females 18 years of age and older compared to 0.8% of their male counterparts had experienced stalking in the past 12 months. Together, it was estimated that over 3,300,000 stalking victimizations occurred annually! This victimization data conforms to perpetration statistics, since research indicates that the vast majority of perpetrators are men.[57] This means, in other words, that stalking is mostly about men stalking women. There are also a few differences in the extent to which stalking was experienced across race/ethnic groups, since a number of studies, for example, have found that Native American and Alaskan Native women were more likely than other groups to experience stalking, while Asian and Pacific Islander women were least likely to report being stalked.[58] Age also appears to be a factor in this crime, with those under the age of 24 experiencing the highest prevalence of stalking victimization. The majority of unwanted stalking tactics included phone calls.[59] Clearly, stalking represents a serious threat in the United States—particularly to women. In many ways, we can see it as a dangerous correlate to intimate partner violence.

Clearly then, many stalkers are abusers whose desire for control and whose jealousy lead them to interject themselves into all aspects of their victims life by surveilling, contacting, and otherwise monitoring the target of their obsession. So why do they go to such extremes? As with so many other aspects of human behavior, there is no one single answer. Stalkers stalk for a variety of reasons. Research has shown that a recent traumatic event, such as a breakup, the death of a family member, or the loss of a job, can sometimes trigger this behavior.[60] For others, it's all about wanting to control their former intimate and as such, it is another way that an abuser tries to manifest power over their intimate partner, especially after a breakup.[61] Here is how one woman experienced it. "He would follow me every time I went someplace. And he'd drive by and walk by my house every chance he got, every day until I moved to where he couldn't find me. So, I started getting these phone calls at home and at work. And he'd come to my work and sit on a bench outside and just watch me. When I got off at night, he'd follow me home. One night when I came out to my car, there was a note saying, "You'd better think hard before you turn the key." I got in the car and there was a picture of a blown up car on the steering wheel. I didn't move it until a mechanic looked it over and said, "No, it's fine."[62] In this victim's experiences, we can see a number of the stalking tactics reviewed above and get a sense of how frightening and traumatic it can be.

Societal Responses to Stalking

As noted above, California passed the nation's first antistalking legislation in 1990.[63] Prior to this legislation, stalking was not considered a criminal offense in any state and, because of this, police had little power to arrest someone who behaved in a threatening way—even though such behavior caused the victim extreme distress. Although traditionally associated with celebrities, stalking was often a serious problem for women in general, many whom were trying to terminate an abusive relationship. Today, all states and the District of Columbia have some form of legislation in place to protect victims of stalking. These statutes generally define stalking in a similar way to the model antistalking statute developed by the NIJ. The goal of these statutes, of course, is to end this pattern of harassment before it escalates to physical violence. Although there is great variability in antistalking statutes across states, they can generally be classified as being either broad or narrow. A broad antistalking law prohibits conduct that causes mental distress and fear of physical harm, while a narrow antistalking law, in contrast, requires a credible threat and some form of malicious or intentional conduct, such as following or harassing.

Determining how well antistalking statutes actually protect the public is a difficult task. Ideally, to measure the effectiveness of an antistalking statute, one would first need to examine baseline rates of stalking behavior before an antistalking law was implemented in that jurisdiction and then monitor the change in stalking rates after implementation. To control for the effects of other factors that may be related to stalking behavior besides the new law, research should simultaneously monitor stalking behavior in a demographically similar jurisdiction that did *not* implement antistalking statutes during the study period. This would be considered the control group. Only if rates of stalking decreased in the experimental group and not in the control group could the decrease validly be attributed to the effects of the antistalking laws. This research design is called a quasi-experimental design and is often used in evaluation research. Several factors, however, make it impossible to utilize this research design to examine the efficacy of antistalking statutes. Foremost of these is access to reliable base rates of stalking behavior. Since stalking behavior was not illegal prior to the passage of most antistalking laws, criminal justice agencies do not have data on the number of complaints, arrests, and convictions for such behavior. In the absence of such data, it is hoped that these statutes will help to deter stalking by communicating the illegality of this behavior to would-be offenders and to society at large.

Child Abuse

In Focus 5.2 illuminates the most extreme form of **child abuse**—when a child is killed by a parent. However, child abuse takes many forms, including sexual abuse which we briefly review in Chapter 7, physical abuse, and neglect. In this section, we will deal exclusively with the physical abuse of children. As you might imagine, estimating

---

In Focus 5.2

When Mothers Kill

On average, over 500 children aged 5 and under are killed annually. The majority of these murders are committed by a parent, with mothers being as likely to kill their children as fathers. In the past few years, several of these cases have made national headlines, including Andrea Yates, who drowned her five children in the family's bathtub in 2001, Deanna Laney, who stoned two of her young sons to death and seriously injured another in 2003 because she believed God commanded it, and Dena Schlosser, who in November of 2004 cut off her 11-month-old daughter's arms.

The most recent case to make national headlines occurred in the upscale neighborhood of Tampa Palms, in Florida, in March of 2011. There, Julie Schenecker was found on her patio with blood on her white bathrobe.

Inside were the bodies of her two children, 16-year-old Calyx and 13-year-old Beau. She had apparently shot Beau with a handgun the previous afternoon while driving him to soccer practice. Calyx was shot while she was on the computer in her bedroom, one bullet hitting the back of her head and another hitting her in the face. In a note found in the home, Ms. Schenecker indicated that she had also intended to kill herself but never did. Friends and neighbors of the family were shocked because they appeared to be a typical suburban family with all the indicators, including car pools, soccer games, track meets, and so on. One teacher described Ms. Schenecker as "an attentive mother who picked her daughter up from practice, attended team suppers and once surprised him with a birthday cake."[64]

the prevalence of child abuse is even more difficult than estimating rates of intimate partner violence, primarily because many child victims are fearful about reporting their victimizations to an authority figure. And despite the mandatory reporting laws in place in all states, evidence of abuse and neglect can often remain hidden except for extreme cases, such as when broken bones and concussions require medical care. Moreover, the cultural norms regarding the use of physical punishment that exist in the United States are still somewhat ambiguous. Despite the fact that the percentage of parents who believe spanking a child is harmful has increased during the past 30 years, the majority of parents still use corporal punishment to discipline their children. Many of you reading this book probably have had first-hand experience with this, as have the authors. Most of us may think this is normal, but looking at the norms of other countries tells us otherwise. For example, in 1979 Sweden became the first country to ban the spanking of children. Since then, Finland, Denmark, Norway, and Austria have also banned this practice in an effort to end the abuse of children.[65] Physical discipline is not considered a legitimate form of punishment in these nations.

As with other types of family violence, the best place to start when examining the rate of violence against children is with homicide rates. The rate of homicide against children aged 5 and under has remained relatively stable for the past 25 years. The good news, then, is that lethal child abuse has not increased. The bad news is that we have not decreased the rate at which young lives are taken by violence either.[66] Table 5.2 presents the number and percentage of homicides against children aged 5 and under by the gender and relationship of the perpetrator. As can be seen, parents kill the majority of children of this age, with mothers and fathers about equally likely to murder their own children.

Of course, most cases of child abuse don't result in death. But when does punishment cross the line and become abuse? How should we define child abuse? All 50 states and the District of Columbia have laws against child abuse and neglect, but each statute is different. In fact, there appears to be no national or scientific consensus on what constitutes "child abuse," even in research circles. For example, some researchers define an abused child on the basis of having been injured. Others contend that abuse is abuse because of the severity of the assault, regardless of whether it resulted in injury.[67] Barbara Wauchope and Murray Straus define the two as follows:

> Physical punishment is . . . a legally permissible violent act (or acts) carried out as part of the parental role and physical abuse is . . . a violent act (or acts) by a parent that, in our judgment, exceeds the level of severity permitted by law and custom and exposes the child to a greater risk of injury.[68]

The NFVS discussed earlier also asked parents about their behavior toward their children. The actions considered to be physical punishment included children being "pushed, grabbed, shoved, slapped, and spanked. Physical abuse included being kicked, bit, hit with a fist, hit with an object, beat up, burned or scalded, or being assaulted with a gun or knife." According to these definitions, 51% of boys and about 49% of girls experienced physical punishment. Boys, however, had higher rates of physical abuse than girls, with rates of 2.8% and 1.9% respectively. Interestingly, there was no

Table 5.2	The Percentage of Homicides Against Children Aged 5 and Younger by the Gender and Relationship of the Offender, 1980–2008					
Gender of Offender	Parent (%)	Other Family (%)	Friend/ Acquaintance (%)	Stranger (%)		
Male	33	4	23	3		
Female	30	3	5	3		

SOURCE: Cooper and Smith, *Homicide Trends in the United States, 1980–2008*, Bureau of Justice Statistics, 2011.

difference between the rate of abuse by mothers and fathers. Recall that this is consistent with the homicide data revealing that mothers and fathers are equally likely to kill their children aged 5 and under.

Risk Factors for Physical Child Abuse

As we saw in In Focus 5.2, the most extreme cases of physical abuse of children that result in death are often the only cases represented by the media. However, the reasons provided to explain these exceptional cases, such as **postpartum psychosis**, are rare and are not responsible for the majority of physical abuse against children. The risk factors for intimate partner violence discussed earlier in the chapter also relate to child abuse. For example, stereotypical beliefs about men holding dominant positions over women also influence depictions of children as "property." The intergenerational transmission of violence also contends that being abused as a child places a person at a greater risk of abusing their own children. And, similar to IPV, the stress of poverty, a lack of social support, and drug and/or alcohol abuse most certainly increase the risk of parents becoming abusive. There are, however, other risk factors specific to child abuse which are worth noting.

One consistent finding in all research is that younger children, particularly under the age of 3, are at a greater risk of being abused compared with older children.[69] Other situations that appear to increase a child's risk include inadequate bonding between parent and child and/or having a physical or mental disability as well as other health problems, including being born prematurely. Each of these situations places families and parents under tremendous stress, which for some parents may translate into abusive behavior.[70] The reality of course is that many parents in high stress situations do an admirable job of parenting and act with restraint and compassion, while others in less difficult circumstances cross the line and abuse their children.

Societal Responses to Physical Child Abuse

Child abuse was one of the first forms of family violence to be recognized as a social problem. The impetus for this is thought to come from the medical field where the advent of radiology allowed doctors to observe multiple fractures that could not be explained by accidental falls. In 1962, the prestigious *Journal of the American Medical Association* published an article in which the term "The **Battered-Child Syndrome**" was first coined and which provided a means to publicize the problem.[71] Unfortunately, it took the federal government almost 10 years to act. In 1974, the **Child Abuse Prevention and Treatment Act** was implemented by Congress, which established the National Center on Child Abuse and Neglect under the U.S. Department of Health, Education, and Welfare.

Soon afterwards, psychologists and social workers alike began to observe the unintended negative consequences of removing children from their families and lobbied to rectify previous legislation that did not guide this removal. The **Adoption Assistance and Child Welfare Act of 1980**[72] was intended to prevent unwarranted removal of children from their families by making "reasonable efforts" to keep families together or to unify families in a timely manner if placement could not be avoided. This act was soon followed by the **Family Preservation and Support Services Act of 1993** that was mandated to expand the services available to strengthen families as well as to provide additional supports for children who must be placed outside the home.

When the victims of family violence are children, the social service system as well as the criminal justice system becomes involved. Each state has a **Child Protection Services Division** that is mandated to protect and remove children from abusive situations. Increasingly, however, states are removing the abusive parent or caretaker rather than the child in order to prevent the child from feeling punished or stigmatized. The primary objective of the agencies in charge of this mission is to make sure the child is protected and cared for, which distinguishes them from law enforcement agencies that are focused on holding offenders accountable through criminal statutes. All states and the District of Columbia have mandatory reporting laws for these offenses, requiring designated professionals to report cases of abuse and neglect. Any person who has a duty to care for or protect a child may be considered a mandated reporter; this category includes teachers, childcare providers, physicians, and police officers. These mandatory reporting laws vary by state, as does the age at which someone is considered a "child." At the other end of the age spectrum are the elderly who, as we are also finding out, sometimes suffer violently at the hands of loved ones.

Elder Abuse

Edna Zehner, who cared for her 85-year-old father, Frank Altman, lost her temper one day because his television was too loud. He was recording a religious broadcast and apparently wanted to make sure it was picked up by his tape recorder. Unfortunately for Edna, the tape recorder also provided evidence about Frank's murder that day. After a lot of yelling about the volume of the television, Edna was heard to say, "Shut your face! I don't want to hear you! I don't want to see you!" Several impact sounds were heard and were followed by Frank's groaning. It was later surmised that the noises were the sounds of Edna beating her father with a tire iron. Found four days later by a grandson, Frank was discovered lying bruised in his own waste, with a broken arm. He had been without food or water since the attack. He died just over three weeks later.

Elder abuse is one of the most recent types of family violence to be acknowledged as a social problem, and it is one of the most difficult types of violence to uncover for a number of reasons that include the isolation of the victims (i.e., they don't go to school like children) as well as the extreme shame that many elders feel as a result of their victimization.[73] The U.S. National Academy of Sciences has proposed a useful definition of elder abuse:

> (a) intentional actions that cause harm or create a serious risk of harm (whether or not harm is intended), to a vulnerable elder by a caregiver or other person who stands in a trust relationship to the elder, or (b) failure by a caregiver to satisfy the elder's basic needs or to protect the elder from harm.[74]

There are several types of abuse subsumed under this definition, including physical abuse, psychological abuse, material or financial exploitation, and neglect. We will focus exclusively on physical abuse in this section. It is also important to understand that physical abuse of the elderly can occur in many settings, including in their homes, hospitals, and nursing homes. Our attention in this chapter will be focused on abuse occurring in private residences.

There have only been a handful of surveys conducted to examine elder abuse specifically, and estimates of abuse from these studies range from 2% to 10% prevalence rates. Examining the extent of violence perpetrated by known offenders against the elderly from the NCVS and homicide data suggests that, while the elderly continue to experience intimate partner violence, they are generally more vulnerable to assaults by other relatives and other known offenders compared with their younger counterparts, who are more vulnerable to assaults by intimates. In other words, they tend to be more at risk from their children than from their partners.

Risk Factors for Elder Abuse

Research generally indicates that a shared living situation is a major risk factor for elder abuse; elders living alone are at the lowest risk of experiencing physical abuse. Obviously, living with others increases the opportunities for conflict and tension that arise in all living situations. Another consistent risk factor appears to be the mental dementia: Elders with dementia appear to have higher rates of physical abuse compared with elders without this disorder. And, like the physical abuse of intimates and children, social isolation also has been identified as a risk factor for elder abuse. Victims are more likely to be isolated from friends and relatives than nonvictims. The presence of or frequent contact with other people would increase the likelihood that abusive behaviors would be detected.

A risk factor that is unique to elder abuse is that the perpetrators are more likely to be financially dependent on the person they are abusing. In many cases, the abuse results from attempts by the relatives—especially adult children—to obtain resources from the victim.[75] It is important to reiterate, however, that abuse can take place with or without any of these factors present and that the majority of families with these risk factors present do not manifest physical abuse against the elder for whom they may be caring.

Societal Responses to Elder Abuse

In 1965, Congress passed the **Older Americans Act**, which was the first piece of national legislation that expressed society's commitment to protect vulnerable older Americans at risk. When the act was reauthorized in 1992, Congress created and funded a new Title VII, called the **Vulnerable Elder Rights Protection Act**, which expanded the original legislation to include mandates for the prevention of elder abuse, neglect, and exploitation. In the most recent amendments to this act in 2000, Congress called on states to foster greater coordination with law enforcement and the courts. As the years have gone by, this piece of legislation has proven instrumental in promoting public education and interagency coordination to address elder abuse. In 2003, the Senate attempted to pass an act titled the Elder Justice Act, which, among other things, would have established dual offices of elder justice in the U.S. Department of Health and Human Services/Administration on Aging as well as the U.S. Department of Justice to coordinate elder abuse prevention efforts nationally.[76] Unfortunately, no action was taken by the Senate and the law was never passed.

As with all crimes, however, states have the primary responsibility for responding to elder abuse. As with Child Protective Services (CPS), which has primary responsibility for cases of child abuse, all 50 states and the District of Columbia have enacted legislation authorizing the provision of **Adult Protective Services** (APS) in cases of elder abuse. Generally, these APS laws establish a system for the reporting and investigation of elder abuse and for the provision of social services to help the victim and ameliorate the abuse. In most jurisdictions, these laws also pertain to abused adults who have a disability, vulnerability, or other impairment as defined by state law, not just to older persons. As with child abuse, the laws in most states require helping professions in the front lines, such as doctors and home health providers, to be mandated reporters when it comes to cases of suspected elder abuse or neglect. Increasingly, however, states are updating their statutes to require "any person" to report a suspicion of elder abuse.[77] Although most states do not currently have specific laws for the prosecution of elder abuse, all incidents can be adjudicated under other statutes, including laws mandated for rape, assault, and battery.

Conclusions

Violence that takes place within the home has been occurring since the advent of the family. It is a terrible irony that the family—the institution so often portrayed as a place of love, acceptance, and refuge from the outside world—is instead, for all too many, the most dangerous environment they will ever face. Only recently have we, as a society, acknowledged the extent of the problem of violence within the family and taken steps to intervene and prevent its occurrence. We now know that family violence—even witnessed violence—has profound effects on the lives of victims, including increasing the risk of both offending and victimization in adulthood, and increased risk for other negative consequences, such as depression and alcohol and/or drug dependency. Continuing to understand the causes of these forms of violence is therefore extremely important, not just to the families affected by this violence but to society as a whole.

Key Terms

Adoption Assistance and Child Welfare Act of 1980

Adult Protective Services

Battered-Child Syndrome

child abuse

Child Abuse Prevention and Treatment Act of 1974

Child Protection Services Division

civil protection order

Conflict Tactics Scale

coordinated community responses

cycle of violence

elder abuse

Family Preservation and Support Services Act of 1993

family violence

fatality review team

intergenerational transmission of violence theory

intimate partner violence

Kenosha Domestic Abuse Intervention Project

mandatory arrest

Minneapolis Domestic Violence Experiment

National Crime Victimization Survey

National Family Violence Survey

National Intimate Partner and Sexual Violence Survey

National Violence Against Women and Men Survey

Older Americans Act of 1965

patriarchy

postpartum psychosis

primary aggressor

procedural justice

same-sex unions

Spouse Assault Replication Program

stalking

victim empowerment

Violence Against Women Act

Vulnerable Elder Rights Protection Act of 1992

Discussion Questions

1. All 50 states have passed some form of mandatory reporting law for cases of child abuse and neglect. Although many states have also created legislation to make the reporting of elder abuse cases mandatory, there is still a great deal of controversy about these laws. Some believe that elders—like all adults—have the freedom to report or not to report a victimization to police. They contend that by making the reporting of such victimizations mandatory, this freedom is taken away from a subgroup of the population. Others, however, contend that because the elderly population is more likely to suffer particular cognitive disorders that may prevent them from seeking help, these mandatory reporting laws are necessary. Where do you stand on the issue? Is there some way to protect "at risk" groups of the elderly population without taking away the freedom of choice for the entire subgroup of those over a certain age? What are the benefits and costs of such legislation?

2. Go to the U.S. Department of Justice website and find the Office on Violence Against Women (http://www.usdoj.gov/ovw/regulations.htm). Go to the section on federal legislation and find the link for the "Violence Against Women and Department of Justice Reauthorization Act of 2005 (VAWA 2005)." In your opinion, what are the

most important components of the act? What underserved populations are highlighted in the act for increased protection? What provisions does the act stipulate for each crime highlighted?

3. In 2000, the National Center for Victims of Crime (NCVC) developed a Stalking Resource Center. The mission of the program is to raise awareness of stalking and to encourage the development and implementation of multidisciplinary responses to stalking in local communities across the United States. Access this resource center through the NCVC website (www .ncvs.org/src) and examine in detail at least one issue related to stalking, which may include information about state laws and legislation or court cases involving the legality of statutes against stalking. How has legislation evolved to combat stalking while at the same time not compromising personal liberties guaranteed by the Constitution?

4. The status of women and women's health in general are strongly related to the incidence of violence against women. The World Health Organization has published a cross-national study comparing indicators of women's health and violence against women for several countries (www.who.int/gender/violence/who_multicountry_ study/en). Using the report, compare and contrast indicators from at least five different countries. Do indicators of women's health in general correlate with their incidence of victimization? That is, do countries with high rates of health-related problems (e.g., high rates of infant mortality, low life expectancies) also have high rates of victimization? What other national factors may contribute to high rates of violence against women?

Stranger Danger

The fear of crimes of violence is not a simple fear of injury or death or even of all crimes of violence, but, at bottom, a fear of strangers . . . this fear of strangers has greatly impoverished the lives of many Americans, especially those who live in high-crime neighborhoods in large cities.

—The President's Commission on Law Enforcement
and Administration of Justice, 1967[1]

I was a brand-new sheriff. I didn't even know the definition of a hate crime. What I knew was that somebody had been murdered because he was black.

—Sheriff Billy Rowles, Jasper, Texas[2]

I don't think there is any one factor that precipitates the commission of a crime . . . I think it's just the conditions. I think the primary factor is being without.

—Robber in St. Louis, Missouri[3]

Thus far, you have learned that acts of interpersonal violence are often perpetrated by those we love and trust as well as by friends and acquaintances. In this chapter, we focus on the crimes that are most likely to be committed by strangers, at least generally. These include robbery, workplace violence including bank robbery, and violent hate crime. In his classic study of homicide in Philadelphia, Marvin Wolfgang divided homicide into **primary homicides**, which involved intimates, friends, and acquaintances, and **secondary homicides**, which involved strangers. He also coined the phrase "**stranger crime**" for this latter category.[4] Before reading this chapter, it is important for you to remember that the majority of all violent crime, except for robberies, are committed by offenders known to us. For example, recent data from the National Crime Victimization Survey (NCVS) indicates that only 24% of rapes, 42% of aggravated assaults, and 37% of simple assault were committed by unknown offenders.[5] Despite this fact, stranger crime is what we most dread. It is the stranger lurking in the alley or the bushes who captures our imagination and stirs our fears. Strangers are anonymous and dangerous while our friends and acquaintances are known to us and therefore seem to be nonthreatening. Even though the odds are that perpetrators of interpersonal violence are most likely to be those familiar acquaintances, friends, and family, the fact is that we usually don't fear them the way we fear strangers. We begin this chapter with a discussion of robbery. The second part of the chapter focuses on violence perpetrated in the workplace, followed by hate crime, which has received a fair amount of attention in recent years.

Robbery

For many of us, the story of Robin Hood is a familiar tale that we grew up with that recounts the heroic exploits of a robber and his band of merry men who stole from the rich to give to the poor. It is an exciting story about a noble outlaw who was a champion of the poor and oppressed.[6] Unfortunately, the reality of robbery seldom lives up to this romantic image. **Robbery**, as we shall see, can occur in a number of different contexts, including the home, a public location, or a commercial establishment. Sometimes it involves offenders known to their victims, but more often it involves strangers, and the dynamics of each robbery event can vary dramatically.

On February 2, 2006, in Worcester, Massachusetts, a 61-year-old man was walking to work after leaving a Dunkin' Donuts store early in the morning. He noticed a Nissan Sentra following him and driving slowly, so he started walking faster. He turned down a side street thinking he would lose the car when two young men jumped out of the car and approached him. They wore dark clothing, headbands around their faces, and carried large kitchen knives. They demanded his money, and when he told them he didn't have any, they grabbed him from behind and put a knife to his throat. One of the men then punched him in the face and again demanded money. After going through his pockets and finding a small amount of cash, the assailants threw the elderly victim to the ground and fled in the Nissan. The man was able to describe the car and remembered the license plate number. The car was soon found and stopped; a large knife was discovered in the backseat. The two young men were arrested and charged with armed robbery.[7] In many ways, this is a fairly typical type of robbery, although this victim was fortunate because robberies can and sometimes do end in death. On June 2, 2006, seven family members, including three children, were shot dead in their home in Indianapolis, Indiana, during what appears to have been a robbery. The victims represented three generations of a family, from a 5-year-old boy to his 46-year-old grandmother, and the alleged robbers—who were later apprehended—believed the family had a large sum of money hidden in the house, which motivated their crime.[8]

In general, about 23% of homicides in which a circumstance has been identified were the result of another type of felony, most of them robberies.[9] Although most robberies don't result in death, they all involve the use of force or the threat of force. As John Conklin described over three decades ago, the crime of robbery incorporates two threatening elements: "the use of force against the victim and the theft of [their] property."[10] According to the NCVS, robbery is defined as follows: "Completed or attempted theft, directly from a person, of property or cash by force or threat of force, with or without a weapon, and with or without injury."[11] The element of force or attempted force is the reason robberies are considered crimes of violence and not simply property crimes. This violence distinguishes a purse snatching, in which an offender grabs a victim's purse and runs, from a robbery. A **burglary**, in which an offender(s) breaks into a residence and steals a homeowner's belongings, is a property crime because there is no force or threat of force to a person. However, a burglary can become a robbery if an offender finds someone in the house and uses or threatens to use force against that person during the commission of the crime. Unfortunately, this was what led to the terrible fate of the Indianapolis family who just happened to be home when the burglars arrived.

As you can imagine, there is a great deal of variability in the extent to which police officers classify particular victimizations as robberies instead of some other crime. For example, how would you classify a purse snatching that results in the victim sustaining an injury, such as a broken arm? Is this a crime of violence even though the offender did not "intend" to harm the victim? Which is more important? The intention or the outcome? What if a burglar has been casing a home and knows that the house is not occupied between the hours of 10:00 a.m. to 4:00 p.m.? Upon entering the home the next day, he is surprised to find the owner home from work early because she is sick. Should this be classified as an attempted robbery, making it a crime of violence? In many ways, the definition comes down to the discretion and judgment of the law enforcement officers at the scene, and obviously these decisions affect police report data on the prevalence and nature of robberies.

According to the NCVS—which you will recall is based on reports of victimization to interviewers regardless of whether the victimization was reported to police—although rates of robbery have declined since the highs witnessed in the early 1990s, since 2002 they have remained relatively stable. For example, the robbery rate per 1,000 individuals aged 12 and over in 2002 was 2.7 compared to a rate of 2.2 in 2011.[12] This translates into almost 500,000 robbery victimizations every year. Like all violent crime, young adults are more likely to experience a robbery compared to their older counterparts. According to the NCVS, those between the ages of 18 and 24 have the highest rates of robbery. Minority populations, especially African Americans and American Indians or Alaskan Natives, are also more vulnerable to robbery, which is consistent with what is known about various other forms of violence. The poor are more vulnerable to robbery victimizations compared to those with higher family incomes, and minorities who live under the poverty level are extremely vulnerable to robbery. In fact, African Americans whose family incomes are less than $15,000 are almost 10 times more likely than others to become robbery victims.[13] This is most likely because of the fact that robbers—like other types of violent offenders—usually perpetrate their violence in the same communities and neighborhoods in which they live. Additionally, the poor are less likely to be able to afford security systems for their homes and businesses, are more likely to live in apartments that make the residents more vulnerable in stairwells and hallways, and are more likely to shop in stores and eat in restaurants that are considered good locales for robbers because of a lack of adequate lighting or security personnel.

We also know that younger males are at a higher risk of experiencing a robbery compared with their younger female counterparts; however, this is not the case for the elderly. In fact, elderly males and females are equally vulnerable to robbery.[14] As you will see in the next section, the elderly—particularly elderly women—are often targeted by robbers. Marital status and geographical location are also related to robbery victimization. Not surprisingly, those living in urban locations are more likely to experience a robbery compared with either their suburban or rural counterparts. Being single, either through never marrying or being divorced or separated, also increases the risk of robbery.[15] This is probably related to the increased number of leisure activities in which single people engage outside of the home, particularly evening activities that place people at greater risk of victimization.

As we noted earlier, unlike other violent crimes, robbery is more likely to be perpetrated by strangers compared with known offenders. However, when gender-specific robberies are examined, a somewhat different picture emerges. While the majority of robbery victims are attacked by strangers, white robbery victims are more likely to be attacked by known offenders.[16]

While we often fear the nighttime, it is important to note that robberies are about equally likely to occur in the daytime as they are at night. Similarly, over four in 10 robberies occur at or near a personal residence compared to in public spaces. And finally, despite the fact that robberies involve both theft and violence, only about 60% of robbery victims reported their victimization to police.[17] This underscores the deficiency of relying exclusively on police report data to measure crimes of violence, even those most likely to be perpetrated by strangers.

If you were being robbed, what would you do? Would you run? Fight back? Scream for help? Or would you simply hand over what was demanded? According to the NCVS, about two in three robbery victims engaged in some type of **self-protective action**, but this included such things as appealing or reasoning with the

Table 6.1	The Percent Distribution of Robbery Victimizations Involving Strangers by Gender and Race, NCVS
	Percent Strangers
African American Victims	
Males	89
Females	64
White Victims	
Males	74
Females	42

offender. The majority of those who did take some action told interviewers that the action helped the situation in some way, including such things as avoiding injury and protecting their property.

About one in three robbery victims sustained an injury as the result of their victimization. This was true for both males and females. Interestingly, victims robbed by strangers were equally likely to be injured as the result of their victimization compared with those robbed by known offenders.[18] Perhaps this relates to victims being more willing to argue and/or resist a robbery from a friend or acquaintance. The greater familiarity with the perpetrator in these situations might engender less fear. Remember, however, that the NCVS obtains information on nonfatal injuries only and does not include the percentage of robberies that resulted in a victim's death.

Motivations for Robbery

In this section, we will focus exclusively on the motivations for typical street robberies involving individuals, sometimes referred to as **muggings** or **stickups**. While some robbers engage in both individual and commercial robberies, most typically engage in one or the other. Those who victimize primarily commercial establishments are very different in their level of sophistication and modus operandi compared with the typical street robber. In fact, after interviewing incarcerated robbers, Roger Matthews found that those who primarily targeted commercial establishments perceived themselves as more elite than the typical street mugger and even had disdain and contempt for robbers who primarily targeted individuals.[19] Some of the best information on robbers comes from a study by Richard Wright and Scott Decker, who interviewed over 80 active robbers in St. Louis, Missouri.[20] Not surprisingly, they found that, for the majority of those interviewed, the decision to commit an armed robbery was based on the desire to get cash and other valuables. This need for loot, however, was not usually about meeting long-term goals, such as an education or a home, but typically to satisfy immediate and often illicit gratification needs, such as gambling, drug use, or heavy drinking.

The majority of the offenders in Wright and Decker's sample spent most of their time on the street abiding by the "**code of the streets**," a term we discussed earlier in this book.[21] One of the "codes," you will recall, is protecting one's honor and reputation against acts of disrespect, even with violence if necessary. However, this environment is also characterized by other "codes" that members must abide by as well, one of which is what Wright and Decker refer to as "an open-ended quest for excitement and sensory stimulation," which tends to include things such as gambling, drug use, and heavy drinking.[22]

Jack Katz also observed this activity in his study of robbers. In fact, he interpreted the armed holdup as just another form of excitement in the lives of many of the men he studied.[23] Similar to Elijah Anderson, Wright and Decker interpreted this street culture as an attempt by many of the offenders to achieve a form of success in their lives that they could not attain through the legitimate routes to material success (e.g., a college education and good job). Because these traditional means of success were not available to them, the "code of the streets" had replaced the conventional moral order. Others have similarly described the street culture as the "enjoyment of good times with minimal concern for obligations and commitments."[24] This endless pursuit of excitement, of course, can't be pursued for long without money. Most of the offenders in Wright and Decker's study were under constant pressure to find money, which in turn often led them to commit robberies. Acting the part and enjoying the good times is only part of street culture; you also have to look the part. Researchers have found that outward appearances, such as dress and accessories, are also an important part of street culture.[25] A small percentage of the offenders interviewed by Wright and Decker also reported that they committed robbery to buy status items like the correct brand-named clothes and accessories, like jewelry.

Despite this tendency by robbery offenders to use the proceeds of their crimes for short-term gratification and nonessential status symbol items, several offenders in Wright and Decker's sample did rob to get money for essential needs. Some used the money to pay for rent or food, while one offender told Wright and Decker that he had recently committed several robberies in the past month because he was going to trial on assault charges and needed to pay for a private attorney because he didn't trust the ability of public defenders. One has to wonder if this brash young man understands the meaning of irony.

Obviously, robbery is not the only way to obtain money. Why not get a job instead of mugging people? The sample of robbers in Wright and Decker's study were all unskilled and poorly educated and as a result were not able to obtain suitable employment. Most of the jobs available to these individuals were menial with no opportunity for advancement or status. In fact, a third of the offenders claimed that they would stop robbing if they were given a good job. One offender specifically stated, "If I had a union job making sixteen or seventeen dollars an hour, something that I could really take care of my family with, I think that I could become cool with that."[26] We also need to understand that the "rush" or thrill provided by the danger of committing the robbery can also play a part in the decision-making process of robbers, as a number of researchers have found. Robbing someone, because of the inherent risk, can be quite a thrill, and this motivation shouldn't be discounted.

Robbery in Action

How do robbers choose their targets? Wright and Decker discovered that, for most offenders, the decision to rob was usually quick and involved little deliberation. When offenders found themselves in need of cash, they would rob the first suitable target that presented him/herself. **Routine activities theory**, you will recall, contends that there are three elements that are generally necessary for the commission of a crime to occur: a motivated offender; a suitable target; and lack of capable guardianship. Basically, this means that when someone wants to commit a robbery, they are more likely to go after someone they perceive as vulnerable who doesn't have any protective mechanism in place, such as bystanders. Importantly, the majority of the offenders in Wright and Decker's sample preyed upon those involved in criminal activity, such as drug dealing. In the inner city, where the majority of these offenders lived and robbed, drug dealing is a part of the scenery. As Bruce Jacobs notes

> [Drug dealers] deal strictly in cash and tend to have lots of it; drug selling is a high-volume, repeat business. Their merchandise is valuable, portable, and flexible; it can be used, sold, or both . . . Drug sellers cannot rely on bystanders to come to their aid; operative norms dictate that witnesses mind their own business or suffer the consequences. They have no recourse to the police either: black market entrepreneurs cannot be "victims" and therefore lack access to official means of grievance redress.[27]

Of course, robbing other criminally involved people, such as drug dealers, also carries risks. Not surprisingly, drug dealers tend to be armed and are often members of criminal groups that can protect them or retaliate with street justice. Nevertheless, many offenders viewed drug dealers and others engaged in criminal activity as easy targets. Other robbers, however, preferred law-abiding citizens as victims. In selecting a law-abiding citizen as a target, robbers first chose an area for the robbery and then a suitable victim. The areas selected were generally believed to be locations where people were more likely to carry large quantities of cash. Some preferred the downtown locations, where businesses and banks were located, while others preferred to stick to the marginalized and low-income neighborhoods, because the people there were more likely to carry cash compared with credit cards. As you might guess, check-cashing businesses and automatic teller machines were prime targets. In locating victims, offenders generally relied on external signs to identify who was most likely to be carrying cash; clothing, jewelry, and demeanor were indicators of this. For example, one offender described his judgment process like this:

> I'm a pretty good judge of character. I ain't come up empty-handed yet . . . My wife kids me about that: 'How'd you know they got money?' . . . I know by the way they dress and the way they act. They be dressed nice. Got on nice clothes, brand new clothes, and stuff like that. A lot of them act nervous and be walking real fast . . . people that got something you can tell cause they be looking behind them and all that, walking fast trying to get to their car.[28]

Two demographics—gender and age—also affected the vulnerability attached to potential victims. Women were generally thought to be more defenseless than males, and elderly people were perceived as weaker than their younger counterparts. Of these two characteristics, age was probably the most important, as many offenders noted the attraction to elderly victims. For example, one offender noted, "When I need to find a robbery victim, I look for an older person . . . because you don't have to worry about struggling with them and being real forceful with them. They might just give the money to you anyway, to keep from being hurt I guess."[29]

When an appropriate victim has been selected, the next issue for potential robbers is figuring out the best way to pull off the crime without getting caught. To make sure victims comply, robbers must use violence or the threat of violence. The robbers interviewed by Wright and Decker generally used two methods to approach their victims and take control of the situation. The first was to sneak up on their victims, usually from the rear to avoid being detected. In this way, victims had no advance warning and were therefore unable to evade their attackers. The other method used by robbers involved trying to fit into the social setting and looking normal and nonthreatening, sometimes asking the intended victims a question, such as directions or the time. The modus operandi of robbers has not changed much since these tactics were uncovered almost three decades ago by David Luckenbill in his study of robbers and their behavior.[30]

The next step in the robbery was to announce the stickup and establish dominance and control over the situation. According to Wright and Decker, most offenders typically opened their armed robberies with a demand that victims stop and listen to them and then quickly summarize the situation for the victim. For example, one robber often informed his victims, "This is a robbery, don't make it a murder!"[31] The majority of assailants also used a gun, the bigger the better. If a potential victim refused to comply, the robbery offenders most often responded with brutality. One offender stated, "You would be surprised how cooperative a person will be once he been smashed across the face with a .357 Magnum."[32] While a few of the offenders in Wright and Decker's study had been involved in armed robberies that resulted in the death of a victim, these were rare, and the vast majority of offenders never intended to seriously injure, much less kill, their victims. Once the money and/or other goods were taken from the target, robbers need to quickly make their getaway. While some robbers reported that they made the victims leave the scene first, most preferred to be the ones to flee first. To do this successfully, they first had to make sure that the victim wouldn't attempt to follow them or make a scene. Most robbers accomplished this by threatening the victims with their lives, while others tied their victims up or incapacitated them through injury.

Female Robbery Offenders

While the majority of all robbers are male, females represented about 13% of the robbery offenders recalled by robbery victims in the NCVS. To determine whether motivations and methods of offending were different for male and female robbers, Jody Miller analyzed 14 interviews with active female robbers from Wright and Decker's sample described above. Because of this small sample, it is hard to know how representative these women are of female robbers in general, but her research does reveal some interesting gender differences in robbery offending. Miller found that the motivations for robbery were essentially the same for male and female robbers; however, their modus operandi was different.[33] She found that the most common form of female robbery was to rob other females in a physically confrontational manner. While male robbery is more likely to involve guns in all situations, the females in Miller's sample most often relied on knives when robbing other women. Like their male counterparts, female robbers selected female targets primarily because they believed they were less likely to be armed and less likely to resist.

Another tactic employed by female robbers was to target males by appearing sexually available. In these scenarios, the female robbers almost always armed themselves with a gun but kept themselves at a safe distance from their male prey to prevent physical resistance and also to prevent having the gun taken from them.

About half of the female robbers in Miller's sample also robbed other men with male accomplices, although they rarely used accomplices for the robbery of females. In these scenarios, the crime most often resembled the typical male robbery, with close physical contact and frequent use of violence. In sum, female robbers committed their offenses for the same reasons as their male counterparts; however, the way they carried out their crimes was different, depending on the gender of their victims.

Preventing Robbery

Some of the leading theories that attempt to explain criminality were reviewed in Chapter 2, and many of them can be applied to the specific crime of robbery. However, because robberies are all about getting money, valuables, and other resources, those theories that link offending behavior to economic deprivation or to the disjuncture between the material goals of society and the unequal availability of the means to achieve these goals are particularly salient for explaining robbery. These explanations include anomie and general strain theories. Simon Hallsworth, who has extensively studied robbery in Great Britain, outlines the connection between robbery and economics nicely when he states

> the street robbery problem in its contemporary form is a problem of a society that induces young people to desire and covet the very goods they have been pressurized from an early age to associate with the good life. The kind of designer branded objects, in other words, they have been led to desire through their exposure to the capitalist culture industries that target them remorselessly and relentlessly. At the same time . . . this is a society which, while inducing a universal desire on the part of young people to build their lifestyles and establish their identities through consumptions, does not equip everyone with the wherewithal to consume legitimately.[34]

This sentiment is very much like that articulated by Messner and Rosenfeld in their institutional theory of anomie that was discussed in Chapter 2. The assumption behind these theories is that if all citizens had equal access to a quality education and a good job that would allow them to provide a good life for themselves and their families, rates of robbery would most certainly decrease.

Other theories, however, propose alternative measures. Rational choice theory, you will recall, contends that would-be offenders will be deterred from committing an offense if the costs of the crime outweigh the benefits. This theory assumes, of course, that offenders make decisions rationally. The fact that most of the offenders in Wright and Decker's study were under a lot of financial pressure so that the perceived monetary reward of the robbery generally outweighed the perceived risk of incarceration doesn't seem to support this perspective. Similarly, those who engage in robberies in order to maintain their drug and/or alcohol addictions also cannot be said to be rational in their decision-making process. Nevertheless, while the majority of robbers anticipated getting arrested in the future, most of them did not perceive this as a real threat or cost. The offenders in the study spent their lives on the street, and their lives were riddled with insecurity, poverty, and disorganization. In fact, most didn't even have a home and as a result had to depend on the charity of friends and family for a place to stay. As a result, many never slept more than two or three nights in the same place. For them, prison was seen as a "pleasant break from the turmoil and physical dangers that marked their day-to-day existence on the street."[35] When we understand this reality, it's easy to see why the threat of being arrested and sent to prison does not represent a real deterrent to committing robbery. Some may respond to this by recommending that penalties for robbery be increased to make it a more tangible threat. However, the penalties for robbery are already very extreme. Except for the crime of murder, convicted robbers are more likely to be sentenced to prison compared with offenders convicted of other crimes of violence, including rapists.[36] Even if penalties were increased for robbery, remember that these offenders are generally under tremendous financial duress and typically see no other alternative to robbery, so their immediate needs will probably outweigh the threat of formal sanctions they perceive to begin with (i.e., arrest and prison), regardless of how stiff the penalties are.

In contrast to understanding the underlying causes of criminology, **situational crime prevention** seeks to understand technical and structural solutions to crime and in response design environments or products in ways that minimize the risk of victimization.[37] Measures such as installing cameras in crime-prone areas are among such techniques. While cameras have proven effective in some commercial areas, critics contend that their presence simply moves street crime outside the camera range.[38] Other situational changes, such as improving lighting, may also deter some offenders—but again, they may simply move to less well-lit areas to do their dirty deeds. In other words, some of these changes may simply displace crime to other less protected areas.

One interesting idea advanced by Wright and Decker to reduce robbery is to replace cash in the economy with electronic monetary transfers like credit and debit cards. On most college campuses, for example, students can get debit cards that the university uses to pay for meals and other university services. Many states also now administer a form of debit card to food stamp recipients; this serves not only to reduce the risk of robbery but also reduces the stigma associated with paying with food stamps in checkout lines. Wright and Decker state that, "Many armed robbers already regard the theft of checkbooks and credit cards to be more trouble than it is worth. In a truly cashless society, the vast majority of them almost surely would come to view these instruments as having no practical value whatsoever."[39]

Bank Robbery

You only have to think of movies such as *Heat, PointBreak, Set It Off, The Town, Public Enemies,* or *Citizen Gangster* to realize how iconic the bank robber is in popular culture. Part of this can be traced back to the era of the Great Depression when bank robbers such as John Dillinger, Bonnie and Clyde, Pretty Boy Floyd, and others were perceived as latter-day folk heroes who stood up for the ordinary person against the big banks. Banks were associated with big business and government authority and, in an era when poverty, job loss, foreclosures, and hopelessness were prevalent, many bank robbers were seen as underdogs fighting a cruel and unjust system. Times, however, have changed. Nowadays, **bank robberies** rarely capture much media attention unless they result in multiple deaths or a shootout with police that happens to be captured by video. Despite the lack of media coverage and more sophisticated security systems, bank robberies are still relatively common. In 2011, for example, over 200 people were attacked in over 5,000 bank robberies and other financial institutions. Today, California has the highest number of bank robberies compared to other states. For example, in 2011, California had 697 bank robberies compared to the state of New York, which had only 339 robberies.[40] Why California? According to one FBI agent who spent years investigating bank robberies, this is primarily because of the "easy mobility of the freeway culture, the loose state banking regulations that allow a branch bank or a savings and loan or a credit union on nearly every corner—almost 3,500 of them in the L.A. area by the latest count—the laid-back attitudes that discourage banks from installing bullet-resistant Plexiglas bandit barriers or access control doors."[41]

While the majority of bank robbers are males, about 7% are female. The relatively rare female bank robber does tend to generate more media attention simply because of their novelty. For example, images of one young female bank robber, who became known as the "Ponytail Bandit" made media headlines after she had conducted bank robberies in three states: Texas, California, and Washington. The FBI reported, "She's a pretty young woman whose shoulder-length blonde ponytail sprouts from the back of her baseball cap in images captured by banks she allegedly robbed. . . . She approaches bank tellers, demands money, then waits, arms crossed, slouching slightly, as tellers comply."[42] A baseball cap with a ponytail doesn't seem like much of a disguise, but after examining snapshots of bank robberies in action at the FBI website for wanted bank robbers, it is amazing how few of them actually wear disguises that effectively conceal their identity.

❖ Photo 6.1   Wanted photo for an unknown bank robber who robbed a Chase Bank in Houston, Texas on December 20, 2012

The photo of one lone bank robber caught on tape in Houston, Texas after robbing a Chase Bank on December 12, 2012, is but one example. Clearly, this guy, who was armed with a semiautomatic pistol, thought a black baseball cap was enough. Evidently, he wasn't thinking much about security cameras when he planned his crime.[43]

Most bank robberies involve a single individual waiting in line for a teller and passing a note to the teller letting them know that they are being robbed. This kind of robbery happens very quickly, and most customers usually don't even know that a robbery is taking place. A takeover robbery, on the other hand, involves several armed individuals seizing control of a bank. While the risks are greater, there is also a potentially larger payoff, since this kind of robbery allows the perpetrators to gain access to all of the registers as well as the vault.[44] One notorious and extremely violent bank robbery occurred in the North Hollywood section of Los Angeles in 1997. At 9:15 a.m. on Friday, February 8, two heavily armed and masked men entered a Bank of America branch in a takeover bank robbery attempt.[45] The two men were dressed all in black, including ski masks, and had also protected themselves with body armor.

One of the men was a Romanian emigrant named Emil Matasareanu and the other was a young man named Larry Phillips Jr. They had met while bodybuilding at a Gold's Gym and became friends who shared not only their mutual pursuit of weightlifting but a taste for armed robberies as well. The North Hollywood takeover was not their first. They were armed with AK-47 automatic assault rifles and pistols and plenty of ammunition. Upon entering, they began shouting for everybody to get down and cover their eyes. They also opened fire with their AK-47s and shot into the ceiling and the Plexiglas barriers between the lobby and the employee area. The golden rule of bank robberies is that the perpetrators need to leave within two minutes in order to beat the police response time to the silent alarms that are invariably triggered. By the time Matasareanu and Phillips had cleaned out the vault and exited the bank, some 15 minutes had elapsed. This doesn't sound like a long time, but for bank robberies it is an eternity; when the two masked men went outside over two dozen police vehicles and officers confronted them. Instead of surrendering or running back inside, the two young men simply opened fire with their automatic weapons. In a scene inspired by the movie *Heat*, a film often watched by Matasareanu and Phillips, a gun battle erupted which lasted for just under an hour.

The police were dramatically outgunned. So much so, in fact, that a number of officers went to a nearby gun store to acquire heavier weapons. The body armor worn by the two assailants allowed them to shrug off repeated hits to the torso, and after about 40 minutes of exchanging fire with the police, Matasareanu got in the car and began slowly driving while Phillips followed behind and continued to fire. Eventually they split up. Shortly thereafter Phillips shot himself in the head after his assault rifle jammed and he realized that there was no escaping the police. Matasareanu was also unable to escape, since the police shot out his tires, and he was unable to commandeer another vehicle. He was arrested after being wounded more than 29 times. Cuffed and lying face down in the street, he quickly bled to death. Although 11 officers and six civilians were wounded, amazingly, aside from Matasareanu and Phillips, no one was killed.[46] Considering how many rounds were fired, this fact is truly remarkable. Banks, it should be noted, are not the only places of employment that experience violent crime, and it is to the broader issue of workplace violence that we now direct our attention.

Workplace Violence

The most notorious types of workplace violence are mass shootings that receive a great deal of media attention and which are often referred to as "going postal."

Because these types of killing were discussed at length in Chapter 4 as a type of mass murder, they are not the focus of this particular discussion. Generally speaking, except for a few jobs that we typically think of as being dangerous, like policing for example, most of us don't think of the workplace as an inherently risky place. Most violence, as we have seen in this book, tends to occur while people are not working. But we shouldn't ignore the reality that being violently attacked while working is still far from uncommon. In 2011, for example, out of the 4,609 workplace fatalities that occurred around the country, most were caused by accidents, but 780 of these deaths were because of violence. Specifically, 458 were workplace homicides, while 242 were the result of suicide.[47] This means that about 17% of workplace deaths were a consequence of violence, of which homicides account for 10%. The remainder of workplace fatalities were generally the consequence of transportation accidents, fires and explosions, accidental hits by machinery or other equipment, falls, slips, trips, and exposure to toxic substances.[48] Breaking these statistics down further reveals some interesting and important characteristics. Firearms were the most common weapon for both homicides and suicides, at 78% and 45% respectively. As with so many crimes of violence, firearms were the preferred method of killing in the workplace. Important gender differences also emerge when the data from the Bureau of Labor Statistics are examined. In 2011, of the 375 fatal work injuries suffered by females, 21% of them were homicides compared to only 9% homicide fatalities for males. In other words, while males were more likely to die from work-related injuries, rarely (9%) was it the result of a homicide. In contrast, almost one fourth of women who died from injuries sustained in the workplace were victims of homicide. This pattern makes more sense when we look at the relationship pattern of these killings. In almost 2 out of every 5 female workplace homicides, the perpetrator was a relative—almost always an intimate partner or an ex. This can be compared with male homicide victims at work whose relatives perpetrated the crime in only 2% of the cases. One study looking at workplace killings of females from 2003 to 2008 found that the leading cause were robberies, followed closely by intimate partner homicides.[49] Essentially, what we are seeing is that many of the deaths experienced by women while at work are the result of domestic violence.

Table 6.2 presents the percent of workplace violence incidents reported to the NCVS by gender of victim and victim/offender relationship. You can see that female victims of workplace violence are somewhat more likely to face known offenders, even at work, while male victims are more likely to face strangers. Keep in mind that this table also includes nonfatal incidents of violence, whereas the discussion above focused solely on lethal workplace incidents. When nonfatal workplace violence is examined, we find that the majority of these victimizations are assaults, which mirror nonfatal violence in other settings.[50] However, the majority of known offenders for both males and females are people at work, primarily current or former coworkers.

Table 6.2   Percent of Workplace Violence by Gender of Victim and Victim/
            Offender Relationship, NCVS

	Male Victims (%)	Female Victims (%)
Intimate Partner or Family	1.4	2.4
Friend/Acquaintance	11.7	18.9
Work Relationship		
Customer/Patient	5.4	12.5
Coworker	20.1	19.3
Stranger	52.9	40.9
Unknown Relationship	8.5	6.1

SOURCE: Harrell, *Workplace Violence, 2005–2009*, Bureau of Justice Statistics, U.S. Department of Justice.

Which occupations are most vulnerable to workplace violence? To examine the risk of victimization, we can't simply rely on the total number of victims in each occupation category since different jobs employ different numbers of people. We therefore need to control for the total number of people who work in a particular occupation category by generating rates of victimization by occupation. Table 6.3 presents these rates generated from NCVS data for particular types of occupations. As you can see, there is a great deal of variability of risk across occupation categories. When these categories are examined even closer, we find that particular occupations within each umbrella category are responsible for this variability. Not surprisingly, those who teach in elementary schools are much less vulnerable to being attacked compared to high school teachers. One group that might surprise you as being at a relatively high risk is people in health professions, such as mental health workers. Nurses are also particularly at risk, especially those who work in emergency rooms.[51] This tends to make more sense when we realize that people admitted to emergency rooms, for example, are sometimes high or intoxicated, suffering from mental illness, or going through withdrawals and detoxing, all of which can increase the risk of violent assault. Specifically, people in retail sales have the highest risk for robbery victimization, while law enforcement personnel have the highest assault risk.[52] Even within job categories, however, risks can vary. For example, not all retail sales positions are at equal risk for violence. Statistics indicate that within retail sales positions bartenders appear particularly vulnerable to workplace violence as do gas station attendants. Also, while those in law enforcement appear to be especially vulnerable to violence on the job, police officers are over twice as likely to be victimized as corrections officers.

Table 6.3	Rates of Nonfatal Workplace Violence per 1,000 Employed Persons Age 16 or Older, NCVS 2005–2009
Occupation Categories	**Rate**
Medical	6.5
Mental Health	20.5
Teaching	6.5
Law Enforcement	47.7
Retail Sales	7.7
Transportation	12.2
Other	2.8

SOURCE: Harrell, *Workplace Violence, 2005–2009*, Bureau of Justice Statistics, U.S. Department of Justice.

Part of this relative risk depends on the nature of the job. We find that there are certain kinds of job characteristics that increase the likelihood of victimization.[53] These can include interacting with the public in positions that involve money, such as working a cash register. Being alone or with only a few other coworkers is also a risk factor, as is working late at night and early in the morning. Jobs located in high crime areas heighten the risk as well. A position that requires an employee to be out and about in the community, such as driving a taxicab, makes the job a bit more dangerous. Having to deal with criminals and/or people with mental issues is a risk factor. Think of the people that law enforcement has to interact with in the course of patrolling a beat and you get the idea. Guarding property or delivering goods and services increases risk. Keep in mind that these factors don't influence risk individually. A taxicab driver, for example, usually works alone and may be driving in high crime areas at night picking up and delivering passengers who may or may not be criminal or unstable. Needless to say, driving a cab can pose a bit more risk than a job in which a person avoids these kinds of higher risk scenarios.

Violent Hate Crimes

One night in June 1998, James Byrd Jr., a 49-year-old African American, declined a ride home from a friend during a party and later started to walk home alone on Martin Luther King Boulevard in Jasper, Texas. A gray pickup truck driven by Shawn Berry, the 23-year-old manager of a local movie theater, and two other men Byrd did not know pulled up and Berry asked Byrd whether he wanted a ride. When Byrd climbed into the back of the truck, Berry gave him a beer. Byrd's decapitated body was found the next morning; his head and one of his arms were found over one mile away from the rest of his body. At the scene where an obvious struggle had initiated the crime, cigarette butts and a lighter with the symbols for the Ku Klux Klan and the word "Possum" etched in the dirt were found. Later, Berry's written confession detailed the facts: He and two other men, Bill King and Russell Brewer, had picked Byrd up on Martin Luther King Boulevard; they then drove him up to Huff Creek Road, beat him up in a clearing, spray-painted his face black, and then dragged him with a logging chain tied to his ankles about 3 miles before they dumped his body at the side of the road.[54] Byrd's head and arm had been cut off when his body was pulled over a sharp metal culvert.

The nation, the state of Texas, and the town of Jasper were all outraged that such a horrific crime could have taken place. The country showed an outpouring of support for Byrd's family in particular, and for the African American community of Jasper in general. To demonstrate their support, thousands wore yellow ribbons, and at Byrd's funeral, speeches about reconciliation and healing were given by dignitaries, including Jesse Jackson and Senator Kay Bailey Hutchison, and a letter from then President Bill Clinton was read. For their crimes, King and Brewer were sentenced to die and Berry was sentenced to life in prison. In the end, however, James Byrd Jr. was buried on the black side of the Jasper City Cemetery, "still segregated in 1998."[55]

The brutal murder of James Byrd Jr. brought the term "hate crime" to the forefront of public consciousness in the United States. Unfortunately, within four months, the nation would be shocked by yet another brutal murder motivated by hate—this time against gays. The victim in this case was a 21-year-old college student named Matthew Shepard, who attended the University of Wyoming. On the evening of October 7, 1998, Russell Henderson and Aaron McKinney went to a known gay bar with the intent of targeting a gay man for robbery. They met Shepard there and offered him a ride home. Instead of taking him home, however, they took him to a remote area, tied him to a fence post, and pistol-whipped him in the head to unconsciousness and then left him there to die. Shepard was found over 18 hours later by a cyclist. He never regained consciousness and died four days later on October 12. Henderson and McKinney were found guilty of first-degree murder and sentenced to life in prison without the possibility of parole.[56]

Although none of the defendants in the Byrd or Shepard murders received enhanced sentences for their crimes, today nearly every state and the federal government have laws that require sentencing enhancements for offenders who commit crimes motivated by hate. As such, an ordinary crime becomes a **hate crime** when offenders select a victim because of some characteristic, such as their race or religion. Each state has its own definition of what characteristics are included within its hate crime legislation; however, the FBI's definition is a useful starting point:

> A hate crime, also known as a **bias crime**, is a criminal offense committed against a person, property, or society that is motivated, in whole or in part, by the offender's bias against a race, religion, disability, sexual orientation, or ethnicity/national origin.[57]

Many states include other characteristics within their hate crime statutes, including age, gender, political affiliation, and transgender/gender identity. As the statute notes, bias crime is sometimes used as another term for hate crime. The first major hate crime legislation passed at the federal level was called the **Hate Crime Statistics Act of 1990**. The law directed the attorney general to collect data "about crimes

❖ **Photo 6.2** Site where Matthew Shepard was killed

that manifest evidence of prejudice based on race, religion, sexual orientation, or ethnicity." In September 1994, Congress passed the **Violent Crime Control and Law Enforcement Act**, which amended the Hate Crime Statistics Act to include both physical and mental disabilities.

The most recent law enacted at the federal level against hate crimes is called the **Matthew Shepard & James Byrd, Jr. Hate Crimes Prevention Act** that was signed into law by President Obama in March of 2010. The law expanded already existing federal hate crime legislation to include violence based on gender, sexual orientation, gender identity, and disability in addition to the already existing criteria based on race and religion. After signing the legislation, President Obama stated, "After more than a decade of opposition and delay, we've passed inclusive hate crimes legislation to help protect our citizens from violence based on what they look like, who they love, how they pray, and who they are."[58]

As mandated by the **Church Arson Prevention Act of 1996**, the FBI's Uniform Crime Reporting (UCR) program began collecting statistics on offenses motivated by bias against physical and mental disabilities in January 1997. However, remember that the UCR collects data only on those incidents that are reported to the police, which is only a small percentage of victimizations. In 2011, the FBI reported that there were nearly 8,000 incidents of hate crime reported to police. Over half of these were racial/ethnicity bias incidents (56%), around 19% were religiously motivated, and another 21% were bias against sexual orientation.[59] The NCVS also added questions to its interview guide that now asks victims of crime whether they perceive their victimization to have been motivated by hate. From both of these sources of data, we now know more about the characteristics of hate crime victimization in the United States.

The NCVS defines hate crimes as those incidents in which victims believe the offender selected them for victimization because of one or more of their personal characteristics, including race, ethnicity, religion, sexual orientation, or disability. This definition also includes incidents in which the offender perceives the victim as belonging to or associated with a group largely identified by one of these characteristics. Before a crime is classified as hate related, corroborating evidence of hate motivation must also be present at the time of the incident, including at least one of the following:

- The offender used derogatory language.
- The offender left hate symbols.
- The police confirmed that a hate crime had taken place.

Genocide and murder, of course, are the most extreme forms of hate crime and are discussed elsewhere in this book. Most nonfatal violent hate crime described by victims in the NCVS accompanied violent crimes, with the majority of these being assaults. On average, this translates into over 176,000 violent crime victimizations motivated by hatred that occurred in the United States.[60] As such, hate crime represents about 3% of all violent crime annually. Based on both the NCVS data and reports of hate crime to police, the motivation for the majority of hate crimes was racial bias. Similar to the UCR estimates above, over 55% of hate crimes recorded by the NCVS were perceived by hate crime victims to have been motivated by race. About one-third of hate crimes were perceived to have been motivated simply because of the victim's association with persons who have certain characteristics—that is, they were attacked simply because they had a relationship with someone with a hated characteristic, such as race, sexual orientation, or religion. African Americans tend to be the most frequent target of racially motivated hate crimes, while Jews are the most common victims of religiously based attacks.

As we stated at the beginning of the chapter, unlike violent crimes in general, in which the majority of offenders are known to the victim, violent crimes motivated by hate are more often perpetrated by strangers.[61] About 52% of violent hate crimes reported to the NCVS involved strangers. Violent hate crime is also more likely to involve multiple offenders than other violent crime. For example, about 33% of violent hate crime incidents involved more than one offender compared with only 19% of violent victimizations that were not motivated by hate.[62] Although most offenders are prosecuted for hate crimes at the state level, hate crime charges are also brought against offenders at the federal level. Moreover, hate crime prosecutions are successfully being made for victimizations not typically thought of as motivated by hate. For example, on September 20, 2012, Samuel Mullet Sr., a leader of a so-called "renegade Amish sect," along with 15 of his followers was convicted in federal court of hate crimes for terrorizing another Amish community in eastern Ohio by forcefully shaving the beards of men and cutting the hair of both men and women. While the crimes themselves constituted assaults, the jury convicted the "renegade sect members" of hate crime because they were attempting to "suppress the victims' practice of religion." The U.S. attorney described the incidents quite graphically, "The defendants invaded their homes, physically attacked these people and sheared them almost like animals." This is a significant victimization in traditional Amish communities because "men's long beards and women's uncut hair are central to religious identity." One female victim recounted how the attackers forcefully entered her home at night, with several of them holding both she and her husband down, shaved her husband's beard with clippers and then cut his hair while he repeated prayers and then cut her hair with shears used to cut a horse's mane.[63]

Preventing Hate Crime

At some level, all violence is the result of an "us" versus "them" mentality. Perpetrators usually see their victims as being different and somehow of lesser worth or value. They also tend to perceive the victim as having brought on their own victimization. Remember back to Chapter 1 when we pointed out that many who commit violence tend to understand their actions as being necessary or justified.

IN FOCUS 6.1

The Internet, Hate Groups, and the Emergence of the Lone Wolf

The Internet is providing society with a host of new possibilities, but not all of them are positive. Unfortunately the Internet's promise of anonymity provides many hate groups with the visibility often denied them in regular media channels and allows them to introduce their propaganda to thousands. According to the Southern Poverty Law Center, the number of websites devoted to hate group propaganda continues to increase at a rapid pace. The Internet has also allowed hate groups to recruit through mass emailing and to establish a sense of community through cyber bulletin boards and chat rooms for people hundreds of miles apart. Of course, this visibility has also allowed researchers access to their world. Through the messages and images presented on hate sties, we now have more information about how they recruit new members, how they build a sense of community, and how they compel individuals to action.[1]

Tolerence.org delineates five reasons why hate groups and hate speech can flourish on the web. All of these conditions have increased the effectiveness of recruiting so-called "*lone wolves*," who are individuals who take part in a movement but remain largely anonymous. Many hate groups encourage "lone wolf" action by telling their members, "Don't keep membership lists, don't go to rallies or meetings where you can be observed, and, should you decide to break the law, be sure not to tell anyone about it."[2]

1) **Privacy:** Even though many sites remain open for anyone to post information or participate in a chat room, many are now requiring a screening and approval process for participants, thereby allowing greater privacy from public scrutiny.

2) **Persuasion:** Open discussions on the web allow extremists to more personally talk with individuals who may feel alienated from the rest of society, but may not be convinced that an affiliation with a hate group is the way to go. The immediate availability of this communication makes such propaganda much more persuasive.

3) **Anonymity:** Although access to Internet traffic has the potential to be subpoenaed in a court of law, most people do not perceive that this will ever happen to them. Most people believe their interaction on the web will remain anonymous. This perceived anonymity serves to increase participation in hate groups. Obviously, having to attend a meeting, such as a Ku Klux Klan rally, to get involved in an organization would be perceived as more of an obstacle to reluctant participants compared to chatting over the Internet.

4) **Planning:** The Internet allows groups the ability to organize and plan activities, such as rallies, concerts, and lectures, more effectively than traditional methods of communication.

5) **Support:** All of us feel the need to be part of a community. Internet chat rooms facilitate this formation of community for its participants and provide reinforcements for extremist ideas that would not be tolerated in the larger society.

NOTE:

1. For an example of these types of analyses, see J. Adams and V. J. Roscigno, "White Supremacists, Oppositional Culture, and the World Wide Web," *Social Forces* 84 (2005): 759–778.
2. Southern Poverty Law Center, *Intelligence Report: Lone Wolves.* Downloaded February 13, 2007, from www.splcenter.org/intel/intelreport/article.jsp?aid=239

This is a common tendency among many different kinds of offenders, whether the bully in the schoolyard, the genocidal killer, or the hate criminal. The victims are typically seen as having caused the violence against them because of what they've done or said or perhaps simply because of how they look. In their own minds, these offenders are only being violent as a kind of righteous payback or retaliation. We can certainly see this in action when we look at the connection between economic conditions and **xenophobia**, the tendency to have contempt for foreigners or other strangers, which is particularly likely in times of economic hardship, when resources are scarce. Researchers have found that groups tend to develop much more reactive and punitive attitudes during uncertain economic times, periods of high crime rates, and eras of social and cultural change.[64] Uncertainty and fear, in other words, tends to breed and strengthen hostility and anger against those defined as being dangerous, threatening, or different. Thus, although hate crimes may not be directly linked to economic needs like many robberies, tougher economic times do increase the likelihood of hate crimes and other forms of violence. We find, for example, that in the United States, **negative stereotypes** of immigrant populations and crimes against them have both been shown to increase during times of economic depression. For example, during the depressions of 1893 and 1907, the latest immigrants from Italy were the targets, while the depression of the 1920s set the stage for the recent immigrants from the Mediterranean and Slavic nations to become the scapegoats. During more recent economic hard times, Latin American immigrants, both legal and illegal, have become the target of the moment. This correlation between economic hardship and xenophobia has been observed at other times in the United States and in other countries around the world.[65] In many ways, then, certain kinds of hate crimes are motivated by the fear surrounding economic uncertainty and cultural change. Ironically, perpetrators of this kind of violence often define themselves as being the victims and the groups they target are seen as being the perpetrator because of the social, cultural, and demographic changes they represent.[66] This tendency is made easier by preexisting prejudices and stereotypes against minority groups. One particularly potent example of this concerns anti-Semitism.

Anti-Semitism refers to derogatory speech and action targeted against Jews and relies on very old images and prejudices. In fact, anti-Semitism has sometimes been referred to as the longest hatred.[67] Because anti-Semitism has been around such a long time, many people are at least somewhat familiar with the negative images and stereotypes associated with the Jews, even if they are not necessarily anti-Semites themselves. This means that when times get tough or tragedies happen, these old ideas are easily resurrected to explain what happened and why. Globalization, for example, and all of the resulting economic and social changes and dislocation are not always easily understood or explained. They are scary phenomena for many people who see their jobs or way of life being threatened by the changes. This has only been worsened by the 2008 financial collapse and the widespread anger directed against Wall Street and the banking industry. An easy way to make sense of what happened and have a target to focus anger against is to scapegoat a group for the economic downturn. Scapegoating can be used by political, social, and religious leaders in order to capitalize on old prejudices and further their own goals, whatever those might be. One anti-Semitic theme, for example, that has been relied on in recent years portrays the Jews as rich and exploitative industrialists and bankers responsible for our economic problems. After the collapse of Lehman Brothers and other large investment banks, a rumor spread across the Internet that just prior to the collapse, $400 billion dollars was secretly transferred to Israeli banks. Similarly, in the wake of the Bernie Madoff scandal in 2008, a great deal of anti-Semitic postings appeared on various Internet forums.[68] The fact that Bernie Madoff is a Jewish businessman who created a $50 billion Ponzi scheme allowed for a great deal of anti-Semitic comments to be voiced that included, "Just another jew money changer thief. It's been happening for 3,000 years. Trust a Jew and this is what will happen. History has proven it over and over. Jews have only one god—money," and in a similar vein "Madoff is another Jew banker ... The Sec [SEC] is filled with Jewish gatekeepers who routinely turn a blind eye to jewish financial bandits ... It's no conspiracy that the Jews are the source of all the financial troubles in the world."[69] It's no accident that the Anti-Defamation League (ADL) has tracked an increase in anti-Semitic hate crime in the wake of the 2008 downturn. Even the recent shooting at Sandy Hook Elementary was an occasion for anti-Semites to lay the blame for this massacre at the foot of Jews.[70] The problem with the kind of stereotypes and prejudices that lead to hate crimes is that they are remarkably enduring. In many ways they are like a forest fire that, after the flames have been doused, continues to smolder underground for a long time. You think it's been eradicated, but then given the right conditions, those smoldering embers can burst into flame again. So too with prejudice. Education, legal changes, and tolerance training can all be used to combat intolerance and hatred so that it goes underground. But given the right economic, social, and political conditions, those old prejudices can quickly be resurrected. There are many reasons why these ideas persist. One explanation relates to a deep-seated instinct among groups to distinguish between who is and who is not included.

The tendency to separate ourselves into in-groups and out-groups is very strong. Jack Levin and Gordana Rabrenovic state, "If no ethnic or religious differences exist, humans will invent them to set up a hierarchy of those of us who are the richest, most intelligent, most morally superior, best hunters, and so on."[71] However, this predisposition to view the world into "us versus them" does not inextricably result in hate. Levin and Rabrenovic conclude, "Hating 'the other' is learned behavior, pure and simple . . . Haters learn such ideas either early in life from their parents or later in life from their friends, classmates, teachers, religious leaders, and the mass media."[72] As such, the elements responsible for socialization, including family, school, religious organizations, and society as a whole each play roles in creating hate. In fact, we all play a role. It is important to remember that everyday acts of prejudice and bigotry are also related to acts of hate-motivated violence. When we allow bigoted comments and jokes to be told without comment, we are acting as bystanders to hate. When a classmate makes an anti-Semitic comment; when your roommate insults something by saying "That's so gay"; when a coworker uses racial and ethnic slurs in casual conversation; when the coach of a child's baseball team tells a player that he throws like a girl—each of these seemingly small instances helps to foster prejudiced environments where hateful attitudes and behavior are more likely to flourish. Each presents an opportunity to step out of the role of a bystander into one of action. We will have more to say about the role of bystanders in Chapter 10 on genocide.

In U.S. society, the **First Amendment** protects a citizen's right to free speech, including hate speech. This is a fundamental right that we believe should never be jeopardized. Nevertheless, there are ways in which communities can respond to events, such as rallies and other gatherings, which promote hate. The **Southern Poverty Law Center** has published methods that have been successfully used by communities to combat hate groups. For example, if a hate group such as a white supremacist organization plans a demonstration, an alternative event can be organized that encourages multiculturalism. Hate crime victimizations should also be responded to by the community, not just by law enforcement. This is important to not only show unity within the community against hate, but also send a message to the hate crime victims that their community cares about them.[73]

Conclusions

In this chapter, we have provided an overview of several types of interpersonal violence that are more likely to be perpetrated by strangers. It is important to remember that while these crimes are more likely to be committed by strangers, known offenders still perpetrate a significant proportion of these crimes. This chapter has also illustrated the fact that, while robbery is clearly motivated by the prospect of economic gain on the part of the offender, crimes that are not so obviously linked, such as hate crimes, are also inextricably related to economic hardship. Thus, while the installation of crime prevention techniques like closed-circuit cameras in crime-prone areas may reduce the likelihood of crime occurring in particular areas, these attempts do little to ameliorate the underlying sources of violence that exist in society, like inequality. Finally, we concluded the chapter with steps we each can take to promote unity within our communities, thereby promoting an environment where those who hate will not be tolerated.

Key Terms

bank robberies

bias crime

burglary

Church Arson Prevention Act of 1996

code of the streets

First Amendment

hate crimes

Hate Crime Statistics Act of 1990

Matthew Shepard & James Byrd, Jr. Hate Crimes Prevention Act

muggings

negative stereotypes

primary homicides

robbery

routine activities theory

secondary homicides

self-protective action

situational crime prevention

Southern Poverty Law Center

stickups

stranger crime

Violent Crime Control and Law Enforcement Act of 1994

xenophobia

Discussion Questions

1. Go to the FBI website and find the link to information about their Uniform Crime Reporting (UCR) program called "Crime in the United States" (www.fbi.gov/ucr/ucr.htm). Here you can obtain a breakdown of robberies reported to police by state and region of the country. Examine robbery rates by state. Where does your state fall in the ranking? What factors do you think are related to robbery offending in your state? How do these factors differ from those of neighboring states?

2. You have access to your state's statutes for all crimes. One way to access state statutes is through a search engine called LexisNexus, which provides access through its State Capital database. Using this or another search engine, find your state's statutes for hate crimes. What categories are included for special protection against hate in this statute (e.g., race, sexual orientation, religion, gender)? Do you think your state's statute could be more inclusive of other at-risk groups? Why or why not?

3. Go to the FBI website and find the most recent publication and/or data on bank robberies. Has the rate of bank robberies increased or decreased during the past decade? What factors do you think are responsible for this change? If the incidence of bank robberies has not changed, what policies do you think could be implemented to help decrease the rate?

7

Rape and Sexual Assault

Few North Americans deny that there is such a thing as rape or that it should be punished. The problem is that many people feel there is, on the one hand, "real rape," which is commonly portrayed as some greasy guy jumping out from behind the bush; then, there are other rapes that are not so "real."

—Martin D. Schwartz[1]

The opposite of compassion is not hatred, it is indifference.

—Male prison rape victim[2]

In August of 2012, a series of parties were held in Steubenville, Ohio; the majority of those attending were high school students gearing up for the upcoming school year and the much anticipated football season. When morning came, a series of social media postings revealed a young woman being carried around by her wrists and ankles by two star athletes from Steubenville High School. On her body were written the words, "drunk girl" and "rape." She was unconscious and appeared to be under the influence, and was therefore unable to respond to what her body was being subjected to. Photos and videos of the girl naked and in compromising positions were posted online. One attendee posted on Twitter, "Song of the night is definitely Rape Me by Nirvana," while others tweeted "rape" and "drunk girl." By the afternoon, a social media frenzy was erupting in Steubenville, with some people siding with the alleged victim

❖ **Photo 7.1**   Protesters at a rally outside Jefferson County Courthouse in Steubenville, Ohio on February 2, 2013

and others taking the side of the alleged offenders. After finding the videos and photos online, the girl's parents took her to the police station to report the crime, and eventually two high school football players were charged with rape and kidnapping. Evidence for the crimes, however, was difficult to find; the girl had showered several times before a medical examination was conducted and evidence such as semen was absent. Moreover, she acknowledged that she did not remember much of the night of the party because she had consumed so much alcohol, and only one witness came forward to testify against the defendants. In court, the prosecution could clearly illustrate that the girl had no ability to give her consent to any of the things done to her based on the photos and videos, which showed her extreme inebriation. At the time of this writing, the trials are still ongoing. It is important to note, however, that the young woman depicted in the photos has not been able to return to school, "Her friends have ostracized her, and parents have kept their children away from her."[3] Others, however, have stood by her side, writing blogs and holding rallies outside the courthouse (Photo 7.1).

A few months later, in Dabra, India, a 16-year-old lower caste girl was dragged into a stone shelter by eight men and raped for nearly three hours. The rapists took videos of the crimes and circulated them in the village. Upon seeing the video, the girl's father committed suicide, and the girl is now widely regarded in India as a "shamed woman" who is unfit for marriage. As with many cases of rape across the globe, when the media publicized the crime, responses ranged from blaming the victim, blaming the media, or outright indifference. [4]

We are sure that reading about these two cases has evoked many feelings; few crimes arouse such strong and visceral reactions as **rape**.[5] Rape is more than an act of violence; it is also a violation of the most intimate sort and strikes at our identities as women and men. In many ways, it is the ultimate assaultive crime or, as one writer suggests, "Rape strips its victims of her power to make determinations about perhaps the single most intrinsic value in her existence: the right to share intimacy."[6] Rape is also a crime that is subject to a bit more misunderstanding than most. For example, we tend to perceive it solely as having women victims; however, the reality is that, although females represent the majority of rape victims and males represent the majority of rape offenders, both males and females are capable of being both victims and offenders. In addition, rape in the United States is most likely to be perpetrated by people the victim knows rather than strangers. Because of these last two realities, most state **sexual assault** statutes are now gender and relationship neutral. We also tend to think of it largely in terms of forced intercourse, yet the reality is so much more. To illustrate the range of behaviors that comprise rape and sexual assault, we can look at a definition of a sexual act provided by the U.S. federal code (18 U.S.C. § 2245):

> (A) contact between the penis and the vulva or the penis and anus, and for purposes of this subparagraph contact involving the penis occurs upon penetration, however slight; (B) contact between the mouth and the penis, the mouth and the vulva, or the mouth and the anus; or (C) the penetration, however slight, of the anal or genital opening of another by a hand or finger or by any object, with an intent to abuse, humiliate, harass, degrade, or arouse or gratify the sexual desire of any person.

Notice the last section, which emphasizes the element of intent. In the past, rape was often perceived as stemming from sexual desire, rather than the myriad factors that are now known to influence the perpetration of this crime. The first section of this chapter discusses issues related to estimating the magnitude of rape and sexual assault victimization. We next focus on rape within four specific contexts: rape of children; rape on college campuses; rape in prison; and rape within the context of genocide or ethnic cleansing. After this, we move on to a discussion of alternative explanations for rape and sexual assault, with particular emphasis on power and control. In the final sections of the chapter, we examine society's responses to these victimizations, including a discussion of rape law reforms, the adjudication of rape and sexual assault offenders, and sex offender registries. To begin, however, it is important to first examine the ways in which rape statistics are gathered, since our understanding of the nature and prevalence of rape can vary widely depending on the data source upon which we rely.

How Many Victims Are There?

Similar to the assaults and victimizations perpetrated by family members that were discussed in earlier chapters, estimates of rape and sexual assault victimization can be obtained from several different sources. The important question remains, however, which is the most accurate? Recall that the FBI's Uniform Crime Reports (UCR) and its National Incident-Based Reporting System (NIBRS) include only those victimizations that the police find out about, either through the victim or someone else. Because rape and sexual assaults remain the least likely form of violence to be reported to police, our best estimates about how many victimizations there are, and who is most likely to be victimized and by whom, remain problematic. Similar to forms of violence perpetrated in the home, the most reliable information on rape victimization—imperfect and incomplete as it is—comprises the data obtained from social scientific surveys.

Even surveys, however, can have results that vary widely depending on how the questions are worded, the composition of the sample obtained, and the context of the survey. The only survey that monitors rape and sexual assault on an annual basis is the National Crime Victimization Survey (NCVS). However, the questions used to uncover rape are probably the least behaviorally specific. In addition to directly asking respondents whether they have experienced "any rape, attempted rape, or other type of sexual attack," they also ask the following:

Incidents involving forced or unwanted sexual acts are often difficult to talk about. Have you been forced or coerced to engage in unwanted sexual activity by
Someone you didn't know before?
A casual acquaintance?
Someone you know well?

If respondents reply yes to one of these questions, they are then asked, "Do you mean forced or coerced sexual intercourse?" to determine whether the incident should be recorded as a rape or as another type of sexual attack. But this sort of vague and broad question lends itself to different types of interpretation. Perhaps the perpetrator was an acquaintance or even a husband, and the victim may therefore not define it as rape even though it can be considered as such. Or perhaps there was no overt use of force, and so the victim may not define it as an "attack." The word rape itself has a variety of meanings that are used differently depending upon the situation and the individuals involved. Because of this, these types of questions about rape are prone to a great deal of underreporting. In order to avoid this problem, some researchers contend that respondents need to be asked more **behaviorally specific questions** to uncover rape victimizations that may have occurred. Beginning with a study by Mary Koss (1989) that examined the rape victimization experiences of college women, most recent surveys attempting to estimate the magnitude of rape have used very specific question wording. For example, the National Violence Against Women and Men Surveys (NVAWMS) asked the questions displayed in Table 7.1. The National Intimate Partner and Sexual Violence Survey (NISVS) conducted by the Centers for Disease Control further cued respondents to think of unwanted sex that occurred when they were "unable to consent to it or stop it from happening because they were drunk, high, drugged, or passed out from alcohol, drugs, or medications."[7]

Do you think estimates of rape using these questions will be higher or lower compared with estimates obtained using the NCVS questions? If you said higher, you are correct. Estimates are higher because these behaviorally specific questions elicit responses about incidents that may have happened to them that the other questions may not. In addition, there are other reasons why estimates differ. The context in which the survey is introduced to respondents, along with other factors, also affects how many rapes the survey uncovers. For example, the NVAWMS is introduced to respondents as a survey about issues of safety, unlike the NCVS, which is introduced to respondents as a survey interested in crime. These differences result in very different estimates. According to the NCVS, the rate of rape has not changed much over time, with approximately 250,000 people age 12 and older becoming the victims of rape annually. The majority of victimizations reported to NCVS interviewers were never reported to police. In fact, fewer than three in 10 victimizations, according to the NCVS, are ever reported to police. The NVAWMS, on the other hand, estimates that over 900,000 men and women over 18 years of age become the victims of rape annually. This is far more than the number estimated by the NCVS. Clearly, the way

Table 7.1	Questions Used in the National Violence Against Women and Men Surveys to Uncover Incidents of Rape and Sexual Assault

- [For female respondents] (1) Has a man or boy ever made you have sex by using force or threatening to harm you or someone close to you? Just so there is no mistake by sex we mean putting a penis in your vagina.
- [The remaining questions are for all respondents] (2) Has anyone, male or female, ever made you have oral sex by using force or threat of force? Just so there is no mistake, by oral sex we mean that a man or boy put his penis in your mouth or someone, male or female, penetrated your vagina or anus with their mouth.
- (3) Has anyone ever made you have anal sex by using force or threat of harm? Just so there is no mistake, by anal sex we mean that a man or boy put his penis in your anus.
- (4) Has anyone, male or female, ever put fingers or objects in your vagina or anus against your will or by using force or threats?
- (5) Has anyone, male or female, ever attempted to make you have vaginal, oral, or anal sex against your will, but intercourse or penetration did not occur?

in which you ask people about the victimization experiences affects the magnitude of estimates obtained by surveys!

Unfortunately, the only estimates of rape and sexual assault available at most local levels, including state and city levels, are from the less reliable police reports. The problem is that we know victims are reluctant to report to police for many reasons, including the personal nature of the victimization, fear of retaliation from the offender, and the treatment they expect to receive from the media and the criminal justice system. Additionally, many victims often believe that they will not be believed by the police if they report the rape, and many also suffer a sense of shame about their victimization.[8] It is a sad reality that rape victims still suffer from many stereotypes, misperceptions, and the social stigma and embarrassment associated with this crime. With these shortcomings in mind, we now turn to the patterns revealed by the imperfect data available.

Demographic Factors Related to Victimization From the NCVS

As we noted in the beginning of the chapter, females experience much higher rates of rape compared with males. According to the NISVS about 1% of adult women in the United States are raped every year; this translates into more than 1.2 million women. Over 18% of women have been raped in their lifetimes compared to just over 1% of men. For those who identify with one race/ethnicity, American Indians and Alaskan Natives (AIAN) are much more likely to be raped in their lifetimes compared to any other racial/ethnic group. In fact, over 1 in 4 AIAN women have been raped in their lives compared to 22% of African Americans, 19% of whites, and 15% of Hispanic women. The majority of rapes occurred when victims were under 25 years of age and nearly half occurred before age 18. Data also indicates that victims are much more likely to be raped by people they know compared to strangers. In fact, only about 14% of victims reported that they had been raped by strangers. Of course, rape is not a problem unique to the United States, as the case from India briefly reviewed at the beginning of this chapter illustrates. However, it is hard to make comparisons across nations because most countries do not have a national survey that measures rape victimizations and, as such, only police data can be relied upon. Relying on police reports for rape data is even more problematic in certain cultures, including predominately Islamic or Hindu cultures, where victims are often publicly shamed and are therefore unlikely to report their victimizations to police. In fact, many scholars warn against making comparisons of rape rates across countries because police procedures and legal definitions of rape vary so widely. For example, in some countries like Hong Kong and Mongolia, no cases of rape were reported to police in 2010. Does this mean that in those countries, nobody was forced or coerced to have sex against their will? That is highly unlikely. In those countries that are somewhat comparable, such as Great Britain, surveys reveal patterns similar to the United States: Females are more likely to be rape victims than males; and their attackers are much more likely to be known rather than to be strangers.[9]

Rape and Sexual Molestation of Children

When Pennsylvania State University made headlines for child molestation instead of football, it gave many people an up close and personal glimpse into the nature and context of child rape and abuse. Like all rapes, this example illuminated the fact that this form of violence is most often perpetrated by people the victims know and trust. In this case, Jerry Sandusky, an assistant football coach at Penn State, was convicted in June of 2012 of sexually assaulting 10 boys, all who were part of Sandusky's local charity dedicated to mentoring young boys from disadvantaged homes. Sandusky will likely spend the rest of his life in prison. When the victims of rape or sexual abuse are children, the Child Protection Services Divisions of states usually become involved because they are mandated to protect and remove potential victims from abusive situations. Law enforcement agencies are also mandated to hold offenders accountable through criminal statutes. Furthermore, all states have mandatory reporting laws for these offenses, requiring designated professionals, such as school and health officials, to report cases of sexual abuse of children, in addition to acts of physical abuse or neglect. However, it is important to remember that the age at which someone is considered a "child" varies by state. Although all states have their own individual child protection statutes, the federal definition of sexual abuse and exploitation included in the **Child Abuse Prevention and Treatment Act** is illustrative of most state statutes and includes the following:

(A) The employment, use, persuasion, inducement, enticement, or coercion of any child to engage in, or assist any other person to engage in, any sexually explicit conduct or simulation of such conduct for the purpose of producing a visual depiction of such conduct; or

(B) The rape, molestation, prostitution, or other form of sexual exploitation of children, or incest with children . . .[10]

While some estimates of child sexual abuse range from 114,000 to 300,000 cases per year,[11] we should point out that incidence rates of child sexual abuse are even more difficult to estimate than those of adults because children are even more reluctant to tell anyone about these victimizations. This is largely because the perpetrators are usually trusted friends, family members, or neighbors who gain their victims' trust and then typically intimidate them with threats of harm, and it is precisely for this reason that the sexual abuse of children is often considered one of the most heinous of crimes. The

❖ Photo 7.2   Jerry Sandusky, Assistant Football Coach at Penn State, convicted of sexually abusing 10 Boys

people who victimize children are trusted adults, like Jerry Sandusky or other family members, who betray the innocence and dependence of the children in their care. In fact, child sex abuse is often referred to as the "silent crime" because victims are very reluctant to tell anyone.

Studies indicate that about one in five girls and one in 20 boys has been a victim of child sexual abuse. Offenders are overwhelmingly male, and although over one-third of offenders are likely to be juveniles, they range in age from adolescents to the elderly. Similar to rape against adults, only about 14% of child sexual abuse victims were attacked by strangers.[12]

College Women and Rape

We often think of college campuses as being safe and secure locations, immune from the dangers and violent influences of the outside world. But the truth is that college campuses are as dangerous and crime prone as the larger communities within which they exist. In fact, research suggests that women attending college are at greater risk of rape and sexual assault compared with other women of the same age in the general population. Several recent cases have brought media attention to rape on college campuses, including the case highlighted in Focus 7.1 that occurred at Arizona State University.

IN FOCUS 7.1

Arizona State Student Receives Civil Settlement for Rape

According to court documents, in the summer of 2003, a freshman Arizona State University football player named Darnel Henderson was taking a course intended to assist first-year students adjust to college. He was quickly accused of a number of crimes that included grabbing and fondling women in the dorm, exposing himself to female staff members, and threatening other women in the program.

When asked by officials about his behavior, he told them that he wanted "women to fear him" and to "show them their place." Because of this, he was expelled from the program, but the head football coach at the time persuaded ASU to allow Henderson to return to the dorms during the academic year, even though they had a zero-tolerance policy. That spring, Henderson began stalking a female student and repeatedly calling her. In March, he entered her dorm room, found her asleep, and raped her. An emergency room examination revealed that her injuries could "not have occurred in consensual sex." Henderson was eventually expelled from school but was never convicted of rape in a criminal court. A subsequent investigation uncovered the fact that ASU destroyed records in an effort to try and cover up Henderson's misconduct in the summer program, and consequently the victim filed civil suit against ASU alleging that the university had "placed her in a dangerous position, which led to the rape." The case was settled out of court and resulted in the establishment of a women's safety czar for all three major campuses in Arizona and an $850,000 cash settlement to the victim.

SOURCE: http://www.titleix.info/Resources/News-Articles/Arizona-State-Rape-Case-Settled.aspx

Because of the increased vulnerability to rape and other crimes faced by college students, the U.S. Congress passed the **Student Right-to-Know and Campus Security Act of 1990**.[13] This legislation mandates that colleges and universities participating in federal student aid programs "prepare, publish, and distribute, through appropriate publications and mailings, to all current students and employees, and to any applicant for enrollment upon request, an annual security report." The purpose of the report is to communicate campus security policies and campus crime statistics for each institution. This legislation was revised in 1992 and again in 1998, at which time the amendments were officially renamed the **Jeanne Clery Disclosure of Campus Security Policy and Campus Crime Statistics Act**.[14] This act requires institutions to publish more specific policies regarding the awareness and prevention of sexual assault and also requires basic rights to be given to sexual assault victims. The published reports provided by institutions, of course, include only victimizations that are reported to police or campus security. While these numbers may partially reflect relative safety and vulnerability, they are more likely to be indicators of the willingness of students in particular university settings to report their victimizations to authorities.

The U.S. Justice Department realized the problems inherent in official reports of rape and sexual assault victimization on campus and funded a survey called the **National College Women Sexual Assault Victimization Study** (NCWSV) that was carried out by Bonnie Fisher and her colleagues in 1997.[15] The survey involved telephone interviews of 4,446 randomly selected women who were attending a two- or four-year college or university. In addition to rape, the NCWSV asked a series of behaviorally specific questions that sought to assess whether respondents had experienced a range of sexually assaultive victimizations. The questions used to determine whether respondents had experienced a rape or attempted rape were almost identical to those used by the National Violence Against Women and Men Surveys (see Table 7.1). Importantly, this survey had another experimental component in which some respondents were asked the screening questions that were the same as those used by the National Crime Victimization Survey (NCVS). In this way, researchers could determine the effects these different questions had on prevalence estimates. Not surprisingly, it was found that the more behaviorally specific questions yielded significantly more reports of victimization compared with the NCVS questions. Clearly, behaviorally specific questions are more successful in prompting women who have been victimized to be counted as such. Student respondents were asked whether they had experienced any of the victimizations "since school began," and about 2.8% of those interviewed were identified as rape or attempted rape victims. If this rate is projected forwarded for a one-year period, the data suggest that nearly 5% of college women are victimized in any given calendar year. This means that, for every 1,000 women attending these types of institutions, there may be 35 incidents of rape in a given academic year. And what should not be surprising to you by now is the fact that most victims knew their assailants. In fact, nine out of 10 offenders were known to the victims. According to the results of the NCWSV, the majority of the offenders were other classmates, friends, boyfriends, and ex-boyfriends. Similarly, the majority of rapes, regardless of whether they occurred on or off campus, took place in residences. While popular imagery would suggest that women need to fear the stranger lurking in the bushes or the alley, the greater threat actually comes from friends and acquaintances.

Often, these rapes are facilitated by a variety of drugs. Although particular drugs have become known as "**date-rape drugs,**" most experts prefer the term "**drug-facilitated sexual assault.**" We raise this issue because their use has become particularly problematic on college campuses. There are at least three drugs used for this purpose: **GHB** (gamma-Hydroxybutyric acid); **Rohyphol** (flunitrazepam); and **Ketamine** (ketamine hydrochloride).[16] These drugs often have no color, smell, or taste and are easily added to flavored drinks without the victim's knowledge. They can affect a victim very quickly, although the length of time that the effects last can vary, and the drugs serve to render many victims helpless and unable to refuse sex. Importantly, they also hinder victims' memories so they are unable to recall the victimization or adequately testify on their own behalf. While these drugs have become known as date-rape drugs, virtually all drugs affect judgment and behavior and can put a person at risk for unwanted sexual activity. This is particularly true for the legal drug (at least for those over 21 years of age) of alcohol. When under the influence of alcohol, it is harder to think clearly and evaluate a potentially dangerous situation. Drinking too much can also cause blackouts and memory loss, similar to the effects of the drugs discussed above. It is important to remember, however, that even if a victim of sexual assault had too much to drink, they are *not* at fault for being assaulted, and this impaired judgment makes a victim unable to consent to anything, including sex. Looking at all these characteristics, it is probably safe to say that particularly high-risk situations are parties and similar kinds of events when students are socializing with friends and acquaintances and using alcohol and/or other substances. Parties held in dorm rooms, frat houses, or off-campus houses and apartments also offer the convenience of potential seclusion where this type of assault can more easily occur. In about one in five rapes of college students, victims reported sustaining other injuries in addition to the rape injuries. These injuries are most often bruises, black eyes,

❖ Photo 7.3   Friends drinking

cuts, scratches, swelling, or chipped teeth. Despite these injuries, however, very few rapes were reported to law enforcement officials. In fact, less than 5% of all rapes were reported. This should demonstrate the unreliable nature of official reports when trying to estimate the magnitude of rape on college campuses. It also forces us to acknowledge the disturbing reality that most perpetrators go unpunished and remain free to offend further. Another setting in which official reports are even more unreliable is prisons.

Prison Rape

Without question, the facts about inmate-on-inmate sexual abuse are little known by the population at large, even though virtually all correctional officers and wardens are fully aware of the issue. As with the rape of males in general, serious discussion of male **prison rape** typically remains muted in our society. However, a recent series of lawsuits by former prisoners who experienced rape and sexual abuse behind bars has focused attention on the issue (see In Focus 7.2).

IN FOCUS 7.2

Rape in Prison

William Laite was married with a family and had no previous criminal record. He was a former Georgia legislator and business-man. Laite was convicted in Texas of perjury relating to a contract he had with the Fed-eral Administration Housing Authority and was sentenced to serve time in the Terrant County Jail in Fort Worth, Texas. The moment he entered the tank or day room, he was approached by five men. The first comment from them was, "I wonder if he has any guts. We'll find out tonight, won't we? Reckon what her name is; she looks ready for about six or eight inches. You figure she will make us fight for it, or is she going to give up to us nice and sweet like a good little girl? Naw, we'll have

to work her over first, but hell, that's half the fun, isn't it?"

"I couldn't move," said Laite, "I was terri-fied. This couldn't be real. This couldn't be hap-pening to me." Laite was saved from sexual assault when a 17-year-old youth was admitted to the day room as he was about to become the victim of the five men in the tank. The men saw the boy and turned on him, knocked him out, and then, "they were on him at once like jack-als, ripping the coveralls off his limp body. They sexually assaulted him, savagely and brutally like starving animals after a raw piece of meat. Then I knew what they meant about giving me six or eight inches." Laite said the guards never made any attempt to discipline the prisoners.

One such case was brought against the state of Texas by Roderick Johnson. Johnson was a restaurant manager before he was arrested for burglary, writing a bad check, and cocaine possession. After being convicted, he was sent to Allred, a maximum security prison in Texas, even though none of his offenses was a violent crime. According to state prison records, Allred ranked second among the more than 70 Texas prisons in terms of the number of sexual assaults experienced by inmates.

While most prisoners who enter maximum security prisons like Allred prefer to go by names like Monster and Animal, inmates gave Roderick another name upon his entry: "Coco." Not a good sign of things to come. According to court papers, gangs such as The Gangster Disciples made him a sex slave, buying and selling his sexual services. Johnson's suit asserts that he begged several times in writing for prison officials to move him to a unit called safekeeping, but officials told him he had two choices: to fight or to engage in sex. When prison officials were asked by Johnson's representatives why nothing was done to protect him, the response was, "There seems to have been a lot of doubt about his motives and his ability to present evidence."[17] Nearly 300 pages of testimony detail the horrific conditions under which Johnson was forced to exist. Once he was raped by eight men, one after the other. He was raped in cells and stairwells, but he said showers were the worst. He recalled, "It's like throwing a piece of meat to a pack of wolves."[18]

How many prisoners become the victims of rape while incarcerated? There are very few empirical studies that have documented the incidence of rape and sexual abuse in prisons. Estimating incidence rates using the number of grievances submitted to prison officials is almost useless since very few of these victimizations are ever reported. In addition to the terrible stigma attached to becoming the victim of rape in prison, there is an obvious deterrent to reporting instilled by the "**convict culture**" that prohibits such snitching behavior. "Snitches" or "rats" who inform on other inmates are considered the lowest members of the inmate hierarchy.[19] As one inmate told Human Rights Watch

> The first time I was raped, I did the right thing. I went to an officer, told him what happened, got the rectal check, the whole works. Results? I got shipped to [another prison]. Six months later, same dude that raped me is out of seg and on the same wing as I am. I have to deal with two jackets now: snitch and punk. I . . . had to think real fast to stay alive. This was my first two years in the system. After that I knew better.[20]

In the same vein, another inmate asserted that

> I never went to the authorities, as I was too fearful of the consequences from any other inmate. I already had enough problems, so didn't want to add to them by taking on the prison identity as a "rat" or "snitch." I already feared for my life. I didn't want to make it worse.[21]

Even with such obvious hindrances to reporting, a small body of research has been developed. One study of sexual assault in prison conducted by Cindy Struckman-Johnson and her colleagues in Nebraska concluded that 22% of male inmates had been pressured or forced to have sexual contact against their will while incarcerated. Of these, over 50% had submitted to forced anal sex at least once.[22] A later study conducted by Cindy and David Struckman-Johnson found very similar rates of sexual assault in seven Midwestern prisons.[23] The problem with these attempts to estimate the incidence of rape and sexual assault in prison is that they rely on samples that are not randomly drawn, so they are not necessarily representative of those prisons from which they were obtained nor of the prison population in general. This means that, while their conclusions are suggestive, they are certainly not definitive.

Human Rights Watch obtained testimony from over 200 prisoners in 37 states and published its findings in a very graphic account of the reality of rape in prison called *No Escape: Male Rape in Prison*. Because their methodology did not include random sampling, state and national estimates could not be obtained from this study, but what emerged were important narratives and personal accounts of the brutality and fear that many inmates serving time in our nation's prisons must face. The report helps to draw a picture of the dynamics of prison rape. It reveals, for example, that certain physical characteristics mark certain inmates as likely targets for this kind of assault. Being young, small, white, and effeminate are red flags for predatory inmates, as are other qualities such as shyness, passivity, long hair, and having a high-pitched voice. Inmates with more of these qualities have a greater likelihood of being perceived as vulnerable and being attacked. Once victimized, the victim runs the risk of being labeled a "bitch" or "punk," which puts them at greater risk of subsequent victimization. The perpetrators, on the other hand, tend to be incarcerated for more violent offenses and are often linked with gangs. Interestingly, they also do not define themselves as homosexuals, even though their sexual assaults are against other men. Race also appears to be an issue in regard to prison rapes, with white inmates being disproportionately at risk, especially from African Americans.

The Human Rights Watch report prompted Congress to enact a law called the **Prison Rape Elimination Act of 2003** (P.L. 108–79) that requires the Bureau of Justice Statistics (BJS) to develop a new data collection on the incidence and prevalence of sexual assault within correctional facilities.[24] BJS recently reported the first results of a survey of former state prisoners that found almost 10% of former inmates reported at least one incident of sexual victimization during their most recent incarceration. About half of these incidents were perpetrated by other inmates, while the other half were committed by facility staff.[25] These estimates are higher than those reported by inmates who are currently serving time in a correctional facility, probably because former inmates do not have to fear retaliation. However, all survey data indicate that female inmates are more vulnerable to inmate-to-inmate sexual assaults compared to males, while the males are more vulnerable to staff sexual assaults. Interestingly, large differences in vulnerability were found in sexual victimization by an inmate's sexual orientation. Inmates with a sexual orientation other than heterosexual, including bisexual and homosexual, reported much higher rates of both intimate and staff sexual victimization.[26]

Genocide and Rape

Although we review and discuss state-sponsored violence in the second part of the book, this chapter would not be complete without mentioning the use of rape as a means of genocide and war. Throughout history, women have experienced mass rape as a byproduct of war and population annihilation. In the same way that looting and

pillaging have often been seen as a soldier's right and privilege, so too has rape traditionally been defined as a "**spoil of war**" or, as Susan Brownmiller explains

> Women are raped in war by ordinary youths as casually, or as frenetically, as a village is
> looted or gratuitously destroyed. Sexual trespass on the enemy's women is one of the sat-
> isfactions of conquest . . .[27]

As with all rape, sexual violence as a tool of armed conflict primarily affects women
and girls, as the case study in In Focus 7.3 reveals. Although the number of women
and girls raped in contemporary conflicts between nations or between national ethnic
groups will never be known, testimonies from survivors in recent times confirm that
rape is extremely widespread and that hundreds of thousands of victims across the
globe have been individually raped, gang-raped, raped with objects, held in sexual slavery, or sexually mutilated during contemporary wars and ethnic cleansing campaigns.

During the 1994 genocide in Rwanda, one of the worst mass slaughters in recent
history, Tutsi women were often raped after they had witnessed the torture and killings
of their families and the destruction and looting of their homes by Hutu militia groups
and by soldiers of the Rwandan Armed Forces. Hutu officials encouraged HIV-positive
soldiers to take part in gang rapes. According to many witnesses, many Tutsi women
were immediately killed after being raped. Others escaped death only by agreeing
to become sex slaves.[28] While the exact number will never be known, human rights
workers—basing their estimates on the number of pregnancies from rape—suggest
a figure of 250,000 to 500,000. Some have even suggested that almost every surviving
Tutsi woman and female adolescent was sexually assaulted.[29] These rapes were often
extremely cruel and brutal, with the Hutu rapists making use of sticks, rifle barrels,
machetes, and various other implements. Rape during the Rwandan genocide, it
is important to note, was a conscious strategy fomented by Hutu extremist leaders

In Focus 7.3

The Story of Maria—A Survivor of Rape and Genocide

In 1994, 18-year-old Maria was a Hutu woman and a student in Gikongoro, Rwanda. In April of that year, however, her life would change forever. Maria watched the Interahamwe militia kill her grandparents, her two aunts, and her brother. As she was fleeing, she was caught and raped by five militia men, one of whom she knew. When she was found by a Red Cross team, her vagina had been severely slashed with knives and she was hemorrhaging, because the mutilation had destroyed the wall between her vagina and rectum. In 1995, Maria was sent to Belgium for reconstructive surgery where it was discovered that an infection had spread to her uterus and a hysterectomy had to be performed. Her rectal and vaginal injuries were irreparable. Maria also contracted the AIDS virus during the rape. In the end, her rape was also a death sentence.

❖ Photo 7.4 Survivors of the Rwandan genocide

intended to further the goal of the genocide, which was the destruction of the Tutsi population in Rwanda.[30] This kind of tactic has been replicated in many other examples of genocide, such as that which occurred in Bosnia during the early 1990s.

The genocide that was perpetrated in Bosnia was termed "ethnic cleansing" by the Serb forces who wanted to remove all Bosnian Muslims and Croats from the territory they controlled. Rape was an integral part of the genocidal violence and was intended to serve a number of different purposes. It was intended not only to dominate, humiliate, and terrorize the population into submission and flight, but also to destroy the future of the Bosnian Muslim people by impregnating Muslim women with Serb babies.[31] One European commission report estimated that approximately 20,000 women were raped in Bosnia during the violence there.[32] As with the rapes in the Rwandan genocide, the sexual assaults in Bosnia were characterized by excessive and horrific brutality and often ended with the murder of the victim or victims.

Historically, the first time an international court successfully convicted someone for the crime of genocide was in 1998, when the **International Criminal Tribunal for Rwanda** convicted Jean Paul Akayesu. In this verdict, the international court underscored the fact that rape and sexual violence also constitute genocide in the same way as any other act, as long as they are committed with the intent to destroy a particular group. The court defined rape as "the physical invasion of a sexual nature, committed on a person under circumstances which are coercive." The court noted, however, that sexual violence was not limited to physical invasion and that coercive circumstances included "threats, intimidation, extortion, and other forms of duress which prey on fear or desperation."[33]

Unfortunately, there has been no lack of business for the International Criminal Court with regard to rape. A few years later, in 2001, the focus was on the former Yugoslavia. Importantly, this year marked the first time that the international tribunal brought charges against defendants solely for crimes of sexual violence against women when three former soldiers in the Bosnian Serb Army were found guilty of rape, torture, and sexual enslavement.[34] While this case set an important precedent for holding rapists accountable in international courts, there are thousands of offenders who remain at large despite the rape and sexual enslavement of women around the world. Unfortunately, invading troops and perpetrators of genocide are not the only offenders. A number of United Nations Security Council peacekeeping troops have been responsible for participating in and perpetrating rapes, sexual abuse, and sexual slavery in various UN missions around the world. Holding these offenders accountable is difficult because each country which contributes troops has the primary responsibility for its own soldiers, and these nations are often reluctant to prosecute their own troops. There are, of course, legal prohibitions against such offenses; however, as in many situations, legal remedies often take a back seat to political realities, and unfortunately this is not a problem limited to foreign troops since even U.S. soldiers have been implicated in rapes while serving overseas in Iraq.[35]

Reasons for Rape

As this chapter has illustrated, rape is a varied phenomenon, and consequently rapists are a heterogeneous group. This means that no single theory is going to explain all rape. Furthermore, studies based on interviews with convicted rapists in prison cannot be generalized to all rapists because so few rapes are ever reported to police, much less end in the conviction and incarceration of the offender. Research into the motives and mindset of perpetrators is therefore limited. It is possible, however, to glean some insight based on the evidence that is available.

One popular perception holds that rapists are somehow abnormal or sick. Yet the image of most rapists having some psychopathology has not been supported by contemporary research. After reviewing the psychological research, researchers concluded that the link between sexually aggressive men and psychopathology was inconclusive and weak at best.[36] Thus there is little evidence to suggest that rape is a behavior confined to a few "sick" serial rapists. In fact, Diana Scully and Joseph Marolla contend that attempting to explain rape using psychopathological models places emphasis on the wrong things, since "attention is diverted away from culture or social structure as contributing factors. Thus . . . it ignores evidence which links sexual aggression to environmental variables and which suggests that rape, like all behavior, is learned."[37] As we have seen, rape is an act perpetrated by persons from all ranks of society, or as one police investigator stated: "Rapists are where you find them, without regard for appearance, criminal history, or stature in the community."[38]

Another popular misperception about rape suggests that it is a product of sexual desires and needs—or, as A. Nicholas Groth suggests,

> With regard to the offender, he is frequently regarded as a lusty male who is the victim of a provocative and vindictive woman, or he is seen as a sexually frustrated man reacting under the pressure of his pent-up needs, or he is thought to be a demented sex-fiend harboring insatiable and perverted desires. All these views share a common misconception: they all assume that the offender's behavior is primarily motivated by sexual desire and that rape is directed toward gratifying only this sexual need.[39]

The truth, however, is that rape is first and foremost a crime of violence. This is not to suggest that the rapist is not motivated in part by desire and the need for sexual gratification but rather that the sexual elements are woven together with issues of power and dominance in the mind of the rapist. One rape victim put it this way

> When he came in waving his gun, he definitely was in control, no doubt about it. But he didn't use the control to make me grab my cat by the tail and twirl him over my head. He

didn't make me write hot checks. He didn't make me vacuum the apartment. He raped me, dammit. He screwed me without my permission, and threatened to kill me if I resisted. And he didn't leave until he got off. From my view—and it seems like I ought to be in a position to know—it damn well was about sex.[40]

To the rapist, violence and sex are linked in a perverse way that allows them to project their insecurities, fantasies, and frustrations onto the bodies of their victims. Rapists commit their crimes for a variety of reasons, but three themes seem to run through all of them: power, anger, and sexuality. We see this when we examine the typologies of rapists that have been developed by various scholars. One such classification scheme divides rapists into four broad types: power reassurance; anger retaliation; power assertive; and sadistic.[41] Keep in mind that these categories are ideal types and any one offender might have characteristics that fit into several different classifications. This is sometimes referred to as a blending or mixing of types.[42] Additionally, the characteristics reviewed below represent qualities that are often found to be representative of a rapist but not necessarily in all cases.

The **power reassurance rapist** is generally considered to be the most common type of sexual assaulter and is someone who suffers from low self-esteem and feelings of being inadequate.[43] This may be reflected in their personal appearance since they often tend to have bad personal hygiene and wear dirty clothes. They don't typically have a large friendship network, and their interpersonal skills are fairly minimal, which also means that they often find menial jobs without much responsibility and where they don't interact with the public. These individuals are sometimes described as being loners, quiet, and shy. In the act of rape, they try to achieve a sense of personal empowerment. They tend to be the least violent and sometimes fantasize that their victim may actually come to enjoy the rape and may even want to initiate a relationship with their attacker. Because of this, they often try to reassure their targets by engaging them in conversation and encouraging the victim to cooperate and undress themselves, to change sexual positions, and otherwise play along with the fantasy of the rapist that this assault is consensual. They may even demand that the rape victim say things like, "I love you," and "I want you to make love to me."[44] It's all about creating and living out a fantasy in which the attacker is in a relationship with their victim, and this is why they use minimal force and encourage cooperation—it feeds this mental scenario they have created.

The second most common type is the **power assertive rapist** for whom power and dominance are the primary motivating forces. This type of individual is usually very concerned with their physical appearance and tends to be very well dressed and groomed. They may be in good shape and even very athletic. In many ways, they see themselves as being a real "macho" kind of guy, which is often reflected in their choice of cars, what they wear, and even what kind of jobs they do. These offenders, for example, are often in blue collar jobs like the construction industry, the military, or law enforcement and typically like to drive big trucks or sports cars. These individuals can be quite friendly and charming, even when interacting with women, but can change dramatically when they want sex. In the act of rape, these individuals achieve a feeling of control—of having the power of life or death over their victims. Violence, for this predator, is often an intrinsic part of the rape, since it visibly confirms their absolute control over the victim. Whereas the power reassurance rapist asks the victim to do things, this type of attacker doesn't ask. Instead, he demands. Interestingly, this kind of offender has often been married multiple times and is frequently in conflict with his spouse. In a sense, then, their rapes serve as an expression of their anger and desire for power and control.

The **anger retaliation rapist**, on the other hand, is someone who feels a tremendous amount of hostility toward women and consequently uses rape as a vehicle of revenge. Often these men were abused as children and/or come from single-parent homes.[45] It has also been suggested that their generalized hatred of women may stem from a negative relationship with a mother or other significant female. In a very real sense, their victims serve as a stand-in for all women or at least the woman they have a problem with. Because they are usually very impulsive, they frequently rely on a blitz-style attack on any vulnerable target of opportunity. The predator sees a woman out for a walk, strolling across a parking lot, or jogging in a secluded area and initiates a quick surprise attack on that unfortunate victim. For this perpetrator, rape is simply a tool to hurt, humiliate, and degrade women. Because of this, significant physical injuries typically accompany the rape, much more so than with the types of sexual assault discussed above.

The **sadistic rapist,** also known as the anger excitation rapist, is someone who displays extreme violence and cruelty in his attacks. Such rapists enjoy and revel in the pain and humiliation that they inflict on their victims and are potentially the most likely of the different types of rapist to kill their victims. For them violence and sex are intimately linked. Violence, especially against women, is sexually exciting for this offender, but in a larger sense it is the complete control and domination over another human being that they find so stimulating. These offenders tend to be a bit older than many of the other types of rapists and are commonly married with children. To the outside world, they appear to be a typical married man and to all outward appearances look like decent, law-abiding citizens. But this image is a façade that disguises an individual who preys on innocent victims. As opposed to the blitz-style attacks of the anger retaliation types, this rapist spends a great deal of time planning out and preparing their attacks, which often involves the creation of a rape kit that can include a blindfold, condoms, gloves, and duct tape or precut rope. Also included may be a police radio in order to monitor law enforcement.

In addition to these main types of rapists, there are a couple of other types. Opportunistic offenders, for example, are those individuals who perpetrate a rape during the commission of another crime. A person engaged in a burglary may take advantage of their situation to rape a female in the house, but their primary intention in this situation was not the rape but rather the burglary. There is also the gang rapist who commits rape as part of some group, such as a military unit or a sports team. But both of these last two categories represent atypical offenders. Keeping in mind that the ability to generalize from all of these above reviewed types is somewhat limited because of the small samples from which they were drawn, we can still see the intertwined elements of many rapes and the ways in which sexuality and sexual gratification are sometimes fused into a vision of eroticized violence in the minds of many rapists, feeding into their needs for power and domination.

Power and Dominance

Fundamental to many theories, especially feminist thought, is the contention that violence against women—both sexual and nonsexual—is an expression of a **patriarchal** (male-dominant) social structure. Accordingly, this argument argues that the subjugation of women by men is built into the organization of society. Thus several feminist scholars contend that rape is an act of social control, an extension of normative male behavior that defines the traditional male sex role and is integral to the historical powerlessness of women in male-dominated societies.[46] There is some support for this at the societal level. For example, research has found that there are higher rates of rape in societies in which women are excluded from positions of power compared with societies based on the relatively equal distribution of power and mutual respect.[47] Research in the United States has also found that states with higher rates of gender equality have lower rape rates compared with states that have higher rates of inequality.[48]

Other scholars have focused on the socialization process of males and females and argue that traditional socialization practices encourage males to associate aggression, dominance, strength, and virility with masculinity. In contrast, traditional female stereotypes encourage females to be submissive and passive. Further, as Diana Scully explains

> Males are taught to have expectations about their level of sexual needs and expectations for corresponding female accessibility which function to justify forcing sexual access. The justification for forced sexual access is buttressed by legal, social, and religious definitions of women as male property and sex as an exchange of goods. Socialization prepares women to be "legitimate" victims and men to be potential offenders.[49]

In fact, research does support the contention that a belief in traditional sex roles is related to attitudes endorsing violence toward women. For example, Martha Burt interviewed a representative sample of almost 600 adults and found that individuals with a belief in conventional sex-role stereotypes were more likely to

- endorse rape myths such as women are partially responsible for their own rapes, many women enjoy rape, and women who are drunk cannot be raped;
- have attitudes supporting violence against women; and
- believe that sexual relationships are necessarily deceptive, manipulative, and exploitative.[50]

Each of these attitudes has been linked to sexual aggression. In research conducted with college males, it has been found that men who believe in traditional sex roles are more likely to be involved in sexually aggressive activity than those males who do not adhere to these values.[51] One form of rape that has sometimes been linked with this theoretical perspective is marital rape, which, according to some statistics, is perpetrated against 10% to 14% of all married women and accounts for a quarter of all rapes.[52] Many suggest that this form of rape is often accompanied by additional forms of domestic violence and involves a male perpetrator using sexual violence to maintain power and control. Such violence—both sexual and nonsexual—is an attempt to coercively maintain traditional male prerogatives.

One of the most incriminating pieces of evidence that rape is associated with power and dominance comes from Robert Sapolsky, who did extensive fieldwork with baboons living in the wild. Like many primate societies, baboon groups have a top-ranking male, called the alpha male, who presides in the top-ranking position of the baboon community. Females, on the other hand, inherit their rank from their mother. Males who want to reign as alpha male must defeat the existing alpha male in an intimidation showdown that often turns to physical violence. One summer, Sapolsky observed a rape and other acts of violence that occurred after the current alpha male had been dethroned. He describes the incident. (Note that he gave all the baboons in the community names from the Old Testament, and Solomon was the reigning alpha male who was deteriorating with age.)

> Solomon was challenged by another high-ranking male who, two months before, shrank before Solomon's gaze. Solomon won . . . but the threads were unraveling. The next morning, Solomon sat next to Devorah, who was not in estrus that week, not sexually receptive. Obadiah had just taken his first few steps; Rachel was sitting near Job: Miriam, two months pregnant, was grooming her youngest kid, who was throwing a tantrum. A quiet, small-town morning. Uriah appeared and stood a dozen yards from Solomon, staring, [the] town no longer big enough for the two of them. And Solomon, like the script specified, looking neither left nor right, walked toward Uriah, turned around, and groveled belly in the grass, rear end stuck in the air, a male gesture of submission. The transition had occurred. During that day, Uriah sat and groomed with Leah, Naomi, some of the other females. Solomon, without provocation, attacked Benjamin, mauled Job repeatedly, broke the play of Daniel and David, chased the terrified Ruth and Obadiah. I would come to recognize the typical behavior of a male baboon with problems who wants someone else to pay for them. And Solomon did something else, a behavior I would see only once afterward, again on the day that an alpha male lost his primacy . . . Solomon chased Devorah, seized her near an acacia tree, and raped her. By this I mean that she had not presented to him, was not behaviorally receptive nor physiologically fertile at the time, that she ran like hell, tried to fight him off, and screamed in pain when he entered her. And bled. So ended the reign of Solomon.[53]

Solomon was clearly trying to retrieve an element of power that he had lost with his fall from the thrown. This description clearly illustrates that rape in primate society, as in ours, is both an act of violence and an act of power and domination over its victims.

Response to Rape Victims and Offenders

Less than 30 years ago, most state rape statutes required that the victim promptly report her victimization to police, that the victimization be corroborated by other witnesses, that the victim demonstrate that she had physically resisted her attacker, and that judges could provide cautionary instructions to the jury about the difficulty of determining the truth of a victim's testimony. In addition, most state statutes also narrowly defined rape as sexual intercourse with a woman who was not one's wife, by force or against her will. Beginning in the early 1970s, however, education and activism by various feminist groups and other civil rights groups led to a growing awareness about the antiquated nature of rape laws in this country. This awareness provided the impetus for the **rape law reforms** enacted by states which followed. By 1980, most states had passed some form of rape reform legislation. Although the nature and scope of rape law reforms vary significantly across jurisdictions, Cassia Spohn and Julie Horney note four common reform themes:

1. Replacing the single crime code of rape with a series of offenses graded by seriousness with commensurate penalties, usually gender and relationship neutral (e.g., including both rapes against males and females by both stranger and known offenders including intimate partners)

2. Changing consent standards by modifying or eliminating requirements that victims resist their attackers

3. Eliminating corroboration requirements

4. Enacting rape shield laws that place restrictions on the introduction of evidence concerning the victim's prior sexual conduct

The intended goals of rape law reforms have been somewhat diverse. Obviously, different reform groups have had different agendas. In addition to changing the public's perceptions of rape and of rape victims, reformers also intended to modify existing criminal justice practices. In general, it was hoped that legal reforms would serve a symbolic purpose by educating the public about the seriousness of all forms of sexual assault and would decrease the stigma and stereotypes associated with rape victims. Instrumentally, it was also hoped that reforms would eradicate the conditions thought to impede rape prosecutions, such as the ability of defense attorneys to use a victim's sexual history to impeach her character. The impact of both types of reform was also intended to be complementary. For example, changes in public conceptions about what rape "really was" and who "really rapes" were expected to lead to more reports of rape to the police by victims. Simultaneously, jurors were expected to become more sensitive to both the victimization and stigmatization of rape victims. Consequently, it was hoped that rape reports, arrests, convictions, and rates of imprisonment (especially for non-stereotypical acquaintance rapes) would all increase.

Have rape reforms achieved these goals? Surprisingly, there has been little research investigating the effectiveness of rape law reforms. Although earlier studies examining the efficacy of reforms found few changes in the reporting or conviction rates of rape, recent research has shown that women are not as reluctant to report sexual assaults perpetrated by known offenders as they were before the reform movement. Also, according to the NCVS, women who were raped by known offenders were more likely to report that an arrest had been made as a result of their coming forward compared with women who had been raped by strangers. This is a reasonable finding given the greater likelihood of victims being able to identify known offenders compared with strangers, and police thus being more likely to apprehend them. This finding is also supported by recent research that discovered, in a sample of 671 sexual assault complaints made to the Chicago Police Department, the accused was in custody in 62% of the acquaintance cases compared with only 31% of the stranger cases.[54] Do these results indicate that the victim–offender relationship is not important in a woman's decision to report a rape victimization to police or in the criminal justice system's response? It would be premature to conclude that the victim–offender relationship is not important, particularly given the fact that percentage differentials still exist in reporting across relationship categories. However, it would also be remiss to ignore the increasing propensity of women raped by men they know to bring their victimizations to the attention of authorities. Findings from prison inmate surveys lend support to the notion that women are less reluctant to report victimizations by known offenders. For example, one study found that a significantly higher proportion of inmates incarcerated for rape in 1991 knew their victims compared with those incarcerated for rape in the early 1980s. Cumulatively, these findings appear to suggest that women who are sexually assaulted by known offenders may not be as reluctant to report their victimizations to police as they once were. It also implies that the criminal justice system may be treating acquaintance- and stranger-perpetrated rapes more equitably.

The backdrop behind these findings is still troublesome, however. Less than one-quarter of the rape victimizations from the National Crime Victimization Survey are ever reported to police, regardless of the victim–offender relationship. And as we saw, even fewer rape victims on college campuses make reports of their victimizations to police (the rate is less than 6%). These dismal percentages underscore the difficult choice rape victims still face when deciding whether or not to report their victimization to authorities. Clearly, there are other barriers that still prevent rape victims from making a report. Interviews with victims are very informative in illuminating these barriers. For example, in a sample of rape victims, guilt and self-blame were among the primary reasons why victims of acquaintance rape did not report their victimizations to the police. As researchers report

> fear, guilt, and shame to a large extent account for their failure to report. Self-blame is a recurring theme in survivors' comments . . . In some instances, the self-blame was seen reinforced by family or friends, who, on hearing of the assault, overtly or covertly blamed the victim for what occurred. "Why did you invite him to your apartment?" "Why did you go to his house?" "Were you drinking at the time?" These and similar questions, although [they] on the surface appear to be asking for information, in essence are blaming the victim for what happened.[55]

Another reason for not reporting to police acknowledged by women is the lack of confidentiality provided to rape victims who do report. For example, a recent survey suggested that women would be less inhibited about reporting a sexual assault if they could be assured that their names would not appear in the newspaper and that their anonymity would be protected.[56] An obvious policy implication would be to create legal statutes that guarantee a rape victim's right to confidentiality by prohibiting the news media from disclosing their names and addresses. However, because the U.S. Constitution guarantees defendants the right to a public trial and the right to face their accusers, this goal may never be realized, and it is unlikely that the media would take it upon themselves to provide such anonymity without being compelled to do so. A more likely avenue of change may lie in continued educational efforts to further increase societal awareness about rape and to eradicate the persistence of rape myths that still exist in society.

Research examining changes in overall conviction and incarceration rates since reforms have also failed to find consistent results. In Michigan, for example, where the first and most comprehensive reforms were implemented, research has found increases in the number of arrests and convictions for rape but no change in the number of rapes reported to police.[57] In California, early data found an increase in the probability that those convicted of rape would be sentenced to a state institution but no increase in clearance rates for rape or court filings.[58] In a very extensive study of reports of rape and on the processing of rape cases in six urban jurisdictions, Julie Horney and Cassia Spohn concluded that "our overall finding was the overall lack of impact of rape law reforms . . . we have shown that the ability of rape reform legislation to produce instrumental changes is limited."[59] However, using more refined data, such as age- (victims over 18) and gender-specific (male offenders and female victims) incidents of rape, other researchers have found increases in both conviction and incarceration rates of rape offenders at the national level and in three states they examined.[60]

When examining aggregate rape and sexual assault data, it is important to be as specific as possible regarding the age and gender of the rape victim. Most of the research investigating rape from the NCVS as well as data from police reports from single jurisdictions has not excluded rapes of minors under 18 years of age or rapes involving multiple offenders. This poses a very serious interpretive problem. "Rape and sexual assault," as used by most jurisdictions as well as the NCVS, includes such things as incest and other sexual offenses against minors in addition to other dissimilar offenses like sodomy against a male.[61] In fact, a recent Justice Department study concluded that police-recorded incidents of rape in three states showed that 44% of the victims were younger than 18 years and two-thirds of violent sex offenders serving time in state prisons said their victims were younger than 18.[62] In sum, utilizing aggregate data that do not distinguish between these heterogeneous incidents can obviously affect the outcome of the study, particularly when assessing the usefulness of rape reforms. Clearly, more research is needed that utilizes age- and gender-specific incidents of rape to better examine the effectiveness of rape law reforms. In addition to the legal sphere, reform has also affected the response of communities, and it is important to also examine the impact of medical reforms—especially in regard to the ability of communities to respond to victims of rape.

Today, it is not uncommon for jurisdictions to have specialized units that respond to incidents of rape and other sexual assaults. These units have come to be known as **sexual assault response teams** (SART) and often include a coordinated response to the victimization, including victim assistance workers along with special prosecutors and investigators. One recent addition to these teams is the use of **sexual assault nurse examiners** (SANE), who typically provide expert testimony for the prosecution. Although there have been no evaluation studies of SARTs, most believe that such units will only serve to increase the criminal justice system's sensitivity toward sexual assault victims, thereby decreasing the trauma that historically has been associated with reporting a sexual assault to police. For example, the team approach used by many SARTs allows for vertical prosecution, which alleviates the need for a victim to repeatedly relive the trauma by describing the assault to numerous entities along the adjudication process. These changes are real and positive, and they suggest that the usefulness of the reforms should not be judged solely on the basis of changes in reporting.

The Criminal Justice System and Sexual Assault Offenders

Obviously, there cannot be a criminal justice response to rape without the victim or someone else reporting the incident to police. However, we can examine what happens when rape offenders are adjudicated by looking at the **National Corrections Reporting Program** (NCRP), which is administered by the BJS and collects data on this issue. In 2009, the most recent data that are available indicates that in state prisons the average median sentence length for those inmates convicted of some form of rape was 120 months (about 10 years). In that same year, rape offenders who had been released from state prisons for the first time served a median of 74 months in prison at the time of their release. Compared to those convicted of homicide, these sentence length and time served rates are lower. However, they are much higher than similar data for those convicted of other violent crimes, including robbery and other assaults.

It is a stereotypical perception that rape offenders are more likely to recidivate, that is reoffend, after release from prison compared to other violent offenders. When rates of recidivism are examined, however, rates for those convicted of rape are generally lower compared to other offenders. For example, using the BJS recidivism analysis tool, about 5.8% of males with fewer than 2 prior arrests are expected to be convicted of a new crime within one year. In contrast, 12.7% of males released from prison after serving time for other physical assaults are expected to be convicted of a new crime within one year.[63] Despite these low recidivism rates, societal fears of "serial rapists" are widespread, as evidenced by the proliferation of laws attempting to protect victims. Virtually every state now has legislation that includes sanctions, such as adding lifetime GPS monitoring of sex offenders, mandating civil commitment for life, restricting where they live (not near schools and playgrounds, etc.), and mandating registration of websites that are available to the public, to name the most common. Many of these statutes are named for victims, which helps to add urgency to their passage.

For example, in July 1994, Megan Kanka was a 7-year-old living in New Jersey when her neighbor lured her into his home by promising her a puppy. Once he had her in his house, he raped, strangled, and suffocated her. Her body was then stuffed into a plastic toy chest and dumped in a nearby park. Jesse Timmendequas was the man who raped and murdered her, and he was a twice-convicted child offender who lived across the street from the Kanka home and was sharing his house with two other convicted sex offenders he had met in prison. Although the **Jacob Wetterling Act** was in place at the federal level before this incident, this case was the catalyst for many states and the federal government to enact stronger legislation requiring convicted sex offenders to register with law enforcement officials.[64] The Wetterling Act required persons convicted of a criminal offense against a minor or sexually violent offense and persons deemed to be "sexually violent predators" to register a current address with state law enforcement. This information, along with fingerprints, was to be transferred to the FBI. The problem with this act, according to many critics, was that this information was never supposed to be released to the public. In addition, states implemented this act in very different ways and defined "sexually violent predators" in various ways as well.

After Megan Kanka's death, many states and the federal government enacted legislation named after the little girl that was intended to make the registries more effective. For example, the U.S. Congress amended the Wetterling Act by adding what was termed **Megan's Law**. This legislation allows the release of offender information "for any purpose permitted under the laws of the state." This gives states the power to determine what kind and how much of the information about offenders is disclosed to whom and for what purpose.

Another legislative addition passed by Congress was the **Pam Lychner Sexual Offender Tracking and Identification Act of 1996**, in memory of a victims' rights activist who died in the TWA Flight 800 crash off the coast of Long Island, New York.[65] This act mandated the creation of a national database of convicted sex offenders designed to track offenders as they moved from state to state and cover for states not in compliance with the Wetterling Act. The most recent data available for these registries indicate that as of January 1, 2012, there were nearly 747,500 registered sex offenders in 49 states and the District of Columbia. This was nearly a 25% increase in the number registered since 2006. The states with the largest number of registered sex offenders are California, followed by Texas and Florida. Because each state defines what type of offenders will be registered, absolute nationwide number comparisons remain somewhat problematic. However, it is important to note that the absolute number of registrants will continue to grow in each state. Another provision of the Lychner Act was that the registration requirement was changed from a maximum of 10 years to 10 years to life, depending on the number of prior convictions and the type of crime committed. The majority of states and the District of Columbia now have publicly accessible websites containing information on individual sex offenders in a searchable format.

In 2006, Congress passed the **Adam Walsh Child Protection and Safety Act**, which mandated a number of changes including expanding the definition of "jurisdiction" to include federally-recognized American Indian tribes, expanding the number of sex offenses that must be captured by registrations, and established a new office within the U.S. Justice Department to administer the standards for sex offender notification and registration called the Office of Sex Offender Sentencing, Monitoring, Apprehending, Registering and Tracking (SMART). In addition to these statutes passed at the federal level, there are numerous acts that have been passed at the state level.[66] As politicians continue to write more stringent legislation, it is important to note that there is not much research that examines the effectiveness of such legislation in preventing sexual assaults generally or sexual assaults against children in particular. One recent study investigated recidivism practices of a released group of sexual offenders, and using Google Earth, mapped whether their offending could have been prevented with the residency restrictions placed on them. They concluded that the new offenses, like most violent crime, were against victims known to the offenders and the few that did establish new contact with young offenders who were strangers did not do so near a school, park, or playground, all of which are included in residential restriction laws. In explaining why the residential restriction laws do not appear to work at deterring recidivism, the authors explained, "Why does residential proximity appear to matter so little with regard to sexual reoffending? Much has to do with the patterns of sexual offending in general. . . . Sex offenders are much more likely to victimize someone they know . . . one of the most common victim-offender relationships of this study for those who victimized children was that of a male offender developing a romantic relationship with a woman who had children. . . . They used their relationships with these women to gain access to their victims . . . or through babysitting for an acquaintance or co-worker."[67]

In the end, debates about sexual offending legislation are often heated. Some critics argue that states should do more to rehabilitate sex offenders in the first place and that registries and residential restrictions placed on offenders only serve to stigmatize offenders and prevent them from moving on with their lives. Other legal scholars contend that these laws are really nothing more than a second punishment for those who have already paid their debt to society. In a fascinating examination of sex offender legislation over the 20th century, Chrysanthi Leon concluded that all sex offenders, regardless of the contextual circumstances of their crimes, are now classified as "monsters" requiring confinement, which prioritizes the public's belief "that all sexual offending is harmful, dangerous, and caused by deviant desires that are compulsive and beyond control."[68] Today, based on politicians' need to appear tough on crime, such legislation will probably continue to become ever more punitive, regardless of their effectiveness to combat such crimes.

Conclusions

We hope this chapter has eradicated any stereotypes you may have had about rape and sexual assault. Rape is not a rare event and it is used in many arenas as a tool of violence, power, and dominance. We believe we have come a long way as a society in recognizing that these victimizations are no different from other forms of violence. However, we still have a long way to go. When fewer than one in 10 women who meet the legal criteria of being raped on college campuses and fewer than one in four victims in the general population are willing to report their victimization to police, we know that the vast majority of offenders will never be punished and any deterrence value the criminal justice system may have for them and for other would-be offenders is lost. It is hoped that, one day, societal awareness will catch up with legal norms.

Key Terms

Adam Walsh Child Protection and Safety Act

anger retaliation rapist

behaviorally specific questions

Child Abuse Prevention and Treatment Act

convict culture

date-rape drugs

drug-facilitated sexual assault

GHB

International Criminal Tribunal for Rwanda

Jacob Wetterling Act

Jeanne Clery Disclosure of Campus Security Policy and Campus Crime Statistics Act of 1998

Ketamine

Megan's Law

National College
   Women Sexual Assault
   Victimization Study

National Corrections
   Reporting Program

Pam Lychner Sexual
   Offender Tracking and
   Identification
   Act of 1996

patriarchy

power assertive rapist

power reassurance rapist

prison rape

Prison Rape Elimination
   Act of 2003

rape

rape law reforms

Rohyphol

sadistic rapist

sexual assault

sexual assault nurse
   examiners

sexual assault response teams

spoils of war

Student Right-to-Know
   and Campus Security
   Act of 1990

Discussion Questions

1. All 50 states have passed some form of mandatory reporting law for cases of child abuse, including cases of physical and sexual abuse. Although mandatory reporting varies by state, the majority of those specified to report include teachers and other educational service workers, social service workers, law enforcement officials, and other health and mental heath care workers. However, remember that much of the information we have about the true magnitude of sexual assault comes from victimization surveys. Yet some national surveys, including the National Crime Victimization Survey funded by the U.S. Department of Justice, do not require interviewers to report incidents of uncovered abuse against children to authorities. What are the ethical issues that surround such practices? Does the protection of children outweigh the need to gather information on their victimization? Should respondents who report their victimizations also be told about victims' services that may be available in their area?

2. You have access to your state's criminal statutes for all crimes, including rape and sexual assaults. One way to access state statutes is through a search engine called LexisNexus, which provides access to all state statutes through its State Capital database. Using this search engine, find your state's statutes for sexual assault. Based on the reforms made by most jurisdictions that were discussed in this chapter, look at the sexual assault statutes in your state to see how they provide protection to victims. Do they have a form of rape shield law that in some way prohibits information about a victim's past sexual history? Is there gender-neutral language written into the statutes? Is an incident considered a crime regardless of the victim–offender relationship? What type of corroborating evidence, if any, is required?

3. Go to the National Criminal Justice Reference Service, which is sponsored by the U.S. Department of Justice (www.ncjrs.gov) and find the following publication: *Extent, Nature, and Consequences of Rape Victimization: Findings From the National Violence Against Women Survey* (www.ncjrs.gov/pdffiles1/nij/210346.pdf). Using this publication as a resource, discuss how the findings from this survey did or did not conform to what you believed about rape victimizations before you read this chapter and read this publication.

Mob Violence

Accounts of outrages committed by mobs form the everyday news of the times. They have pervaded the country from New England to Louisiana; they are neither peculiar to the eternal snows of the former nor the burning suns of the latter; they are not the creatures of climate, neither are they confined to the slaveholding or the non-slaveholding states. Alike they spring up among the pleasure-hunting masters of Southern slaves, and the order-loving citizens of the land of steady habits. Whatever then their cause may be, it is common to the whole country.

—Abraham Lincoln[1]

The great mystery of all conduct is social conduct. I have had to study it all my life, but I cannot pretend to understand it. I may seem to know a man through and through, and I still would not dare to say the first thing about what he will do in a group.

—F. Bartlett[2]

Men, it has been well said, think in herds; it will be seen that they go mad in herds, while they only recover their senses slowly, and one by one.

—Charles Mackay[3]

On the 4th of August, 2011, a 29-year-old British man named Mark Duggan was shot and killed by police in Tottenham, a northern suburb of London. Because Duggan was black and the shooting occurred under somewhat suspicious circumstances in a community with a history of troubled race relations, Tottenham locals responded with outrage and began clashing with police. In subsequent days, the unrest spread to other communities throughout England and descended into widespread rioting that included arson, looting, and violent confrontations with police. All told, the disturbances resulted in widespread property damage, a number of deaths, many injuries, and thousands of arrests. While law enforcement, government officials, and the media defined it as rioting, some supporters labeled the upheaval as an insurrection, a protest, and even as an "English Spring," a reference to the "Arab Spring" of 2010 that brought down a number of governments in North Africa and the Middle East. A better comparison, however, might be with the riots in France that had taken place a few years earlier.

On October 27, 2005, two Muslim teenagers died by electrocution while allegedly trying to hide from police in an electricity substation in a Paris suburb characterized by high rates of poverty and unemployment.[4] Their deaths sparked resentment in the mostly immigrant community, leading to protests that quickly turned into riots. Most scholars contend that, while the boys' deaths acted as the trigger point, the real reason for the riots was attributable to the enduring poverty and sense of hopelessness that many Muslim immigrants endured in these "ghettoized" suburbs.[5] Within two days, violence had spread to other cities in France. After nearly two weeks of rioting, nearly 1,500 vehicles had been burned along with several businesses and a school. The riots left many injured and at least one person dead.[6]

Closer to home, in Cincinnati, Ohio, on April 7, 2001, Timothy Thomas, an unarmed African American man, was shot and killed by a police officer who had confronted Mr. Thomas in a dark alleyway. The officer asserted that he was in fear for his life since he thought Mr. Thomas was reaching for a gun in his pants and the officer said "his gun just went off."[7] Like many other similar incidents across the United States, some of the public did not buy the explanation. For the next several days, the city of Cincinnati exploded in riots, with fires burning in many places, people pulled out of their cars and beaten, looting, and police in riot gear unable to control the mass hysteria and violence. In the end, hundreds of people were jailed and dozens were injured, including one police officer, who was shot.[8]

As these relatively recent riots illustrate, mob violence is not something that belongs to the distant past. The fury of the mob continues to haunt our society and our world. Like all violence, mob violence is not unique to any nation or the modern era. History is replete with examples of communal violence wracking cities, communities, and entire regions as crowds erupted into uncontrolled and destructive violence in countless places and at numerous times for many different reasons. From ancient times to the present, many societies have confronted the problem of group violence. Ancient Greek society experienced it so often that the dramatist Euripides suggested that "mobs in their emotions are much like children, subject to the same tantrums and fits of fury."[9] Rome had so many riots that the Roman emperors resorted to ruinously expensive gladiatorial games in large part because they wanted to keep the mobs happy with "bread and circuses," to borrow the Roman poet Juvenal's famous phrase. England and France both suffered dreadfully from mob violence throughout their long histories. In fact, the historian Julius Ruff asserts that riots "represented a serious threat to the political and social stability of early modern Europe."[10] The danger was so bad that many European nations passed laws limiting the right of ordinary citizens to assemble, rightly fearing that demonstrations or protests could easily get out of hand and devolve into a riot.[11] In June of 1780, for example, the **Anti-Catholic Gordon Riots** took place in and around London. In less than a week, mobs burned, pillaged, and looted, leaving around 500 people dead—the army was finally called in to quell the disorder.[12] In France, one historical study found around 450 to 500 riots occurring between the years 1590 and 1715.[13] In short, **mob violence** has been a relatively common occurrence within most societies throughout history.

Because we are social creatures who need to live and work within groups, there is something fundamentally frightening about large groups of people engaging in what we perceive as mindless and excessive brutality. We need to trust and rely on our friends, neighbors, and fellow citizens; we want to feel safe. Mob violence, however, calls into question our security within these same groups. It makes us wonder about the behavior of these same friends, neighbors, and fellow citizens. How can we function within groups when they are potentially so dangerous? By their very nature, riots target anybody and anything unlucky enough to be in the wrong place at the wrong time. In these situations, no one is safe. Seemingly rational and reasonable people appear to act irrationally and unreasonably. But is this an accurate picture? Do crowds simply "erupt" into violence or is there something more to it? Why do some crowds explode into violent behavior while others do not? Are there specific identifiable triggers that play a role in sparking the transformation of a crowd into a mob? This chapter is largely concerned with exploring these kinds of questions. In this chapter, we examine three of the most well-known forms of mob violence: **riots**, **lynch mobs**, and **vigilante groups**. All three are forms of collective behavior that are relatively spontaneous and unplanned (although there are exceptions), and the groups are relatively unorganized. First, however, we need to spend some time discussing and defining crowds and mobs.

Mobs and Crowds

What is the difference between a **mob** and a **crowd**? Simply put, a crowd is nothing more than a collection of individuals who may or may not share a common purpose.[14] Groups waiting for a bus, standing in line, or listening to a concert are all crowds. They are usually temporary in nature and do not usually act in a unified and singular manner. A mob, on the other hand, has very different connotations. The term "mob" carries with it a tremendous amount of implicit condemnation. In fact, the word "mob" comes from the Latin *mobile vulgus*, which literally means "the movable common people" and was meant to refer to the fickleness or inconstancy of the crowd.[15] Other terms often used synonymously have been "rabble," "herd," and "the common masses," none of which is particularly positive in meaning. From these unflattering portrayals, we can see that mobs are often associated with the lower classes, disorder, and a lack of respect for the law. They are usually portrayed as being uncontrolled, unorganized, angry, and emotional. Historically, these arguments and images were typically used by those in positions of power and authority to remove any legitimacy from these mass gatherings. Many riots throughout history have mostly been responses to injustice and oppression. As such, it was in the best interests of those in power to portray mob violence as an expression of blind rage rather than a form of protest and resistance.[16] The term "mob," therefore, is a politicized word as much as it is a descriptive one. Because of its common usage, however, in this chapter we use the term "mob" for convenience's sake. To summarize, then, essentially a crowd is any gathering of people, while a mob is a crowd that is seen as being out of control. Put another way, a mob is a crowd waiting for a trigger to set it off.

Sid Heal suggests a typology that organizes crowds and mobs into specific subtypes, which is summarized in Figure 8.1. This way of organizing and categorizing groups is best understood as a continuum of collective behavior that ranges from the most violence prone (escape mobs) to the least (casual crowds).[17] Keep in mind that these are fluid classifications since it is possible for a group to move from one type to another given the right circumstances. As we shall see, there are a number of different catalysts that can set off a crowd, and when this happens, various mechanisms occur that help shape the behavior of individuals in mobs.

Mob Mentality

Why do we often behave differently in crowds than we do when we are alone? A number of different theories on the behavior of crowds have been suggested, but one of the first theories was suggested by Gustave Le Bon, who is sometimes referred to as the "grandfather of collective behavior theory."[18] In fairness, Le Bon was not the first to comment on the behavior of crowds. The ancient Greek lawgiver and poet Solon, for example, suggested that Athenians were as clever as foxes when minding their own affairs, but as soon as they congregated they lost their wits. The playwright Aristophanes also described his fellow Athenians as reasonable old men at home and as fools in the assemblies. Le Bon, however, was the first to explore the behavior of crowds more systematically. He attempted to explain the transformation of reasonable individuals into seemingly out-of-control and violent people when in a mob.

The crowd, Le Bon felt, develops a mind of its own, and individuals become highly vulnerable and suggestible to the will of the collective group. In Le Bon's view, crowd behavior is essentially contagious, so if one person gets excited, angry, or violent, others will quickly pick up on these emotions and actions. In a way, he was suggesting

❖ **Figure 8.1** Continuum of Mob Violence

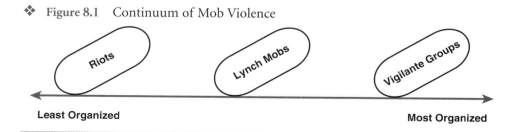

that individuals in a crowd are easily swayed by the mood and behavior of the group because at an unconscious level we are programmed to do so. Individual conscious personality disappears and is replaced by a collective mind that, in Le Bon's view, is credulous, impulsive, emotional, without moral responsibility, less intelligent than individuals, and blindly obedient to charismatic leaders who "hypnotize" and mobilize a crowd into action.[19] He suggests that

> We see, then, that the disappearance of the conscious personality, the predominance of the unconscious, the turning by means of suggestion and contagion of feelings and ideas in an identical direction, the tendency immediately to transform the suggested ideas into acts; these we see, are the principal characteristics of the individual forming part of a crowd. He is no longer himself, but has become an automaton who has ceased to be guided by his will.[20]

The work of Gustave Le Bon was later expanded by Herbert Blumer, who sketched out the transformation of a crowd into a mob.[21] He contended that the first element in the transformation must be a trigger; something happens that is exciting or interesting and able to draw people together, such as a police shooting in a minority neighborhood or an unpopular court verdict, to borrow a few examples from recent U.S. history. Next, the focus of the crowd converges on a common element as emotions strengthen. United around an object or issue, individuals may escalate into behavior that will quickly be mirrored by others. Perhaps someone throws a rock or smashes a car window and others in the crowd, caught up in the moment, also unleash their aggression and begin acting violently; thus a mob is born. The criticism of Le Bon's and Blumer's work, however, is that they tend to simplify the actions of the mob and focus exclusively on the emotional and irrational elements of crowd behavior while downplaying the more instrumental aspects of the violence. In other words, their work begs the question, "Is there purpose and reason to mob violence?" Do people caught up in mobs think about the consequences of their action?

Recent work on individuals in mobs portrays them as being much more rational than the earlier conceptualizations. Clark McPhail, for example, after extensively reviewing the major theories of and perspectives on crowd behavior, emphatically asserts, "Individuals are not driven mad by crowds; nor do they lose cognitive control!"[22] Instead, he suggests that much crowd behavior is basically a rational attempt to accomplish or prevent some sort of social change. Importantly, he also acknowledges that this rationality is influenced and shaped by emotions and beliefs. Similarly, the historian Paul Gilje points out that mobs are often very selective in their choice of victims and targets, which does not support the notion of mindless violence. He says,

> Riotous crowds do not act merely on impulse and are not fickle. There is a reason behind the actions of the rioters, no matter how violent those actions may be. This rationality has two major components. First, the mob's tumultuous behavior is directly connected to grievances of those involved in the riot. A tumultuous crowd does not ordinarily engage in wanton destruction of persons and property. Instead they seize upon some object or objects that represent the forces that propelled them into the riot originally.[23]

While acknowledging that crowds are affected by emotion and may sometimes get out of control, these more recent perspectives reveal that they are also fundamentally rational responses to specific political, social, religious, racial, and/or economic catalysts. Consider for example the recent riots in Egypt that erupted in the city of Port Said in January 2013. The previous year at a soccer game on February 1, 2012, between Port Said's al-Masry team and Cairo's al-Ahly team, rival groups of hard-core fans engaged in a full-blown riot that left 74 people dead and over a thousand injured.[24] Some of these fans, known as Ultras because of their loyalty to their club and propensity for violence, smuggled weapons into the soccer stadium and began attacking supporters of the other team.[25] Things escalated after the violence spilled out on to the field and the crowd panicked. As thousands tried to escape, they created a stampede that resulted in many injuries and death, with some people falling from the bleachers to their death, while others were crushed or suffocated as the escape mob tried to squeeze down stairwells and through the exits. In the wake of this disaster, 75 participants were charged with murder and attempted murder for those deaths, and on January 26, 2013, 21 of the defendants were sentenced to death. Rioting broke out almost immediately after the verdicts were announced, with relatives storming the prison where the condemned were being held. The violence soon spread throughout Port Said, and over the course of the next several days hundreds were injured and at least 38 individuals were killed. While the specific trigger for the violence was the imposition of a death sentence on so many of the convicted, in a larger sense many believe that the rioting was much more about dissatisfaction and disillusionment with President Mohamed Morsi's Islamist government that failed to live up to the expectations created by the Arab Spring and which has seemed to be becoming more authoritarian and intolerant.[26]

Another way to assess this issue is to identify some of the reasons why individuals come to participate in these types of group violence. Sid Heal, for example, has suggested that there are eight specific psychological factors that serve to lower or remove our prohibitions against violent behavior and thus facilitate individual participation in mob violence:[27]

- *Novelty*: Some people may come to participate in riots and other group behavior simply because they are bored and riots provide a sense of excitement and novelty. It's a break from routine.
- *Release*: Even though an individual may not be very concerned with a specific grievance or cause, they may participate because participation offers a release for more generalized feelings of hostility, anger, and/or frustration that they may harbor.
- *Power*: Mobs feel empowered by the violence and destructiveness they unleash. Joining in large-scale violence can confer upon somebody intoxicating feelings of control, domination, and supremacy.
- *Justification*: The sense of power created by mob violence can also lead to feelings of righteousness and legitimacy.
- *Suggestibility*: Many individuals in a mob may not be fully aware of what is going on or why and so may be open to the answers provided by others who may appear to better know or understand the situation.
- *Stimulation*: The emotions and sentiments of crowds can be infectious, and individuals caught up in the group can easily find their own emotions aroused and stimulated.

- *Conformity*: Not only do individuals have a natural tendency to conform to the demands of a group, rioting mobs also have a tendency to attack and victimize those who resist or don't conform, which tends to increase the pressures toward going along with the throng.
- *Deindividuation*: In groups, individual identity tends to be diffused into the larger collective identity. When combined with feelings of anonymity, participants may feel released from normal constraints on their behavior.

These facilitators suggest that individuals participate in riots for many different reasons. Importantly, this involvement is also influenced by the historical and social context within which the group behavior is situated. That aggression, however, can take a number of related yet different forms and meanings.

As we stated earlier, this chapter will examine three types of mob violence: riots, lynch mobs, and vigilante groups. Each can be differentiated by its level of organization, as seen in Table 8.1. Riots tend to be the most spontaneous and the least organized; lynch mobs

Table 8.1	Typology of Crowds and Mobs
Casual crowd	• No common purpose • Members define themselves as individuals • Requires a great deal to provoke this kind of crowd into violence
Cohesive crowd	• Gathers for a common purpose • While members still define themselves as individuals, more of a collective spirit prevails • Rarely engages in violence
Expressive crowd	• Members share a common purpose • Members share collective sense of anger and/or frustration • Is quickly moved to action and violence
Aggressive crowd	• Members share a common and strong sense of purpose • Individual identity is muted or lost • Group tends to be impulsive and emotional and easily aroused to violence
Aggressive mob	• Targets of this group can be property, people, or both • The violence of this group is motivated primarily by emotion • Tends to be fairly short lived
Expressive mob	• Violence is seen as a means to express anger, resentment, and frustration • Violence and rioting are ways for members to give voice to their sentiments • Violence and rioting are seen as legitimate expressions of collective emotions
Acquisitive mob	• Motivated by greed and a desire to acquire goods • Looters use the anarchy of a riot to plunder and steal • Is more easily controlled by authorities
Escape mob	• Characterized by panicked behavior • Very dangerous • The only type of group that can be instantly aroused into mindless violence

fall somewhere in the middle of the continuum; while vigilante groups are often the most planned and organized. It is important to emphasize that these are generalizations and there are plenty of exceptions to the rule. Any particular example can involve varying levels of organization. The infamous **New York City Draft Riots of 1863** began with a pre-planned and organized protest of the draft and then spontaneously evolved into a race and class riot.[28] We also need to keep in mind that these are somewhat arbitrary distinctions and that many of the qualities of riots, lynchings, and vigilantism are virtually indistinguishable from each other. Many riots involve lynchings, and lynch mobs often define their actions as a form of vigilantism. In other words, we discuss them as separate entities for conceptual clarity and for ease of discussion, but we cannot forget that they are variations on a common theme. Each can contain elements of the others, and the boundaries between them are sometimes indistinct and unclear. That being said, we begin with riots.

Riots

Riots have been defined a number of different ways. The Federal Criminal Code, for example, defines a riot as

> A public disturbance involving (1) an act or acts of violence by one or more persons part of an assemblage of three or more persons, which act or acts shall constitute a clear and present danger of, or shall result in, damage or injury to the property of any other person or to the person of any other individual or (2) a threat or threats of the commission of an act or acts of violence by one or more persons part of an assemblage of three or more persons having, individually or collectively, the ability of immediate execution of such threat or threats, where the performance of the threatened act or acts of violence would constitute a clear and present danger of, or would result in, damage or injury to the property of any other person or to the person of any other individual.[29]

Every state has its own definition of a riot, and these sometimes vary significantly from each other and from the federal code. Arizona, for example, defines a riot as occurring as follows: "A person commits riot if, with two or more other persons acting together, such person recklessly uses force or violence or threatens to use force or violence, if such threat is accompanied by immediate power of execution, which disturbs the public peace."[30] For Arizona, then, a riot needs only two participants. Not everyone necessarily agrees with such an inclusive definition.

Paul Gilje, who has studied riots extensively, asserts that riots are "any group of twelve or more people attempting to assert their will immediately through the use of force outside the normal bounds of law."[31] While setting the threshold for a riot at 12 people appears somewhat arbitrary, it does reinforce the idea that riots are a form of crowd violence.

Charles Tilly, on the other hand, writes that the word "riot . . . embodies a political judgment rather than an analytical distinction. Authorities and observers label as riots the damage-doing gatherings of which they disapprove, but they use terms like demonstration, protest, resistance, or retaliation for essentially similar events of which they approve."[32] Tilly's work reminds us that the meaning of a riot can vary tremendously depending upon who is involved, the reasons for the violence, and the social audience. Riots, in other words, occur in particular political and social contexts that influence how they are perceived and

❖ Photo 8.1   Illustration depicting a man being beaten during the New York Draft Riots

BRUTAL MURDER OF COL. H. T. O'BRIEN, NEAR HIS RESIDENCE, JULY 14.

defined. This is as true today as it was in the past. Not surprisingly, riots—like many other forms of collective violence—have been a fairly common feature of U.S. history. From the earliest days of this nation to the present day, riots have often been a featured part of U.S. life. Romanticized examples of civil disobedience, such as the Boston Tea Party and the Boston Massacre are perhaps more accurately remembered as riots. In their behavior, the colonists were simply reflecting common attitudes and practices that had been a traditional part of English life. As Gilje summarizes, "Scholars now know that the boisterous crowds of the 1760s and 1770s built upon popular practices inherited from English traditions that were well rehearsed in the years before resistance began."[33]

During the Civil War, the infamous draft riots occurred in New York City when President Lincoln imposed the draft (see In Focus 8.1). These traditional forms of civil unrest and destruction continue into the present day. The 20th century was no exception to this practice and was filled with many different examples, some of which we will examine in more detail below.

As we alluded to previously, riots happen when a group of people react to some trigger or grievance and become violent and destructive. It is usually spontaneous, although it sometimes can be orchestrated and set in motion by those who are trying to achieve some political or social goal. It is also important to remember that not every crowd descends into violence. Eruptions of group violence can and do occur in a number of different contexts, such as around sporting events or in prison settings, but in this chapter we are going to focus on one of the most destructive and widespread manifestations of rioting, those that revolve around race.

IN FOCUS 8.1

The New York Draft Riots

The New York Draft Riots are one of the best known historic examples of rioting in U.S. cities, thanks in part to Martin Scorcese's film, *Gangs of New York*. They also are considered by some to be the worst example of riots and civil unrest that this nation has seen.

In the summer of 1863, the Civil War had been raging for two years and casualties had been mounting for the North. The war had proved monumentally expensive in lives, and the Union had lost many men in battles, such as the First and Second Bull Run, the Seven Days Battle, Fredericksburg, and Chancellorsville, to name but a few. At the battle of Antietam alone, the Union had over twelve thousand casualties. To make good these losses, President Lincoln and Congress passed an act of conscription which authorized the draft of every able-bodied male citizen between the ages of 20 and 35 and unmarried men between 35 and 45. Terrible stories of the horror and privations of the war enjoyed wide circulation in the North and, consequently, volunteers were becoming ever harder to attract. Conscription seemed like the only alternative.

The draft was determined by lottery in each congressional district and, even though all able-bodied men were eligible, a $300 fee exempted those who could afford it. Clearly, this policy discriminated against the underprivileged, and they didn't like it since it ensured that the poor would do the bulk of the fighting and dying. Monday, June 13, 1863, was the second day of the draft, and when the draft offices opened at 10:00 a.m., crowds of laborers had already gathered around the provost's offices where the names were being selected. The large and restless crowds quickly descended into violence and, after destroying the provost's offices, spread out and began attacking police stations as well. While initially targeting only military and government facilities, the rioters soon began widening the focus of their violence. African Americans, for example, were a particular target of the mobs, and many suffered from horrendous tortures and cruelty before being murdered. The rioters also began looting and pillaging the homes of the wealthy and privileged. It soon became clear that various groups saw in the violence their opportunity to settle scores or unleash their aggression against those with whom they had grievances and problems, whether it was the police, African Americans, the wealthy, Republicans, or anyone who made the mistake of trying to oppose the mob. Badly outnumbered, the police could not contain the rioting mobs. Finally, soldiers were force marched from the Gettysburg battlefield (the battle had just taken place) and took back the city, street by bloody street. It wasn't until the 16th that the riots were finally brought to an end.

SOURCES: Herbert Asbury, *The Gangs of New York* (New York: Thunder's Mouth Press, 1998); Iver Bernstein, *The New York City Draft Riots: Their Significance for American Society and Politics in the Age of the Civil War* (New York: Oxford University Press, 1990).

Race Riots

Race has been one of the most problematic features of U.S. life, and the discontent perceived by some minority group members has often been expressed through rioting and accompanying violence. In the United States, these outbreaks of communal violence reflect deep-seated discontent and frustration with the inequalities and injustices of society. And there have been many. Between 1900 and 1949, there were at least 33 cases of significant racial unrest, the most deadly of which occurred in Tulsa, Oklahoma, at the end of May 1921.[34]

Tulsa in the 1920s was a thriving boomtown and had grown strong and rich on oil and hope. The African American quarter of the city, known as Greenwood, was a healthy and vibrant place with many African American-owned businesses and attractions.[35] But racial tensions existed in Tulsa as they did for the nation at large. Race riots had been occurring all over the country in those years in places such as Houston, Chicago, Washington, DC, and Duluth. The **Tulsa Race Riot of 1921** began after a young African American man named Diamond Dick Rowland stumbled into a white lady as he was entering an elevator and unwittingly grabbed her arm. Unfortunately, the young lady assumed the worst and quickly claimed that he had assaulted her. Dick Rowland was arrested the next day by police and placed in the city jail, and that's when the trouble began. Earlier that year, an African American man who allegedly murdered a cab driver had been forcibly taken from the Sheriff, driven out of town by a mob in a caravan that reportedly stretched over a mile, and was lynched. The Tulsa police arrived just before the killing, but preferred to direct traffic rather than save the intended victim.[36] It also didn't help that the local paper ran a lurid and completely fictional account of the elevator attack that strongly insinuated a sexual element to the supposed attack. The paperboys selling the paper sold copies by yelling, "EXTRA! EXTRA! TO LYNCH NEGRO TONIGHT! READ ALL ABOUT IT!"[37] Given this kind of reporting, the recent lynching, and the racially charged atmosphere of the times, a number of African Americans decided to arm themselves and go to the jail in order to ensure that Rowland wasn't lynched. Not surprisingly, this behavior was seen as an extremely provocative act by many of the white citizens of Tulsa, and when a scuffle broke out at the jail and a gunshot sounded, it almost immediately escalated into a full blown gun battle. Within minutes, around 20 whites and blacks were dead or wounded. After the African Americans retreated to Greenwood, mobs of whites armed themselves and marched on Greenwood, precipitating some of the ugliest and most destructive racial violence this country has ever seen. Homes, businesses, and churches were looted and destroyed. African Americans—even the very young and the elderly—indiscriminately shot. At one point, the National Guard set up machine guns and began pouring fire into Greenwood. The damage was summarized by one commentator:

> Thirty-eight were confirmed dead, including ten whites, but the true figure was well over that, perhaps even three hundred. More certain is the destruction of property: 1,256 houses were burned in a thirty-six block area of Greenwood, including churches, stores, hotels, businesses, two newspapers, a school, a hospital, and a library—in short, all the institutions that perpetuated black life in Tulsa. The burned property was valued between $1.5 million and $1.8 million—more than $14 million in 2000 dollars.[38]

Unfortunately, none of the rioters was ever held legally accountable for their actions, even though many of the main actors were well known.

Race riots exploded into the U.S. consciousness again during the 1960s and yet again in the 1990s. From June 1963 to May 1968, for example, 239 riots took place that involved over 200,000 participants, 8,000 injuries, and 190 fatalities.[39] The historian of U.S. violence, Richard Maxwell Brown, summarizes the worst of these riots beginning with

> The August 11–16, 1965, Watts riot in the Los Angeles area, with thirty-four killed and $35,000,000–$40,000,000 in property damage. Other notable riots of the traumatic 1965–1968 period were the Chicago and Cleveland uprisings of 1966; the gigantic 1967 riots in Newark with twenty-three killed and $10,250,000 in property damage and in Detroit with forty-three killed and $40,000,000–$45,000,000 in property damage. Following the assassination of

Martin Luther King on April 4, 1968, there was a massive wave of 125 riots (led by those in Washington, Baltimore, Chicago, and Kansas City, Missouri), with 46 deaths and $70,000,000 in property damage.[40]

This catalogue of death and destruction is by no means complete, especially if we add the riots from our more recent past. In 1992, for example, the city of Los Angeles exploded in the wake of the acquittal of four police officers who had been on trial for the beating of Rodney King. Rodney King was an African American motorist who was stopped by the Los Angeles police on the evening of March 3, 1991. Originally spotted driving at over a hundred miles an hour, Rodney King led law enforcement officers on a high-speed chase before he was finally forced to stop.[41] While the two passengers quickly complied with instructions from police officers to exit the vehicle and lie face down on the ground, Rodney King, the driver of the vehicle, did not comply and instead advanced on the officers. Believing him to be under the influence of PCP and/or alcohol, the officers swarmed over King, jolted him with a taser, beat him with nightsticks, and kicked and stomped him, even after he was lying on the ground clearly stunned and helpless. The incident was captured on videotape by a private citizen and quickly created a firestorm of bad publicity. Ultimately, the district attorney of Los Angeles pressed charges against the four officers for using excessive force. Because of the media coverage of the case, the trial was moved to Simi Valley, a predominantly white suburb. This change of venue gave the impression to many, especially within the African American community, that the case was being stacked in favor of the police officers. The officers were ultimately acquitted of all the charges save one. After the verdicts were read, protests broke out almost immediately in various parts of the city and rapidly spread, although much of the unrest occurred in the largely minority south Los Angeles neighborhoods known collectively as South Central. Surprisingly, given the history of riots in Los Angeles, the buildup of tension leading up to the verdict, and the widespread belief within the LAPD that the city would burn, the Los Angeles Police Department was caught unprepared for the violence that followed the acquittal. As the violence flared up and officers were increasingly subjected to thrown bricks, bottles, and rocks, officers received orders to retreat from the affected areas. Instead of regrouping and returning to the rioting neighborhoods, the police stayed largely outside of the affected zones, not even setting up a perimeter. This allowed many unwary motorists to drive into the rioting and become victims. The rioting involved large-scale looting, arson, and violence directed against whites, Asians, and Latinos unfortunate enough to find themselves within South Central during the violence, many of whom were literally dragged from their vehicles and attacked. One of the most emblematic images of the riot was created when Reginald Denny, a white truck driver, was pulled from his vehicle at an intersection and horribly beaten, all of which was captured by a news helicopter hovering overhead. Gun battles erupted as Korean store owners banded together to fight the rioters. Korean businesses and liquor stores were particular targets of the mob, partially because of the prospect of looting offered by these establishments but also because they had been the focal point of various tensions and hostility. Black-owned businesses, while not spared from looting, were largely spared from arson. One post-riot study suggested that more than 2,000 Korean

American-owned business were destroyed, with the damage valued at $400 million. It was almost a week before police and national guardsman stopped the violence. In the end, between 50 and 60 individuals were killed and many thousands injured, not to mention the extensive property damage. Over 800 structures were damaged or destroyed to the tune of $900 million in property losses.

The **Los Angeles City Riot of 1992**, like many other earlier riots, revolved around racial issues. It is important to note that race riots are ultimately class riots as well, since race and poverty are so closely related in our country. In other words, while the riots were manifestations of racial discrimination and hostility, they were also about poverty, a lack of economic opportunities, and the frustration and alienation that often accompany such conditions. In this sense, race riots have not been purely spontaneous or completely irrational events. We find instead that they can best be understood as a response to historic and ongoing problems of racism and discrimination experienced by African Americans. The poet Langston Hughes once asked, "What happens to a dream deferred?" Many of the riots in our cities provide an answer to that question. When entire communities feel disenfranchised and discriminated against, they are primed for civil unrest and protest; it only takes a catalyst or triggering event to convert that pent-up anger and frustration into violence. In the case of the Los Angeles riot of 1992, the acquittal of the police officers was merely the specific spark that allowed a long-simmering rage and frustration to be released. The underlying factors that influenced the riot included very high rates of unemployment in South Central Los Angeles because of an economic downturn in the 1980s and a widespread perception that the LAPD was racist and brutal. For example, the LAPD had been in the news for its use of chokeholds, which had resulted in 17 deaths in six years, 13 of which were African American.[42] More immediate precipitants included the shooting of Latasha Harlins, a 15-year-old African American teenager who had been shot in the back of the head by a Korean owner of a deli store after a dispute. The suspended sentence received by the deli owner was perceived as lenient by the African American community and served to further reinforce the belief that African Americans were subject to different standards of justice compared with others. Very much in the same vein, we can point out that the Paris riots of 2005 or the British riots of 2011 occurred under similar economic conditions along with the same perceptions of inequality. In fact, we find very similar triggers for many of the other famous examples of riots:

- The 1965 Watts riot was instigated by a drunk driving arrest.
- The Newark riot of 1967 began with the arrest of an African American taxicab driver.
- The Detroit riot in 1967 was sparked by a police raid on an after-hours club.
- The 1980 Liberty City riot in Florida was started by the police killing of an unarmed African American who ran a red light.
- The 1989 riot in Miami occurred after police shot an unarmed African American motorcyclist.
- The 1997 looting and rioting in Nashville were precipitated by police officers shooting a young black suspect.
- The 2001 rioting in Cincinnati was the result of the police shooting an unarmed black man (noted at the beginning of the chapter).[43]

While none of these incidents should have been enough to begin a riot, they were triggering events because they were the most visible and inflammatory examples of the racism and brutality perceived to be employed by the police in many minority neighborhoods. In fact, in many minority neighborhoods, the police are seen as a hostile occupying army, not as public servants whose job it is to protect and serve.[44] This is not to suggest, however, that rioters act solely or even primarily out of a sense of injustice and for political and racial motivations. Many participants in riots see the violence as an opportunity for excitement, crime, and/or personal enrichment. To recognize the emotional elements of a riot, however, doesn't invalidate the underlying structural conditions that form the backdrop for race riots in this country. Historically, race riots—especially those directed against minority groups—have also often contained elements that may best be understood within the context of lynching, and it is to this form of mob violence that we turn next.

Lynching

Lynching is an imprecise term and has been used and misused in many ways. However, it can roughly be defined as an extralegal execution by a mob. This, of course, is not what Supreme Court Justice Clarence Thomas was referring to when he called his nomination hearings a "high tech lynching." Lynching is a type of collective violence in which a group of individuals circumvent the law and punish individuals for real or imagined crimes. Initially nonlethal in nature, it usually involved punishments such as whippings and tarring-and-feathering, but over time it evolved to become a much more lethal form of social control—one which typically included torture, mutilation, hanging, and burning.

While there are a couple of possible contenders, the origin of the term "lynching" most likely comes from Judge Charles Lynch who fought against the Tories during the Revolutionary war.[45] Tories were colonists who supported the British against the revolution. A Virginia magistrate, legislator, and colonel in the militia, Lynch and his sympathizers rounded up and punished Tory sympathizers, even though they had no jurisdictional authority to do so. As Lynch himself reported after one extralegal expedition, "Shot one, hanged one, and whipt [*sic*] several."[46] Because of the relatively high social status of those perpetrating the acts and a superficial adherence to formality and impartiality, many people felt that their actions were legitimate and carried the force of law, even if the technical legality was missing. This type of violence soon became known as Lynch's law, later shortened to Lynch law, and still later to the verb lynching.

After the revolution, lynching began appearing on the frontier as the newly formed nation began its inexorable expansion westward, but in character and tone lynch law remained largely unchanged and was a relatively infrequent occurrence. Lynching at this time, it should be noted, was rarely perpetrated against blacks but was instead perpetrated against various other groups that were perceived as threatening some established order. There was no need to lynch slaves, since the laws and customs of slaveholding states and territories provided many legal mechanisms intended to keep blacks in their place and under control. This all changed, however, after the end of the Civil War and the beginning of Reconstruction.

On April 9, 1865, General Robert E. Lee surrendered to Ulysses S. Grant at Appomattox courthouse and, to all intents and purposes, ended the American Civil War. In December of the same year, Congress had ratified the Thirteenth Amendment and officially abolished slavery, completing the process begun with President Abraham Lincoln and the Emancipation Proclamation. African Americans were finally free to participate in the economic, social, and political life of the nation. Unfortunately, many white Southerners resented and hated the newly won rights of their former slaves. Under slavery, whites had enjoyed a privileged position that was protected by the laws and institutions of the slaveholding states. The Civil War and Reconstruction put an end to that and, as one historian of lynching asserts

> The conclusion of the war and the subsequent abolition of slavery unleashed an unprecedented wave of extralegal violence. Many white southerners, embittered by defeat and unsettled by the turmoil of Reconstruction, responded by expanding antebellum customs of communal violence to meet new conditions. Thus, the events of the postbellum era served both to perpetuate and to expand the role of extralegal violence in southern culture. At the root of the postwar bloodshed was the refusal of most whites to accept the emancipated slaves' quest for economic and political power. Freed from the restraints of planter domination, the black man seemed to pose a new and greater threat to whites. During a period when blacks seemed to mock the social order and commonly understood rules of conduct, whites turned to violence to restore their supremacy.[47]

Lynching, then, was a way for white Southerners to reassert control over the African American population—or, in other words, it was a tool for protecting certain traditional values that placed blacks in a subordinate role to whites. This **extralegal means of social control** was also buttressed by a host of legislative initiatives in the Southern states known as the "Black Codes" that were intended to limit the rights of African Americans. Congress attempted to hamper these codes by passing the Civil Rights Act of 1866 that gave blacks citizenship and full rights, even overcoming a presidential veto to do so.[48]

❖ Photo 8.2   Two men are lynched in Marion, Indiana. After being accused of murdering Claude Deeter, 23, and assaulting his girlfriend Mary Ball, 19, two young African American men are taken from the Grand County Jail and lynched in the public square.

In short, in the aftermath of the Civil War, Southern whites began relying on violent and repressive tactics, of which lynching was the most lethal manifestation, in order to protect their privileged way of life relative to blacks. Although there were many organized groups that fought to retain white supremacy during this time, the **Ku Klux Klan** (KKK) is probably the most well known. The KKK was founded in 1866, its main purpose being to fight Reconstruction efforts. Today, the number of members in various organizations related to the KKK has dwindled; however, the Klan is still alive and well, holding annual rallies and marches across the country. You can even order Klan jewelry and figurines from various Klan websites. The organization's scope of intolerance has widened since the time of Reconstruction following the Civil War, and the Klan now professes to be anti-Jewish, anti-Catholic, anti-gay, anti-immigration, and anti-Muslim.

As a tool for maintaining social control, lynchings in U.S. history were not isolated incidents. In fact, lynchings by small groups of whites or mobs were so prevalent between 1880 and 1930 that Stewart Tolnay and E. M. Beck have referred to these years in U.S. history as the "Lynching Era."[49] Tolnay and Beck found that there were 2,805 people lynched between 1882 and 1930 in ten Southern states.[50] While the vast majority of these victims were African Americans, other victims were those from the North who came down South to assist the black population during **Reconstruction**, white Southerners who sympathized with Reconstruction and efforts to integrate blacks into Southern society, and others. In the view of Tolnay and Beck, these nearly 3,000 victims represented only the tip of the iceberg of the violence and intimidation faced by Southern blacks on a daily basis. It is therefore a mistake to see lynchings as spontaneous eruptions of **communal violence**, although they were often portrayed as such—especially by many Southern newspapers.[51] Instead, we must recognize that lynching often served some very real social, political, and economic goals.

Examining the patterns of lynchings in the South, we find that, up until World War I, most lynchings of African Americans were concentrated in the areas in which cotton was the dominant crop. In fact, the number of lynchings at any given time has been found to be influenced by fluctuations in the price of cotton. Specifically, lynchings against Southern blacks increased during tougher economic times in those regions of the South where the dominant cash crop was cotton. Keep in mind that cotton cultivation depended heavily on cheap African American labor. While never overtly about labor conditions, the violence against African Americans certainly helped reinforce white domination over the African Americans and helped maintain the plantation owners' supply of cheap labor. Lynchings also varied by time of year, and this seasonality also reflected the needs of the planters. As Tolnay and Beck assert

> Although plantation production was extremely labor intensive, the demand for labor was not uniform throughout the year. It is likely that landlords and planters perceived greater need to maintain control over workers during periods of peak labor demand . . . Although the manifest function of lynchings might well have been to rid the white community of offending blacks who violated the moral order, the latent function was to tighten the reins of control over the black population, especially during times when whites most needed black labor to work fields of cotton.[52]

In many ways, then, we can see lynching as operating on a number of different levels. One of the primary purposes was to strike fear into the hearts of blacks in the post-Reconstruction period as they were attempting to integrate into white society and assert their economic and political independence. Lynchings helped intimidate the black population and made them easier to control within the labor force. This reign of terror also made many blacks hesitant about agitating for higher wages and/or better working conditions. It also served as a means to maintain white supremacy over the black population because it helped to discourage African Americans from challenging the status quo of white privilege more generally. In addition, some have suggested that as the prices of cotton fell and Southern whites were under more economic stress, blacks were more likely to be scapegoated for the problems and economic misfortunes of whites who lynched out of frustration and misplaced anger.[53] This is not to suggest, however, that these instrumental reasons were articulated overtly. Instead we find a whole host of rationales and justifications used to paint the lynchings in a positive light. The victims of lynchings were almost always portrayed as dangerous and brutish offenders who had called down the righteous wrath of the community by their actions. Perpetrators of violence, we must remember, almost always portray their behavior as justified and righteous, and in this the lynch mob was no different. Local newspapers, for example, often portrayed the actions of a lynching in the best possible light. After one lynching in 1886 in Louisiana, for example, the local paper wrote

> While we deplore the necessity for mob law, we must commend it in this instance, for if the accused had been convicted of an "attempt at rape," the penalty would only have been two years in the Penitentiary, which is worse than farce . . . the action of the mob is approved by the best people in the parish. As we have said before, "the will of the people is the law of the land," and all such monsters should be disposed of in a summary manner.[54]

Ostensibly, as Tolnay and Beck point out, African Americans were lynched for a variety of real or alleged crimes, such as murder, theft, or rape, or for appearing to challenge their position within society by being uppity, insolent, or rude. The image of black men defiling white women was a particularly potent symbol and was often used to justify violence against African American males. One Texas editorial even went so far as to write, "Almost every day some negro brute assaults a white woman in this state, and often one to a half-dozen murders are committed in an effort to hide the crime . . . If rape and murder by brutish negroes are to become common, the negro must expect extermination."[55]

Some may be tempted to argue that lynchings were simply a form of **popular justice**—that lynch mobs were simply making sure that justice was served in cases where a crime had been committed. However, this premise is almost impossible to justify since the majority of lynching victims were taken from jails or some other form of law enforcement authority.[56] As such, most victims were already facing legal sanctions in some form or another, even though many victims had not been tried or convicted of an offense. Moreover, a significant number of lynchings involved more than a mere hanging; many involved symbolic mutilations, burning, and torture of the body, which was always displayed in a place that was easily visible to the black community. In sum, the purpose of lynching against the blacks during this time was not solely to impose justice but to create a reign of terror within the African American community and to make a political statement that blacks who did not submit to white rule would be severely dealt with.

Another peculiar element of lynchings was the often carnival-like atmosphere that frequently accompanied these murders. Hundreds, if not thousands, of spectators who often included children, watched some lynchings. Spectators sometimes came from miles around to join in the festivities, and the crowd would often pose for photographs with the bodies of the victims—which would sometimes be turned into postcards. After the lynching, spectators would often fight for scraps of clothing, rope, and bone to take home as souvenirs. As repellent as this is to us, it should be noted that this kind of behavior was also often seen at legal executions performed in public and was part of a long tradition of public conduct.

As we noted earlier, African Americans were not the only victims of lynch mobs in the United States. At various times and in various locations, Cubans, Mexicans, Native Americans, union organizers, Northern sympathizers, and many others were victims of lynch mobs.[57] In all cases, however, lynching represented an attempt to maintain an unequal social hierarchy without the protection of the law. It is important to remember that while ritualistic lynchings are mostly relegated to our past, killing in the name of hate still continues as examples from this book illustrate. Moreover, ritualistic lynchings have not disappeared entirely, as the case of Michael Donald illustrates. In Mobile, Alabama in 1981, an African American man charged with the murder of a white police officer resulted in a hung jury. The KKK believed that the jury was unable to convict the defendant because some of the jury members were African American. To avenge the policeman's death, two Klan members, Henry Hays and James Knowles, went to Mobile to seek revenge. After cruising for victims, they found 19-year-old Michael Donald walking home from the store after getting his sister a pack of cigarettes. At the time, Donald was attending a vocational school and working part-time at the local newspaper. Hays and Knowles forced him into their car and drove him to the next county where they beat him with a tree limb, slit his throat, and then hung him from a tree. Donald's death was originally attributed to a drug deal gone bad, but Donald's mother fought tirelessly to get her son's murder investigated. It took two-and-a-half years, but the FBI finally linked Hays and Knowles to the murder and both were ultimately convicted; Hays was sentenced to death and Knowles was sentenced to life in prison. The Southern Poverty Law Center also filed a wrongful death suit against United Klans of American on behalf of Beulah Donald, Michael's mother. The jury ruled that the Klan was responsible for Donald's death and awarded his mother 7 million dollars.[58]

Vigilantism

The last of the three related types of group violence that we explore in this chapter is vigilantism. Briefly, vigilantism can be defined as an organized extralegal movement in which the participants take the law into their own hands.[59] Typically conservative in orientation, these groups were intended to protect the status quo by applying their own brand of law and justice to outlaws and others who threatened the establishment of social order. Vigilante movements generally arose in times and places where the established authority or government was perceived to be ineffective in protecting traditional rights of property, possessions, and personal safety. Not surprisingly, the heyday of U.S. vigilantism was in the mid- and late 19th century in the American West as the process of settlement and industrialization required the eradication of widespread criminal elements and gangs.[60] In Focus 8.2 illustrates one case that reveals many of these qualities.

In Focus 8.2

Vigilantism in Flagstaff

Flagstaff is a quiet university town set in the mountains of northern Arizona. Nestled in the largest ponderosa pine forest in the world, the scenic beauty belies the turbulent history of this Western community. In the late 1800s, Flagstaff was a raucous and wild place, with the downtown known as Whiskey Row because of the large number of saloons and gambling halls. In the evenings and on weekends, the loggers and the ranch hands came into town eager to drink, gamble, and engage the services of the "fallen doves." The problem was that these young men coming into town for an evening's fun were often preyed upon by a large and aggressive population of criminals who would assault and rob the often intoxicated pleasure seekers. At that time, Flagstaff had only one deputy sheriff who was unable to deal effectively with the situation. Concerned citizens and local business leaders called for action and held meetings, but nothing came of it, and by 1885 the situation reached a head when some of the victims, angered at their treatment, threatened to burn the town down. In response, six saloon owners formed a volunteer committee to take care of the situation. They recruited a rancher named McMillan from out of town to come in and pose as an easy mark. Varying his appearance, pretending to be drunk, and flashing a lot of money, this undercover cattleman was victimized numerous times, but each time he made note of who the perpetrators were. Eventually, the volunteer committee made a list of the most prolific offenders and posted a warning on the doors of local businesses that read, "Notice: Tinhorns have 24 hours left!" Tinhorn was the term used at that time for criminals. Predictably, the warning was ignored, and so at 3:00 a.m. on the morning of August 28, the vigilantes went to work. Squads of men fanned out throughout Flagstaff in order to apprehend the ten worst offenders. Only one of the men on the list was not apprehended because he escaped by breaking through a window and into the night. The nine prisoners were taken to a large ponderosa pine at the outskirts of town and summarily hanged from a long branch. Left dangling for most of the day, the bodies were finally cut down and buried without caskets or markers. The violence had its intended effect, with many of the other reputed criminals leaving town for safer pastures. When the sheriff came up from Prescott to investigate the killings, not a single person he interviewed admitted knowing anything about the hangings, and they remained an open secret until 1928 when one of the participants wrote a letter detailing the activities of this frontier vigilante group.

SOURCE: Gladwell Richardson, "Flagstaff Vigilantes," Xerox, n.d.

While there is often a great deal of overlap between vigilantism and lynching, vigilantism often represents an attempt to impose some sort of law in a lawless setting, while lynchings typically involve an attempt to get around established law and order. In fact, many lynching victims were actually broken out of jail in order to punish them for some real or alleged crimes. This often happened with the tacit approval and assistance of law enforcement officers but nonetheless involved an attempt to circumvent legitimate legal proceedings. Vigilantism, on the other hand, typically does not involve groups trying to short-circuit legitimate avenues of justice. Instead, vigilante groups try to create a legal process where none is perceived to exist. Historically, some vigilante groups even went so far as to put the accused criminals on trial. As imperfect and as rough and ready as these trials may have been, they at least adhered to the semblance and process of legality. The famous **San Francisco Vigilance Committee** certainly illustrates this point.

San Francisco in the mid-19th century was the epitome of a wild frontier community. The California gold rush had swelled the population of San Francisco into a large city that included not only those seeking their fortune in the gold fields but many seeking their fortunes by robbing others. The criminal element also included a large number of criminals who often made their living by robbing miners, setting fires, and from various other criminal enterprises. In desperation, a number of businessmen formed a vigilance committee in the spring of 1851 to protect the lives and property of San Franciscans. They even created a constitution and bylaws and notified the community via the local newspaper that they would punish criminals. Their first action was to put on trial an Australian named John Jenkins who had been caught stealing a safe. After being found guilty, he was hung in front of a crowd.[61] This was followed by a fair number of other hangings as well as some deportations. Largely supported by the community and the newspapers, the vigilance committee helped pressure the official law enforcement agencies to take a stronger stance against crime. Over time, the San Francisco Vigilance Committee died out, but it was resurrected a number of times whenever the crime rate rose again; it was always distinguished by an adherence to formalities of justice, including providing a trial.

Not all vigilante groups were the same, however. Some adhered more to the formalities of law while others were much less concerned with following the proprieties. The motivations for these groups also varied, as illustrated by the typology developed by Rosenbaum and Sederberg who suggest three main types of vigilante groups.[62] The first type is labeled **crime-control vigilantism** and is the type most often associated with this form of collective violence—targeted as it is with the elimination of crime. The second kind of vigilante group is known as **social group-control vigilantism** and describes groups whose goal is to keep some population group in their place, usually within the lower levels of class structure. This is the kind most closely akin to lynch mobs. The third and last type is **regime-control vigilantism**, which concerns groups that engage in violence in an effort to control the government if it strays from an acceptable course of action and policy. Typically composed of middle- and upper-class elites who want to protect their prerogatives, this type of vigilante group defines its role as keeping the regime in check.[63] Each type of vigilante group, as this typology makes clear, is a conservative organization in the sense that it doesn't try to subvert law and order; rather all types of group try to enforce it, though each has a different goal in mind as it engages in violence. We also should not think that vigilantism is a relic of the past. Vigilantism is alive and well, both in the United States and around the world. Today, however, we more often hear about cases of individual vigilantism compared with actions of an organized group. While not as acceptable as it once was, vigilantism still represents a kind of violence that springs up in certain kinds of scenarios. In Brazil during the 1970s, for example, off-duty police officers were implicated in the murder of between 500 and 1,200 habitual criminals. They felt that the courts were too easy on criminals and that the people they had killed could not be rehabilitated. Amazingly, 60% of residents in the city in which the vigilantes were operating approved of their actions.

In contemporary America, the **Guardian Angels**, a group founded in 1979 in the Bronx, is still active in a number of communities. Identified by their red berets, its members patrol the subways, streets, and neighborhoods in order to prevent crime and have sometimes been labeled vigilantes by police. Nevertheless, new Guardian Angels chapters continue to thrive and operate in many communities in the United States and around the world. Instead of group vigilantism, we more often hear of individuals engaging in vigilantism in contemporary society. **Sex offender registries**, which all states have available in some form (see Chapter 7), make convicted sex offenders particularly easy targets for individuals bent on delivering their own brand of justice. For example, in April of 2006, within a five-hour period, 20-year-old Stephen Marshall killed two men he found registered on the state of Maine's sex offender registry. One of the victims was William Elliott, a 24-year-old man who had been convicted of statutory rape when he was 19 because his girlfriend was under 18 years of age. Marshall later killed himself, while police were closing in on him on a bus in Boston. As we learned earlier in Chapter 7, other registered sex offenders have experienced vigilante justice, including two men who were killed in August 2005 in the state of Washington when a self-styled vigilante gained access to their homes by posing as an FBI agent.

Conclusions

As we have seen, mob violence—as exemplified by lynchings, vigilantes, and riots—has a long history in this country. While lynchings are not as prevalent as they once were, they nevertheless remain as potent manifestations of collective violence perpetrated outside of the boundaries of official governmental authority. Moreover, while ritualistic lynchings by hanging and burning have faded, we know that hate-motivated killings remain an ever-present part of all societies. We also know that the primary purpose of lynchings is not to seek some form of popular justice but to instill a climate of terror in marginalized populations. It is a sad reality that mob violence, in its various guises, is still very much a part of our contemporary landscape.

Key Terms

acquisitive mob	conformity	extralegal means of social control
aggressive crowd	crime-control vigilantism	
aggressive mob	crowd	Guardian Angels
Anti-Catholic Gordon Riots	deindividuation	Ku Klux Klan
casual crowd	escape mob	Los Angeles City Riot of 1992
cohesive crowd	expressive crowd	lynch mobs
communal violence	expressive mob	mob

mob violence	Reconstruction	sex offender registries
New York City Draft Riots of 1863	regime-control vigilantism	social group-control vigilantism
	riots	
popular justice	San Francisco Vigilance Committee	Tulsa Race Riot of 1921
race riot		vigilante groups

Discussion Questions

1. Conduct a case study of a recent incident of mob violence from somewhere around the world. It is probably best to access news sources to find recent cases, including such sources as the BBC (www.bbc.co.uk), the *Washington Post* (www.washingtonpost .com), CNN (www.cnn.com), or some other national or international source of news.

What societal conditions were present before the violence? What groups were involved in the incident(s)? Which were perceived by the media as the primary offenders, and which were perceived primarily as the victims? What factors can you identify as those that are common contributors to mob violence in general?

2. The Southern Poverty Law Center, which started out as a small civil rights law firm, is now a large internationally known organization devoted to tracking hate groups and pursuing civil and criminal remedies against hate. Go to the center's website (www .splcenter.org) and search for "lynching." One of the locations to which you will be guided will provide you with details of the civil trials the center has pursued against acts of racial injustice, including modern-day lynchings. Conduct a case study of one of the incidents listed on the site. To find out more information about the case, search the web for information from local news media that covered the case (it is probably best to use the plaintiffs' and/or victims' names as the keywords). Discuss how civil remedies have been used to wage a war against these criminal incidents.

3. David Haddock and Daniel Polsby are professors of law at Northwestern University. They published an article titled "Understanding Riots" for the Cato Institute in the *Cato Journal*, which can be accessed at www.cato.org/pubs/journal/cj14n1-13. html. According to the article, what factors are typically necessary for a riot to ensue? What factors can be used to stop a riot? What policies do they recommend for preventing riots? In your opinion, what other factors may be useful in preventing riots?

Terrorism

Hostility toward America is a religious duty, and we hope to be rewarded for it by God. To call us Enemy #1 or #2 does not hurt us. I am confident that Muslims will be able to end the legend of the so-called superpower that is America.

—Osama bin Laden[1]

Communist dictatorships, socialist democracies, and capitalist systems must all face the problems of terrorism. Skyjackings, assassinations, bombings, extortions, and sabotage do not stop at any national or regional borders.

—Irving Louis Horowitz[2]

After the attacks of September 11, 2001, on the United States, President Bush declared a "war on terrorism" that has understandably loomed large in the minds of most Americans. But what else comes to your mind when you think of **terrorism**? The bombing of the **Alfred P. Murrah Federal Building** in Oklahoma City in 1995? The hostage taking and killing of school children in Beslan, Russia in 2004? The killing of the American ambassador to Libya along with other staff members in 2012? The bombs set off at the finish line of the Boston Marathon on Monday, April 15, 2013? The all too frequent suicide bombings experienced across the Middle East? Whatever thoughts and perceptions you have are obviously based on the assumptions and definitions you have about what terrorism is and who the terrorists are. Defining terrorism, however, is not such an easy task.

Defining Terrorism

Defining terrorism is difficult, and it is a task that has yet to be resolved to the satisfaction of all. As such, terrorism is no different from the other types of violence we have already discussed in this book. All violence is inherently terrifying, so what differentiates "terrorism" from other forms of violence? Is terrorism simply the intersection between violence and politics or is there more to it than that?

Many different definitions of terrorism have been proposed by various scholars, politicians, law enforcement officials, and others. In fact, one writer identified over 100 different definitions of terrorism that had been created between 1936 and 1983.[3] The current number of definitions is even greater. What makes defining terrorism so difficult? Why, in the words of Philip Herbst, does it defy "precise, complete, objective definition"?[4] There seem to be several reasons for this problem.

First, we have to remember that terrorism encompasses many different types of behavior perpetrated for many different reasons. It can include intimidation, assassinations, bombings, hijackings, theft, military-style attacks, kidnappings, and any number of other violent or threatening acts. Yet, at the same time, not all bombings, killings, thefts, and kidnappings are acts of terrorism. How do we distinguish between acts that are terrorism and others that are not? Does it have to do with the intent and motivation of the act, is it more about the perpetrators and victims, or is it some combination of these? If we examine the motives of terrorism, we find a wide range of reasons that involve a combination of political, religious, ethnic, racial, or ideological purposes. Different terrorist organizations engage in their destructive behavior for a variety of reasons. This complexity and variation mean that terrorism defies simple, easy, or absolute definition.

Second, terrorism is a continuously evolving phenomenon. During the 19th and early 20th centuries, for example, most terrorism was nationalistic and focused on helping a population group achieve political independence and sovereignty. At that time, the targets of terrorism were not usually selected indiscriminately but tended to be military and political leaders who represented the government system in power. During the 20th century, however, the character of terrorism changed and came to include a broader spectrum of organizations, including right-wing fascist groups, religiously motivated groups, and even criminal groups, such as those involved in the drug trade.[5] The 20th century also saw terrorism move away from being primarily directed against political and military leaders and become ever more indiscriminate in selecting its targets.[6] Civilians and noncombatants now comprise the most common victims of terrorist attacks. The organizational structure of terrorist groups has also changed. Whereas in the past terrorist groups were usually centrally organized and cohesive organizations—albeit secret ones—they now tend to be much more diffuse and autonomous groups networked and connected by modern information technologies, such as the Internet.[7] All of these changes make it more difficult to capture the essence of terrorism in a few sentences or paragraphs.

Third, defining terrorism depends in large part on your particular point of view. Do you agree with the actions of the group? Do you support their cause? If so, you may have a hard time defining them as terrorists. The old adage that "one person's terrorist is another's freedom fighter" has some truth to it, although we strongly believe that injustice never justifies atrocity. This phrase simply points out that definitions of terrorism are largely a matter of perception. As such, we need to recognize that terrorism has many meanings for the people involved. For example, do you think about terrorism when you think about the American Revolution? Probably not. However, in writing about political extremism, John George and Laird Wilcox suggest

> If one were to describe the American Revolution as a seditious conspiracy fomented by a band of extremists, misfits, malcontents, and troublemakers dedicated to the overthrow of recognized authority, one might well be right on the mark. For many people, the words used to describe behavior have a lot to do with how they view it.[8]

The word "terrorist" is inherently a negative term with tremendous power to remove whatever legitimacy or moral authority an organization or movement may have. Governments and politicians often use the word to undermine the support a group may have among a larger population. Conversely, those who support a cause will work hard to avoid using the word terrorism. Bruce Hoffman points out that many terrorist groups try to avoid being labeled as terrorists and instead try to link themselves with the concepts and language of freedom and liberation, armies and military organizations, self-defense, and justified retribution.[9] Many Muslims, for example, do not feel that **Al Qaeda** is a terrorist organization or that Osama bin Laden was a terrorist. Rather, they perceive them as heroes fighting against what they see as a powerful and unjust enemy: the United States. One study conducted by the Arab news station Al Jazeera found that only 8.7% of the 4,600 who participated in the survey saw Osama bin Laden as a terrorist. Instead they defined him as a hero and freedom fighter.[10] Suliman Abu Geith, a spokesman for Al Qaeda, certainly didn't perceive the attacks of September 11 as terrorism when he asserted, "Those youths who did what they did and destroyed America with their airplanes, they've done a good deed. They have moved the battle into the heart of America."[11]

❖ Photo 9.1 Osama bin Laden, founder of the Al Qaeda terrorist organization

Obviously, he sees Al Qaeda as fighting a war and therefore defines its fighters as soldiers rather than as terrorists. Similarly, Ramzi Yousef, the mastermind of the first World Trade Center attack, asserted in a newspaper interview that he was a warrior.[12] Again, we see in his choice of words a viewpoint that seeks to legitimize his actions. One member of the Lebanon-based **Hezbollah**, after reading a newspaper article in which his organization was referred to as a terrorist group, reacted by asserting, "We are not terrorists. We are fighters," while another leader of the group suggested, "We don't see ourselves as terrorists. We don't see resisting

IN FOCUS 9.1

September 11 and Al Qaeda

The American landscape was horrifically changed on September 11, 2001, when the United States was the victim of a deadly series of terrorist attacks. The first indication that something was wrong occurred when United Airlines Flight 11, a Boeing 767 flying from Boston to Los Angeles and carrying 81 passengers and 11 crew members, flew into the North Tower of the World Trade Center at 8:45 a.m. Five men armed with box cutters had taken over the plane and intentionally piloted it into the building, causing massive destruction.[1] Based on surreptitious phone calls made by flight attendants, we know that the hijackers, who had been sitting near the front of the plane, stabbed a number of flight attendants, cut the throat of a first class passenger, and stormed the cockpit. They also threatened to use a bomb if the people on board didn't cooperate.[2] At 9:03 a.m., a second hijacked plane, United Airlines Flight 175 with 56 passengers and nine crew members on board, crashed into the South Tower of the World Trade Center. A third plane, American Airlines Flight 77, loaded with 58 passengers and six crew members, was also taken over and flown into the Pentagon building at 9:43 a.m. The last plane to be hijacked was United Airlines Flight 93, with 38 passengers and crew members. Its destination is uncertain because the plane crashed into a field in rural Pennsylvania, although it seems likely that the destination was either the White House or the Capitol building in Washington, DC. Based on cell phone calls made by passengers of that flight, the passengers attempted to retake the aircraft, and either they or the hijackers crashed the plane into the ground. Not ten minutes after Flight 93 plowed into the field, both Twin Tower buildings collapsed. A large number of police officers and firefighters as

well as those workers from the building who had not been able to get out in time were killed in the collapsing buildings.

These well coordinated and effective attacks produced a terrible toll in human lives, as 2,788 people were killed, making this the single most deadly act of terrorism ever perpetrated. This day ranks as the deadliest single day for Americans since the Civil War, and it is important to remember that the victims of the attacks included hundreds of citizens of countries from all over the world. September 11 was not just a U.S. tragedy but an international and human one as well. Beyond the human cost, the repercussions will be felt for years. Americans suddenly awoke to the realization that we are not immune to terrorism. Even though the nation was shocked and alarmed when the Twin Towers were bombed for the first time in 1993 and when the Alfred P. Murrah Federal Building in Oklahoma City was destroyed by a homemade bomb in 1995, these acts of terrorism seemed like singular aberrations and did not truly affect our sense of security and well-being. It still seemed that most terrorism occurred in faraway places and didn't intrude into our daily lives. But the September 11 attacks changed that perception.

It quickly became evident that the hijackers were members of a Middle Eastern-based terrorist group known as Al Qaeda, which translates roughly as "The Base."[3] The origins of Al Qaeda lie in the invasion of Afghanistan in 1979 by the Soviet Union, which was interested in supporting a puppet socialist government that had recently come to power in that country. Many Muslims around the world, however, were outraged that a secular communist state had invaded an Islamic nation, and a resistance movement quickly sprang up that was

(Continued)

(Continued)

dedicated to the violent ousting of the Soviets. The membership of these groups included not only native Afghanis but Muslims from other countries as well, and they became known as the *Mujahideen* or "holy warriors."[4] The importance of this event for future Islamic terrorism cannot be overstated. For the first time, young men from all around the Muslim world came together to fight for a common Islamic cause and developed lasting connections and friendships that would serve them well in the coming years. Ironically, the United States helped support these *Mujahideen* through the Central Intelligence Agency (CIA), which funneled money to the Pakistani Security Services (ISI), which in turn funded and supported various *Mujahideen* groups.[5] In fact, the vast majority of money, weapons, and training were provided courtesy of just three countries: Pakistan, Saudi Arabia, and the United States.[6]

Among the international volunteers was a wealthy young Saudi named Osama bin Laden, who helped cofound an organization called the Maktab al-Khidmat, or the Afghan Services Bureau, which was based in neighboring Pakistan and helped recruit and train Muslim fighters for the war in Afghanistan.[7] While Osama bin Laden initially limited himself to raising funds and organizing the fighters, as the war progressed he involved himself increasingly in combat operations and quickly became recognized as a fairly successful military leader. Ultimately, in 1989, the *Mujahideen* were successful in forcing out the Soviet military, which, after 15,000 soldiers killed in action, thousands more dead of disease, and several hundred thousand wounded, finally packed it in and left the country.[8] It was around this time that Osama bin Laden established Al Qaeda out of his most dedicated fighters in order to continue the holy war and protect Muslims around the world. Bin Laden envisioned an organization that would help to create a unified Islamic world order under the rule of a Caliph, and Al Qaeda's goals reflect this vision of a world dominated by Islam.[9] Specifically, Al Qaeda seeks to overthrow corrupt regimes in the Middle East, especially those that do not follow Islamic law know as *Shari'a*, and Saudi Arabia heads the list since it is considered too secular, too corrupt, and too cozy with Western powers. Second, the group intends to destroy the United States because it is seen as a foreign and corrupting influence and an impediment to the creation of an Islamic world order. Third, Al Qaeda intends the destruction of Israel and its replacement with a Palestinian state.[10] Organized around four primary committees—military, financial, religious, and media—Al Qaeda soon began providing resources, training, and financing to Muslim terrorist groups around the world.

After the Soviet withdrawal from Afghanistan and disgusted by the squabbling between the victorious Afghan warlords, bin Laden returned to Saudi Arabia where, after Iraq's invasion of Kuwait, he offered the services of his fighters to the Saudi government. The Saudi government politely but firmly refused the offer.[11] Osama bin Laden was outraged that the assistance of experienced Muslim fighters was rejected in favor of American troops who began flooding into Saudi Arabia in preparation for what would become the First Gulf War. Osama bin Laden had long harbored anti-American feelings, and these now blossomed into a full-blown hatred directed against not only the United States but the Saudi monarchy as well. In this he was joined by many other Saudis who spoke out against the Saudi Arabian monarchy and engaged in various protest activities until the government finally cracked down on the dissenters.[12] Some were imprisoned; however, bin Laden—because of his family connections—was only forced into exile in the Sudan, where a hard-line Islamic government had recently come to power. It was during this time that Al Qaeda became operational and began mounting attacks against the United States. Without really being aware of it, America had entered a new era of terrorism—one in which the United States was a primary target.

It began in December of 1992 when a tourist hotel in Yemen was bombed by Al Qaeda and two tourists were killed. The intended targets were American troops deploying for Somalia.[13] Earlier that year, an Al Qaeda operative named Ramzi Yousef traveled from Pakistan to New York and met with Sheikh Omar Abdel Rahman, a blind Egyptian cleric known for his radical views. Along with a number of others who attended the Sheikh's mosque in New Jersey, they plotted an attack on the World Trade Center, a potent symbol of America's economic might. Their plan involved filling a Ryder truck with $300 worth of homemade explosives. On February 26, 1993, it was parked in an underground garage below Tower One and detonated just after noon. The terrorists had added sodium cyanide to the bomb in the hope that it would be distributed as cyanide gas throughout the building. Fortunately, the sodium cyanide was destroyed in the blast or the casualties would have been far greater. The death toll would also have been far higher if the building had collapsed as the terrorists had intended.[14] Around 40,000 people worked in the Twin Towers on a daily basis, and if the cyanide gas had worked or the buildings collapsed, the death toll would have been immense. As it was, six people were killed in the attack and over a thousand injured.[15] The next Al Qaeda-inspired attack occurred on June 25, 1996, when a truck bomb exploded outside the Khobar Towers, a housing complex in Dhahran, Saudi Arabia that housed U.S. Air Force personnel. Nineteen service personnel were killed and 372 wounded.[16]

Al Qaeda issued a manifesto which stated that one of its goals was:

To kill Americans and their allies—civilians and military—is an individual duty for every Muslim who can do it in any country in which it is possible to do it, in order to liberate the al Aqsa mosque and the Holy Mosque [in Mecca] and in order for their armies to move out of all the lands of Islam, defeated and unable to threaten any Muslim.[18]

This manifesto was essentially a call to arms against the United States and were intended to provide legitimacy for the actions of Al Qaeda by framing anti-American acts of terrorism within a military, religious, and political framework.

The attacks against the United States continued, with two suicide truck bombs that exploded outside of the U.S. embassies in Kenya and Tanzania on August 7, 1998.[19] Several hundred people were killed, 12 of whom were American. In retaliation, President Bill Clinton launched cruise missile attacks against a Sudanese pharmaceutical plant that was mistakenly suspected of making chemical weapons and against six Al Qaeda terrorist camps in Afghanistan. According to some reports, Osama bin Laden narrowly missed being on the receiving end of the attack, having left one of the targeted camps just an hour earlier.[20] Finally, in October 2000, a suicide bomb damaged the 505 foot *USS Cole* in Aden Harbor, and 17 sailors were killed and 39 wounded. The warship was in the process of refueling when a small boat came alongside with two men in it who stood up and waved at the sailors above them as they came alongside. They then detonated hidden explosives that blew a forty by sixty foot hole in the side of the ship, killing themselves and 17 Americans.

In hindsight, these Al-Qaeda terrorist attacks—terrible as they were—were only the prelude to far worse violence. The September 11, 2001, attacks literally exploded out of the blue and shocked and surprised not only the United States but the world

(Continued)

(Continued)

community as well. One result was the subsequent declaration of a war against terrorism that, in the words of President George Bush

is a different war from any our nation has ever faced, a war on many fronts, against terrorists who operate in more than 60 different countries. And this is a war that must be fought not only overseas, but also here at home.[21]

While the United States has been largely successful in attacking and killing most of the senior leadership of Al Qaeda, including Osama bin Laden in 2011, the movement itself has become less centralized and more of a loosely affiliated movement, with many autonomous and largely independent groups that share a common vision of holy war or *jihad*.[22] This means that Al Qaeda remains a threat. Clearly, the United States has entered a new era of conflict, which pits U.S. military might against a nebulous enemy—one which is hard to identify and whose plans are difficult to uncover and prevent. At the same time, the problem of confronting terrorism is complicated by our desire to protect the civil liberties and freedoms that are so important to our way of life.

NOTES:

1. Christoph Reuter, *My Life Is a Weapon: A Modern History of Suicide Bombing* (Princeton, NJ: Princeton University Press, 2004).
2. Paul Thompson, *The Terror Timeline: Year by Year, Day by Day, Minute by Minute. A Comprehensive Chronicle of the Road to 9/11—and America's Response* (New York: Regan, 2004).
3. Harvey W. Kushner, *Encyclopedia of Terrorism* (Thousand Oaks, CA: Sage, 2003).
4. The term *Mujahideen* is derived from *mujahidid*, which is someone who is engaged in fighting to defend his honor, his country, and his faith. See Kushner, *Encyclopedia of Terrorism*.
5. Steve Coll, *Ghost Wars: The Secret History of the CIA, Afghanistan, and Bin Laden, From the Soviet Invasion to September 10, 2001* (New York: Penguin, 2004).
6. Jane Corbin, *Al-Qaeda* (New York: Thunder's Mouth Press, 2003).
7. Corbin, *Al-Qaeda*; Rohan Gunaratna, *Inside Al Qaeda: Global Network of Terror* (New York: Berkley, 2003); Paul L. Williams, *Al Qaeda: Brotherhood of Terror* (New York: Alpha, 2002).
8. Corbin, *Al-Qaeda*.
9. Kushner, *Encyclopedia of Terrorism*.
10. Kushner, *Encyclopedia of Terrorism*.
11. Corbin, *Al-Qaeda*.
12. Daniel Benjamin and Steven Simon, *The Age of Sacred Terror: Radical Islam's War Against America* (New York: Random House, 2002).
13. Thompson, *The Terror Timeline*.
14. Harvey W. Kushner, *Terrorism in America: A Structured Approach to Understanding the Terrorist Threat* (Springfield, IL: Charles C Thomas, 1998).
15. Simon Reeve, *The New Jackals: Ramzi Yousef, Osama Bin Laden and the Future of Terrorism* (Boston: Northeastern University Press, 1999).
16. Steven Strasser, ed., *The 9/11 Investigations: Staff Reports of the 9/11 Commission* (New York: Public Affairs, 2004).
17. Benjamin and Simon, *The Age of Sacred Terror*.
18. Cited in Jason Burke, *Al-Qaeda: Casting a Shadow of Terror* (London: I.B. Taurus, 2003), 158.
19. Jonathan Randal, *Osama: The Making of a Terrorist* (New York: Alfred A. Knopf, 2004).
20. Some analysts suggest that Osama was in one of the targeted camps only an hour earlier while others suggest that he was nowhere near the camps. See Randal, *Osama*.
21. Taken from President George Bush's speech, which is reprinted on the web at www.whitehouse.gov/news/releases/2001/11/20011108–13.html.
22. Burke, *Al-Qaeda*.

the occupier as a terrorist action. We see ourselves as **Mujahideen** [holy warriors] who fight a Holy War for the people."[13] Philip Herbst summarizes this point when he writes that

> Very few of those today who are labeled terrorists see themselves as such. They wrap themselves instead in the images of "freedom fighter" or "soldier" . . . they belong to "armies" or "brigades," and they believe their cause to be just, reflecting the will of their people—even sanctioned by God.[14]

As you can see, to portray the essential elements of terrorism in a few definitive words is a difficult task. Yet, for all their shortcomings, definitions still offer some help in trying to understand the nature of terrorism. They help us organize our thoughts by allowing us to build a mental picture of what is and is not terrorism, even though that understanding may not be complete or absolutely accurate. It is therefore worthwhile to examine some of the definitions that have been proposed, which are displayed in Table 9.1. Examining some of the more common definitions reveals some interesting and important commonalities.

Even though the definitions in Table 9.1 vary on a number of points, they still share a number of ideas that can be used to construct a working understanding of terrorism and a mental image of the essential qualities of terrorism, which should be sufficient for our purposes. First, terrorism is a violent activity. At its core, terrorism is about destruction and harm, whether of people or property or both. Terrorists have chosen violence as their preferred method of accomplishing their goals. While there are all kinds of nonviolent ways to help bring about change within a society, terrorists have settled on violence as the preferred method to achieve their agenda.

This brings us to the second point, which is that terrorism is intended to achieve some goal, whether it is political change or some other cause. There is purpose and reason to it. The violence is instrumental and, therefore, we need to recognize that terrorism is rational. This is not to say that it should be condoned or accepted, but rather that terrorist acts are not simply the senseless actions of crazy people. Terrorists engage in extreme acts of violence because they think it will help them to achieve some goal. Remember that this is a common thread or theme that is consistent across many of the different examples of violence we examine in this book, such as lynchings and genocide. Many of the definitions in Table 9.1 suggest that the goals are usually political. Even terrorist groups that are ostensibly religious in orientation, such as many contemporary Islamic terrorist groups, have political change or reform as part of their motivations. Al Qaeda, for example, is in the pursuit of an Islamic world order and intends to replace corrupt and secular Muslim regimes with regimes free of Western and secular influences and which are true to **Shari'a** or Islamic law. Muslim extremists do not subscribe to a separation between church and state, so for them religion is politics and political violence is also religious.[15] They are part and parcel of the same package.

Third, terrorism usually targets defenseless victims. Victims are not typically those with the training or resources to defend themselves, such as the military or police—although these groups are also sometimes attacked. Far more common, however, are civilian and noncombatant targets who are placed in the crosshairs precisely because

Table 9.1	Definitions of Terrorism

- Terrorism is the use of force (or violence) committed by individuals or groups against governments or civilian populations to create fear in order to bring about political (or social) change.[1]
- A synthesis of war and theater; a dramatization of the most proscribed kind of violence—that which is perpetrated on innocent victims—played before an audience in the hope of creating a mood of fear; for political purposes.[2]
- The intentional generation of massive fear by human beings for the purpose of securing or maintaining control over other human beings.[3]
- The unlawful use of force and violence against persons or property to intimidate or coerce a government, the civilian population, or any segment thereof, in furtherance of political or social objectives.[4]
- Premeditated, politically motivated violence perpetrated against noncombatant targets by subnational groups or clandestine agents, usually intended to influence an audience.[5]
- Political terrorism is the use, or threat of use, of violence, by an individual or a group, whether acting for or in opposition to established authority, when such action is designed to create extreme anxiety and/or fear-inducing effects in a target group larger than the immediate victims with the purpose of coercing that group into acceding to the political demands of the perpetrators.[6]
- The deliberate creation and exploitation of fear through violence or the threat of violence in the pursuit of change.[7]
- The use of unexpected violence to intimidate or coerce in the pursuit of political or social objectives.[8]
- Terrorism is the use or threat, for the purpose of advancing a political, religious or ideological cause, of action which involves serious violence against any person or property.[9]
- Terrorism is an anxiety-inspiring method of repeated violent action, employed by (semi-) clandestine individual group or state actors, for idiosyncratic, criminal or political reasons, whereby—in contrast to assassination—the direct targets of violence are not the main targets. The immediate human targets of violence are not the main targets. The immediate human targets of violence are generally chosen randomly (targets of opportunity) or selectively (representative or symbolic targets) from a target population, and serve as message generators. Threat- and violence-based communication processes between terrorists (organization), (imperiled) victims, and main targets are used to manipulate the main target (audience[s]), turning it into a target of terror, a target of demands, or a target of attention, depending upon whether intimidation, coercion, or propaganda is primarily sought.[10]

NOTES:

1. Harvey W. Kushner, *Terrorism in America: A Structured Approach to Understanding the Terrorist Threat* (Springfield, IL: Charles C Thomas, 1998), 10.
2. Cindy C. Combs, *Terrorism in the Twenty-First Century,* 3rd ed. (Upper Saddle River, NJ: Prentice Hall, 2003), 10.
3. H. H. A. Cooper, "Defining Terrorism in the New Era," in *The New Era of Terrorism: Selected Readings*, ed. Gus Martin (Thousand Oaks, CA: Sage, 2004), 55–63.
4. U. S. Department of Justice, Federal Bureau of Investigation, *Terrorism 2000/2001,* publication #0308 (Washington, DC: FBI, 2001).
5. U.S. State Department definition.
6. Grant Wardlaw, *Political Terrorism* (New York: Cambridge University Press, 1989).
7. Bruce Hoffman, *Inside Terrorism* (New York: Columbia University Press, 1998).
8. Ted Robert Gurr, "Political Terrorism: Historical Antecedents and Contemporary Trends," in *Violence in America: Protest, Rebellion, Reform,* Vol. 2, ed. Ted Robert Gurr (Newbury Park, CA: Sage, 1989).
9. David J. Whittaker, ed., *The Terrorism Reader* (New York: Routledge, 2001).
10. Thomas J. Badey, "Defining International Terrorism: A Pragmatic Approach," *Terrorism and Political Violence* 10 (1998): 90–107 at 91.

they are civilians and noncombatants and therefore vulnerable. In military terminology, they are "**soft**" **targets,** also called defenseless targets, as opposed to "**hard**" **targets** that are more difficult to assault because they are protected.

Figure 9.1 shows the relative frequency with which different groups are victimized and reveals that civilian/commercial targets are by far the most frequent focus of terrorist attacks around the world. Their status as innocents increases the dramatic qualities of the act. When soldiers or police officers are killed, it is recognized as being a horrible tragedy, but at some level there is the sense that they knew the risks and had taken on their dangerous responsibilities by choice. The killing of noncombatants, on the other hand, is often perceived as more terrible because these victims did not choose to be in harm's way but were simply in the wrong place at the wrong time. These sentiments tend to be heightened when the victims are children and women. This innocence serves to increase the impact of a terrorist attack.

The fourth element that runs through all definitions presented in Table 9.1, even though it might sound redundant, is that the purpose of terrorism is to terrorize. In other words, terrorist groups want to create a climate of fear within a society. The indiscriminate nature of the attacks coupled with civilian targets exacerbates the fear and vulnerability of the population, which doesn't know when or where the next attack is coming. If people everywhere feel that they could be a victim, then terrorists will have made an impact. Creating a climate of fear throughout a society is one way that these groups can project an image of strength and pervasiveness that is not based on actual capabilities. This is also the reason why attacks are often chosen for their dramatic qualities and their symbolism, both of which increase the impact of the attacks and also provide the terrorists with an aura of power and influence. The intended target of terrorist attacks always extends beyond those individuals who are on the receiving end of the violence to include the society at large.

❖ Figure 9.1   Terrorist Attacks by Type of Target, 2002–2011

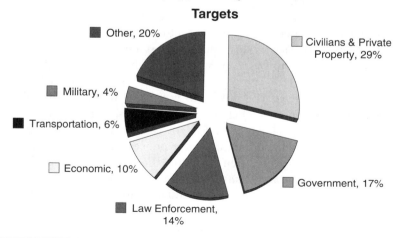

SOURCE: Adapted from data from The Institute for Economics and Peace, "2012 Global Terrorism Index: Capturing the Impact of Terrorism for the Last Decade."

❖ Photo 9.2   Alfred P. Murrah Federal Building in the aftermath of a bomb attack by members of the Patriot Movement

Fifth, terrorism is systematic. An isolated event, even though it might be terrifying, is not necessarily considered terrorism. Instead, terrorism is a recurring phenomenon. For example, the political scientist Thomas Badey suggests that, whereas the first World Trade Center attack was an act of terrorism, the Oklahoma City bombing was not.[16] Because the February 26, 1993, bomb attack on the Twin Towers was perpetrated by individuals who have since been implicated in other attacks against the United States, Badey defines it as an act of terrorism. In contrast, the Oklahoma City bombing is not considered terrorism because it was apparently an isolated event or, as Badey asserts, "the Oklahoma City bombing at present can be classified as an act of terror, but not as terrorism."[17] Terrorism, in short, is part of a pattern of violence because the fear terrorists hope to instill in a population must periodically be renewed with further threats and acts intended to provoke alarm, fear, and anxiety.

The definitions in Table 9.1 also share one weakness: They tend to ignore state-perpetrated terrorism. Governments engage in terrorism in order to suppress dissent, quash a social or political movement, or intimidate a population. This is sometimes termed **authorized terror** or **repressive terror**, or even **enforcement terror**.[18] Most definitions, however—especially those proposed by government agencies—focus almost exclusively on terrorism that is geared toward changing a society rather than that used to try to maintain a status quo. Yet governments can and do unleash terror on civilian populations. During the 1970s, for example, the military *junta* that ruled Argentina engaged in what has been termed a "**dirty war**" against its own citizens. Originally focused on suppressing leftist revolutionaries, the government soon began to attack journalists, writers, intellectuals, students, union organizers, and supporters—in short, anyone who was even suspected of being a leftist sympathizer or of not supporting the state.[19] The government was quite blatant in its intent to terrorize the population; one general put it this way, "First we kill all the subversives; then we will kill their collaborators; then their sympathizers; then . . . those who remain indifferent; and finally we will kill the timid."[20] You can't get much more explicit than that. The vast majority of all the perpetrators were police officers and military personnel who kidnapped, tortured, and often murdered those they defined as the enemy. Their victims became known as the ***Desaparecidos***, or "disappeared ones." One method of disposing of victims involved drugging individuals, loading them on planes, stripping them, and then throwing them alive into the ocean.[21] Estimates of the number of victims range from a low of 10,000 to a high of 30,000.[22] This era of repression cannot be described as anything other than state terrorism, and we believe any reasonable definition of terrorism must include this type of political violence. In fact, some have even suggested that the problem of terrorism is primarily a problem of state terrorism rather than the more commonly studied revolutionary terrorism.[23]

Terrorism and Guerrilla Warfare

It is important to note that terrorism is not guerrilla warfare. Even though the words are sometimes used synonymously in the media, terrorism and **guerrilla warfare** are not the same thing, even though there may be a fair amount of overlap between their goals and methods. The term "guerrilla" literally means "little war" and originated in the Napoleonic wars after the French army invaded Spain as part of Napoleon's attempt to conquer Europe. Deposing the Spanish monarchy and setting up his brother as King of Spain, Napoleon earned the undying hostility of the Spanish people, who rose up and began a nontraditional war that was characterized by ambushes and small-scale localized attacks on the French forces. The French military responded with policies of mass reprisals and atrocities that only served to increase the hatred of the Spanish for the French. Since that time, there have been many examples of guerrilla warfare, but its essential character has remained the same. Generally speaking, guerrilla war—which is also sometimes called **low-intensity warfare** or **insurgency warfare**—is usually different from terrorism in that it involves larger, military-style forces that tend to attack the military forces of their enemy and often seek to hold and control territory.[24] Terrorist organizations tend to be smaller, do not usually operate in the open, target primarily noncombatants, and generally do not hold territory and exercise sovereign political authority over the land and people they control or influence.

There is, of course, overlap between terrorism and guerrilla war. For example, guerrilla forces sometimes use terror tactics in their military campaigns, and terrorist groups may organize in military-style units. Government forces also may resort to repressive terrorism to deprive guerrilla forces of support. During Guatemala's civil war of the 1970s and 1980s, when the government was fighting to wipe out a popular guerrilla movement, the state engaged in wholesale terrorism against the rural civilian population in an effort to destroy the popular support upon which the guerrilla forces depended.[25] Individuals and movements can also move from one type to the other; a good example of this is Osama bin Laden and Al Qaeda. During the 1980s, bin Laden was a guerrilla leader who successfully attacked Soviet forces in Afghanistan and helped force them out of Afghanistan. His guerrilla fighters also formed the nucleus of Al Qaeda. After the war in Afghanistan ended, however, Osama bin Laden and Al Qaeda increasingly turned to terror tactics as their goals shifted and evolved. Last, some organizations are large enough that they can encompass both terrorist and paramilitary wings of the organization. Hezbollah, for example, is an Islamic group based in Lebanon, and their organization includes a political arm, social services, and a paramilitary branch and engages in traditional-style terrorism.

Clearly, as this preceding discussion shows, defining terrorism can be quite tricky. Despite this, however, the fact that terrorism generally shares a number of common qualities allows us to have a working understanding of terrorism, which is all we really need for purposes of discussion in this chapter. To further develop our understanding of what terrorism is, it might be helpful to understand a little about its historical origins, and it is to that issue that we now turn.

History of Terrorism

Violence, as previous chapters have shown, has been around for about as long as human communities have existed, and terrorism is no exception to this general rule. On the contrary, terrorism is a very old strategy for creating social and political change. In this section, we review several historic examples that can assist in illuminating the dynamics of this particular type of violence. Historical examples are also relevant because the actions of many modern terrorists are heavily influenced by previous generations whose tactics and ideas have proved enduring and who have provided the inspiration for a number of contemporary terrorists.

Any starting point will be somewhat arbitrary, but a good beginning can be made with ancient Rome, since some scholars have suggested that the first recognizable terrorist group was found in Roman-occupied Judea or Palestine—present-day Israel. Here, a group of Jewish rebels known as the **Zealots** used assassination and terror to fight the Roman occupation. After Rome abolished the Jewish monarchy and took control of Palestine, an unorganized and spontaneous resistance movement sprang up. Predictably, Rome reacted with heavy-handed tactics that further escalated the violence. Eventually, a radical Jewish group known as the Zealots emerged from out of this unstructured conflict. The word Zealot has come down through the ages to refer to anyone who is a fanatic for a particular cause. When looking at the tactics of the Zealots, it is easy to see why their name has become synonymous with uncompromising extremism.[26] Their favorite weapon was a short, curved knife known as a Sica from which they derived their other name, the **Sicarii**. They attacked Roman administrators and soldiers, Jewish collaborators, and Jewish priests and leaders who were seen as being supportive or sympathetic to Roman rule. They made a point of assassinating people in the middle of the day even if that person was amongst friends and supporters. The Sicarii wanted people to feel that anyone could be a victim at any time. These Zealots also wanted to provoke the Romans into harsh repressive measures, and in this they were also successful. All attempts at compromise and conciliation were frustrated by the terrorist tactics of the Zealots, who succeeded in inflaming suspicion and hostility between Jews and Romans.[27] Sicarii violence came to an end when almost a thousand of them committed mass suicide in the fortress of Masada after enduring a long siege by the Romans.[28] Guided by religious beliefs and motivated by a political vision of a sovereign Israeli state, the Sicarii were the precursors of the modern religiously inspired groups that use terrorism to achieve political goals based on religious principles. Their desire to create a climate of fear through their daring and often suicidal tactics is also a strategy that has persisted over time.

Rome was not just a victim of terrorism—far from it, in fact. The Romans often used state terrorism to protect their interests and maintain their empire. One of the more well-known examples concerns the slave revolt led by the gladiator Spartacus. In the spring of 73 BC, Spartacus, a Thracian gladiator who probably had some military experience, broke out from a gladiator school in Capua and created an army of gladiators and runaway slaves.[29] Successfully defeating a number of Roman legions, they held out for several years before finally being defeated by a Roman army. Selecting 6,000 captured fighters at random, the victorious Roman general had them crucified on crosses in a line that stretched all the way from Capua, the city where the rebellion began, to the gates of Rome. The bodies of the dead were left to rot on the crucifixes as an object lesson on the perils of rebellion.[30] Essentially, this act of state-perpetrated terrorism was designed to send a message to the thousands of slaves throughout the Roman territories about the dangers of challenging their enslavement.

Another example of early terrorism concerns an 11th century radical Shiite Islamic sect known as the Nizari Isma'ilis or more colloquially as the **Assassins**.[31] Based in what is now Iran, Iraq, and Syria, they were dedicated to creating a pure Islamic state and used terrorism against Muslim officials and Christian crusaders alike.[32] Founded by Hasan ibn al-Sabbah to spread a radical interpretation of Islam, this sect's adherents were famous for their ability to strike with stealth and surprise and to disguise themselves effectively. Because they controlled a number of mountain castles, their leader, Sabbah, was known as "The Old Man of the Mountains."[33] So effective were they that one of their contemporary Muslim enemies said that

> To kill them is more lawful than rainwater. It is the duty of Sultans and kings to conquer and kill them, and cleanse the surface of the earth from their pollution. It is not right to associate or form friendships with them, nor to eat meat butchered by them, nor to enter into marriage with them. To shed the blood of a heretic is more meritorious than to kill seventy Greek infidels.[34]

The Assassins reportedly always used a dagger and never tried to escape, instead seeking their own martyrdom. Contemporaries were amazed at the dedication of these killers who might spend years working in the household of their eventual targets, perhaps even becoming fast friends with their victims before the fatal day of the assassination. Chroniclers of the time suggested that this amazing dedication was accomplished by having recruits drugged and then taken to a secret and beautiful garden that had been filled with fountains, streams, fruit trees, and beautiful women. In that wondrous place, these future killers were told that they had been taken to paradise and could only return after they had fulfilled their mission. Another example of their dedication was that, in order to impress visitors, their leader sometimes ordered individuals to jump off a cliff or to stab themselves, which they invariably did.[35] The Assassins also presaged the modern incarnation of Islamic terrorists who, perhaps inspired by the legends of this sect, continue to see martyrdom in the service of Islam as a viable political weapon. The name "assassin" comes from the Arabic word *hashashin*, which literally means "hashish-eater" and comes from the fact that the followers of this order supposedly used hashish in preparing for their martyrdom.[36] Wielding great political power and instilling widespread fear, they ultimately were destroyed by Mongol invaders in the 13th century.[37]

The first use of the word terrorism does not actually emerge until the late 1700s in France. On the eve of the French Revolution, France was an unhappy place with many millions living in grinding poverty while a few thousand lived lives of tremendous luxury and excess.[38] Suffering from high rates of taxation, endemic disease, and a chronic lack of adequate food, the populace finally revolted and kicked down the door of the monarchy in 1789.[39] In the wake of the revolution, King Louis XVI was put on trial and sentenced to death. As he ascended the steps to the guillotine on January 21, 1793, he is reputed to have said, "People, I die innocent of all the crimes imputed to me! I pardon the authors of my death, and pray to God that the blood you are about to shed may not fall again on France."[40] Unfortunately, his plea fell on deaf ears for France would see rivers of blood flow as the country plunged into what became known as The Great Terror. The humanistic and republican ideals of the early revolution were forsaken as the revolutionary government found itself beset on all sides by enemies and resorted to ever more brutal methods, proving the truth of George Bernard Shaw's words when he asserted, "Revolutions have never lightened the burden of tyranny: they have only shifted it to another shoulder."[41]

Facing insurrection from royalist nobles and Catholic priests among others, an uprising in the Vendee region of central France and a war against Austria, the revolutionaries increasingly relied on the **Committee of Public Safety and the Revolutionary Tribunal**.[42] Comprising 12 men, the Committee of Public Safety was invested with more and more dictatorial powers. Its most influential member was a man named Maximilien Robespierre, known to all as "the Incorruptible." It was he who asserted that

> If the spring of popular government in time of peace is virtue, the springs of popular government in revolution are at once virtue and terror: virtue, without which terror is fatal; terror, without which virtue is powerless. Terror is nothing other than justice, prompt, severe, inflexible; it is therefore an emanation of virtue; it is not so much a special principle as it is a consequence of the general principle of democracy applied to our country's most urgent needs.[43]

With these words, Robespierre unleashed a reign of terror that took thousands of lives and destroyed the brief flowering of democratic values that the revolution had begun. Some estimates suggest that up to 40,000 people met their fate on the guillotine and several hundred thousand died in prisons around the country.[44] Anybody could be arrested and executed on the flimsiest of evidence. In the mind of Robespierre and his fellow extremists, terror in defense of the revolution was a civic virtue. More than that, it was seen as a necessity. For them, terrorism—when perpetrated for the right reasons—was nothing more than justice and therefore legitimate. Robespierre and his fellow extremists, known as the **Jacobins**, even executed a large number of their fellow revolutionaries who had been calling for more moderation. In revolutionary France, we see an early incarnation of a government using terror as a means to protect a set of values and beliefs. Linking violence to national security and defense is a long-standing method by which governments justify violence and terror. The revolutionaries of France wanted to create a just and virtuous society founded upon the principles of "Liberty, Equality, and Fraternity," but in seeking to foster and protect this utopian vision from its enemies—both real and imagined—its defenders resorted to extreme violence and terror and ultimately destroyed the very ideals they were trying to protect. In the process, they left us the legacy of the word terrorism and a case study that illustrates the lengths to which a government may go in protecting its interests.

Modern terrorism also owes a great deal to the ideas and tactics of the Russian terrorists from the late 19th and early 20th centuries. Intent on destroying the Russian monarchy and the Tsar, groups such as **Narodnaya Volya** or the People's Will employed terror and violence in the cause of anarchy and nationalism. These groups defined the violence of terrorism as a justified response to governmental oppression and despotism. Inspired by the writing of theorists, such as Mikhail Bakunin, Sergey Nechayev, and others, these groups were responsible for repeated assassination attempts and bombings against various Russian leaders and government officials. They hoped to expose the corruption and weakness of the Tsarist government through the assassination of government officials and of the Tsar. It was believed that this would impel the peasantry to rise up and create a revolution.[45] They succeeded in killing Tsar Alexander II on March 1, 1881, but their success proved their undoing, as the government was finally mobilized into rounding up and executing many of the revolutionaries in the aftermath of the Tsar's death. Their ideas, however, lived on and influenced later generations of terrorists around the world who read the writings of people such as Sergey Nechayev, whose *Catechism of the Revolutionist,* published in 1869, became the manual of professional revolutionaries for much of the next century.[46] In part, the creed he espoused asserted that a terrorist or revolutionary

- is an implacable enemy of this world, and if he is continues to live in it, that is only to destroy it more effectively;
- the revolutionary is a dedicated man, merciless toward the state and toward the whole of educated and privileged society in general; and he must expect no mercy from them either;
- must have but one thought, one aim, night and day—merciless destruction;
- is not a revolutionary if he feels pity for anything in this world.[47]

These kinds of words inspired a generation of revolutionaries who strove to be cold, merciless, and devoid of sentimentality. By eliminating weaknesses and impurity within themselves, adherents of this philosophy hoped to better be able to violently overthrow the existing social structures that they defined as bourgeois, corrupt, and weak. More modern groups, such as the German **Baader-Meinhof Gang** and the **Japanese Red Army,** were profoundly influenced by these earlier ideals.

While significantly influenced by the past, terrorism continues to evolve and change according to the times so that the modern face of terrorism reflects the present political and social realities of our contemporary world. This also means that, in the present day, terrorist groups subscribe to a wide range of motives and agendas. As we have seen in other chapters, estimating the prevalence of terrorism is inextricably related to how it is defined and measured. As you read the next section, remember how difficult it is to define terrorism and how our perceptions can change depending upon who is doing the counting and which definition is being applied.

How Frequent Are Terrorist Acts?

Since the September 11 attacks on U.S. soil and the subsequent war on terror, the fear of terrorism has become much more prevalent. Similar to all perceived threats, however, our perceptions are sometimes not based in objective reality—or, as one journalist put it, "Sensible calculation of real-world risks is a multidimensional math problem that sometimes seems entirely beyond us."[48] In other words, our fears are out of all proportion to real risk. We tend to be more fearful of things that aren't likely to happen, and surprisingly unconcerned about dangers that are more likely to happen. Most of us are more fearful of flying than of driving, for example, even though we are more at risk of being injured or killed when we get into our cars every day compared with boarding an airplane. In the wake of the September 11 attacks, many people stopped flying and began driving instead. According to one calculation, about a thousand more people died on our nations highways in the three months following the attack than would have died if the usual patterns of travel had stayed in effect.[49] It's important to keep this in mind when looking at the real dangers and risks of terrorism. So how much are we really at risk from terrorism? The FBI reports that between 1980 and 2001, there were 294 terrorist attacks in the United States and another 55 suspected terrorist incidents.[50] Keep in mind, however, that the FBI definition is not necessarily the most inclusive of standards, which affects what gets counted and reported. From 2002 to 2011, the United States was the site of another 127 terrorist attacks, which resulted in 23 fatalities and another 76 injured.[51] It is important, however, to point out that this only counts those perpetrated on U.S. soil and excludes attacks against Americans in places like Iraq and Afghanistan. Obviously, if attacks in these war zones were included, the figures would be much, much higher.

Figure 9.2 traces the number of terrorism attacks within the United States from 1998 through 2009. It includes events from both domestic groups as well as international organizations but excludes those that were foiled before being carried out, such as that which occurred on December 25, 2009, when passengers on a Delta Airlines plane prevented a Nigerian passenger from detonating an explosive device as the plane was on approach to land in Detroit. As you can see, Figure 9.2 reveals that the actual number of attacks that the United States suffers in any given year tends to be rather limited, especially when compared with terrorist activities in other parts of the world—although, as the September 11 attacks illustrate, any single attack or series of attacks can be quite destructive in its own right.

In other words, most terrorism occurs outside the United States, and in fact, between 1969 and 2009, only 7.8% of all terrorism attacks in the world were directed against the United States, which means that 92.2% of terrorism around the world did not involve U.S. targets. This understanding is further reinforced when we examine Figure 9.3, which tracks the total number of terrorism events from 1969 through 2009 by region of occurrence and clearly shows that terrorism occurs much more frequently on the international stage than it does in the United States. Contrary to our fears, North America is in fact the safest part of the world. Obviously, this doesn't mean that the United States is immune to terrorist activity but simply that most terrorism incidents occur in other parts of the world. Also apparent is the fact that every region of the world suffers from the problem of terrorism, and what varies are the local and regional dynamics that affect the specific intent and motivation. When terrorism does occur in the United States, we also need to understand that it is not always foreign terrorists who are targeting us. Figure 9.4 traces the number of terrorism attacks in the United States perpetrated by domestic groups and reveals that this is often a homegrown problem, albeit one that has been diminishing in recent years. The first Oklahoma City bombing certainly illustrates the nature of this problem.

❖ **Figure 9.2**   Acts of Terrorism Within the United States, 1998–2009

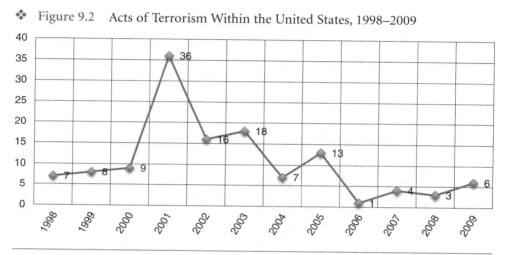

SOURCE: Adapted from data from "The Rand Database of Worldwide Terrorism Incidents," www.rand.org

❖ **Figure 9.3**   Terrorism Events by World Region, 1969–2009

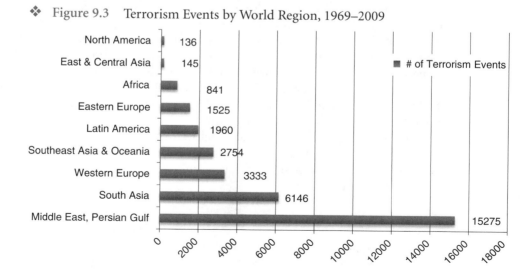

SOURCE: Adapted from data from "The Rand Database of Worldwide Terrorism Incidents," www.rand.org

❖   Figure 9.4   Domestic Terrorism in the United States, 2001–2009

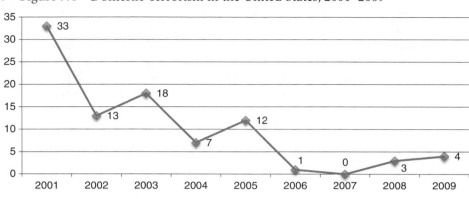

SOURCE: Adapted from Data from "The Rand Database of Worldwide Terrorism Incidents," www.rand.org

On April 19, 1995, a rental van blew up in front of the Alfred P. Murrah Federal Building in Oklahoma City, Oklahoma, killing 168 people and wounding another 850.[52] Almost by pure luck, just a short time later a highway patrol officer pulled over a vehicle for driving without a license plate and speeding. When the officer saw that the driver was carrying a handgun in a shoulder holster, he arrested the man for carrying a concealed weapon, without realizing that he had just nabbed the man responsible for the bombing. Ironically, the perpetrator of this bombing was not some foreign extremist, but was instead a decorated former soldier named Timothy McVeigh. Fueled by antigovernment resentment and hatred, and with coconspirator Terry Nichols, McVeigh planned and implemented the act of terrorism in Oklahoma City. In doing so, they felt that they were responding to the government handling of the siege of the Branch Davidian compound in Waco, Texas and the siege of Randy Weaver's cabin at Ruby Ridge. Ultimately convicted of the attack, McVeigh was sentenced to death and executed in 2001, while Terry Nichols received life in prison. In perpetrating this homegrown terrorist attack, McVeigh was following in the footsteps of a long line of domestic terrorist groups who have seen violence as a legitimate response to their perceptions of governmental abuse. From the Ku Klux Klan to Posse Comitatus, and from the Puerto Rican nationalist group the Macheteros to the antiabortion group Army of God, this country has seen plenty of terroristic violence from a variety of United States–based groups. As with international terrorism, domestic terrorism occurs for many different reasons, and the best way to examine this is to take a look at the typologies or categories of terrorism that have been developed to explain the various goals motivating terrorist groups.

Types of Terrorism

While many typologies of terrorism exist, one of the best is provided by Jerrold Post, who suggests that there are three main types of terrorism: political, criminal, and pathological (see Figure 9.5).[53]

Criminal terrorism, as the name implies, refers to terrorism committed to achieve some illicit goal or to protect an illegal operation. The best contemporary example of this involves the Medellin drug cartel of Pablo Escobar. Before he was finally tracked down and killed in December 1993, Escobar had been waging a campaign of terror against the government of Colombia. Threatened with extradition to the United States because of his drug smuggling, he had unleashed a wave of terror that included widespread bombings and the assassination of political candidates, judges, attorneys, journalists, police officers, and military leaders.[54] He even had an airliner blown out of the sky because he thought a presidential candidate would be on board. He paid a guerrilla movement known as **M19** to attack the Palace of Justice and take members of Colombia's Supreme Court hostage.[55] Terrorist organizations sometimes engage in crimes in order to help fund their activities. Some groups support their operations through widespread kidnappings for ransom, while others are actively involved in crimes such as credit card fraud or smuggling in order to bring in revenue.[56]

Pathological terrorism, on the other hand, concerns acts that are perpetrated because of some sort of mental illness. A good example of this type of terrorism was committed by Ted Kaczynski, more infamously known as the **Unabomber**. Between 1978 and his arrest in 1996, the Unabomber sent homemade explosive devices to a variety of executives and scientists in his misguided campaign against technology. Before being captured by the FBI, he killed three individuals and wounded 29 others. His behavior was in all likelihood the result of mental illness—probably paranoid schizophrenia. It is important to underscore the fact that this type of terrorist represents only a very small fraction of all types of terrorism.

The last category is **political terrorism**, of which there are three subcategories: substate; state-supported; and regime or state. **Regime or state terrorism** refers to the actions of a government in using terror to intimidate and suppress dissent. As indicated earlier in this chapter, the actions of the Argentinean government during its "Dirty War" certainly fit into this category. Another example concerns the government of South Africa during the years of **apartheid**. Apartheid was a legal system developed to keep the races apart and maintain white privilege in a country in which white Africans were outnumbered four to one by black Africans. Throughout the 1970s and 1980s, the government, through its security services, engaged in a protracted campaign of murder, torture, kidnapping, intimidation, and subversion that only came to a halt with the end of apartheid in 1994.[57] Subject to abject poverty and overt racial discrimination, many black South Africans organized marches, strikes, and demonstrations during the latter years of apartheid, while others supported more militant organizations, such as the African National Congress. Told they were defenders of their way of life and that the unrest was engineered by the Soviet Union, the police and military reacted with startling brutality and violence, secure in the knowledge that they were protecting their society and way of life. The leader of one government death squad, Eugene de Kock—nicknamed "Prime Evil"—described himself as a "crusader" while later being interviewed about his activities.[58]

State-supported terrorism is terrorism that is assisted by a government. Historically, many nations have provided money, a safe haven, training, and resources for terrorists and organizations. As of January 2013, The U.S. Department of State designated the following countries as state sponsors of terrorism: Cuba, Iran, North

❖ Figure 9.5   Typology of Terrorism

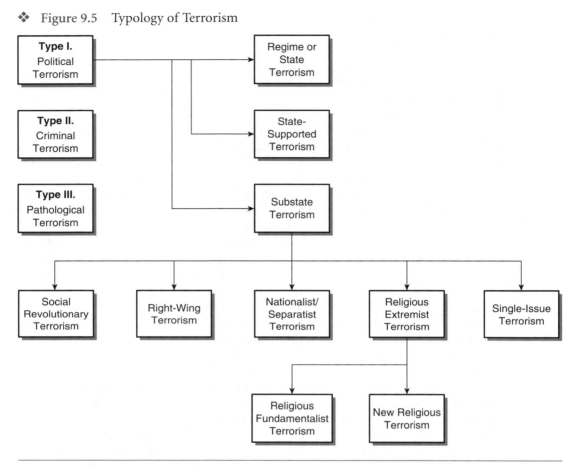

SOURCE: Jerrold M. Post, *Leaders and Their Followers in a Dangerous World: The Psychology of Political Behavior* (Ithaca, NY: Cornell University Press, 2004).

Korea, Syria, and Sudan. Iran, for example, provides financial and other support to Hezbollah, Hamas, and several other Middle Eastern terrorist groups.[59]

Substate terrorism is the designation Jerrold Post uses to indicate terrorism perpetrated by nongovernmental groups and is further divided into five subtypes: social revolutionary terrorism; right-wing terrorism, nationalist-separatist terrorism, religious extremist terrorism, and single-issue terrorism.

Social revolutionary terrorism is the type of terrorism most people envision when they think about terrorism. It invariably involves groups trying to overthrow an established order. For this reason, it is often considered leftist—especially since many of these groups have espoused Marxist or socialist agendas. During the 1980s, for example, a terrorist group emerged in Peru known as the Tupac Amaru, or more formally the **Tupac Amaru Revolutionary Movement** (MRTA). The name was taken from Peruvian history: Tupac Amaru was an Incan noble who in the 1780s led a revolt against Spanish rule.[60] Admirers of the Cuban revolution, and of Che Guevara in particular, members of this group wanted to get rid of the Peruvian government and install a Marxist-inspired one. Their most notorious attack happened in 1996, when 14 MRTA terrorists stormed the Japanese embassy and took 700 people hostage. The resulting hostage crisis lasted four months and only ended when military forces attacked and killed all the terrorists. Similar examples of this type of terrorist organization include Germany's Red Army Faction, Italy's Red Brigades, and Mexico's Zapatista Army for National Liberation.[61]

On the other side of the spectrum, **right-wing terrorism** refers to conservative organizations that seek to preserve a political system or to return society to some past or mythic time of greatness. Organizations such as the Ku Klux Klan (KKK) fit into this category. Originally created at the end of the Civil War by a Confederate cavalry general from Mississippi named Nathan Bedford Forrest, the name is derived from the Greek word for circle, *kuklos*.[62] Founded in order to combat reconstruction and protect Southern whites from the transgressions of the newly freed slaves and from Northern carpetbaggers, its members were hooded and dressed in robes to make African Americans think they were the ghosts of Confederate soldiers. They lynched, threatened, and otherwise intimidated those who tried to exercise their newfound rights.[63] Soon disbanded because of political infighting, the Klan was reborn in 1915 when D. W. Griffith's film *The Birth of a Nation* sparked a renewed interest in the organization, and over the years the Klan has continued to promote a nativist and racial agenda through violence and intimidation.

Nationalist-separatist terrorism is exemplified by groups that attempt to create a nation or achieve political autonomy and independence for their people. A good example of this involves the violence in **Chechnya**. In 1991, as the Soviet Union was disintegrating, the republic of Chechnya in the Caucasus Mountains declared independence under the leadership of a retired Soviet Air Force general named Dzhokhar Dudayev.[64] In 1994, Russian forces invaded in an attempt to force a reunification, and since that time the region has been wracked by an ever more vicious campaign of state terror perpetrated by the Russians, which is countered by Chechen terrorists who have staged ever more destructive acts of their own.[65] In October 2002, for example, 700 people were taken hostage in a Moscow theater by Chechen terrorists. Russian commandos ended up using an experimental gas as a prelude to storming the theater. Some 129 hostages and 41 terrorists were killed in the assault, most from the effects of the gas. More recently, in September of 2004, Chechen terrorists took 1,300 hostages—most of them children—when they took control of a school in the town of Beslan in Russia. The siege ended horrifically, with large numbers of the hostages killed and many others wounded. Other examples of nationalist-separatist terrorists include the Irish Republican Army (IRA), the Tamil Tigers in Sri Lanka, and the Kurdish PKK.

Single-issue terrorism concerns groups that are focused on only one particular topic. Earth First!, the Earth Liberation Front, and the Evan Mecham Eco-Terrorist International Conspiracy (EMETIC) are all radical environmental organizations that have engaged in what has been called ecoterrorism, which involves acts of violence and sabotage in order to protect the environment.[66] One might also include antiabortion terrorist groups within this category, although they are also often motivated by underlying religious convictions. The **Army of God** is one such group that has been implicated in the bombing of abortion clinics—"abortuaries" in the group's parlance—and the murder of doctors who perform abortions. Single-issue terrorism is often not concerned with overthrowing a government, but rather with changing specific policies or laws.

Religious extremist terrorism can further be broken down into **fundamentalist terrorism** and **new religions terrorism**. The latter is best exemplified by the Japanese group **Aum Shinrikyo**, which means "Supreme Truth." Led by Shoko Asahara, a former yoga teacher who preached that the end of the world was coming, this group came to believe that it needed to purify humanity for the coming apocalypse by killing those who were sinful and impure. In a perverse way, the killings the group performed were defined by the cult as being altruistic and even compassionate. To their way of thinking, the deaths were helping the victims experience a positive rebirth and brought the world closer to a cleansing cataclysm and the subsequent renewal of the earth.[67] Members who tried to leave were threatened and intimidated and in more than a few cases killed.[68] Aum Shinrikyo also experimented with and collected various chemical and biological agents, including sarin nerve gas, anthrax, and the Ebola virus, culminating in the March 1995 release of sarin nerve gas in the Tokyo subway system. Cult members carried bags filled with the gas, punctured them with umbrellas, and left. Twelve people were killed and thousands injured. Asahara was arrested by the Japanese Police in May 1995, put on trial, and finally sentenced to death by hanging in early 2004.

The last category of Post's typology is fundamentalist terrorism, and it is this type that has come to dominate the attention of the world community because of the attacks of September 11. Fundamentalism is a belief in the literal and absolute truth of the sacred scriptures of a religion and typically involves attempts to return that faith to its founding beliefs and principles. Over time, all religions have modified their rituals, beliefs, and practices in response to social, cultural, and political changes. The religious sensibilities of today are not those of yesterday. This is particularly true in the developed world, where various secularizing forces have moved religion out of the public realm and into the world of private life.[69] Antimodernist in orientation, fundamentalism rejects these changes because they are seen as moving a religion away from the true path. All religions have an idealized vision of the perfect religious society according to traditions, scriptures, and other holy writings, and fundamentalism is intended to bring that vision into reality.

While fundamentalism is often linked with religious-inspired violence, such as terrorism, it must be understood that not every fundamentalist organization is violent. According to Jerrold Post, fundamentalists tend to be either quietist or activist.[70] Quietists are those who await the fulfillment of God's word, while activists try to bring it about, often through violence. Believing in the absolute and infallible truth of their doctrine, fundamentalists acknowledge no moral complexity. The religious scholar Charles Kimball points out that claims of absolute truth, which fundamentalists tend to believe, are closely linked with violent religious extremism.[71] From the point of view of violent religious extremists, there is no ambiguity because all other points of view are wrong and displeasing to God. There is also no room for compromise because that is perceived as a negation of truth. Manichean or dualistic in outlook, fundamentalism divides the world into two easily understood camps: good and evil; right and wrong;

light and dark. To the true believer, violence in pursuit of fundamentalist goals is perpetrated in defense of God's word and so is not wrongful. Those who do not share the same vision of their faith are by definition spiritually and morally inferior, and are therefore legitimate victims of righteous violence. From this perspective, the suffering and harm caused to innocent victims can be justified as God's will in bringing about a more moral world.[72]

All religions provide powerful justifications and legitimacy for violence. We merely have to look at examples of religiously inspired violence such as the Crusades or the Inquisition for confirmation of this fact. Christian fundamentalist terrorists have been involved in the killing of doctors and others at abortion clinics. Believing it is their duty to create a Christian theocracy so that Jesus Christ can return to establish the Kingdom of God, members of groups such as the Army of God believe they are obligated to fight abortion with violence because "the government of the United States has become a godless and apostate body" to which the only answer is violence to destroy its "Idolatry."[73] They believe that their violence is defensive in nature—that is, they see themselves as protecting the life of the unborn children from murderers.[74]

Similarly, Jewish fundamentalist terrorists have been involved in attacks not only against Palestinians and other Muslims but also against fellow Jews. On November 4, 1995, the Prime Minister of Israel, Yitzhak Rabin—who the previous year had won the Nobel Peace Prize—was shot and killed by a young Jewish law student named Yigal Amir who believed that the policies of the government violated Judaic law. In his own words, Amir stated, "According to Jewish law the minute a Jew betrays his people and country to the enemy, he must be killed."[75] In Amir's view, the killing was demanded by God because, in giving up control of the West Bank, Rabin had violated a central tenet of Jewish fundamentalist theology that posits that the Holy Land was given solely to the Jews, His chosen people, by God, and therefore anyone who gave it away deserved to be killed. We also see Jewish fundamentalist-based terrorism in the actions of Gush Emunim (Movement of the Faithful), which in the 1980s was involved in many terrorist attacks against Palestinians, including a foiled plot to blow up the Dome of the Rock in Jerusalem, one of Islam's holiest sites.[76]

Fundamentalist terrorism is also an issue within Islam. Most contemporary Islamic terrorism is connected, at least in part, to a larger **Islamic *Salafi Jihad*** that is essentially a fundamentalist movement inspired by visions of a holy war in the name of Islam. *Salafiyyah* is an Arabic word that means "ancient one" and refers to those who accompanied the prophet Muhammad, and the use of this word in this context clearly indicates a desire to resurrect a more traditional version of Islam.[77] Desiring a return to Islamic greatness, this movement holds that Islam has declined, especially relative to the West, because it left the true path and displeased Allah. In many ways, Islamic fundamentalist violence is all about recapturing a golden age. Western nations—especially the United States—are seen as corrupting and malignant influences on the Islamic world. This revivalist movement has taken a number of different forms, depending on the country in which each was formed. On the Arabian Peninsula, it is known as **Wahhabism** after Muhammad ibn Abd al-Wahhab, an 18th century Arabian who preached a puritanical vision of Islam and influenced many generations of Muslims, including Osama bin Laden.[78] In Egypt, the movement was heavily influenced by Sayyid Qutb among others, who believed that Islam and Western secularism could not coexist peacefully.[79] Executed in 1966 for conspiring against the Egyptian government and inciting violence, his legacy nevertheless continues to influence present-day Islamic fundamentalists and terrorists. The leader of a radical fundamentalist group known as the **Muslim Brotherhood**, Qutb, believed that not only was violence justified against Western influences, but it was also justified against Muslims who did not abide by his strict interpretation of Islam. In 1981, a group known as al-Jihad, inspired by the ideas of Qutb, assassinated Anwar Sadat, then President of Egypt, while he was reviewing a military commemoration ceremony. Even though Sadat was a devout and practicing Muslim, he was killed because he pursued policies of accommodation with the West and wanted to modernize Egypt.[80] In the eyes of Islamic fundamentalist terrorists, the killing of Muslims and nonbelievers is justified in the name of *jihad*. Generally speaking, *jihad* refers to a struggle or a striving, and one common view holds that there exists a greater and a lesser *jihad*. Greater *jihad* refers to an internal struggle that someone might go through in trying to become a better Muslim and live a life based on the five pillars of Islam: professing faith; regular prayer; fasting during the holy month of Ramadan; charity; and making a pilgrimage to Mecca known as the Haj.[81] But *jihad* can also refer to an armed struggle on behalf of Islam. This lesser form of *jihad* has historically encompassed conflict in order to protect Islam and expand its influence, and it is to this latter form of *jihad* that Islamic terrorists turn in order to justify their destructive actions.

Jerrold Post's typology helps teach us that terrorist groups engage in their violent behavior for a number of different reasons, although it should be pointed out that these are not mutually exclusive categories. Any particular group can be made to fit into several different categories because their goals and methods may encompass overlapping means and intentions. In other words, the lines are often blurred. This typology, however, does not tell us why and how individuals come to join these groups, and it is to this issue that we now turn.

Who Becomes a Terrorist?

What kind of person becomes a terrorist? What makes a person decide that the killing of noncombatants is a legitimate way to accomplish some goal or goals? Is there a profile of a "typical" terrorist? Although our gut reaction may often be "are they crazy?" research indicates that the majority of terrorists do not suffer from psychological problems such as schizophrenia.[82] This makes sense, for what terrorist group would want to recruit someone who was psychologically unstable? These individuals would pose a significant security risk for the organization.[83] This is not to say that the violence they inflict does not brutalize the perpetrators, nor that some don't come to enjoy the violence. If there is any single truth to violence—both collective and individual—it is that violence has a corrupting influence and has a tendency to transform those who engage in it. People who rely on violence become used to it and may even come to enjoy and revel in it.[84]

❖ Photo 9.3   Photo of Mohamed Atta obtained by the FBI

Despite the absence of mental illness, a number of scholars have suggested that the roots of terrorist activity may lie in the psychological makeup of certain individuals. Some believe, for example, that terrorists suffer from a narcissistic personality disorder that renders them somewhat sociopathic, arrogant, and without care or concern for others.[85] Keep in mind that this doesn't necessarily mean that they are "crazy" but rather that they have certain personality traits that allow them to more easily engage in this kind of violence. The suffering they cause doesn't really touch them in an emotional way. In short, they have a hard time empathizing with others. One component of this type of individual is that they tend to externalize the source of their difficulties in a process known as splitting. Because of difficulties suffered in childhood, these individuals feel inadequate, yet project those inadequacies on others and make them the subject of their anger and blame. Post's analysis of German terrorists of the 1970s reveals that many of them lost a parent at a young age, often clashed with authorities, and had many difficulties in school and work—all of which seems to anecdotally support this argument for at least some terrorists.[86] Other researchers have borrowed from Erikson's ideas about the ways in which individual identity is created and suggest that terrorists adopt a negative identity. Because of disappointments and rejection, these individuals come to embrace destructive forces as a way to express their anger and frustration.[87] Essentially, terrorism involves a rejection of the values and ideas that mainstream society holds as important.

However, as appealing as these arguments may be, we cannot rely exclusively on psychological explanations to understand why people become terrorists. Terrorists come in all shapes and sizes. While some come from poor backgrounds, others come from relatively well-to-do families. Osama bin Laden, for example, was a multimillionaire who came from one of the wealthiest families in Saudi Arabia. Some terrorists have little formal education while others are college educated and some have even earned PhDs and medical degrees. One study of Islamic terrorists found that the majority of those studied came from the upper or middle classes, which calls into question the belief that terrorism is primarily motivated by poverty.[88] Consider, for example, Mohamed Atta, who is discussed in In Focus 9.2 and whose biography graphically illustrates these points. In short, there is no single background, upbringing, or life experience that all terrorists share. Instead we find that terrorist profiles vary depending upon the context, the cause, and the individual involved.

Portrait of a Terrorist: Mohamed Atta

Tracing the trajectory of Mohamed Atta's life, one would not expect this person to have ended up as the operational commander of one of the most devastating terrorist attacks of the last 50 years, the September 11, 2001, attacks on the World Trade Center and the Pentagon. Yet that is precisely what Mohamed el-Amir Awad el-Sayed Atta[1] became. Born in 1968 to a respectable middle-class family, Atta was the youngest of three siblings, having two older sisters. His father was a lawyer who was able to establish the family in a faded, but still fairly well-to-do, section of Cairo. The family was not overly religious and would certainly never be characterized as extremist or fundamentalist. Growing up, Mohamed Atta did not have many friends, since his father—a strict disciplinarian—insisted that his children spend their time studying. One relative of the family described the children in this way: "They respected their father's determination and demands on them. It was a house of study. No playing, no entertainment. Just study."[2] Ultimately, the Atta children did well academically, with one sister ending up as a Professor of Botany and the other as a cardiologist. Mohamed, on the other hand, went into engineering, and ultimately graduated in 1990 from Cairo University in the middle of his class. Interestingly enough, during his time at the university Mohamed Atta apparently steered clear of the Muslim Brotherhood, which actively recruited at the campus. It seems that, at this stage in his life, Atta was not much interested in fundamentalist Islam. After graduation and unable to go to graduate school because of his mediocre grades and unable to get a job because of the weak Egyptian economy, Atta left for graduate school in Germany in 1992. Evidently he wasn't keen on going. As his father explained, "My son is a very sensitive man; he is soft and was extremely attached to his mother. I almost tricked him to go to Germany to continue his education. Otherwise, he never wanted to leave Egypt. He didn't want to go."[3] Hamburg was Atta's destination, where he enrolled at Hamburg Technical University and also got a part-time job at Plankontor, an urban planning control company where he worked as a draftsman.

Sheltered, shy, away from his family and with few friends, Atta was at a vulnerable point in his life, and it didn't help that many of his fellow students found him stiff, intolerant, and prudish. Atta also found German culture, with its open and permissive attitudes toward sexuality, women, and entertainment, distasteful and perhaps even frightening. Looking for some recognizable traditions and customs, Atta sought refuge at the Al Quds mosque in a working-class section of Hamburg where he found solace and comfort in the familiarity of Islam. Al Quds, however, espoused a brand of radical Islam, and some of the preachers had links with terrorist groups. It was here, according to all the evidence, that Mohamed Atta was recruited into the cause of Islamic terrorism. Islamic terrorist groups have long used mosques as fertile grounds for recruiting inexperienced, impressionable, and needy young men into their movements. Alienated and alone, Mohamed Atta proved an ideal candidate.

In 1995, in response to the ever-increasing role of Islam in his life, Atta made his *haj*, or pilgrimage, to Mecca and found it a powerful experience. After his return, he began growing the beard without a mustache that often indicates a man is a fundamentalist. He also spent less time on his studies and more time at the mosque teaching religious courses and

(Continued)

(Continued)

praying. It was on his return that he also wrote out a will that was recovered after his death and in which he makes clear his commitment to Islam. For example, he cautions his family not to mourn his death because it negates his religious beliefs: "I don't want anyone to weep and cry or to rip their clothes or slap their face because this is an ignorant thing to do."[4] He went on to also give detailed instructions on how his body was to be washed and that no women be allowed at his grave.

During this transformation from a student to a terrorist, Atta became friends with a number of other Islamic students, including Marwan al-Shehhi and Ziad Jarrah, who were to become fellow September 11 hijackers. Increasingly, many of these young men spent all their time reading, thinking, and talking about their faith. They listened to audiotaped sermons and chants about holy war, many of which glorified martyrdom. One line from a chant, for example, went: "When I die as a martyr, I die as a better human being."[5] Spending all their free time together, limiting their exposure to outside influences, and deepening their commitment through this self-reinforcing group process, it is not surprising that some of these individuals would begin to explore more extreme and violent ways

of expressing their beliefs. Over time, their radical and violent views of Islam acted as a catalyst for them to engage in more aggressive action. A number of these young men, including Atta, also went to Al Qaeda training camps in Afghanistan where they learned the basics of terrorist tactics. In this setting, not only did they learn the techniques of terrorism, but they were further immersed into a culture that glorified violence, sacrifice, and holy war or *jihad*.

After his return to Germany, the group further coalesced around Atta's involvement with Al Qaeda and ultimately resulted in Mohamed Atta becoming operational commander of the plot that would result in the attacks of September 11. Mohamed Atta was not a monster in the sense that he was psychologically different from other people. Rather, we see in his life the transformation of a sheltered and somewhat socially awkward young man into someone who believed fervently in the notion of sacrificing himself and the lives of others in the cause of a holy war. It was a vision fostered by his exposure to a radicalized version of Islam preached and sustained in the Mosque of Al Quds and given potency by the sense of isolation and estrangement he experienced in Germany.

NOTES:

1. There are many variants of Atta's name and this is one formal version.
2. Terry McDermott, *Perfect Soldiers* (New York: HarperCollins, 2005), 13.
3. McDermott, *Perfect Soldiers*, 19.
4. Jane Corbin, *Al-Qaeda: In Search of the Terror Network That Threatens the World* (New York: Thunder's Mouth Press, 2003), 128.
5. Quoted in McDermott, *Perfect Soldiers*, 49.

To better understand terrorism, we have to take into account social, political, religious, and even cultural factors in addition to the psychological arguments. Looking at Islamic terrorist groups, for example, we find that many rank and file members join for a mix of reasons. One common element involves belief. Many of the individuals who join these groups are devout Muslims who see their participation as a duty to their faith—a duty that includes the anticipation of heavenly rewards if they are killed as well as monetary rewards for their families. The families of martyrs (usually suicide bomb-ers), for example, may receive cash payments for the death of their child. Participation in terrorist activity, then, may be seen as an expression of faith by some, who are also able to materially benefit their families. For others, the desire for adventure and the prestige and status of belonging to a violent group are significant factors. Within many communities, terrorists and terrorist groups enjoy a heroic standing with tremendous popular support. Among the Palestinians, for example, Yehiya Ayyash, better known as The Engineer, was a member of Hamas and a hero to many who idolized him for his ability to lead attacks against Israel. After he was killed by Israeli security services with a booby-trapped cell phone in 1996, he received a lavish funeral attended by over 100,000 supporters. Other Palestinian suicide bombers have posters and hip hop videos dedicated to them and achieve with their martyrdom a kind of posthumous pop stardom that may be a significant enticement for many. Young men and women who grow up in these communities where the terrorists and the dead are celebrated and made into heroes may find the idea of participating in terrorism appealing and intoxicating. In this sense, young men who join terrorist groups are no different from young men who join other kinds of groups, such as street gangs. Within these groups, they find acceptance and belonging, a sense of purpose, and prestige. The influence of friendship should also not be discounted. Many terrorists are recruited into terrorist cells through friendship networks and, once within the groups, the bonds of friendship help maintain their membership. During their time as students in Germany, many of the leaders of the September 11 attacks became close friends who clearly enjoyed each other's company.[89] Additionally, for many young men who feel powerless in their own lives, membership in a terrorist organization and the weapons and violence that are part and parcel of that membership can provide a sense of power and mastery.[90]

To these elements discussed above we can add the effects of poverty, oppression, despair, and hopelessness. While these do not cause terrorism in and of themselves, they certainly contribute to the appeal of terrorism as a means of addressing per-ceived wrongs and injustice. As terrorism expert Jessica Stern asserts, "Hopelessness, deprivation, envy, and humiliation make death, and paradise, seem more appealing."[91] Another expert, speaking about Palestinian suicide bombers, put it this way: "What prompts a 20-year-old to blow himself up and kill as many Israelis as he can in the process? It definitely takes more than a belief in God to turn a boy into a martyr. It takes desperation, anger, loss of hope. It's believing that your life is not worth living anymore."[92] While it is true that many of those in leadership roles in terrorist groups may be from middle- and upper-class families and be fairly well educated, it is also true that most of the lower ranking operatives—the foot soldiers, as it were—are typically derived from the ghettos, slums, and refugee camps of the world's dispossessed.

Tactics and Weapons

Terrorists employ a wide variety of tactics and weapons to perpetrate their brand of violence. They range from nonlethal assaults and campaigns of intimidation to mas-sively deadly attacks using bombs and firearms or, as we saw, airplanes. In many ways, the tactics are largely dictated by the goals of the organization. Choices are made based on the impact that a particular weapon will be likely to have. Figure 9.6 reviews the methods favored by terrorists in 2008 and reveals that the two most common tactics in that year were armed assaults and bombings. Bombs, in particular, have long been a favored weapon of terrorist groups and can range from small pipe bombs, such as those detonated at the 1996 Summer Olympic Games in Atlanta, Georgia, to much more powerful vehicular bombs and improvised explosive devices (IED) that have been used with such lethal effect in Iraq and Afghanistan.

One specific kind of bombing attack that has received a great deal of attention in recent years is suicide bombings. According to the Combating Terrorism Center, an independent research institute at the West Point military academy, there were approximately 1,944 suicide bombings worldwide from 1981 through 2008. [93] The report concluded that the majority of attacks occurred in Iraq, Afghanistan, and Pakistan, with increasing numbers in the latter countries compared to Iraq. In total, over 21,000 people have been killed by these attacks, and nearly 50,000 seriously injured. Although suicide bombings generally represent less than 5% of all terrorist attacks, these attacks generally account for nearly half of all fatalities from terrorist attacks.[94] Thus, while they may be relatively infrequent compared with other types of terrorist attacks, they represent almost half of all fatalities exacted by terrorists. That is probably why the term "suicide bomber" has become synonymous with terrorism.

Suicide bombings are not a new phenomenon. Throughout history, men and women have been willing to sacrifice their lives in the service of a cause or their faith. In addition to the examples of the Zealots and the Assassins discussed earlier, we can also refer to the Kamikaze pilots of World War II. In the closing years of the war, with the tide swinging against Japan, the Japanese military began sending out pilots who were trained to fly their airplanes directly into U.S. ships in an effort to stem the allied

❖ Figure 9.6   Terrorism by Method, 2008

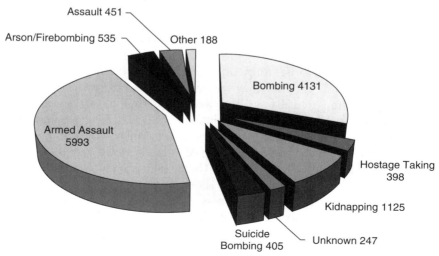

advance. By sacrificing their lives, they hoped to make the cost of victory so expensive in lives that the Americans would negotiate for peace.[95]

The modern era of suicide bombing began in the 1980s when Hezbollah, a Lebanese group, began using suicide bombers against Israel and the United States. They were inspired by Iran which, in their war with Iraq, had used young boys to march through mine fields in order to clear them with their bodies. The most notable of Hezbollah's many suicide bombings occurred on October 23, 1983, when a truck loaded with explosives was driven into the U.S. Marine barracks at the Beirut airport. A total of 241 marines were killed in the resulting explosion.[96] Since that time, many suicide bombings have occurred, including the most deadly of all, the September 11, 2001, attacks by airplanes that crashed into a Pennsylvania field, the Pentagon, and the Twin Towers of the World Trade Center.

When people think of suicide bombings, they tend to think of Middle Eastern terrorist groups—mostly Palestinian bombers—but in reality, most suicide bombing has been perpetrated by a Sri Lankan terrorist group known as the Liberation Tigers of Tamil Eelam, better known as the **Tamil Tigers**.[97] A Marxist separatist organization, this group fought the government of Sri Lanka from 1983 until 2009, when they were finally defeated by the Sri Lankan military. Renowned not only for its use of **suicide bombers**, including women and children, this group was also known for issuing cyanide capsules to its fighters so that they could commit suicide if in danger of being captured.[98] This also illustrates that suicide attacks are not exclusively an Islamic phenomenon. Instead, we must acknowledge that many philosophies and creeds are capable of inspiring members and believers to sacrifice their life for a cause in which they believe.

There seem to be a number of reasons for the recent increase in the use of suicide bombers by terrorist groups around the world. First, it works. As a tactic designed to help an organization achieve its goals, suicide bombing has proved remarkably effective. Robert Pape's research indicates that, out of 13 suicide bombing campaigns instituted by various terrorist groups, roughly half resulted in significant political gains for their cause.[99] Hezbollah, for example, was successful in forcing the United States and France out of Lebanon in the early 1980s, largely through its reliance on suicide bombers.

Second, terrorist groups often learn from each other. The Tamil Tigers began using suicide bombings after they sent members to train with the Palestinian Liberation Organization in Lebanon and were impressed by the success of groups such as Hezbollah in using this tactic. Similarly, Al Qaeda has been influenced by the suicide bombings of Hezbollah, Hamas, and other similar organizations.

Third, suicide bombing is easy. All it takes is a willingness to die for a cause on the part of a young man or woman. There really is no technical training required. Often, explosives are placed in a backpack or satchel with a hand-operated detonator. Other times, they wear a special harness or vest that can easily be concealed under clothing and which distributes the explosives around the body. In either case, the terrorist simply needs to go to a public area, such as a park, restaurant, or bus, and detonate the device. For these reasons, suicide bombings have become the weapon of choice for many modern terrorist organizations. Learning that it is an effective way to make progress toward their goals, terrorists have adopted this method of destruction and have employed it around the world. But it is not the only weapon available to them, nor is it potentially the most destructive. The most destructive weapons that terrorist groups could conceivably use are known generically as **weapons of mass destruction** (WMD).

Weapons of Mass Destruction

Many terrorism experts fear terrorist organizations will acquire and use weapons of mass destruction with even more horrific results than the September 11 attacks of 2001. Weapons of mass destruction include nuclear, chemical, and biological agents, the scariest of which are usually considered to be nuclear weapons. In her book *The Ultimate Terrorist,* terrorism expert Jessica Stern describes the effects of a 1 kiloton nuclear blast detonated at the Empire State Building in New York City.[100] A fireball 300 feet in diameter would ignite and destroy the building and the 20,000 people who work in it. A shockwave would spread out and collapse buildings for 600 feet around. The flying debris would act as shrapnel and wound and kill many thousands more. Individuals up to a quarter of a mile away would be killed and injured as their clothes burst into flames or melted from the intense heat. The updraft would suck radioactive material into the air that would then descend over the next several days. Depending upon the wind, people as far away as 9 miles would receive a lethal dose of radiation and die within the next two weeks, and individuals as far as 18 miles away would suffer from radiation sickness. Stern suggests the death count from "fallout alone might kill up to 100,000—in addition to those killed by blast, heat, or initial radiation close to the explosion. The death toll might easily reach twice that."[101]

This is a horrific scenario and one which would make all previous attacks—even September 11—pale in comparison. But is it likely? Terrorist groups can acquire nuclear weapons in one of three ways. First, they can build one, but that is a technically difficult job—one which is out of the reach of most organizations. Second, an organization can steal one; and third, an organization can buy one. All three of these scenarios offer difficulties, especially the first. But we must remember that, since the fall of the Soviet Union and the end of the Cold War, nuclear weapons are less well protected than in earlier eras, and the black market now contains experts, parts, and radioactive materials.[102] But even though evidence suggests that various groups, such as Al Qaeda, have attempted to acquire nuclear devices, as of now it appears that they have been unsuccessful. More likely, perhaps, is a situation in which a terrorist organization detonates what is known as a "**dirty bomb.**" This is a conventional type of explosive, but one that is laced with radioactive elements that would be dispersed by the blast. Radioactive material is much easier to acquire than a nuclear device. Evidence of this type of planning includes the American Jose Padilla, who was arrested in May 2002 for allegedly being an Al Qaeda operative and planning to build and detonate a dirty bomb in the United States.

Chemical and biological weapons, on the other hand, are somewhat easier to obtain and produce, yet they could potentially still have the same devastating effect as a nuclear device. Many nations have already developed them. Additionally, they tend to be easier to convey to a target and to use. For that reason, they are sometimes referred to as the poor man's nuclear weapon. Of the two, biological weapons have the longer pedigree, having been used as early as the Middle Ages when attackers besieging a castle or city would sometimes hurl diseased livestock or people into the city in an effort to induce a plague.[103] While not in use for as long, chemical weapons have also been used. In World War I, for example, the Germans used chlorine and mustard gases to mixed effect.[104] In the 1980s, Saddam Hussein used poison gas against several Kurdish villages, including mustard gas, sarin, tabun, and VX.

Chemical weapons generally fall into one of four categories: **nerve agents**, **blood agents**, **choking agents**, and **blistering agents**.[105] Choking agents, such as phosgene gas and chlorine gas—both of which were used during World War I—kill by damaging the lungs and causing them to fill with mucus. Its victims literally drown in their own secretions. Blister agents, such as mustard gas, on the other hand, kill by burning whatever parts of the body come into contact with them—such as the skin, eyes, and lungs. Blood agents, as the name implies, kill by affecting the blood after being inhaled. Specifically, these chemicals—such as hydrogen cyanide and cyanogen chloride—prevent the body from utilizing the oxygen in the blood. Last are the nerve agents, such as tabun and VX, which kill by inhibiting the functioning of an important enzyme that regulates nerve functioning. These tend to be the most dangerous form of chemical weapons because they are lethal, even in extremely small doses.

Biological weapons such as anthrax, smallpox, plague, and Ebola can also provide terrorists with extremely potent and deadly weapons. It is worth noting that the leader of the September 11 attacks, Mohamed Atta, had earlier explored the possibility of buying a crop-dusting plane, presumably to be able to spray chemical or biological weapons over an urban area. It is also worth pointing out that Aum Shinrikyo, prior to the sarin nerve gas attack on the Tokyo subway, also worked on acquiring and developing various other chemical and biological weapons and even experimented with their release.[106]

Conclusions

Given its long history, terrorism is likely to be a problem for the United States and the world for a considerable time. Islamic fundamentalist terrorism is merely the latest manifestation of this age-old tradition and is unlikely to be the last type we must confront. The difference between today's terrorism and that of the past is that the stakes are so high in the modern era. The weapons of mass destruction that exist in such proliferation in so many troubled parts of the world mean that this ancient tactic of violence may be able to exponentially increase the lethality and destructiveness of its attacks.

Key Terms

Alfred P. Murrah Federal Building

Al Qaeda

apartheid

Army of God

Assassins

Aum Shinrikyo

authorized terror

Baader-Meinhof Gang

blistering agents

blood agents

Chechnya

chemical and biological weapons

choking agents

Committee of Public Safety and the Revolutionary Tribunal

criminal terrorism

Desaparecidos

dirty bomb

dirty war

enforcement terror

fundamentalist
terrorism

guerrilla warfare

hard targets

Hezbollah

insurgency warfare

Islamic *Salafi Jihad*

Jacobins

Japanese Red Army

low-intensity warfare

M19

Mujahideen

Muslim Brotherhood

Narodnaya Volya

nationalist-separatist
terrorism

nerve agents

new religions terrorism

political terrorism

regime or state terrorism

religious extremist terrorism

repressive terror

right-wing terrorism

Shari'a

Sicarii

single-issue terrorism

social revolutionary
terrorism

soft targets

state-supported
terrorism

substate terrorism

suicide bombing

Tamil Tigers

terrorism

Tupac Amaru Revolutionary
Movement

Unabomber

Wahhabism

weapons of mass
destruction

Zealots

Discussion Questions

1. You can obtain detailed information about foreign terrorist organizations from the U.S. State Department (www.state.gov/s/ct/rls/fs/37191.htm). Examine the criteria necessary for an individual to be included on the list. What factors are necessary to get an organization listed as a terrorist organization? Do you believe these criteria are overly broad or too narrow? What are the implications for such organizations when they make the list?

2. The Federal Bureau of Investigation (FBI) is one of the primary agencies responsible for combating terrorism in the United States and for prosecuting cases when they occur. Go to the FBI's website on counterterrorism (www.fbi.gov/terrorinfo/counterrorism/waronterrorhome.htm). What programs do they have in place to prevent terrorism in the United States? In your opinion, which may be more effective than others? Does the agency have programs in place to combat domestic terrorist activity?

3. The Department of Homeland Security (DHS), developed after the September 11 terrorist attacks, is the newest U.S. agency devoted to combating terrorist activity (www.dhs.gov/index.shtm). Go to the DHS website and examine the programs they have implemented to combat terrorist activity. How are these programs different from those implemented by the FBI? What programs does the DHS fund at the state level? Find out what programs in your area are primarily being funded by DHS to combat a terrorist attack in your city/state. Is there any information about these initiatives on your state's website? What other policies has your state implemented to combat local terrorist threats? In your opinion, are there other policies that would be more effective?

10

Genocide

Confronting the problem of state-sanctioned mass killing is often tantamount to facing the fact that one's own nation has engaged in it.

—Eric Markusen and David Kopf[1]

Genocides stand at the center of our contemporary cultural crisis. They challenge our hopes for a peaceful, tolerant co-existence among diverse peoples; they raise the deepest fears that the modern world we inhabit is not a site of continual improvement in the human condition but the very cause of more intense, seemingly unstoppable violence against civilian populations.

—Eric D. Weitz[2]

Of all the acts of **collective political violence** that plague this world, none is quite so terrible or destructive as genocide. This may come as a surprise to those who probably define war as the worst example of organized group violence, but it is **genocide** that tops the list—at least regarding the magnitude of killing. During the 20th century, for example, some estimate that genocide killed almost four times as many people as all the wars, revolutions, and civil wars combined for the same time period.[3] In addition to all of the dead, this collective violence has also been accompanied by floods of refugees trying to flee the violence. In 1995, for example, there were approximately 27 million refugees worldwide, which represented approximately one out of every 280 people on earth.[4] These displaced people did not just include the victims but the killers as well. During the genocide in Rwanda, for example, many Tutsis fled to neighboring countries in order to escape the destruction. However, after losing power, many Hutu perpetrators also fled to the same refugee camps set up by their former victims and continued their violent attacks. In the Congo, this chain of events helped destabilize the region and sparked a series of conflicts that have continued, on and off, to the present day and has killed approximately 5 million people. Similarly, the violence in Kosovo resulted in more than a million Kosovar Albanians being forced from their homes, many never to return.[5]

Genocide, in short, has been the most lethal form of collective violence in recent history. The political scientist Roger Smith summarizes it this way: "The twentieth century is an age of genocide in which 60 million men, women, and children, from many different races, religions, ethnic groups, nationalities, and social classes, and living in different countries, on most of the continents of the earth, have had their lives taken because the state thought it desirable."[6] The first decade of the 21st century appears to be no different, with genocides occurring in places such as the Darfur region of the Sudan. But before we move on, it is important to define exactly what we mean by genocide. As with other forms of violence, defining genocide can be somewhat tricky.

Defining Genocide

The term "genocide" is often misused. In recent years, the word has been applied to such widely disparate and inappropriate subjects as integration, sterilization, bisexuality, dieting, suburbanization, hysterectomies, urban sprawl, and family planning, among other things.[7] Genocide is such a powerful and symbolic word that people have come to rely on it when trying to strongly condemn or call attention to some situation or policy. It has come to symbolize the worst possible type of destructive violence and has become the go-to word when someone or some group wants to claim that some action, event, or policy is absolutely wrong or evil. While metaphors like this are not uncommon (e.g., comparing a perceived evil person to Hitler), this type of rhetorical excess contributes to the definitional confusion surrounding the word.

Another definitional difficulty is that it is sometimes hard to distinguish between genocide and related types of crimes, such as **human rights violations** and other **war crimes**. Genocide, for example, typically happens during the middle of an armed conflict, such as a civil war, and it is sometimes hard to distinguish between massacres that are considered war crimes and others that might better be understood as genocide. A great deal of overlap exists between these crimes as they are defined in international law. Torture and medical experimentation, for example, are specifically listed as war crimes, yet during the Holocaust various kinds of experiments were performed on unwilling victims, the same victims who were sent en masse to be killed in gas chambers. Do we consider these experiments to be war crimes or genocide? Do we perceive genocide as a type of human rights violation, or do we see it as a distinct and separate type of phenomenon? As you can see, it isn't always easy to classify these events. Adding to this kind of definitional confusion is the fact that politicians, social commentators, and even scholars use the term differently and apply the definition selectively, depending on the nature and politics of the situation. Historically, for example, U.S. political leaders have been reluctant to employ the term when our allies were perpetrating it because of concerns about pressures to intervene or because of Cold War politics. A good case in point concerns the Chinese invasion of Tibet on

October 7, 1950. Portraying Tibet as a former part of its territory, China argued that it was simply reclaiming a past province and liberating Tibet from the evils of feudal rule and Western imperialism.[8] Not surprisingly, given the overwhelming strength and size of the Chinese People's Liberation Army, Tibet appealed for help to Nepal, Great Britain, India, and the United States. Even though Chinese forces halted their advance to see what the international reaction would be, every nation—with the sole exception of El Salvador—rejected Tibet's pleas for assistance and refused to raise any objections or challenge China, which then proceeded to quickly conquer Tibet. Since that time, the Chinese have starved, executed, and tortured over a million Tibetans in the course of their occupation.[9]

There was a similar silence and lack of condemnation when the Indonesian military invaded East Timor in 1975. East Timor was on the road to independence when the Indonesian government sent in the army to occupy and take over the former Portuguese colony.[10] It is estimated that, after only four years, over 120,000 East Timorese had been killed, and that between the years 1975 and 1991 the population decreased by around 12% due to the fighting, massacres, and executions.[11] During this time, the United States was in the middle of the Cold War against the Soviet Union. As a result, this violence was not condemned as an act of genocide; instead, the governments of Australia and the United States actually encouraged and gave approval to the Indonesian government because of economic interests and because the Indonesian military was a staunch ally against communism. In fact, several days ahead of the invasion, President Ford and Henry Kissinger had met with and given approval to the president of Indonesia for the invasion.[12] Even though numerous advocates for the East Timorese lobbied the **United Nations** to apply the language of genocide to the violence, they were unsuccessful. The world community carefully avoided defining the ongoing violence as genocide, since to do so would have called attention to the situation and increased pressure to intervene.[13] These are just two examples of world powers ignoring an act of genocide before their very eyes. Unfortunately, they continue today. For example, in about one hundred days in the spring and early summer of 1994, almost one million Rwandans, mostly from the Tutsi minority, were murdered by fellow Rwandans from the Hutu majority in what was clearly a case of genocide. Over time what has become abundantly clear is that the United States, the United Nations, and the larger world community were fully aware of the planning for the genocide and its execution and chose to do nothing, largely because it was easier to plead ignorance than to intervene.[14]

Although the act of genocide is as old as human civilization, the term genocide is relatively new. It was first coined in 1944 by the Polish lawyer Raphael Lemkin, in his book *Axis Rule in Occupied Europe*. Lemkin tried to bring attention to the atrocities being perpetrated by the Nazis.[15] He did not believe that other preexisting terms, such as "mass murder" or "massacre," fully captured what the Nazis were doing, so he coined the word genocide from the Greek *genos,* which means race or tribe and the Latin *cide,* which translates as killing. The term genocide therefore refers to the killing of a race or tribe. Genocide, in short, is about destroying populations, and this is what separates it from many other types of large-scale violence. In addition to developing the word, Lemkin was also instrumental in helping to provide the impetus for the international community to outlaw this crime.

The United Nations Definition of Genocide

The United Nations (UN), on December 9, 1948, approved the **Convention on the Prevention and Punishment of the Crime of Genocide.**[16] The entire convention can be read in the In Focus 10.1 box, but for our purposes the most important part of the document is article II, which defines genocide as

> Any of the following acts committed with intent to destroy, in whole or in part, a national, ethnical, racial or religious group, such as: (a) Killing members of the group; (b) Causing serious bodily or mental harm to members of the group; (c) Deliberately inflicting on the group conditions of life calculated to bring about its physical destruction in whole or in part; (d) Imposing measures intended to prevent births within the group; (e) Forcibly transferring children of the group to another group.[17]

This definition reveals a number of important points that help us understand the nature of genocide. First, it makes it very clear that genocide is about destroying populations. Crimes such as massacres, as abhorrent and terrible as they are, are not considered genocide unless they are part of a larger program intended to destroy a group. An important aspect of this first issue is that genocide is also considered to have taken place even if the goal was not to kill every single member of that group. Destroying part of a specific population can still be genocide. The problem with applying the phrase "in whole or in part" is that it leaves undefined what "in part" means. How do we legally define "in part"? How many members of a group need to be targeted before something is defined as genocide? Is there a specific percentage of a population that must be killed for the word genocide to be applied? If so, what is that percentage—10%, 20%, 30%? The answer is left undefined by the United Nations' definition of genocide.

IN FOCUS 10.1

Genocide Convention

Convention on the Prevention and Punishment of the Crime of Genocide

Approved and proposed for signature and ratification or accession by General Assembly resolution 260 A (III) of 9 December 1948 Entry into force: 12 January 1951, in accordance with article XIII

The Contracting Parties,
Having considered the declaration made by the General Assembly of the United Nations in its resolution 96 (I) dated 11 December 1946 that genocide is a crime

(Continued)

(Continued)

under international law, contrary to the spirit and aims of the United Nations and condemned by the civilized world,

Recognizing that at all periods of history genocide has inflicted great losses on humanity, and

Being convinced that, in order to liberate mankind from such an odious scourge, international co-operation is required,

Hereby agree as hereinafter provided:

Article I

The Contracting Parties confirm that genocide, whether committed in time of peace or in time of war, is a crime under international law which they undertake to prevent and to punish.

Article II

In the present Convention, genocide means any of the following acts committed with intent to destroy, in whole or in part, a national, ethnical, racial or religious group, as such:

(a) Killing members of the group;
(b) Causing serious bodily or mental harm to members of the group;
(c) Deliberately inflicting on the group conditions of life calculated to bring about its physical destruction in whole or in part;
(d) Imposing measures intended to prevent births within the group;
(e) Forcibly transferring children of the group to another group.

Article III

The following acts shall be punishable:
(a) Genocide;
(b) Conspiracy to commit genocide;
(c) Direct and public incitement to commit genocide;
(d) Attempt to commit genocide;
(e) Complicity in genocide.

Article IV

Persons committing genocide or any of the other acts enumerated in article III shall be punished, whether they are constitutionally responsible rulers, public officials or private individuals.

Article V

The Contracting Parties undertake to enact, in accordance with their respective Constitutions, the necessary legislation to give effect to the provisions of the present Convention, and, in particular, to provide effective penalties for persons guilty of genocide or any of the other acts enumerated in article III.

Article VI

Persons charged with genocide or any of the other acts enumerated in article III shall be tried by a competent tribunal of the State in the territory of which the act was committed, or by such international penal tribunal as may have jurisdiction with respect to those Contracting Parties which shall have accepted its jurisdiction.

Article VII

Genocide and the other acts enumerated in article III shall not be considered as political crimes for the purpose of extradition.

The Contracting Parties pledge themselves in such cases to grant extradition in accordance with their laws and treaties in force.

Article VIII

Any Contracting Party may call upon the competent organs of the United Nations to take such action under the Charter of the United Nations as they consider appropriate for the prevention and suppression of acts of genocide or any of the other acts enumerated in article III.

Article IX

Disputes between the Contracting Parties relating to the interpretation, application or fulfillment of the present Convention, including those relating to the responsibility of a State for genocide or for any of the other acts enumerated in article III, shall be submitted to the International Court of Justice at the request of any of the parties to the dispute.

Article X

The present Convention, of which the Chinese, English, French, Russian and Spanish texts are equally authentic, shall bear the date of 9 December 1948.

Article XI

The present Convention shall be open until 31 December 1949 for signature on behalf of any Member of the United Nations and of any non-member State to which an invitation to sign has been addressed by the General Assembly.

The present Convention shall be ratified, and the instruments of ratification shall be deposited with the Secretary-General of the United Nations.

After 1 January 1950, the present Convention may be acceded to on behalf of any Member of the United Nations and of any non-member State which has received an invitation as aforesaid.

Instruments of accession shall be deposited with the Secretary-General of the United Nations.

Article XII

Any Contracting Party may at any time, by notification addressed to the Secretary-General of the United Nations, extend the application of the present Convention to all or any of the territories for the conduct of whose foreign relations that Contracting Party is responsible.

Article XIII

On the day when the first twenty instruments of ratification or accession have been deposited, the Secretary-General shall draw up a procès-verbal and transmit a copy thereof to each Member of the United Nations and to each of the non-member States contemplated in article XI.

The present Convention shall come into force on the ninetieth day following the date of deposit of the twentieth instrument of ratification or accession.

Any ratification or accession effected subsequent to the latter date shall become effective on the ninetieth day following the deposit of the instrument of ratification or accession.

Article XIV

The present Convention shall remain in effect for a period of ten years as from the date of its coming into force.

It shall thereafter remain in force for successive periods of five years for such Contracting Parties as have not denounced it at least six months before the expiration of the current period.

Denunciation shall be effected by a written notification addressed to the Secretary-General of the United Nations.

Article XV

If, as a result of denunciations, the number of Parties to the present Convention should become less than sixteen, the Convention shall cease to be in force as from the date on which the last of these denunciations shall become effective.

Article XVI

A request for the revision of the present Convention may be made at any time by any Contracting Party by means of a notification in writing addressed to the Secretary-General.

(Continued)

The General Assembly shall decide upon the steps, if any, to be taken in respect of such request.

Article XVII

The Secretary-General of the United Nations shall notify all Members of the United Nations and the non-member States contemplated in article XI of the following:

(a) Signatures, ratifications and accessions received in accordance with article XI;

(b) Notifications received in accordance with article XII;

(c) The date upon which the present Convention comes into force in accordance with article XIII;

(d) Denunciations received in accordance with article XIV;

(e) The abrogation of the Convention in accordance with article XV;

(f) Notifications received in accordance with article XVI.

Article XVIII

The original of the present Convention shall be deposited in the archives of the United Nations.

A certified copy of the Convention shall be transmitted to each Member of the United Nations and to each of the non-member States contemplated in article XI.

Article XIX

The present Convention shall be registered by the Secretary-General of the United Nations on the date of its coming into force.

SOURCE: United Nations website (www.ohchr.org/english/law/genocide.htm).

The UN definition also makes clear that genocide includes a number of different behaviors, not just mass murder. While it is commonly thought that only murdering members of a group counts as genocide, the definition includes a variety of actions and policies, some of which are not immediately lethal. Imposing measures intended to prevent births within a group, for example, commits no overt act of violence against individuals yet is ultimately deadly for the survival of the group. Forced programs of sterilization would certainly fall into this category.[18] Similarly, the practice of sending American Indian children to boarding schools where they were forbidden to speak their language, practice their religion, or otherwise engage in aspects of their traditional culture can also be defined as genocide.[19] This type of policy left the individual alive but destroyed the ties that connected groups together as a people.[20] Borne out of a policy of **forced assimilation**, this policy of taking children away from their families and educating them to be "good citizens" was not intended to physically harm anybody. Rather, the intent was to destroy their native cultures. As one commentator wrote, "The kind of education they are in need of is one that will habituate them to the customs and advantages of a civilized life, . . . and at the same time cause them to look with feelings of repugnance on their native state."[21] This particular type of genocide has sometimes been defined as **cultural genocide** or as ethnocide.

Another major element of the UN definition concerns the issue of intent. As you can see, similar to murder, intent must be established before genocide can be prosecuted as a crime, and intent is a difficult concept to prove in a court of law. This is exacerbated by the fact that the UN Genocide Convention definition does not specify any criteria for identifying or proving intent beyond the point that the intention must be to destroy, in whole or in part, one of the groups listed.[22] Moreover, genocide requires a special kind of intent. Essentially, the Genocide Convention specified a level of intent that is referred to as *specific intent, special intent (dolus specialis)* or even *genocidal intent.*[23] For an atrocity to qualify as genocide, therefore, the destructive acts must have been specifically meant to wipe out a group. This is an important point. Potentially, this means that perpetrators of genocide can argue that they never intended to commit genocide but were only trying to acquire land or defend their people.[24] The destruction of the Aché Indians of Paraguay illustrates this well. In this case, even though genocidal crimes had been documented, the government claimed that no genocide had been committed because they had never intended to destroy the Aché, even though evidence indicated that government-sponsored death squads had killed an estimated 85% of the 25,000-member tribe.[25]

It is always difficult to infer intent, even in individual acts of murder. At the group or state level, intentions to commit genocide can be inferred from documents, speeches, and policies. The preparation necessary for genocide to take place and the scale of the killing also allow intent to be uncovered indirectly. In 1998, the genocide conviction of Jean-Paul Akayesu, a Rwandan mayor, by the International Criminal Tribunal for Rwanda illustrates that proving intent is not necessarily any more difficult than proving intent for other types of crime. Nevertheless, intent remains a potentially problematic aspect of the UN definition of genocide.

It is also important to point out that, according to the convention document, genocide can only occur against national, ethnic, racial, or religious groups. This means that destroying other types of collectives or populations does not count as genocide. Political parties, for example, are a type of group excluded from the official UN definition of genocide because it was suggested that they did not have the same permanence and stability as the listed groups.[26] This is a problem since crimes may appear to be genocidal but may not be defined as such because of the nature of the group involved. The mass killings in Indonesia in 1965 that we highlighted earlier illustrate this problem well. In that year, a number of military generals were captured and killed, ostensibly by members of the Indonesian Communist Party (PKI).[27] The PKI was the third largest Communist Party in the world, behind only China and the Soviet Union, and in the Cold War atmosphere of the times the Indonesian military saw it as a threat to Western interests in the region. The murder of the generals provided a pretext for what happened next. The military began rounding up known and suspected members of the PKI as well as those believed to be sympathetic to the PKI movement and murdered them in a series of massacres that killed approximately half a million people.[28] Because the Indonesian military was seen as a strong ally of the United States in its Cold War fight against communism, U.S. diplomats in Indonesia compiled a list of 5,000 suspected communist agents that was turned over to the Indonesian military so those listed could be killed.[29] This violence has all the hallmarks of genocide and is virtually indistinguishable from similar violence that has been defined as genocide, but because the targeted population was based on political affiliation, it was not defined as such. We can compare the Indonesian violence with the 1988 Iraqi government's attacks against Iraq's Kurdish population.[30] The Kurds are a distinct ethnic minority who live primarily in the mountainous northern region of Iraq and had been struggling for greater political power within the largely Arabic country as well as a separate Kurdish nation. Because the Iraqi government saw them as assisting and conspiring with the Iranians during the Iran–Iraq war, it authorized a series of attacks and massacres that involved the use of chemical weapons and the displacement and incarceration of thousands. If we compare this example with the violence in Indonesia, they seem very similar. The PKI and the Kurds were both seen as potential enemies and traitors within their respective countries. Both were targeted for destruction by their respective governments. Yet the violence against the Kurds was considered genocide because they were ethnically homogeneous, but the violence against the Indonesian communists was not because their group was politically defined.

Because of these problems with the United Nations' definition of genocide, many scholars have proposed other definitions of the crime, which can be found in Table 10.1. These definitions provide a range of alternative perspectives on the nature of genocide. It is important to point out, however, that none of these carries the force of international law, as does the UN Genocide Convention. As such, these alternative definitions may help us better understand genocide, but their practical usefulness is somewhat limited. Perhaps a more useful method for understanding the dynamics and nature of genocide is to examine some of the better known examples of 20th century genocide.

Twentieth Century Genocide

The first recognized genocide of the 20th century was that of the **Hereros** in what was then known as German South-West Africa, present-day Namibia. A German colony, German South-West Africa was home to a Bantu tribal group known as the Hereros, whose pastoral life revolved around their villages and cattle.[31] In 1904, the Hereros rose in revolt against German rule because they were increasingly losing their lands, sinking into insurmountable debt, and suffering from the racist policies of the German administration. In January of that year, the Hereros attacked German farms, villages, and military outposts and forts. The Germans responded with heavy-handed efficiency and brought in more troops to wage a campaign of utter destruction. Their policy was to take no prisoners; instead, they killed all the men, women, and children they were able to find. First relying on machine guns, artillery, and rifles, the Germans next forced the surviving Hereros out into the desert and denied them access to the watering holes. In the two years it took to stamp out the Hereros as a people, only 20,000 of the original 80,000 survived. This case illustrates the fact that weaponry is only one means of genocidal destruction; starvation also is commonly used, particularly in arid regions of the world.

The next major genocide of the 20th century occurred in Turkey, when the Armenian population was targeted for destruction by the Turkish government.[32] The Young Turks had taken power in 1913 and believed Turkey needed religious and ethnic purification. Minority groups, such as the Armenians, simply did not fit into their vision of a homogenous and modern Turkish state. These sentiments were brought to a

Table 10.1   Definitions of Genocide

Author	Definition of Genocide
Vahakn Dadrian	The successful attempt by a dominant group, vested with formal authority and/or with preponderant access to the overall resources of power, to reduce by coercion or lethal violence the number of a minority group whose ultimate extermination is held desirable and useful and whose respective vulnerability is a major factor contributing to the decision of genocide.[1]
Robert Melson	A public policy mainly carried out by the state whose intent is the destruction in whole or in part of a social collectivity or category, usually a communal group, a class, or a political faction.[2]
Frank Chalk and Kurt Jonassohn	A form of one-sided killing in which a state or authority intends to destroy a group, as that group and membership in it are defined by the perpetrator.[3]
Helen Fein	Sustained purposeful action by a perpetrator to physically destroy a collective directly or indirectly, through interdiction of the biological and social reproduction of group members, sustained regardless of the surrender or lack of threat offered by the victim.[4]
Israel Charny	The mass killing of substantial numbers of human beings, when not in the course of military action against the military forces of an avowed enemy, under conditions of the essential defenselessness and helplessness of the victims.[5]
Irving Louis Horowitz	A structural and systematic destruction of innocent people by a state bureaucratic apparatus.[6]

NOTES:

1. Vahakn Dadrian, "A Typology of Genocide," *International Review of Modern Sociology* 5 (1975): 204.
2. Robert Melson, *Revolution and Genocide: On the Origins of the Armenian Genocide and the Holocaust* (Chicago: University of Chicago Press, 1992), 26.
3. Frank Chalk and Kurt Jonassohn, *The History and Sociology of Genocide: Analyses and Case Studies* (New Haven, CT: Yale University Press, 1990).
4. Helen Fein, *Genocide: A Sociological Perspective* (London: Sage, 1993), 24.
5. Israel W. Charny, "Toward a Generic Definition of Genocide," in *Genocide: Conceptual and Historical Dimensions*, George J. Andreopoulos (Philadelphia: University of Pennsylvania Press, 1994), 64–94 at 75.
6. Irving Louis Horowitz, *Taking Lives: Genocide and State Power*, 4th ed. (New Brunswick: Transaction, 1997), 74.

head when Turkey entered World War I in 1914 on the side of Germany and Austria and soon suffered a number of military setbacks and defeats. The 3,000-year-old Armenian population of Turkey had a long history of persecution because of its distinct religious and social identity; these factors were exacerbated by the people's demands for social and political equality before World War I. As Turkey's wartime situation deteriorated, the government, hateful and suspicious of the Armenian population in its midst, planned and then implemented a genocide.[33] It began by rounding up Armenian males serving in the military and transferring them to penal battalions where most were soon killed. Next to be targeted were the leaders of the Armenian community, such as doctors, lawyers, politicians, and educators, who were ordered to report to government offices where they were arrested, jailed, and then murdered. Finally, the women, children, and elderly who remained were marched out into the remote interior areas of Turkey where they died from exposure and starvation, and were preyed upon by bandits, and various police and military units.[34] It is estimated that over a million Armenians died during this genocide.[35] Amazingly enough, the present-day Turkish government continues to deny the **Armenian genocide**. Not only that, but in December 2005, the Turkish government put its country's best-known novelist, Orhan Pamuk, on trial for denigrating Turkishness because in an interview with a Swedish newspaper he asserted that his country had killed a million Armenians.

Perhaps the best-known and most deadly of 20th-century genocides involved the Nazi attempt to eliminate the Jews of occupied Europe. Even though there have been more than 40 examples of genocide since 1945,[36] it is the **Holocaust** that remains the preeminent example of genocide. The Nazis and their supporters had long scapegoated the Jews for many of Germany's problems, and in this the Nazis were building upon a long history of anti-Semitism present in Europe. After taking power in 1933, the Nazis began a long process of marginalizing the Jews legally, economically, politically, and socially in order to make them more vulnerable to further persecution. These legalistic maneuvers were punctuated by periodic outbursts of violence against Germany's Jewish population, such as the infamous **Kristallnacht, or Night of Broken Glass**, on November 9, 1938. After a young Jewish man shot and killed a Nazi diplomatic aide in Paris, the Nazis orchestrated a series of attacks over the next few days that resulted in an estimated 7,500 Jewish businesses being looted, over 1,000 synagogues destroyed, just under 100 murders, and some 30,000 Jews being sent to concentration camps.[37] Mass killings, however, did not occur until after the Nazi invasion of the Soviet Union in June 1941. Special extermination squads known as *Einsatzgruppen* followed behind the German army and were tasked with rounding up all Soviet political figures and Jews and then executing them en masse. The mass shootings perpetrated by the Einsatzgruppen were not, however, efficient enough for the Nazis who had also not counted on the brutalizing effect of the killing on their own troops, who were increasingly suffering from nervous breakdowns, developing ulcers, becoming drunks, and even sometimes committing suicide.[38] Accordingly, to increase the efficiency of the killing process and to spare their men, the Nazi government created a number of death camps such as **Auschwitz**, Treblinka, and Sobibor[39] which employed gas chambers to kill millions of Jews and others. The killing only ended with the defeat and collapse of Nazi Germany at the end of World War II. In the space of a few short years, the **Nazis** and their helpers managed to murder many millions of Jews, Sinti and Roma (gypsies), Slavs, homosexuals, communists, and other assorted enemies of the Reich by shooting, gassing, torture, execution, and various other destructive means. In fact, the political scientist R. J. Rummel calculates that the Nazis killed approximately 21 million people through genocide, killing hostages, reprisals, forced labor, euthanasia, starvation, exposure, experiments, and various other means in the concentration and death camps.[40] Of these, over 16 million were victims of genocide alone.[41] Keep in mind that these numbers don't include the over 28 million European war dead.[42] It seems that the greatest talent of the Nazis was in filling mass graves throughout Europe. Sadly, while the Holocaust was the impetus for the creation of international law banning genocide, the years since have not been free of this crime. Instead, "never again" has turned into "again and again."

Another well-known example of genocide occurred during the 1970s when the U.S. war in Vietnam spilled over its borders and helped destabilize the government of Cambodia. In the early 1970s, the United States had begun bombing Viet Cong bases in neighboring Cambodia and had even sent in ground troops, all of which resulted in many deaths as entire villages were destroyed. This helped the **Khmer Rouge** or Red Khmers, a Cambodian communist group, win popular support and brought them many new recruits.[43] In 1975, the Khmer Rouge was able to overthrow the government and established Democratic Kampuchea, which was anything but democratic. The Khmer Rouge had decided it wanted to create a utopian communist Khmer nation, free from what they saw as corrupting and foreign influences. The party began by emptying the cities and then killing everyone associated with the previous government, military officers, students, teachers, journalists, doctors, lawyers, priests, business leaders, ethnic Chams, ethnic Chinese, and anyone else who didn't fit in or who somehow challenged the creation of the new state. Over a four-year period, the Khmer Rouge systematically starved, beat, worked to death, tortured, and murdered between one and two million of its own citizens. Since the total population of Cambodia was only around 8 million, this genocide ranks as one of the most lethal of the 20th century in terms of the proportion of the population killed.[44]

The next example of genocide takes us to Rwanda, a tiny nation in Africa. A former Belgian colony and one of the most densely populated nations of Africa, Rwanda is home to two major ethnic groups: the Tutsi and the Hutu. A minority, the Tutsi, have historically been seen as a privileged group compared with the more numerous Hutu. In the early 1990s, Rwanda was in the midst of a civil war between the Hutu-dominated government of President Juvenal Habyarimana and the Tutsi-led Rwandan Patriotic Front (RPF), which had invaded from neighboring Uganda in 1990.[45] Because of military reverses and setbacks as well as international pressure, Habyarimana soon began negotiations with the RPF. These negotiations were resented by hardliners within his party, so much so that, upon his return from one of the discussions, his plane was shot out of the sky—quite possibly by members of his own government, although absolute responsibility has never been established.[46] Hutu extremists had been preparing for just such a moment and, within hours of the assassination, military forces, police, and militias began killing moderate Hutus as well as every Tutsi they found.[47] Long resented and scapegoated, the Tutsi were murdered in their homes, at roadblocks, and in the churches where they took refuge. Over the course of the next 90 days, almost a million Rwandans were bludgeoned, shot, but mostly hacked to death with machetes.

As horrific as these examples are, they are not the only genocides of the previous century. Table 10.2 provides a somewhat more comprehensive overview of

❖ Photo 10.1   Human remains in a church in
                 Nyamata, Rwanda

the different examples of 20th century genocide. But even this is not complete. Because of definitional difficulties, various genocides may never be counted because they fall on the margins of genocide. As we've discussed, genocide is a slippery concept and it isn't always clear whether or not a specific example of mass killing constitutes genocide. Additionally, we need to be aware that sometimes genocides occur in out of the way places to groups of people who do not have access to media outlets. Much like the experience of American Indians in North America during the European colonization process, indigenous peoples in Central and South America have faced destruction as their homelands have been opened up for economic exploitation and their traditional ways of life targeted for eradication because they are perceived as primitive and dangerous.[48] Yet very few people know about their plight because they live in obscure, remote places that do not receive much media attention. Since most of these victims are part of nontechnological cultures, their suffering and demise usually remain unseen and unheard by the larger world community.

In short, it is clear that genocide has exacted a terrible cost in human life and suffering during the 20th century and continued to do so in the first decade of the 21st, as illustrated by the **genocide in the Darfur region** of the Sudan.

Although we have highlighted the most recent century, genocide is actually a very old phenomenon even though the word wasn't coined until quite recently. The type of collective violence described by this word has been in existence since earliest times, and its perpetrators include the ancient Babylonians, Assyrians, Israelites, Greeks, Romans, and Mongols, among many others.[49] During his eight years fighting the Gauls of modern-day France, Julius Caesar was estimated by Plutarch to have destroyed 800 towns and killed or enslaved over 3 million people.[50] The Mongol hordes of Genghis Khan and his successors were renowned for putting to the sword all the inhabitants of towns and cities that had defied them. In one case, it was reported that it took almost two weeks to kill the 1.3 million inhabitants of the city of Merv.[51] At Genghis Khan's death, it was said, "The Conqueror of the world had for his funeral rites the massacre of an entire people."[52]

One of the best known historical examples of genocide involves the destruction of the **Cathars** of Southern France during the early 13th century. During the Middle Ages, a number of Christian sects and variations sprang up throughout Europe, one of the most popular and prevalent being the Cathars. Out of step with the rest of Medieval society in regard to their understanding of God and Satan, the Cathars believed that the world was evil and that people should live a frugal and ascetic life in order to avoid being corrupted by the world. Because they believed in reincarnation,

Table 10.2   Selected 20th Century Examples of Genocide and Genocidal-Like Atrocities

Location	Years	Perpetrators	Victim Group	Death Count
South West Africa	1904–1905	German military	Hereros	60,000
Turkey	1915–1923	Turkish military and police	Armenians	1 million
Soviet Union	1932–1933	Soviet police	Ukrainians	3–7 million
Nazi-occupied Europe	1941–1945	Nazis and collaborators	Jews, Gypsies, Slavs, homosexuals	21 million
Indonesia	1965–1966	Indonesian military and police	Indonesian Communists	500,000
Guatemala	1968–1993	Guatemalan military and police	Mayans	200,000
Bangladesh	1971	Pakistani military	Bengalis	1–3 million
Burundi	1972	Tutsi military, police, and paramilitaries	Hutu	100,000–150,000
East Timor	1975–1999	Indonesian military	East Timorese	200,000
Cambodia	1975–1979	Khmer Rouge	Ethnic Chinese Ethnic Vietnamese Ethnic Chams Buddhist Monks Educated Classes	1–2 million
Iraq	1988	Iraqi military	Kurds	500,000–100,000
Bosnia	1992–1995	Bosnian Serbs	Bosnian Muslims	250,000
Rwanda	1994	Hutu military, police, and paramilitaries	Tutsis	800,000

they treated men and women equally, since a woman in one life might have been a man in a previous one and vice versa. They abhorred war and the death penalty and in fact were so opposed to all killing that they practiced a strict form of vegetarianism. In 1204 Pope Innocent III began preaching for a crusade against these heretics in order to suppress their threat to the dominance of the church. Named after the city of Albi, a Cathar stronghold, the **Albigensian Crusade** was led by nobles from the north of France who saw an opportunity for land and enrichment in addition to serving their faith and the church. Characterized by numerous massacres, this crusade saw the virtual depopulation of Southern France as entire communities were annihilated. No attempt was made to weed out heretics from nonheretics: All were killed indiscriminately. One abbot, who was the Papal Legate, reportedly told the crusaders to "kill them all. God will recognize his own."[53]

The ancient world is full of similar kinds of genocidal practices and policies. However, in case you are tempted to think that genocide is a problem limited only to far-away places, we should remember that the United States has had more than its fair share of experience with genocide. Perhaps the most obvious example concerns various policies and practices against various American Indian tribes. The influence of European settlement in North America on the indigenous populations was catastrophic and in some cases clearly genocidal. Disease was the largest killer, but massacres, forced relocations, famine, and starvation also played significant roles in the destruction of the native peoples. After gold was discovered in 1848 in California, for example, thousands of Anglos flooded into the region searching for wealth and increasingly came into conflict with the local natives. When the American Indians fought back, the settlers reacted with genocidal ferocity. They formed private militias that hunted down and killed any natives they came across and organized widespread massacres. The state government, rather than trying to stop them, voted to cover many of their expenses and even paid a bounty for every scalp.[54] We can also look at the boarding school system forced upon many native tribes that was intended to "civilize" American Indians but that essentially served to create a cultural form of genocide to those who survived the experience.[55] The purpose was clear as articulated by one advocate who said, "*Give the Indian a white man's chance. Educate him in the rudiments of our language. Teach him to work. Send him to his home, and tell him he must practice what he has been taught or starve. It will in a generation or more regenerate the race. It will exterminate the Indian but develop a man.*"[56]

In summary, it seems that there is hardly a corner of the world or a period in history that has not been touched by this form of collective violence. This includes the United States.

At this point, you may be asking, is genocide more rampant today than in the past? According to the sociologist Helen Fein, genocide has unfortunately tripled and has become more the norm than the exception.[57] Similarly, Eric Weitz suggests that, beginning with the Armenian genocide of the early 20th century, "genocides have become more extensive, more systematic, and more thorough."[58] This argument asserts that genocide has been enabled by the processes of modernity, which have served to separate the use of violence and power from ethics and morality.[59] The modern era is one in which our thinking is dominated by cold-blooded, rational, scientific, and bureaucratic calculations that serve to distance us from human considerations, and this has increased the likelihood of governments pursuing genocidal policies. Others disagree. William Rubinstein contends that genocide has actually decreased in the modern era and was much more common in earlier eras.[60] He asserts, "Genocide in the contemporary world has not been commonplace—we do not live in an age of 'genocide'—but it has occurred rather unpredictably and haphazardly."[61] Rubinstein sees the contemporary period as one characterized by democratization, with a greater emphasis on human rights. Rubinstein's argument is aligned with the work of Norbert Elias, who sees in

❖ Photo 10.2   Sioux children arrive at the
                Carlisle School, October 5, 1879

modern Western history a civilizing process that has made the modern world
much less violent.[62] This argument has
recently been supported by the work of the
psychologist Steven Pinker, who also
argues that the world today is safer and
less violent than in the past.[63] How can
there be such differing views? In part,
much of this debate relates to the different
meanings and understandings that people
give to genocide. It all comes down to how
you define genocide and which examples
you include in your estimates.[64] Not in
doubt, however, are the various reasons
why genocides are perpetrated.

Why Do Genocides Happen?

Genocide goes so far beyond normal and acceptable behavior that it appears incom-
prehensible to most people. Because of this, we often think of it as being fundamentally irrational. How else can we explain such apparently senseless and extreme
violence? Underneath, however, genocides are rational attempts to achieve a specific
goal. In fact, all the examples we have provided so far reveal a perverted logic motivating the killing. That logic, of course, is usually flawed since it is typically influenced by various nationalistic and racial ideologies, historic perceptions of injustice
and persecution, a desire for revenge, and a host of other emotional issues. In other
words, genocides are not completely objective and rational because old hatreds and
prejudices often guide the thinking processes of leaders intent on gaining or achieving
some ambition.

We must also recognize that genocide does not simply happen in a historical
vacuum even though it is often reported that way. The mass media typically portray
genocide as a catastrophe that suddenly explodes into violence because of ancient
ethnic or racial hatreds or tribalism. News reports, for example, described the Bosnian
genocide as a spontaneous and unplanned eruption that was the result of longstand-
ing hatreds and antagonisms between different populations that suddenly flared into
a new round of violence.[65] Essentially, the media suggested that Serbs and Muslims
had hated and fought each other for hundreds of years, and this was merely the latest incarnation of that hostility. This portrayal was also relied upon by a number of
Western politicians who used it to suggest that there was nothing that could be done
to stop the killing. One prominent U.S. politician, for example, said, "They have been
killing each other with a certain amount of glee in that part of the world for some
time now," while another asserted that the violence was "terrifying, and it's centuries
old. That really is a problem from hell."[66] This portrayal is completely false, however.
In reality, genocide requires a tremendous amount of planning and organization that
occurs weeks, months, and even years before the actual killing takes place, and Bosnia

was no exception to this. This planning is usually initiated by a government (or factions within a government) that has decided upon genocide as a way of achieving some goal. Of course, this doesn't mean that old hatreds don't play a role. They do. Governments resurrect and use preexisting prejudices to help stir up resentment and fear of a minority group. But the causes of genocide lie in the present, not in the past. So what are the goals that genocide is intended to accomplish? Why is genocide planned and perpetrated?

Generally speaking, a number of motivations have been identified as providing the rationale for genocide. Helen Fein, a leading scholar of genocide, suggests four types of genocide in terms of motivation: developmental, despotic, ideological, and retributive. **Developmental genocides** are those in which the targeted groups are seen as an impediment to the colonization and/or exploitation of a given geographic area. This happens most often against indigenous peoples who may be perceived as being in the way of progress. In Central and South America, many native peoples have been subjected to genocidal policies as various nations have attempted to remove them from land found to be rich in oil and valuable minerals. In Colombia, for example, the Fourth International Russell Tribunal of 1979 found that the government was perpetrating genocide against the indigenous peoples of the Amazon headwaters. The violence included navy riverboats machine-gunning the banks of the rivers and massacres perpetrated by government forces and private citizens alike.[67] This tribunal also found that similar kinds of genocidal violence were occurring in other South American countries as these nations worked to open up their rainforests for economic exploitation.

Despotic genocides, on the other hand, involve situations in which a government uses genocide as a weapon against rivals for political power. This kind of genocide may often be found in revolutionary situations where a new group has achieved power and works to eliminate any opposition to its authoritarian rule. Much of the violence in the Stalinist Soviet Union clearly fits into this category as Stalin and his minions attempted to destroy all members of various political, economic, and national groups because they were perceived to be a threat to Stalin's consolidation of power. This kind of violence was also mirrored in other communist states such as China and Cambodia, which also relied upon systematic violence and murder to eliminate real and imagined enemy groups.[68] This should not be surprising since many communist movements came to power after long and brutalizing struggles that taught their leaders the usefulness of violence and created a sense of persecution, which often develops after years of being hunted. The mindset engendered by this kind of experience was therefore paranoid and encouraged revolutionary leaders to feel unsafe until any and all resistance to their rule was suppressed and eliminated. We find the same kind of mindset is often present among the members of terrorist groups, who tend to perceive the world in the same kinds of ways because of the similarity of their experiences. They also rely on violence and are used to being hunted.[69]

Ideological genocide, in contrast, refers to the attempted destruction of a population because of a belief system. At some level, all genocides are ideological, so this type is worth discussing in some detail. While the specifics may vary, we can assert that genocide and related kinds of atrocities are often motivated, at least in part, by some form of ideology. Even for genocides that are neither exclusively nor predominantly ideological, belief systems supporting persecution are still used because they provide the necessary intellectual framework that motivates and justifies the persecution of the targeted group. These beliefs may include a variety of nationalistic, historical, scientific, and religious ideas that validate the violence. Very often that ideology is utopian in nature.

The word "**utopia**" comes from Thomas More, the English lawyer who, in his book *Utopia*, described a society that was rationally organized and in which all property was communally held. In this Utopia, there were no lawyers and only a few laws because, in the absence of conflict, they were not needed. Because of the striking nature of this imagery, the term has come to refer to any vision of a perfect and unattainable society. Utopianism has been a significant ideological factor in many of the worst examples of genocide and other human rights violations. The Nazis, the Khmer Rouge, the Soviets, and a number of others all perpetrated their excesses in the name of building a better society. The Nazis saw themselves as revolutionaries who would create a new Germany—a Germany of wealth, prosperity, and order based on notions of racial hygiene and purity. As we discussed earlier, in pursuit of this goal, the Nazis attempted to eliminate from the nation everyone who was seen as an obstacle to achieving this new social order. Part of this ideology involved scientific and medical beliefs about the supposed racial superiority of the Aryan people. Jewish people were seen as a threat to the genetic purity of the Aryan race, and the Nazi answer to this ideological imperative was the Holocaust. Similarly, the Khmer Rouge was utopian in outlook because it wanted to return Cambodia or Kampuchea to a historic and mythic era of greatness when the ethnic Khmer empire ruled the region. The Khmer Rouge attempted to achieve this through the destruction of all corrupting and oppositional influences within Cambodian society, including all ethnic Chinese, Khams, Monks, the educated, and so on. In short, many perpetrators of genocide are utopian idealists intent upon creating their vision of a perfect society. Their beliefs rest on the notion of the perfectibility of society, and in many ways the perpetrators are idealists who are attempting to implement radical policies of social, political, and economic change. In their own minds, and in the minds of their followers, they are creating a better world of prosperity and of ideals. Unfortunately, creating this beautiful world has almost always necessitated the destruction of entire populations.

The last category of Helen Fein's typology concerns **retributive genocides**, which were the most common type in the second half of the 20th century.[70] These are genocides perpetrated by one group against another engaged in a struggle for political and social power. In contrast to despotic genocide, where power has already been taken and the enemies are often imaginary, this particular class of genocide concerns an ongoing struggle. The **Rwandan genocide** is illustrative of this type since the **Hutu** government instigated the genocide against the **Tutsi** population partially because it was trying to maintain power during a civil war. Similarly, the genocide of the Herero at the beginning of the 20th century was triggered by the Herero uprising against German rule. In both examples, the government violence was defined by the perpetrators as retaliation and self-defense. They were, as they perceived it, striking back at those who threatened them.

Helen Fein's typology of genocide indicates that genocides are perpetrated for rational, if reprehensible, reasons. Ultimately, genocide occurs because governmental officials decide that it is the preferred solution to a real or perceived problem and a way they can achieve a variety of political, economic, and/or social goals. While it may appear to be completely unjustified and irrational to outsiders and the larger world community, to those officials advocating the destructive policies of genocide, it makes perfect sense. Of course, not all governments use genocide as a means to achieve the kinds of goals discussed above. In fact, most don't. So what factors can explain why some states resort to this crime and others do not? What are the identifying characteristics or qualities that are common to genocidal states?

Precursors to Genocide

While every genocide is unique and occurs within a specific historical, cultural, and political context, there are common threads that run through most examples, and these commonalities can help us understand the dynamics of this violence. One of the most important factors concerns the relationship between genocide and types of political systems. The political scientist R. J. Rummel has suggested that genocide and similar types of mass violence are crimes perpetrated almost exclusively by totalitarian states. He specifically asserts that "as the arbitrary power of a regime increases massively, that is, as we move from democratic through authoritarian to totalitarian regimes, the amount of killing jumps by huge multiples."[71] While this is somewhat simplistic, Rummel correctly points out that the totalitarian regimes of the last century have been the most lethal in recent history. Stalin's Soviet Union, Mao's China, Pol Pot's Cambodia, and Hitler's Germany, to name a few prominent examples, were some of the worst 20th century human rights offenders—so much so, in fact, that Rummel labels the leaders of these lethal governments as **megamurderers**.[72]

We shouldn't be surprised that dictatorships and totalitarian governments are more prone to genocide. These kinds of governments are often based on fear and coercion, and leadership is typically concentrated in just a few hands. Generally, the more centralized power is, the fewer limits there are on how that power is used, which provides greater freedom in pursuing genocidal policies. Democratic states, on the other hand, tend to have more checks and balances that constrain the ability of leaders to implement and carry out policies, especially those that are considered extreme. Rummel's argument, however, ignores the fact that democratic states sometimes aid, abet, and encourage the genocidal actions of others. Michael Mann's recent work on **ethnic cleansing** and democracy suggests that the relationship is a complex and dynamic one in which ostensibly democratic governments can perpetrate genocide. For example, democracies can define rights and protections as only applying to certain groups within a society, and those excluded may be vulnerable to victimization. Second, democratic states may start out as democratic but may devolve into ethnic cleansing and in the process become less democratic and more authoritarian.[73] The point of Mann's argument is that democracies may have a dark or pathological side that does not preclude them from perpetrating genocide.

Another factor that links genocidal violence is war. While not every nation at war commits genocide and not every genocide occurs during a war, war does make it easier for a government to carry out this violence. War tends to heighten nationalistic and patriotic feelings, and all too often those feelings come at the expense of minority groups. When a nation is fighting a war, it is not such a huge step to expand the definition of the enemy to include vulnerable and scapegoated minority populations, especially if there is a long history of hostility toward that group. Nationalism and patriotism, let us remember, are often xenophobic and call into sharp relief differences between various population groups. While war brings certain segments of a population closer and increases their feelings of togetherness, that increased solidarity often comes at the cost of other groups that are increasingly marginalized and excluded from what Helen Fein calls the "**universe of obligation**."[74] These feelings of segregation are heightened during wartime when a government and population may feel under threat and therefore more inclined to scapegoat a group that can be blamed for the problems and misfortunes of the larger community.

War also produces tremendous amounts of psychological and/or social dislocation. During times of upheaval, normal conventions and constraints on deviant or criminal behavior are weakened or removed and often replaced with an attitude of "anything goes." The formal and informal rules of social control are not seen as being relevant to the extraordinary experiences of individuals and communities during wartime, and in these circumstances prohibitions against victimizing others are severely diminished. We also need to recognize that war is inherently brutalizing and dehumanizing. Human life becomes much less valued when people are exposed to a great deal of death and suffering. Hardened to violence and killing, populations may be more willing to support—or at least tolerate—pressures toward genocide. For all of these reasons, it becomes much easier for citizens to become perpetrators and accomplices to genocide during times of war.

Perpetrators of Genocide

We have seen that states perpetrate genocide for a variety of rational reasons. In many ways, individual perpetrators also exhibit the same flawed rationality of purpose. So who are these perpetrators of genocide? Contrary to popular mythology, most of them are not monsters. Individuals who participate in genocide are generally not psychopaths, even though the crimes they commit are horrendous. Sadists and psychopaths often contribute to the genocidal violence, but they are far outnumbered by ordinary citizens who come to participate and help in the killing of their fellow citizens. The evidence indicates that most of the individuals who participate in genocide are normal people who believe in the necessity of their actions. Just as states sometimes rationalize their genocidal violence as necessary self-protection, individual perpetrators of genocide also have usually accepted a worldview that portrays their participation as an act of self-defense and protection. For example, many Serbs in Bosnia believed the nationalistic propaganda from government-controlled radio and television stations that suggested the Bosnian Muslims were planning to attack and enslave the Bosnian Serbs. Similarly, the Nazis depicted the Jews as intent on destroying the German race and achieving world dominance. In Rwanda, the Hutu were told that the government had uncovered a plot by the Tutsi to massacre all the Hutu, which led one killer to assert, "I defended the members of my tribe against the Tutsi."[75] These arguments provided a rationale for the killers to accept their actions as necessary and justified. This perception of self-defense, we should remember, is heightened when your family, friends, neighbors, community leaders, and others also reinforce this same view about the necessity and rightness of the violence. It is the rare individual who is able to resist defining the victim group as the enemy in the face of such overwhelming social pressure.

The rationality of perpetrators can also be revealed from other evidence. First, genocide requires the participation of literally thousands of individuals from all walks of life, and it is impossible to characterize all of these people as being sociopaths. Second, most of the instigators of genocide are government officials and highly placed bureaucrats; again, it is unlikely that they all suffer from some sort of mental illness. Third, post-genocide trials indicate that the individuals being held accountable are remarkably normal people. Hannah Arendt's famous characterization of "the **banality of evil**" regarding Adolf Eichmann comes to mind here. Adolf Eichmann was the Nazi official who was responsible for much of the logistical organization and planning of the Holocaust genocide. During his trial in 1960 in Israel, he was revealed to be a fairly bland and unremarkable bureaucrat whose decisions nevertheless resulted in the death of millions.[76] Recognizing that the perpetrators of genocide tend to be ordinary folks leads to a disturbing understanding that anyone has the potential to participate in this horrible crime.

How, then, do individuals come to participate? Why do they go along and help in the killing? There is no one answer to this because individuals come to participate for a number of different reasons. Michael Mann suggests that there are nine primary motivations for participation in genocide and classifies the killers according to those reasons:

• **Ideological perpetrators** are true believers who find their justification for participation in a belief system that demands the destruction of a group. This kind of killer is most typically drawn from among the social elites.

• **Bigoted perpetrators** are those who have prejudices against the populations being targeted for destruction. Often these hatreds and stereotypes are long standing and ancient, being rooted in history.

• **Violent perpetrators** are those individuals who enjoy perpetrating violence. While clearly in the minority, some who participate in genocide can clearly be classified as sadistic or psychopathic. Some of these may be drawn to the violence because of innate tendencies, while others may find that their sensitivities are brutalized in the killing. People may also be attracted to the pleasure of having life and death power over others.

• **Fearful perpetrators** lend their help to the killing because they genuinely fear that they will be hurt or killed if they don't participate. In both Rwanda and Bosnia, for example, some Hutu and Serbs were killed when they opposed the killing or refused to participate.[77] One hesitant Serb was told, "If you are sorry for them, stand up, line up with them, and we will kill you too."[78] In the same vein, a Rwandan perpetrator said, "You were told you had the duty to do this or you'd be imprisoned or killed. We were just pawns in this. We were just tools."[79]

• **Careerist perpetrators** are those who become perpetrators because they can advance their careers and get promotions and choice assignments through participation. For these individuals, assisting in the persecution of the victims is simply a way to get ahead professionally.

• **Materialist perpetrators** are those who try to profit from the genocide. During the violence in Bosnia, many participants helped themselves to the homes, cars, and appliances of their victims. In the Rwandan genocide, many Hutu saw participation as a means to acquire livestock and land.[80] In a country in which open land was in short supply, this was a powerful incentive.

- **Disciplined perpetrators** are those who participate because of the need to conform within certain institutional settings where obeying orders is the norm and disobedience is punished. This is perhaps most applicable to police officers, military personnel, and militia members—all organizations in which obedience is very important.

- **Comradely perpetrators** take part in the killing because they don't want to let down their comrades and friends. This kind of killer participates because his bonds to the other members of the group or unit are stronger than any prohibitions he may have against participation. As with the disciplined perpetrators, this motivation is most commonly found among military and police units.

- **Bureaucratic perpetrators** are those who participate in genocide because they work in organizations that are called upon to take part in the apparatus of killing. Their participation may be fairly small, mundane, and appear fairly harmless—such as scheduling trains or compiling lists—but it is nonetheless ultimately lethal.[81] In Germany, this kind of person has sometimes been described as a *schreibtishtater* or desk murderer.

As you can see, individuals may participate in genocide for a variety of reasons. People rarely act for one single reason but instead are influenced by many factors that all play a role in inducing a specific action. Mann's typology can therefore best be understood as illustrating some of the more common themes that help shape individual participation. We must also remember that genocide doesn't happen in a vacuum. The motivations of the perpetrators are supported and encouraged by the social context of their society. Perpetrators are influenced by radio, television, and newspaper stories that reinforce the perception of the target group as the enemy and the danger they pose. Friends, neighbors, and political leaders all reiterate the same kinds of messages. In many ways, the choices made by individuals are largely guided and shaped by their understanding of the situation, and these choices are profoundly affected by the environmental influences of the genocidal society. The historian Mari Sandoz put it this way:

> Properly conditioned, any people will produce a good percent of men (including women) who look upon the extermination of those who differ from them (and have something they want) as the proper destruction of a predatory animal. It is not only the Nazis that do these things, or the wool hat boys of the South. We can all be led down this path if the approach is insidious enough.[82]

Victims of Genocide

Victim groups are often selected for extermination because they fall into a stigmatized social category. It is the ultimate way to dehumanize someone because individual characteristics do not matter; individuals are victimized solely because they fit into a category that has been slated for destruction. They are killed because of how they are defined, not for what they have done. Importantly, self-definition is irrelevant to victimization. Many German Jews saw themselves first and foremost as Germans, not as Jews. Similarly, Bosnian Muslims typically identified themselves as Yugoslavs, Europeans, or Sarajevans, not necessarily as Muslim. It is not how individuals define themselves that dictates victimization but rather how they are defined by others.

Typically, the groups that are chosen are relatively powerless because their members have been socially and politically marginalized. One particularly vulnerable type of minority tends to be "**middleman minority groups**" who serve as intermediaries between producers and consumers in a society and whose role therefore alienates them from the mainstream society. Often acting as traders, small businessmen, or lenders, these groups are usually composed of immigrant populations who fill needed and vacant economic positions, which also tends to breed resentment and hostility from the rest of the population. During the Middle Ages, for example, Christians were prohibited from acting as moneylenders by the church because it was considered un-Christian to charge interest on loans. Jews therefore often filled this role, yet were resented by those who relied on their services and who found themselves having to pay back the loans with interest.

As we noted earlier, victim groups typically have long histories of persecution and stigma. For example, the Jews of Europe had been victims of anti-Semitic ideas and stereotypes for hundreds of years, and the Nazis were able to play upon these images in their persecution of the Jews. Similarly, the Bosnian Muslims were also subject to a great deal of historic resentment dating back to a famous battle in the 1300s. These historic prejudices are not the sole cause of genocide but instead provide a reservoir of hatred that can be manipulated and harnessed and more readily allow a group to be stereotyped, scapegoated, and victimized.

When People Do Nothing: The Bystanders to Genocide

In addition to victims and perpetrators, genocide also depends on bystanders. Albert Einstein once wrote, "The World is too dangerous to live in—not because of the people who do evil, but because of the people who stand by and let them." Genocide cannot take place unless the vast majority of a population allows it to take place. One Rwandan stated, "Everybody in the village was an accomplice, by silence or by looting, and it is impossible to divide the responsibility."[83] All genocides depend upon the active participation of the few and the passive acceptance of the many. It is not uncommon for many to claim that they did not know what was going on after genocide is brought to light, even when the evidence suggests that the killing was so widespread and systematic that it would have been impossible for them not to have known. So why do most people stand by without intervening? There are probably many reasons why people choose not to do anything, several of which seem to be common to most people.

First, we have a built-in predisposition to defer to authority figures, and the government is one of the most powerful of authority figures. In his groundbreaking work on obedience to authority, which you read about in Chapter 2, Stanley Milgram powerfully illustrated this tendency. Importantly Milgram found that

> Of a sample of average Americans, nearly two-thirds were willing to administer what they believed to be life-threatening shocks to an innocent victim, well after he lapsed into a perhaps unconscious silence, at the command of a single experimenter with no apparent means of enforcing his orders.[84]

When a regime tells a population that a certain group represents a threat and that segregating and/or killing its members is necessary, many people are predisposed to believe it since it is their government that is communicating this message. Over time, the authority of the state can win people over who might not have initially believed the propaganda. This is why one Rwandan Hutu could say, "I did not believe the Tutsis were coming to kill us, but when the government radio continued to broadcast that they were coming to take our land, were coming to kill the Hutus—when this was repeated over and over—I began to feel some kind of fear . . . We believed what the government told us."[85]

The second factor related to inaction is that most people believe that there is nothing that can be done, that they are too powerless to prevent and/or stop the violence. How does one stop or hinder something so massive and destructive? These feelings of helplessness are often combined with large amounts of fear. Resisting or questioning the genocidal policies of a government intent on mass murder can carry serious risks of being ostracized and imprisoned at best and physical harm and death at worst. This is made worse when the risks of aiding those targeted for elimination extends to your entire family. Not many people would knowingly risk the safety of their entire family in order to assist strangers who are being persecuted. Because of these factors, the majority of people in any population choose to remain bystanders. Despite this reluctance to intervene, we know that ordinary citizens can and often do make a difference. For example, rescuers in occupied Europe saved many thousands of Jews who would otherwise have died in the gas chambers.[86] In fact, bystanders can even bring a halt to genocidal violence. In the 1930s, the Nazis began a euthanasia program against the mentally and physically handicapped. After information about this policy became known, ordinary Germans protested and forced the regime to stop the euthanasia plan.[87]

Unfortunately, many within a society may agree with the policies of destruction that result in genocide. These individuals become bystanders because they believe that the targeted group is evil and poses a danger. These beliefs tend to be reinforced by friends, families, and neighbors and to echo the official messages of the government.

IN FOCUS 10.2

The Genocide in Darfur

As we write, the western Sudanese region of Darfur is acknowledged to be in a state of human rights crisis. Marginalized and poor, in recent years inhabitants of the region have also faced a loss of crop land and resources brought about by climate change. This has resulted in an intensification of a conflict over resources that often revolves around racial and lifestyle distinctions. While a great deal of intermingling has occurred, the issue of race is an important subtext to the current violence. In 2003, two Darfur-based rebel groups, the Sudan People's Liberation Army/Movement (SPLA/M) and the Justice and Equality Movement (JEM) began attacking police stations and military bases in a desperate bid to demand greater economic and political power. Membership came largely from non-Arab tribes, such as the Fur, Masalit,

(Continued)

(Continued)

and Zaghawa. The government reacted with genocide. They organized militia groups known collectively as the Janjaweed and began a campaign of dispossession, looting, rape, and wholesale murder. Overwhelmingly, the victims are the non-Arab groups from which the SPLA/M and the JEM drew their membership. The typical scenario involves an early morning attack by Janjaweed militia and government forces that move in and sweep through a village from one end to the other or else attack from two sides, pinning the villagers in the middle. The men are usually killed outright while the women are subject to gang rape, after which many are also murdered. The livestock are usually taken away while the homes and other buildings, together with the crops and food stores, are destroyed. The survivors of these attacks have been forced to hide out and have often been subjected to follow-up attacks as the militia and government troops scour the countryside looking for survivors. If the victims manage to survive, they often end up in overcrowded humanitarian camps with little water and food and poor sanitary conditions. In recent years, the genocide in Darfur has evolved somewhat. At this point, most of the villages of the targeted tribes have been destroyed and the violence has become smaller scale and more localized, often involving harassing and attacking the Internally Displaced Persons Camps that are located in the region. According to estimates from the United Nations, almost three million Darfuris have been displaced and close to five million rely on international humanitarian aid. One estimate suggests that almost half a million people have died from violence, malnutrition, and disease.[88] The international community remains deeply divided over what to do in Darfur. In October 2004, the United Nations established a commission to investigate the allegations in the region. The commission established that the government of the Sudan

and the Janjaweed were responsible for serious violations of international human rights and humanitarian law amounting to crimes under international law. In particular, the commission found that government forces and militias conducted indiscriminate attacks, including killing of civilians, torture, enforced disappearances, destruction of villages, rape, and other forms of sexual violence, pillaging, and forced displacement throughout Darfur. These acts were conducted on a widespread and systematic basis and therefore may amount to crimes against humanity. The extensive destruction and displacement have resulted in a loss of livelihood and means of survival for countless women, men, and children. In addition to the large-scale attacks, many people have been arrested and detained and many have been held *incommunicado* for prolonged periods and tortured.

Is the Sudanese government engaging in genocide? The UN Commission at this time deemed that the crucial element of genocidal intent appeared to be missing, at least as far as the central government authorities were concerned. Generally speaking, the policy of attacking, killing, and forcibly displacing members of some tribes does not evince a specific intent to annihilate, in whole or in part, a group distinguished on racial, ethnic, national, or religious grounds. The commission concluded that those who planned and organized attacks on villages pursued the intent to drive the victims from their homes primarily for purposes of counter-insurgency warfare. On the other hand, in March of 2009, the International Criminal Court indicted the president of Sudan, Omar al Bashir on crimes against humanity and war crimes charges. These were later amended in 2010 to include genocide. This marks the first time that a sitting head of state has been so indicted, although at the time of this writing, he remains in power and at large.

SOURCES: Joyce Apsel, ed., *Darfur: Genocide Before Our Eyes* (New York: Institute for the Study of Genocide, 2005); and United Nations Executive Report on Darfur, www.ohchr.org/english/docs/darfurreport.doc.

We also need to recognize that the international community often acts as a bystander to genocide as well. Recent examples of genocides have been perpetrated with the full knowledge of the world community. Genocides don't usually happen in secret. At the time of writing (as In Focus 10.2 in the box shows) an ongoing genocide is being conducted in the Darfur region of the Sudan while international bodies such as the United Nations and individual governments, including the United States, have been unable and/or unwilling to bring an end to the killing. As we noted earlier, governments may plead ignorance, but they usually know full well what is happening and for various reasons are either unwilling or unable to prevent the killing or intervene effectively. This was certainly the case during the recent Rwandan and Bosnian genocides, when journalists, politicians, and human rights workers reported on the violence, and media outlets brought the genocide into our homes nightly. Because we now live in a global community through the use of satellite technology, we are all bystanders to the tragedies that unfold around the world. Hopefully, this will make us much more aware of these crimes, which in turn will allow us to bring accountability to the perpetrators of genocide through international law, which is the topic to which we now turn.

International Law and Genocide

The problem of justice at an international level has emerged as one of the most important and pressing problems of the new century, especially around the issue of genocide. In this section, we illustrate the importance of international law in combating genocide and holding those who perpetrate it accountable with a few recent cases.

On April 16, 2002, something remarkable and unprecedented happened. The Dutch government collapsed. Or, more specifically, the entire Dutch Cabinet resigned. Why? Because of a report that had been released the previous week that blamed the Dutch government for its signal failure to prevent the 1995 massacre at Srebrenica, Bosnia, a town located in a narrow valley in the eastern part of Bosnia. Surrounded by hills, the town is about 2 miles long and approximately half a mile wide and has long been a center for mining; its name means "Silver City." When the fighting broke out in 1992 after Bosnia declared independence, the town had a population of around 9,000. Slobodan Milošević, then President of Yugoslavia, helped organize, fund, arm, and train Bosnian Serbs who were violently opposed to an independent Bosnian state. Almost immediately after the Bosnian declaration of independence, Bosnian Serbs declared the territory as the Republika Srpska and began "cleansing"—which is a euphemism for exterminating—this territory of Muslims.[89]

Paramilitary groups such as **Arkan's Tigers** rampaged through Muslim-dominated towns, such as Bijeljina, Brčko, and Zvornik, killing, torturing, and raping (see Chapter 7 for accounts of genocide and rape). These militias and paramilitary groups committed unspeakable atrocities upon their former neighbors and friends. Arkan's Tigers attacked and took Srebrenica on April 18, 1992, but a couple of days later Muslim residents of the town who had hidden out in the local forests retook the town from the Serb forces. Led by Naser Orić, a 25-year-old police officer, these forces established a perimeter and launched a number of attacks on surrounding Serb communities. This enclave swelled to over 40,000 Muslims by February 1993, as refugees from ethnically cleansed communities made their way to this isolated and besieged island. The UN began airlifting in supplies and foodstuffs to the inhabitants of the beleaguered city. After the French General Philippe Morillon visited **Srebrenica** as a UN representative, he declared, "You are now under the protection of the United Nations," and also stated, "I will never abandon you." He then arranged a ceasefire with Serbian President Milošević that lasted a short while before the Bosnian Serb forces again began shelling. Shortly thereafter, the UN Security Council passed a resolution declaring Bosnia a "safe area," along with five other encircled cities. In Srebrenica, first Canadian and then Dutch troops were sent to defend this enclave. One immediate job they undertook was to placate the Serbs by disarming the Muslim defenders of the community. This safe area held out until July 1995 when the Serb forces under Ratko Mladić attacked the enclave and took 30 Dutch peacekeepers hostage.[90]

The Dutch called in air strikes, but the UN's top military commander, French Lieutenant General Bernard Janvier, and the UN special representative Yasushi Akashi limited the planes to two bombs total. The Dutch retreated to their base followed by many of the Muslims from the "safe area." Many Muslim men tried to undertake a 40-mile march through the forests to Bosnian Muslim territory, but most were killed as they tried to break through the lines and make their way to safety. When the Serb forces arrived at the Dutch base in July, they began a rampage of rape against the Muslim women and led the young men away, most never to be seen alive again. During these actions, the Dutch peacekeepers, outnumbered and demoralized, did nothing.

The best estimates from the Yugoslavia tribunal suggest that between 7,000 to 8,000 men were murdered. Many were taken to ditches and mass graves where they were machine gunned to death, while others were packed into warehouses and other buildings, where they were slaughtered by grenades and automatic weapons fire. Many of these mass graves have been and continue to be excavated by teams working for the War Crimes Tribunal.[91]

In the fall of 1996, the Dutch government—in response to a public outcry—commissioned the **Netherlands Institute of War Documentation** to investigate the Srebrenica massacre. Their final report, which took six years to publish, placed the blame for the massacre squarely on the shoulders of the Dutch Government and senior military leaders. After the report was published, government officials decided to take responsibility and resigned their positions en masse. While this was primarily a symbolic gesture, it remains an amazing act and illustrates a sense of accountability often lacking among political leaders.

This accountability is also evident in the case of the man who orchestrated the genocide in Bosnia, Slobodan Milošević. In April of 2001, Milošević surrendered to Serb police after losing an election the previous fall to Vojislav Koštunica, the leader of the Democratic Opposition of Serbia (DOS). Koštunica quickly found himself under tremendous international pressure to extradite Milošević to the International Criminal Tribunal located in The Hague. Koštunica attempted to appease the international community by placing the former dictator on trial for financial irregularities, misusing customs duties, abusing his powers, and causing damage to the Serbian economy. However, the pressure continued to mount until Milošević finally was surrendered to the UN War Crimes Tribunal and transported to the Hague where he stood for trial in response to three indictments: one for crimes against humanity and violations of the laws or customs of war for Kosovo; one for crimes against humanity,

❖ Photo 10.3   Milošević makes his initial appearance at the War Crimes Tribunal

grave breaches of the Geneva Convention, and violations of the laws or customs of war for the region known as the Krajina; and the most important for genocide, crimes against humanity, grave breaches of the Geneva conventions, and violations of the laws or customs of war for the campaign of "ethnic cleansing" in Bosnia-Herzegovina.[92] The trial continued until his untimely death on March 11, 2006—in all likelihood from a heart attack. The trial was tremendously important because it involved a former head of state being put on trial in an international forum for crimes committed while he was the acting and legitimate president of a sovereign nation. More recently, the Serb general in charge of the forces that committed the massacre, Ratko Mladić, was arrested by police on May 26, 2011, after many years on the run. He is currently on trial at The Hague for genocide, crimes against humanity, and war crimes.

These cases are important because they show the growing power of international human rights law. There is no statute of limitations on genocide or war crimes, so indicted individuals may be arrested years after the offenses took place. For example, throughout the 1990s trials have been held in countries such as Italy and France for crimes committed during the Nazi years, more than fifty years ago. NATO troops have arrested suspected war criminals in Bosnia, such as the Bosnian Serb generals Radislav Krstić and Stanislav Galić, in accordance with the Dayton Peace Accord, and remanded them into the custody of the **International Criminal Tribunal at The Hague**.[93] Argentinean military and police officers have also been indicted for their role in the torture and murder of thousands of people during that country's so-called "Dirty War" during the 1970s.[94] And in Laredo, Texas, in 1996, Elizaphan Ntakirutimana, a Rwandan living in the United States, was arrested for participating in the Rwandan genocide. As you can see, government officials and leaders can no longer consider themselves immune from prosecution for their actions while in power, even if their violence was sanctioned by domestic laws and even if the conflict was a purely domestic one.

Conclusions

In sum, international law—especially in the area of human rights—has gained a new potency and preeminence in recent years. These developments are part of an evolutionary process that continues to redefine the nature of international relations and justice and that hopefully will help prevent the perpetration of genocide in the future.

Key Terms

Albigensian Crusade

Arkan's Tigers

Armenian genocide

Auschwitz

banality of evil

bigoted perpetrators

bureaucratic perpetrators

careerist perpetrators

Cathars

collective political violence

comradely perpetrators

Convention on the
    Prevention and
    Punishment of the
    Crime of Genocide

cultural genocide

despotic genocides

developmental genocides

disciplined perpetrators

Einsatzgruppen

ethnic cleansing

fearful perpetrators

forced assimilation

genocide

genocide in the
    Darfur region

Hereros

Holocaust

human rights violation

Hutu

ideological genocide

ideological perpetrators

International Criminal
    Tribunal at The Hague

Khmer Rouge

Kristallnacht or Night of
    Broken Glass

materialist perpetrators

megamurderers

middleman minority
    groups

Nazis

Netherlands Institute of
    War Documentation

retributive genocides

Rwandan genocide

Srebrenica

Tutsi

United Nations

universe of obligation

utopia

violent perpetrators

war crimes

Discussion Questions

1. In this chapter, you have seen that acts of mass killing need to satisfy several criteria to be classified as cases of genocide. Unless each of these criteria is met, cases of mass killing are very difficult to prosecute as cases of genocide. The organization Prevent Genocide has a link on its website that provides a detailed discussion of the laws against genocide (www.preventgenocide.org/law). Examine the laws specified by the International War Crimes Tribunal and discuss how at least one act of mass killing in the world (e.g., in Rwanda; in the former Yugoslavia) does or does not meet the legal standard of genocide.

2. We have provided several cases of genocide that have occurred in the 20th century. You can also find out more detailed information about these cases and others at the Amnesty International website (www.amnesty.org). You can also find information on genocides from other organizations, including the United Nations and Human Rights Watch. Conduct case studies of at least two cases of genocide that were alleged to have occurred after 1960. What are the factors that were present in these cases that were the precursors to the mass killings? How long did the killing go on before the

international community introduced mechanisms to stop them? What policies could the international community have in place that would better be able to prevent such atrocities in the future?

3. In February 2007, the International Court of Justice of the United Nations acquitted Serbia of committing genocide in Bosnia and Herzegovina during the Balkan war of the 1990s but found it guilty of failing to prevent genocide in the massacre of more than 7,000 Bosnian Muslims in the town of Srebrenica. Go to the United Nations website to find out information about the case (www.un.org). You can search the site for genocide in general or for genocide in Bosnia in particular. What factors were instrumental in the court's decision? What factors were necessary for a guilty verdict according to international law?

Toward Violence Prevention

As in ecological theory, a web of life connects us to each other across all living things, across and within species. This web of life connects each person to another across groups, structures, and systems. The web of violence is the antithesis to the web of life.

—Peter Iadicola and Anson Shupe[1]

We must put some good into the lives of those people who are prone to violence, especially the young, and prevent them from becoming tomorrow's offenders. Good people should speak up in defense of the many victims who are part of an unending genocide and should force the makers of society to finally address the real issue at the roots of crime. It is long overdue!

—George Palermo[2]

The more I learn about other people's lives, the more I realize that I have yet to hear the history of any family in which there has not been at least one family member who has been overtaken by fatal or life-threatening violence, as the perpetrator or the victim—whether the violence takes the form of suicide or homicide, death in combat, death from a drunken or reckless driver, or any other of the many non-natural forms of death.

—James Gilligan[3]

Crime is a social problem that is interwoven with almost every aspect of American life; controlling it involves changing the way schools are run and classes are taught, the way cities are planned and built, the way businesses are managed and workers are hired. Crime is a kind of human behavior; controlling it means changing the hearts and minds of men. Controlling crime is the business of every American institution. Controlling crime is the business of every American.

—President's Commission[4]

There is no "silver bullet" or "cure" for violence. As we have seen, the human experience—both individually and collectively—is inextricably linked with violence. But that doesn't mean there is nothing that can be done to prevent violence or at least reduce it. One thing that should be clear by now is that while we all have the potential for violence, not all of us act on these impulses. In fact, many individuals living under conditions that are ripe for violence (e.g., residing in crime infested and impoverished neighborhoods) never act aggressively in their lives. Furthermore, two individuals can react quite differently to the same situation—one violently and one not. An insult to one person can call forth a violent response, while the same provocation or an even worse one to another individual can result in nothing more than a verbal comeback. At the community level, this book has also shown that levels of crime vary tremendously across states and regions in this country and across nations around the world. What this tells us is that even though the *potential* for violence exists everywhere, *actual* levels of violence can be affected by a number of different issues—many of which have been covered in earlier chapters. The important question that we focus on in this last chapter is "where do we go from here?" This isn't an easy question to answer since there are as many different solutions to preventing violence as there are policy makers passing laws. We are therefore not going to review and assess all of the specific policies intended to ameliorate all types of violence. There are simply too many to even contemplate including in this discussion. In addition, most antiviolence strategies need to be developed specifically for individual types of violence, and we have already covered many of these more specific policy initiatives in individual chapters.

The goal of this chapter is to discuss in a more general and philosophically, the ways in which we as individuals and as communities can rethink our responses to the enduring problem of violence. Because we have examined specific types of criminal justice-related responses to violence within this text, in this chapter we have chosen to examine violence primarily from a public health perspective. From this perspective, the **Centers for Disease Control and Prevention** list homicides and other assaultive violence as a leading cause of death for all young Americans and *the* leading cause of death for African American young people.[5] For far too long we have endured the tremendous costs that violence and premature death from violence have inflicted on our lives and assumed that there was nothing that could be done. The tragic reality is that we routinely accept a level of harm and cost that would be considered unacceptable if it came from some other source. Before presenting prevention strategies from a **public**

health perspective, it is important to first highlight the price U.S. society pays for our high rates of violence.

Costs of Violence

We shouldn't fool ourselves into thinking that the costs of violent crime in our society are minimal or that they are only limited to those individuals and families directly involved. The reality is that we all pay the costs of violence in many ways, even if we are not directly involved as perpetrators or victims. In purely economic terms, one estimate suggests that in 2010, murder, rape, assault, and robbery cost over $42 billion in medical expenses, law enforcement, courts, and correctional facility expenses, and lost earnings.[6] This translates into $137 dollars for every single American. Keep in mind, that this doesn't include intangibles, such as pain, suffering, and a loss of life quality. A recent analysis of eight U.S. cities (Boston, Chicago, Dallas, Houston, Jacksonville, Milwaukee, Philadelphia, Seattle) estimated the intangible costs of violent offenses and arrived at a total of $13.9 billion every year for only these locations.[7] The enormity of this estimate is heightened when we realize that this is only for the eight cities in the study and does not include all of the indirect costs for the rest of the country. Nationwide, it is estimated that the intangible costs of violent crime are around the order of $156 billion per year.

Table 11.1 breaks down both direct and indirect costs for eight cities regarding violent crime. After examining the estimates in this table, it quickly becomes evident that violent crime is extremely expensive in terms of both direct and indirect costs.

Table 11.1 Direct and Indirect Costs in Millions of Violent Crime For 8 Selected Cities, 2010

	Direct Victim Costs	Criminal Justice System Direct Costs	Direct Criminal Costs	Total Direct Costs	Indirect Costs	Total Direct and Indirect Costs
Boston	72	102	24	198	734	932
Chicago	426	547	132	1105	4206	5311
Dallas	145	175	43	363	1444	1807
Houston	268	393	91	752	2655	3407
Jacksonville	78	100	24	202	802	1004
Milwaukee	92	115	27	234	900	1134
Philadelphia	299	351	86	736	2970	3706
Seattle	21	56	12	89	216	305
Totals	1401	1839	439	3679	13927	17606

SOURCE: Adapted from R. J. Shapiro and K. A. Haslett, *The Economic Benefits of Reducing Crime: A Case Study of 8 American Cities* (Washington, DC: Center for American Progress, June 2012).

One of the more costly crimes is generally considered to be rape, which some estimates suggest costs $127 billion a year.[8] For example, estimates suggest that a rape costs around $110,000, which breaks down as follows:

- Short-term medical care: $500
- Mental health services: $2,400
- Lost productivity: $2,200
- Pain and suffering: $104,900

As you can imagine, a mere $104,900 doesn't really touch the pain and suffering a rape victim experiences, so this estimate is very conservative. What these dry and impersonal numbers conceal is the very real and often long-term impact of criminal victimization on those who suffer at the hands of violent offenders. Much higher rates of depression and anxiety disorders are closely linked with women who experience sexual assault,[9] and victims of rape are from 50% to 90% likely to develop **post-traumatic stress disorder (PTSD)**. According to the *Diagnostic and Statistical Manual* of the American Psychiatric Association (DSM-IV), PTSD is defined as

> The development of characteristic symptoms following exposure to extreme traumatic stress or involving direct personal experience of an event that involves actual or threatened death or serious injury, or other threat to one's physical integrity; or witnessing an event that involves death, injury, or threat to the physical integrity of another person; or learning about unexpected or violent death, serious harm, or threat of death or injury experienced by a family member or other close associate.[10]

This means that individuals who experience an extreme and distressing event can develop a set of symptoms that include recurrent dreams and nightmares, flashbacks, avoidance behaviors, psychological numbing, outbursts of anger, difficulty concentrating, a heightened startle response, and various other problems that can dramatically affect their ability to function and maintain relationships and jobs.[11] It should be noted that research shows crime victims do not tend to recover from PTSD without treatment, and the effects can last many years after victimization.[12] Victims of violent crime in general, not just sexual assault, often suffer from this type of psychological distress. In fact, up to 20% of *all* mental health spending is used to treat victims of violent crime.[13] We shouldn't be surprised at this. Crisis theory tells us that after a violent victimization, a person is often in a state of shock and confusion that is coupled with a sense of loss. Roberts and Green point out that all of us live our lives based on certain assumptions, and violent victimization often shatters these assumptions about being in control of our lives, feeling a sense of safety and security, and notions of fairness and justice.[14] When these are lost, it may precipitate a crisis in our emotional state of well-being.

If we look at the physical injuries of violent crime, we find that while the majority of victims of violent crime suffer relatively minor physical harm, a significant number do indeed suffer significant bodily harm, as illustrated in Table 11.2. The other important thing to notice in this table is that offenders we know and sometimes love, including family members, are more likely to cause injuries than strangers and just as likely to cause serious injuries.[15]

Table 11.2	Violent Victimizations Involving Injury by Victim–Offender Relationship, 2005–2010	
	Offenders Were Strangers	**Offenders Were Known to Victims**
Serious Injury*	4%	4%
Minor Injury**	16%	25%

* Includes gunshot wounds, knife wounds, internal injuries, unconsciousness, broken bones, and other injuries that required hospitalization for more than 2 days.
** Includes bruises, cuts, and other injuries that required hospitalization for less than 2 days.
SOURCE: Harrell, *Violent Victimization Committed by Strangers, 1993–2010,* Bureau of Justice Statistics, 2012.

We must also recognize that one of the costs we all experience is the loss of our sense of freedom and safety. Do you sometimes limit where you go or restrict your activities because of safety concerns? Do you think you would feel different in in a place like Japan or Sweden, which have much lower violent crime rates than ours? Studies have shown that 72% of Americans fear becoming a victim of violent crime when traveling, 61% fear being attacked when out alone at night in their communities, and 60% acknowledge fear even when they are at home.[16] Furthermore, 60% of people surveyed limit where they go, while approximately a third of respondents are careful about when and where they go shopping. Around one in five respondents will only work in certain locations because they do not want to take jobs in places they think are dangerous. On top of this, over one in four people have installed home security systems, and one in five has purchased a weapon for self-defense.[17] In other words, in the land of the free, we often don't feel free to travel and work wherever we want. This apprehension about violence also impacts our worldview and often results in a more cynical and mistrustful view of others. In turn, this makes us less willing to interact and extend ourselves for the benefit of our fellow citizens and community members. Mistrust does not encourage taking risks on behalf of others or of giving them the benefit of doubt. Because of violence, in other words, we are less social and communal and we do not see the world as a safe and just place.

In short, the costs of violence are many, and the final bill is extremely expensive—indeed, almost incalculable. The costs are individual and collective, direct and indirect, monetary, physical, and emotional. So what is to be done? Before addressing this question, two main points need to be emphasized.

First, any attempt to address the problem of violence must confront it on a number of different levels. Hopefully, you have learned in this book that there is no single root cause of violence, and as a result, simplistic and one-dimensional answers cannot even begin to address the problem. We can see this principle in action when we examine the literature on **bullying** and school aggression. Bullying has emerged as an important area of concern, especially in light of the spate of school shootings that have happened in recent years, since many of the perpetrators have had a history of being bullied by other students.[18] Because of the media attention to this issue, many strategies have been developed from a variety of perspectives, but all seem to agree that individual strategies are most effective when they are part of a comprehensive package of prevention and intervention.[19]

This should make perfect sense. Bullying does not occur in isolation but instead takes place in a social context, as illustrated in Figure 11.1. The impact of bullying extends far beyond specific perpetrators and victims. Instead, the ripples of bullying spread out to family and friends, school, community, culture, and even the larger society (think, for example, about the impact of the Columbine, Virginia Tech, or Sandy Hook shootings on the entire country). Importantly, notice that the arrows in Figure 11.1 point both ways because the nature and frequency of bullying are also impacted by these very same factors. What this means is that trying to prevent bullying by only intervening with bullies and/or victims is not as effective as simultaneously working with families and bystanders as well as the larger community. Children who bully are profoundly influenced by their peers and families, for example, and ignoring those influences means that the effectiveness of any strategy implemented by the school is doomed to either failure or, at the very least, only partial success. This is why most experts agree that the best way to deal with bullying is through what is often termed a **whole-school approach** that involves all of the factors represented in Figure 11.1.[20]

❖   **Figure 11.1   Social Context of Bullying**

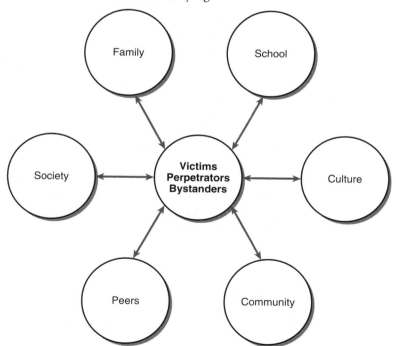

As we have seen in this book, the roots of violence are complex and involve a great many social, economic, political, cultural, psychobiological, and historical factors, to name a few; any attempt to ameliorate violence should therefore take into account as many of these variables as possible. A good example of a well-intentioned policy that failed in this regard is the famous Minneapolis experiment.

In 1980, Richard Berk and Lawrence Sherman conducted a test in Minneapolis, Minnesota, to determine whether arrest was an effective deterrent for intimate partner assault. At the time, the normal police routine for misdemeanor assaults of this nature was simply to separate the victim and offender and leave the scene.[21] The findings of the **Minneapolis experiment** suggested that arresting a perpetrator resulted in a deterrent effect of 50% for a six-month time span. With these results widely hailed as a breakthrough by activists and concerned legislators, many jurisdictions subsequently adopted mandatory arrest policies that forced police officers, when called to a domestic violence situation, to arrest someone if evidence of physical violence was present. In the years after the first experiment, however, six follow-up studies were conducted that extended the original in various ways and in different locations. The effects of arrest on future incidents of intimate partner violence were inconsistent at best. In some locations, a deterrent effect for arrest was found, while others found no deterrent effect and one location even found an increase in violence for arrested batterers who had a low stake in conformity (e.g., the unemployed). The results of the replication experiments seemed to suggest that only certain kinds of individuals were deterred by arrest. Ironically, many scholars—including Lawrence Sherman—now recommend repealing mandatory arrest policies in order to allow a greater range of responses to intimate partner assault.[22] Others suggest that more attention needs to be applied to developing more inclusive system-wide responses to domestic violence, rather than relying solely on law enforcement.[23] The point we are trying to illustrate through this example is not that arrest doesn't work or that it can't contribute to reducing the amount of domestic violence. It can but perhaps not for everyone. Instead, the lesson is that arrest should be one of a number of criminal justice and social service responses that should be used and that the criminal justice approach should be one of a number of broader remedies intended to address this enduring problem.

The second major point that we want to make is that prevention is always better than intervention. While intervention is useful, it is by definition a backward-looking approach to the problem of violence, while prevention tends to be more forward-looking. In other words, where violence is concerned, intervention is all about catching and punishing perpetrators and sometimes assisting those who are victimized. But there is a fundamental problem with this kind of approach—it is always *after* the fact. The harm has already been done. Yet all too often in the United States, our approach has been primarily, if not exclusively, concerned with intervening after the fact. Criminal justice, by its very nature, is largely reactionary in orientation. The police, for example, have historically focused on traditional forms of patrol that are largely reactive. During the 1970s, when crime rates increased dramatically, many police departments judged their effectiveness by how quickly they could respond to citizen calls as measured by elapsed time till arrival at a crime scene or site of a citizen complaint.[24] In more recent years, however, many departments have shifted to more proactive forms of policing that involve developing greater connections with the community and focusing on problem-oriented strategies designed to prevent crimes. This strategy has been called problem-oriented policing or community-oriented policing.[25] The more recent trends in community policing are to some extent based on the "Broken Windows" theory of crime that was articulated in 1982 by criminologists James Q. Wilson and George L. Kelling. They suggested that when neighborhoods are allowed to fall into disrepair with graffiti, abandoned and stripped vehicles, broken-out windows, and similar visible indications of neglect, two things happen. First, criminals learn that criminal activity is tolerated and second, community residents become fearful and are less likely to try to fix things.[26] Consequently, one community policing strategy emphasizes a crackdown on what are sometimes termed quality-of-life crimes, such as panhandling, public intoxication, loitering, and graffiti. By focusing on these types of relatively minor crimes, police departments have tried to prevent the perpetration of more serious crimes that they felt were encouraged by the urban decay so characteristic of many crime-ridden communities. While not without controversy and problems, the **"Broken Windows" strategy** of policing is nevertheless clearly an example of a more proactive approach to the problem of violence and criminality.

In short and to summarize, approaches to the problem of violence should ideally do two things: They should address the issue comprehensively and from a number of different levels; and they should stress preventative measures over purely interventionist strategies. One way of dealing with the issue of violence that involves both of these concerns is utilizing a public health perspective to address the problem of violence.

Violence as a Public Health Problem

As we have pointed out, our societal response to violence has largely been shaped by the classification of violence as solely a criminal justice issue, with our primary attention focused on deterrence and punishment. James Gilligan summarizes it this way:

> For the past four millennia, since the time of the first law-givers—Hammurabi and Moses, Drakon and Solon, Plato and Aristotle, Cicero and Justinian—humanity has been engaged in a great social experiment, testing the hypothesis that we could prevent violence, or at least diminish its scale and intensity, by labeling it "evil" and "criminal": ordering people not to engage in it; and then, when they commit acts of violence anyway, retaliating with more violence of our own, which we call "punishment" and "justice."[27]

This "experiment," as Gilligan terms it, has not been completely successful, and moreover, has had many unintended consequences. Mandatory minimum sentences have filled many state prison facilities to overflowing conditions. In fact, in 2010 the Supreme Court ruled that California's prison system was so over-crowded that prisoners were existing in conditions that amounted to "cruel and unusual punishment" and demanded they reduce their prison population by 30,000.[28] Today, over 7.2 million people are under some form of correctional supervision in the United States, and more than 700,000 are released back into their communities every year with diminished potential for finding a job that pays a living wage. Unfortunately, many will return to prison within 3 years. In fact, a recent evaluation of a large federally funded reentry initiative to develop projects to improve the reentry prospects of offenders to the community called the "Serious and Violent Offender Reentry Initiative (SVORI) has not been promising. Overall, the evaluation project indicated that there were only modest effects on recidivism for offenders exposed to enhanced reentry programming 15 months post-release compared to those who did not receive the enhanced programming.[29] Because of this failure, various scholars and antiviolence activists have increasingly suggested that truly effective violence prevention programs need to approach the issue from a completely different paradigm than that used in the past, namely the public health paradigm.

The public health approach to the issue of violence is fundamentally different from the criminal justice approach. Importantly, it does not pay attention solely or even primarily to the perpetrator but rather attempts to examine a wider range of factors that influence violence. Just like other diseases, a public health approach examines the factors that are related to the prevalence of violence and tries to prevent them. In the words of one report, "Efforts to address individual aspects of the problem, however laudable, must pale compared with the power that can be brought to bear in a coordinated effort by all elements of the community to address the problem as a whole."[30] This somewhat belated awakening is entirely appropriate since violence remains one of the most significant threats to the health of Americans. Rather than accepting violence as an inevitable fact of life, the public health paradigm assumes that violence is a social problem that can be remedied using the same kinds of community-wide and multilevel strategies that have been so successfully used against other social problems, including drunken driving, smoking, drug use, seat belt laws, and childhood immunization and nutrition issues.[31]

Another important difference between the two responses to violence is that the criminal justice response to violence embodies a moral perspective, while the public health response does not.[32] Criminal justice is about punishing bad behavior perpetrated by criminals and deviants. Even the terminology and imagery of the criminal justice approach are laden with the powerful moral symbolism of judgment and condemnation. The public health orientation, on the other hand, tends to be empirical and focuses on epidemiological research to identify and understand the causes of violence. It therefore relies on the language of understanding rather than that of judgment. For example, criminal justice practitioners define certain kinds of violence as crimes, while public health personnel perceive violence as a form of intentional injury that places it within a larger category of health problems.[33] And finally, the traditional legal/moral approach is often preoccupied with deciding whether or not a perpetrator had a guilty or evil mind (*mens rea*), whereas public health practitioners are usually more concerned with identifying the individual biological, psychological, and environmental factors that intersect with various social experiences to produce violent behavior.[34] In fairness, we should point out that the criminal justice system has sometimes created processes and policies derived from a standpoint that criminologists have sometimes termed "**restorative justice**," which is largely concerned with repairing the harm and damage caused by violence and criminality.[35] This approach generally relies on cooperative rather than punitive and judgmental processes and often involves mediation, restitution, and similar forms of healing. However, these kinds of programs also tend to be few and far between, and our characterization of the justice system generally holds true.

In developing preventative measures, the public health approach usually relies on six main elements. These measures are outlined in Table 11.3. This table illustrates a number of important issues regarding public health work. First, as mentioned above, it is philosophically oriented toward a preventative stance rather than a punitive one. Second, similar to the search for risk factors associated with the spread of diseases like AIDS, it is empirically based, since it depends upon the collection of information to identify both risk and protective factors. All too often, our national debates on violence are based on ideology, myths, stereotypes, and outright falsehoods. The public health approach, grounded as it is in nonjudgmental empirical data, offers an important reality check for our policy decisions. Third, it doesn't assume that recommended strategies will be effective in preventing violence. Instead, it depends upon rigorous tracking and monitoring to determine whether policies are working and to refine and alter them as needed. As such, public health initiatives tend to be fairly pragmatic and rooted in practical considerations. An example of this is the **Blueprints for Violence Prevention Project** established in 1996 by the University of Colorado at Boulder's Center for the Study and Prevention of Violence (CSPV). This project created a national program intended to identify **violence prevention** programs that were effective. To date, they have identified 11 **prevention** and **intervention** programs that meet a strict set of criteria, include clear documented evidence of reduced violence that has been tested rigorously, demonstrated effects that are sustained over time, and have involved multiple site replications to make sure that the program can be generalized to other locations.[36] These programs are proven to work and can serve as models for other possible initiatives.

Another way of looking at a public health approach to violence involves looking at the different levels of prevention.[37] The first tier of prevention is called **primary prevention** and involves reaching out to the population at large. This level concerns the implementation of society- or community-wide preventative measures regardless of individual risk factors. In order to fight disease, for example, public health practitioners recommend and promote mass inoculation and sanitation campaigns that have been shown to be very effective in reducing and in some cases almost eradicating certain

---

Table 11.3	Fundamentals of a Public Health Approach

1. Rely on community-based methods to identify root causes and sources of the problem.
2. Generate data to identify patterns of risk and protective factors.
3. Identify and monitor trends in the frequency and nature of risk factors.
4. Implement multilevel community interventions grounded in empirical data designed to reduce or eliminate risk factors or strengthen protective factors.
5. Evaluate and monitor the effectiveness of intervention strategies and revise tactics accordingly.
6. Educate the public about the problems and issues as well as what has been shown to be effective for intervention.

diseases and illnesses. Primary prevention of violence involves some of the same kinds of widespread initiatives that involve wholesale and fundamental changes in the organization of our society. A number of scholars, for example, suggest that a fundamental preventative measure would involve reducing **inequality** in U.S. society to substantially reduce violence.[38] The sociologists Peter Iadicola and Anson Shupe put it this way:

> inequality itself may be a cause of violence as offenders learn to define others as of less worth than they, and as they themselves have been defined by others. The structures of inequality that we experience, that we learn to accept, and that we maintain and extend through our everyday interpersonal interactions and in role performances within institutions, contribute to our ability to separate from others and define others as in need of control, punishment, or subjugation.[39]

Defining inequality broadly, Iadicola and Shupe suggest that violence is linked to the varied ways in which our society keeps individuals and groups in unequal conditions. They argue that not only is inequality built into the very structures of our society, but it is also reflected in our culture, ideology, and values, and that all of these serve to create the conditions necessary for violence to flourish. In other words, they suggest that not only does the deprivation and hardship brought about by economic inequality help produce violent behavior but that our perceptions and definitions are also fundamentally affected by systems of inequality. These perceptions, in turn, affect which behaviors we define as violent. For example, certain forms of institutional and structural violence, such as racism and discrimination, and product and production violence, such as the sale of dangerous products and work-related injuries, are usually not even defined as violence, yet they are very destructive in their consequences.[40] Elijah Anderson summarizes the impact of poverty on violence eloquently:

> The inclination to violence springs from the circumstances of life among the ghetto poor—the lack of jobs that pay a living wage, limited basic public services (police response in emergencies, building maintenance, trash pickup, lighting, and other services that middle-class neighborhoods take for granted), the stigma of race, the fallout from rampant drug use and drug trafficking, and the resulting alienation and absence of hope for the future. Simply living in such an environment places young people at special risk of falling victim to aggressive behavior.[41]

In a very similar vein, James Gilligan asserts that strategies of primary prevention need to focus on reducing poverty. Acknowledging that a great deal of violence is connected with economic deprivation, he argues that

> It has been shown throughout the world, both internationally and intranationally, that reducing economic inequities not only improves physical health and reduces the rate of death from natural causes far more effectively than doctors, medicines and hospitals; it also decreases the rate of death from both criminal and political violence far more effectively than any system of police forces, prisons, or military interventions ever invented.[42]

In a capitalist society such as the United States, this is a radical idea to say the least. But there is clear evidence that poverty is linked to a number of social problems, including violence. Time and again, we have seen how many forms of violence seem to be disproportionately concentrated among the ranks of the poor. While the middle and upper classes certainly do become offenders and victims of violence, their rates of perpetration and victimization are usually much lower for most acts of interpersonal and collective violence. If we are truly interested in reducing the amounts of violence in our society, we will have to address the issue of inequality at some point, no matter how unrealistic it might seem at first glance. Is it possible? There are many places we can start. Practically speaking, specific strategies, such as improving access to health care and educational opportunities, and ensuring that all citizens have basic necessities, such as food and housing, are just a few ways to ameliorate the negative effects of poverty. We should also consider that various other social problems associated with income inequality, such as drug abuse and suicide, may be remediated by the same kinds of solutions.

Others who recommend a public health approach to the problem of violence in our society suggest that violent images in the media be sharply reduced or eliminated. Of course, in a society such as ours that prides itself on freedom of speech, this smacks of censorship, but can we afford not to address this point? We do, in fact, set limits on certain kinds of sexual images in the media, whether it is nudity or simulated and/or real sex acts, yet we do not limit acts of violence. We allow movies and television shows to portray incredibly realistic and graphic acts of dismemberment, mutilation, and torture, yet we do not allow the same movies and television shows to reveal frontal nudity or individuals engaged in lovemaking. In many European nations, however, the reverse is true. In some nations, graphic acts of violence will be edited out of the media while explicit sexuality is not prohibited. The point here is that we are somewhat selective and arbitrary in our willingness to accept censorship and restrictions on the content of media images. We note this because the research is now overwhelmingly clear that violence in the media does affect behavior, as has been discussed in earlier chapters, especially Chapter 3. It is no longer in doubt that mass media violence teaches proviolence attitudes and behaviors, distorts our perception of the nature and consequences of violence, and portrays heroic role models as needing to rely on violence and aggression to solve problems.[43] If we are truly interested in reducing the amount of violence in our country, we need to stop training ourselves in its language and imagery, which serves to make it so familiar and comfortable and also serves to desensitize us to its use.

The second level of prevention is, not surprisingly, **secondary prevention**, which focuses on intervention strategies for those who are at an elevated risk of engaging in violence. Thus it is somewhat more targeted than primary prevention methods, since those are intended for a broader population regardless of risk. With regard to secondary prevention, we find, for example, that we now know a great deal of information about those youth who are at increased risk of violent behavior as both victims and perpetrators. Table 11.4 illustrates what these identified risk factors are for young people, while Table 11.5 lists factors that serve to decrease the risk of violence for youth. Secondary prevention programs seek to identify and engage young individuals who have a preponderance of these risk factors and a minimum of protective factors. Obvious secondary prevention programs should focus on seeking to lower some of the

Table 11.4   Risk Factors for Youth Violence

Individual Risk Factors

- History of violent victimization or involvement
- Attention deficits, hyperactivity, or learning disorders
- History of early aggressive behavior
- Involvement with drugs, alcohol, or tobacco
- Low IQ
- Poor impulse control
- Deficits in social cognitive or information-processing abilities
- High emotional distress
- History of treatment for emotional problems
- Antisocial beliefs and attitudes
- Exposure to violence and conflict in the family

Family Risk Factors

- Authoritarian child-rearing attitudes
- Harsh, lax, or inconsistent disciplinary practices
- Low parental involvement
- Low emotional attachment to parents or caregivers
- Low parental education and income
- Parental substance abuse or criminality
- Poor family functioning
- Poor monitoring and supervision of children

Peer/School Risk Factors

- Association with delinquent peers
- Involvement in gangs
- Social rejection by peers
- Lack of involvement in conventional activities
- Poor academic performance
- Low commitment to school and school failure

Community Risk Factors

- Diminished economic opportunities
- High concentrations of inequality and/or poor residents
- High level of transience (e.g., people moving in and out)
- High level of family disruption
- Low levels of community participation
- Socially disorganized neighborhoods

risk factors faced by youth and maximize or increase the protective factors. Looking at Table 11.5, for example, we find that a couple of protective factors for young people involve commitment to school and involvement in social activities. One strategy, therefore, could involve increasing participation in after-school activities by making them more available and accessible. In recent years, many after-school programs have been cut or reduced because of costs, but if these kinds of activities reduce the risk of

Table 11.5   Protective Factors for Youth Violence

Individual Protective Factors

- Intolerant attitude toward deviance
- High IQ or high grade point average
- Positive social orientation
- Religiosity

Family Protective Factors

- Connectedness to family or adults outside of the family
- Ability to discuss problems with parents
- Perceived parental expectations about school performance are high
- Frequent shared activities with parents
- Consistent presence of parent during at least one of the following: when awakening, when arriving home from school, at evening mealtime, and when going to bed
- Involvement in social activities

Peer/School Protective Factors

- Commitment to school
- Involvement in social activities

violent behavior—which we know has huge costs—perhaps it is time to rethink some of these short-term savings. Another area where secondary prevention programs can make a difference is around the issue of alcohol.

As we discussed in Chapter 3, alcohol is one variable that is a frequent companion to a great deal of interpersonal violence. For example, in Chapter 7, on rape and sexual assault, we pointed out that college women are at greater risk of being victimized by these crimes than women of the same age in the general population, and that a common context for these attacks is parties where alcohol is present. We also know that college students tend to drink a lot and that they often engage in what is often called binge drinking. One report, for example, suggests that around 44% of college students are heavy drinkers, which was defined as five or more drinks consumed in a row for men and four or more for women.[44] This type of drinking is culturally patterned in that it is largely shaped by students' expectations and beliefs about what it means to be college students and what the college experience is all about. In other words, many students see getting drunk and partying as an integral part of being at college. This kind of perception is something that is often amenable to education designed to heighten awareness of the dangers of this kind of drinking. Many universities and colleges have implemented programs that attempt to change the situation or, as one commentator states

> Institutions of higher education are increasingly implementing creative programs and aggressive policies to curb AOD [alcohol and other drugs] use and its associated negative consequences. Many campuses and communities have begun comprehensive prevention approaches that go beyond traditional educational programs to emphasize strategies aimed at changing the physical, social, legal, and economic environment on campus and in surrounding communities.[45]

The **U.S. Department of Education's Higher Education Center for Alcohol, Drug Abuse, and Violence Prevention** suggests that schools adopt the following specific initiatives to reduce binge drinking on campuses. These have been summarized by Daniel Ari Kapner:

- Offer and promote social, recreational, extracurricular, and public service options that do not include alcohol and other drugs.
- Create a social, academic, and residential environment that supports health-promoting norms.
- Limit alcohol availability both on and off campus.
- Restrict marketing and promotion of alcoholic beverages both on and off campus.
- Develop and enforce campus policies and local, state, and federal laws.[46]

These recommended strategies are clearly rooted in a public health approach designed to reduce or prevent heavy drinking practices and are very illustrative of secondary intervention techniques.

The third and last level of prevention is **tertiary prevention**, which isn't really preventative as its name suggests but rather is geared toward intervening in the lives of those who have been impacted by violence. Importantly, this means not only working with victims of violent crime but with the perpetrators as well. Unfortunately, however, this type of intervention tends to be less effective than the previous two levels, since at this level of prevention the harm has already been done. With regard to tertiary public health approaches to the arena of domestic violence, for example, we find many communities have adopted various methods of helping the victims of intimate partner violence that often includes financial assistance with medical costs, counseling, job training, and numerous other strategies designed to help victims cope with and overcome their history of victimization. In the same arena, we see another example of tertiary prevention-based programs that focus on batterers instead of victims.

The mandatory arrest policies that began in the wake of the Minneapolis experiment of 1981 resulted in a large number of abusers ending up in court. Out of this situation, a number of **Batterer Intervention Programs (BIPs)** and **Spouse Abuse Abatement Programs (SAAPs)** were introduced as an alternative to traditional criminal justice responses that were exclusively punitive.[47] One of the earliest and most well known of these is the **Duluth Program**, which has been the model for most of the BIPs across the country. Based on a feminist perspective on battering, these programs work to teach men about the nature and impact of patriarchy and resocialize them into adopting more equal and nonviolent intimate relationships.[48] Over the years, a number of other approaches have also been created and adopted by these programs, including cognitive-behavioral-based intervention programs, and most recently batterer typology or profile-based intervention programs; however, it is the Duluth model that remains the standard.[49] While the specific emphasis of these programs varies, they are essentially all tertiary prevention programs intended to prevent the offender from reoffending. So how effective are these BIPs? Unfortunately, the research results are largely inconclusive and can't definitively let us know whether or not these programs actually work. True to a public health perspective, however, evaluative research continues to be conducted in order to determine the efficacy of these intervention strategies.

There is one last program we want to mention that combines all three of the prevention components to combat violence in communities. While initiated by the criminal justice system, the programs use rewards and incentives for reducing violence to balance the punishments meted out by the criminal justice system. The first program of this nature was launched in Boston, Massachusetts, in the early 1990s and termed "**Operation Ceasefire.**"[50] The approach combines strategic law enforcement along with community involvement and social service provisions all working together to target "hot spots" in cities that have high rates of violence, particularly youth violence. Since its inception, many countries across the world have adopted it. How does it work? The first part of the program invests a great deal of effort in understanding the dynamics and players involved in the violence. In Cincinnati, for example, the first part of the program used mapping techniques and interviews with police officers to identify who was responsible for the majority of the violence in the city. They identified 69 gangs, which were believed to contain over 1,000 people who were also identified by name. Once identified, certain "moral authorities" in the community, such as ministers, ex-offenders, and other outreach workers who have street credibility within the community, are typically brought in to compel the young offenders to do the right thing. This is not done in isolation, however. Another facet of the program is providing help to those want it, including educational assistance, job opportunities, drug treatment, and the like. And finally, a dose of deterrence is also added. For example, in many cities, gang members were told that if one more shooting occurred, the entire gang would take the blame. Although none of these strategies appears to be very effective at preventing violence on their own, when they are combined into one program, results indicate that they are extremely effective in reducing violent crime, including homicides. Importantly, approaches like this must engage the community so that partnerships between law enforcement and social support networks can be combined to combat violence.

These above reviewed prevention strategies (primary, secondary, and tertiary) provide only a brief and selective sample of programs and priorities that apply a public health approach to the problem of violence. They should suffice, however, to provide you with a sense of the direction and potential applications of the approach we are advocating.

Conclusions

The emphasis we have placed in this chapter on a public health approach to violence is not to suggest that such approaches should completely supplant criminal justice responses. As the ceasefire program indicates, there are a few promising strategies that are being implemented by the criminal justice system that hold promise for the future. Moreover, we are not so naïve as to suggest that we don't need police, courts, and prisons. Society does need to be protected against those who would harm and injure others. People who are actively engaged in violent behavior and who do not respect the lives and physical safety of others need to be restrained and prevented from harming others. Those who have inflicted violence on others also need to be held accountable for their actions. On the other hand, this shouldn't be the only way we choose to protect ourselves. Instead, a greater reliance on public health strategies can enhance and broaden our ability to deal with both the causes and consequences of violent behavior and lessen the burden on the criminal justice system. Instead, what we are advocating is a synthesis of the two approaches. Because neither the criminal justice nor the public health approaches can completely eliminate the problem of violence alone, both working in concert with each other can make our society a dramatically safer place.

Key Terms

Batterer Intervention Programs (BIPs)

Blueprints for Violence Prevention Project

"Broken Windows" strategy

bullying

Centers for Disease Control and Prevention

Duluth Program

inequality

Minneapolis experiment

Operation Ceasefire

post-traumatic stress disorder (PTSD)

prevention versus intervention

primary prevention

public health perspective

restorative justice

secondary prevention

Spouse Abuse Abatement Programs (SAAPs)

tertiary prevention

U.S. Department of Education's Higher Education Center for Alcohol, Drug Abuse, and Violence Prevention

Violence Prevention

whole-school approach

Discussion Questions

1. Design a program to combat a type of violence of your choice that will cover both elements of primary and secondary prevention. What factors of your program are directed toward primary prevention, and what factors are directed toward secondary prevention? What elements could you add to the program that would provide tertiary prevention?

2. The World Health Organization (WHO) has declared violence a global public health problem. You can find information about this declaration in a publication titled *Violence: A Global Public Health Problem* on the WHO website (http://whqlibdoc.who .int/publications/2002/9241545615_chap1_eng.pdf). The first chapter in the document details how the WHO has defined violence. What behaviors are included in its definition? What typologies of violence are presented by the WHO? What sources of data does the WHO recommend to monitor violence?

3. The journal *Health Affairs* is an academic journal devoted to policy issues in the health sphere. In a recent issue, an editorial by Mark Moore was published that was titled "Violence Prevention: Criminal Justice or Public Health." You can access a copy of the editorial on the journal's website (http://content.healthaffairs.org/cgi/reprint/12/4/34.pdf). What roles does Moore believe the health field can play in combating violence? What roles does he believe the criminal justice system should retain? How does he believe both systems can complement each other? In your opinion, are these feasible goals that can be achieved? What obstacles may need to be overcome for such an approach to be successful?

End Notes

Chapter 1

1. David T. Courtwright, *Violent Land: Single Men and Social Disorder From the Frontier to the Inner City* (Cambridge, MA: Harvard University Press, 1996), 1.

2. Richard Maxwell Brown, *Strain of Violence: Historical Studies of American Violence and Vigilantism* (New York: Oxford University Press, 1975).

3. Inga Clendinnen, *Dancing With Strangers: Europeans and Australians First Contact* (Cambridge, UK: Cambridge University Press, 2005).

4. David Svaldi, *Sand Creek and the Rhetoric of Extermination: A Case Study in Indian–White Relations* (Lanham: University Press of America, 1989); Gregory F. Michno, *Encyclopedia of Indian Wars: Western Battles and Skirmishes, 1850–1890* (Missoula, MT: Mountain Press, 2003); Stan Hoig, *The Sand Creek Massacre* (Norman: University of Oklahoma Press, 1961).

5. Quoted in Svaldi, *Sand Creek and the Rhetoric of Extermination*, 291.

6. James Allen and others, *Without Sanctuary: Lynching Photography in America* (Santa Fe, NM: Twin Palms, 2003).

7. Bernard Lefkowitz, *Our Guys: The Glen Ridge Rape and the Secret Life of the Perfect Suburb* (Berkeley: University of California Press, 1997).

8. Dan Bilefsky, "Wife Who Fired 11 Shots is Acquitted of Murder," *The New York Times*, October 6, 2011, http://www.nytimes.com/2011/10/07/nyregion/barbara-sheehan-who-killed-husband-is-found-not-guilty-of-murder.html?pagewanted=all.

9. Manny Fernandez and Marc Santora, "Gunman Showed Signs of Anger," *New York Times*, April 18, 2007, www.nytimes.com/2007/04/18/us/18gunman.html.

10. Michael E. Ruane and Chris L. Jenkins, "Gunman Sent Video During Lull in Slaughter." *Washington Post*, April 19, 2001, A01.

11. Dan Frosch and Kirk Johnson, "Gunman Kills 12 in Colorado, Reviving Gun Debate," *The New York Times*, October 6, 2011, http://www.nytimes.com/2012/07/21/us/shooting-at-colorado-theater-showing-batman-movie.html?pagewanted=all.

12. Jeffrey H. Goldstein, *Aggression and Crimes of Violence* (New York: Oxford University Press, 1986).

13. Jake Page, *In the Hands of the Great Spirit: The 20,000-Year History of the American Indians* (New York: Free Press, 2003); David E. Stannard, *American Holocaust: The Conquest of the New World* (New York: Oxford University Press, 1992).

14. Svaldi, *Sand Creek and the Rhetoric of Extermination*, 293.

15. Ruane and Jenkins, "Gunman Sent Video," A01.

16. Jack Katz, *Seductions of Crime: Moral and Sensual Attractions in Doing Evil* (New York: Basic Books, 1988).

17. Lefkowitz, *Our Guys*, 2.

18. Bruce A. Jacobs and Richard Wright, *Street Justice: Retaliation in the Criminal Underworld* (New York: Cambridge University Press, 2006).

19. For example, if we examine domestic violence we find that previous violence is a significant predictor for subsequent violence. See Jacquelyn Campbell et al., "Risk Factors for Femicide in Abusive Relationships: Results from a Multisite Case Control Study," *American Journal of Public Health* 93 no. 7 (2003): 1089–1097; Jacquelyn Campbell, "Prediction of Homicide of and by Battered Women," in *Assessing Dangerousness: Violence by Sexual Offenders, Batterers and Child Abusers* (Thousand Oaks, CA: Sage, 1995), 96–113; Martie P. Thompson, Linda E. Saltzman,

and Holly Johnson, "Risk Factors for Physical Injury Among Women Assaulted by Current or Former Spouses," *Violence Against Women* 7 no. 8 (2001): 886–899; Angela Browne, *When Battered Women Kill* (New York: Free Press, 1987); D. Dutton and others, "Wife Assault Treatment and Criminal Recidivism: An 11-Year Follow-Up," *International Journal of Offender Therapy and Comparative Criminology* 41 (1997): 9–23; Peter Chimbos, *Marital Violence: A Study of Interpersonal Homicide* (San Francisco: R&E Research Associates, 1978); A. E. Daniel and P. W. Harris, "Female Homicide Offenders Referred for Pre-Trial Psychiatric Examination: A Descriptive Study," *Bulletin of the American Academy of Psychiatry and Law* 10 (1982): 261; Desmond Ellis and Walter DeKeseredy, "Rethinking Estrangement, Intervention and Intimate Femicide," *Violence Against Women* 3 no. 6 (1997): 590–609; Rosemary Gartner, M. Dawson, and M. Crawford, "Woman Killing: Intimate Femicide in Ontario, 1974–1994," *Resources for Feminist Research* 26 (1999): 151–173; L. Langford, N. E. Isaac, and S. Kabat, "Homicides Related to Intimate Partner Violence in Massachusetts," *Homicide Studies* 2 (1998): 353–377; Holly Johnson, *Dangerous Domains: Violence Against Women in Canada* (Toronto: Nelson, 1996); Kathryn E. Moracco, Carol W. Runyan, and John D. Butts, "Femicide in North Carolina, 1991–1993: A Statewide Study of Patterns and Precursors," *Homicide Studies* 2 no. 4 (1998): 422–446; Jane Totman, *The Murderess: A Psychosocial Study of Criminal Homicide* (San Francisco: R&E Research Associates, 1978); Margo Wilson, Martin Daly, and Christine Wright, "Uxoricide in Canada: Demographic Risk Patterns," *Canadian Journal of Criminology* 35 (1993): 263–291; Marvin E. Wolfgang, *Patterns of Criminal Homicide* (Philadelphia: University of Pennsylvania Press, 1958); Marvin E. Wolfgang, "An Analysis of Homicide-Suicide," *Journal of Clinical and Experimental Psychopathology and Quarterly Review of Psychiatry and Neurology* 19 no. 3 (1958): 208–218; Marvin E. Wolfgang, "A Sociological Analysis of Criminal Homicide," in *Studies in Homicide*, ed. M. E. Wolfgang (New York: Harper & Row, 1967).

20. Taken from Tyson's official website, www.michaeltyson.com/quotes.html, accessed July 1, 2005.

21. Nancy Montgomery, "Reports of Family Violence, Abuse Within Military Rise," *Stars and Stripes*, July 10, 2011, www.stripes.com/reports-of-family-violence-abuse-within-military-rise-1.148815.

22. William J. Bowers, *Legal Homicide* (Boston: Northeastern University Press, 1984); William J. Bowers and G. L. Pierce, "Arbitrariness and Discrimination Under Post-Furman Capital Statutes," *Crime and Delinquency* 26 (1980): 563–635; Darrell Cheatwood, "Capital Punishment and the Deterrence of Violent Crime in Comparable Counties," *Criminal Justice Review* 18 (1993): 165–181.

23. Bowers, *Legal Homicide*, 274.

24. Dane Archer and Rosemary Gartner, *Violence and Crime in Cross-National Perspective* (New Haven, CT: Yale University Press, 1984); Dane Archer and Rosemary Gartner, "Violent Acts and Violent Times: A Comparative Approach to Postwar Homicide Rates," *American Sociological Review* 41 (1976): 937–963; Rosemary Gartner, "The Victims of Homicide: A Temporal and Cross-National Comparison," *American Sociological Review* 55 (1990): 92–106; S. Landau and D. Pfefferman, "A Time Series Analysis of Violent Crime and its Relation to Prolonged States of Warfare," *Criminology* 26 (1988): 489–504; V. W. Sidel and R. C. Wesley, "Violence as a Public Health Problem: Lessons for Action Against Violence by Health Care Professionals from the Work of the International Physicians Movement for the Prevention of Nuclear War," *Social Justice* 22 (1996): 154–170.

25. Others have more specifically argued that policies and practices of a government can serve to foster violence against subcultural groups, minorities, and women. For a discussion of this, see: Susan L. Caulfield, "The Perpetuation of Violence Through Criminological Theory: The Ideological Role of Subculture Theory," in *Criminology as Peacemaking*, eds. H. E. Pepinsky and R. Quinney (Bloomington: Indiana University Press, 1991); Susan L. Caulfield and Nancy A. Wonders, "Personal and Political: Violence Against Women and the Role of the State," in *Political Crime in Contemporary America: A Critical Approach*, ed. K. D. Tunnell (New York: Garland Publishing, 1993); L. L. Tifft and L. Markham, "Battering Women and Battering Central Americans: A Peacemaking Synthesis," in *Criminology as Peacemaking*, eds. H. E. Pepinsky and R. Quinney (Bloomington: Indiana University Press, 1991).

26. Archer and Gartner, *Violence and Crime in a Cross-National Perspective*.

27. Quoted in Robert Elias, "A Culture of Violent Solutions," in *The Web of Violence: From Interpersonal to Global*, eds. Jennifer Turpin and Lester R. Kurtz (Urbana: University of Illinois Press, 1997), 118.

28. Murray A. Straus, *Beating the Devil Out of Them: Corporal Punishment in American Families* (New York: Lexington Books, 1994).

29. Straus, *Beating the Devil Out of Them*, 9.

30. For a good review, see Amy E. Nivette, "Violence in Non-State Societies: A Review," *British Journal of Criminology* 51 (2011): 578–598.

31. L. M. Friedman, *Crime and punishment in American History* (New York: Basic Books, 1993), 173.

32. Donald Black, "Crime as Social Control," *American Sociological Review* 48 (1983): 34–45.

33. Leslie W. Kennedy, "Going It Alone: Unreported Crime and Individual Self-Help," *Journal of Criminal Justice* 16 (1988): 403–412; W. G. Skogan, "Reporting Crimes to the Police: The Status of World Research," *Journal of Research in Crime and Delinquency* 21 (1984): 113–137.

34. Julia T. Wood, "Monsters and Victims: Male Felons' Accounts of Intimate Partner Violence," *Journal of Social and Personal Relationships* 21 no. 5 (2004): 555–576.

35. Making many of the same points, criminologists Neil Weiner, Margaret Zahn, and Rita Sagi suggest that any definition of violence needs to consider six factors:
1. The degree and type of injury
2. The intent of the participant(s) to apply or to threaten to apply force
3. The object of the force
4. The causes of and motivations and justifications for the behavior
5. The number of people involved
6. Whether the behavior is an act of commission or omission

See Neil Weiner, Margaret Zahn, and Rita Sagi, *Violence: Patterns, Causes, Public Policy* (San Diego, CA: Harcourt, Brace, Jovanovich, 1990).

36. Leslie W. Kennedy and David R. Forde, *When Push Comes to Shove: A Routine Conflict Approach to Violence* (Albany: State University of New York Press, 1999).

37. See, for example, Leonard D. Eron, "A Psychological Perspective," in *Aggression and Violence: An Introductory Text*, eds. Vincent B. Van Hasselt and Michael Herson (Boston: Allyn & Bacon, 2000), 23–39.

38. Curt R. Bartol and Anne M. Bartol, *Criminal Behavior: A Psychosocial Approach* (Upper Saddle River, NJ: Pearson Prentice Hall, 2005).

39. Peter Iadicola and Anson Shupe, *Violence, Inequality, and Human Freedom* (Lanham, MD: Rowman & Littlefield, 2003), 26.

40. Iadicola and Shupe, 23.

41. This is most important for the individualistic forms of violence reviewed in the first half of the book and much less so for the collective forms discussed in the later chapters. Our understanding of murder, rape, and robbery, for example, is largely dependent on the sources of information discussed in this section, while the collective forms of violence—given their nature—are not as dependent upon the same sources of information.

42. Clayton J. Mosher, Terance D. Miethe, and Dretha M. Phillips, *The Mismeasure of Crime* (Thousand Oaks, CA: Sage, 2002).

43. Mosher, Miethe, and Phillips, *The Mismeasure of Crime.*

44. Ronet Bachman, "A Comparison of Annual Incidence Rates and Contextual Characteristics of Intimate-Partner Violence Against Women from the National Crime Victimization Survey (NCVS) and the National Violence Against Women Survey (NVAWS)," *Violence Against Women* 6 no. 8 (2000): 839–867.

45. NCVS screening instruments and incident reports can be found at the following BJS website, http://bjs.gov/index.cfm?ty=dcdetail&iid=245#Questionnaires.

46. James F. Short Jr. and Ivan Nye, "Extent of Unrecorded Juvenile Delinquency: Tentative Conclusions," *Journal of Criminal Law, Criminology, and Police Science* 49 (1958): 296–302.

47. Delbert S. Elliott, *National Youth Survey* (Boulder, CO: Behavioral Research Institute, 1983).

48. Jennifer L. Truman and Michael Planty, *Criminal Victimization, 2011* NCJ 239437 (Washington, DC: BJS, U.S. Department of Justice, 2012).

49. TV Turnoff Network, "Facts and Figures About Our TV Habit," www.tvturnoffnetwork.org

50. Violence in Media Entertainment. www.mediaawareness.ca/english/issues/violence_entertainment.cfm?

51. See, for example, Madeline Levine, *Viewing Violence* (New York: Doubleday, 1996); Dave Grossman and Gloria DeGaetano, *Stop Teaching Our Kids to Kill: A Call to Action Against TV, Movie, and Video Game Violence* (New York: Crown, 1999).

52. Iadicola and Shupe, *Violence, Inequality, and Human Freedom.*

53. James Gilligan, *Violence: Our Deadly Epidemic and Its Causes* (New York: Grosset/Putnam, 1996), 5.

54. Arthur M. Eastman and others, eds., *The Norton Anthology of Poetry* (New York: W.W. Norton & Co., 1970), 737.

55. Peter L. Berger and Thomas Luckmann, *The Social Construction of Reality: A Treatise in the Sociology of Knowledge* (New York: Anchor, 1966).

56. For a more detailed discussion of the nature of culture, see Clifford Geertz, *The Interpretation of Cultures* (New York: Basic Books, 1973); A. L. Kroeber and Clyde Kluckhohn, *Culture: A Critical Review of Concepts and Definitions* (New York: Vintage, 1952).

57. See, for example, Richard Maxwell Brown, *No Duty to Retreat: Violence and Values in American History and Society* (New York: Oxford University Press, 1991); Brown, *Strain of Violence*; James William Gibson, *Warrior Dreams: Paramilitary Culture in Post-Vietnam America* (New York: Hill and Wang, 1994).

58. Marvin Wolfgang, *Patterns of Criminal Homicide* (Philadelphia: University of Pennsylvania Press, 1958), 188–189.

59. Courtwright, *Violent Land*; Richard E. Nisbett and Dov Cohen, *Culture of Honor: The Psychology of Violence in the South* (Boulder, CO: Westview, 1996); Bertram Wyatt-Brown, *Honor: Ethics and Behavior in the Old South* (Oxford, UK: Oxford University Press, 1982).

60. The phrase is evidently an old one. It was H. Rap Brown who, during the 1960s, suggested that violence was as American as cherry pie. See www .phrases.org.uk/bulletin_board/5/messages/1406 .html

61. James Gilligan, *Violence: Our Deadly Epidemic and Its Causes*, 5.

62. Ray Surrette, *Media, Crime, and Criminal Justice: Images and Realities* (Belmont, CA: West/ Wadsworth, 1998).

63. Surrette, *Media, Crime, and Criminal Justice*.

64. Tom Hayden, *Street Wars: Gangs and the Future of Violence* (New York: Free Press, 2004).

65. Stephen Cain, "Murder and the Media," in *The Human Side of Homicide*, eds., Bruce L. Danto, John Bruhns, and Austin H. Kutscher (New York: Columbia University Press, 1982).

66. For a good discussion of this issue, see Barry Glassner, *The Culture of Fear: Why Americans Are Afraid of the Wrong Things* (New York: Basic Books, 1999).

67. Glassner, *The Culture of Fear*, 27.

68. Glassner, *The Culture of Fear*, 27.

69. See Philip Jenkins, *Using Murder: The Social Construction of Serial Homicide* (New York: Aldine de Gruyter, 1994); Joel Best, *Threatened Children: Rhetoric and Concern About Child Victims* (Chicago: University of Chicago Press, 1990).

Chapter 2

1. Anthony Stevens, *The Roots of War and Terror* (London: Continuum, 2004), 12.

2. *Webster's New Explorer Dictionary of Quotations* (Springfield, MA: Federal Street Press, 2000).

3. Edward O. Wilson, *On Human Nature* (Cambridge, MA: Harvard University Press, 2004), 100.

4. Albert J. Reiss Jr. and Jeffrey A. Roth, eds., *Understanding and Preventing Violence* (Washington, DC: National Academy Press, 1993).

5. Scott Shane, "Suspects With Foot in 2 Worlds, Perhaps Echoing Plots of Past," *The New York Times*, April 20, 2013. Downloaded from http://www.nytimes.com/2013/04/21/us/boston-suspects-confused-identities-and-conflicting-loyalties.html?pagewanted=all

6. Deborah Sontag, David M. Herszenhorn, and Serge F. Kovaleski, "A Battered Dream, Then a Violent Path," *The New York Times*, April 27, 2013.

7. Richard Wrangham and Dale Peterson, *Demonic Males: Apes and the Origins of Human Violence* (Boston: Mariner Books, 1996).

8. Wrangham and Peterson, *Demonic Males*.

9. Wrangham and Peterson, *Demonic Males*.

10. Jane Goodall, *The Chimpanzees of Gombe: Patterns of Behavior* (Cambridge, MA: Harvard University Press, 1986).

11. Wrangham and Peterson, *Demonic Males*.

12. Wrangham and Peterson, *Demonic Males*.

13. Wrangham and Peterson, *Demonic Males*, 146.

14. Wrangham and Peterson, *Demonic Males*, 146.

15. Alex Alvarez and Ronet Bachman, *Murder American Style* (Belmont, CA: Thomson/Wadsworth, 2003). See also Elijah Anderson, *Code of the Street: Decency, Violence, and the Moral Life of the Inner City* (New York: W. W. Norton, 1999).

16. Jeffrey H. Goldstein, *Aggression and Crimes of Violence* (New York: Oxford University Press, 1986).

17. See, for example, Stephen Jay Gould, *The Mismeasure of Man* (New York: W. W. Norton, 1996).

18. Frank Schmalleger, *Criminal Justice Today*, 7th ed. (Upper Saddle River, NJ: Prentice Hall, 2003).

19. Gould, *The Mismeasure of Man*, 153.

20. Elof Axel Carlson, *The Unfit: A History of a Bad Idea* (Cold Spring Harbor, NY: Cold Spring Harbor Laboratory Press, 2001); G. K. Chesterton, *Eugenics and Other Evils: An Argument Against Scientifically Organized Society* (Seattle: Inkling Books, 2000); Michael W. Perry and Daniel J. Kevles, eds., *In the Name of Eugenics: Genetics and the Uses of Human Heredity* (Cambridge, MA: Harvard University Press, 1995).

21. Debra Niehoff, *The Biology of Violence: How Understanding the Brain, Behavior, and Environment Can Break the Vicious Circle of Aggression* (New York: Free Press, 1999), 51.

22. For a good review of the research literature on serotonin and aggression, see Niehoff, *The Biology of Violence*; Jan Volavka, *Neurobiology of Violence*, 2nd ed. (Washington, DC: American Psychiatric Association, 2002).

23. Niehoff, *The Biology of Violence*.

24. E. Aronson, T. D. Wilson, and R. M. Akert, *Social Psychology*, 5th ed. (Upper Saddle River, NJ: Prentice Hall, 2005).

25. T. Banks and J. M. Dabbs, "Salivary Testosterone and Cortisol in Delinquent and Violent Urban Subculture," *Journal of Social Psychology*, 136 (1996): 49–56.

26. Niehoff, *The Biology of Violence*.

27. Niehoff, *The Biology of Violence*.

28. Niehoff, *The Biology of Violence*.

29. Niehoff, *The Biology of Violence*.

30. Gary M. Lavergne, *A Sniper in the Tower: The Charles Whitman Murders* (Denton, TX: University of North Texas Press, 1997).

31. Volavka, *Neurobiology of Violence*; Nathaniel Pallone and James Hennessy, "Brain Dysfunction and Criminal Violence," *Science* 35 (1998): 21–27; Adrian Raine, Monte Buchsbaum, and Lori LaCasse, "Brain Abnormalities in Murderers Indicated by Positron Emission Tomography," *Biological Psychiatry* 42 (1997): 495–508.

32. D. Williams, "Neural Factors Related to Habitual Aggression," *Brain* 92 (1969): 503.

33. Discussed in Steven A. Egger, *The Killers Among Us: An Examination of Serial Murder and Its Investigation*, 2nd ed. (Upper Saddle River, NJ: Prentice Hall, 2002).

34. Both the terms "psychopath" and "sociopath" have been superseded in the *Diagnostic and Statistical Manual of Mental Disorders* with the term "antisocial personality disorder." For a thorough discussion, see Robert I. Simon, *Bad Men Do What Good Men Dream: A Forensic Psychiatrist Illuminates the Darker Side of Human Behavior* (Washington, DC: American Psychiatric Press, 1996).

35. James Blair, Derek Mitchell, and Karina Blair, *The Psychopath: Emotion and the Brain* (Malden, MA.: Blackwell Publishing, 2005).

36. Simon, *Bad Men Do What Good Men Dream*.

37. R. J. R. Blair, "The Emergence of Psychopathy: Implications for the Neuropsychological Approach to Developmental Disorders," *Cognition* 101 (2006): 414–442.

38. James Allen Fox and Jack Levin, "Serial Murder: Popular Myths and Empirical Realities," in *Homicide: A Sourcebook of Social Research*, eds. M. Dwayne Smith and Margaret A. Zahn (Thousand Oaks, CA: Sage, 1999), 165–175.

39. D. G. Cornell and others, "Psychopathy in Instrumental and Reactive Violent Offenders," *Journal of Consulting and Clinical Psychology* 4 (1996): 783–790.

40. R. J. Blair, "Facial Expressions, Their Communicatory Functions and Neuro-Cognitive Substrates," *Philosophical Transactions of the Royal Society of London. Series B. Biological Sciences* 358 (2003): 561–572.

41. Simon, *Bad Men Do What Good Men Dream*.

42. Simon, *Bad Men Do What Good Men Dream*.

43. G. T. Harris, M. E. Rice, and V. L. Quinsey, "Psychopathy as a Taxon," *Journal of Consulting and Clinical Psychology* 62, (1994): 387–397; T. A. Skilling, V. L. Quinsey, and W. M. Craig, "Evidence of a Taxon Underlying Serious Antisocial Behavior in Boys," *Criminal Justice and Behavior* 28 (2001): 450–470.

44. D. J. Simourd and R. D. Hoge, "Criminal Psychopathy: A Risk-and-Need Perspective," *Criminal Justice and Behavior* 27 (2000): 256–272.

45. M. Delisi, *Career Criminals in Society* (Thousand Oaks, CA: Sage, 2005).

46. David Farrington, "Family Background and Psychopathy" in *Handbook of Psychopathy*, ed. C. J. Patrick (New York: Guilford Press, 2006), 229–250.

47. Quoted in Henry H. Brownstein, *The Social Reality of Violence and Violent Crime* (Boston: Allyn & Bacon, 2000), 120.

48. Roy F. Baumeister and W. Keith Campbell, "The Intrinsic Appeal of Evil: Sadism, Sensational Thrills, and Threatened Egotism," *Personality and Social Psychology Review* 3 (1999): 210–221.

49. Baumeister and Campbell, "The Intrinsic Appeal of Evil."

50. Jack Katz, *Seductions of Crime* (New York: Basic Books, 1988).

51. Curt R. Bartol and Anne M. Bartol, *Criminal Behavior: A Psychosocial Approach*, 7th ed. (Upper Saddle River, NJ: Pearson/Prentice Hall, 2005).

52. L. Berkowitz and A. LePage, "Weapons as Aggression-Eliciting Stimuli," *Journal of Personality and Social Psychology* 7 (1967): 202–207; L. Berkowitz and K. Heimer, "On the Construction of the Anger Experience: Aversive Events and Negative Priming in the Formation of Feelings," in *Advances in Experimental Social Psychology*, ed. L. Berkowitz, Vol. 22 (New York: Academic Press, 1989); L. Berkowitz, "Guns and Youth," in *Reason to Hope: A Psychosocial Perspective on Violence and Youth*, eds. L. E. Eron, J. H. Gentry, and P. Schlegel (Washington, DC: American Psychological Foundation, 1994); L. Berkowitz, "Frustration-Aggression Hypothesis: Examination and Reformulation," *Psychological Bulletin* 106 (1989): 59–73; M. Carlson, A. Marcus-Newhall, and N. Miller, "Effects of Situational Aggression Cues: A Quantitative Review," *Journal of Personality and Social Psychology* 58 (1990): 622–633; R. W. Rogers and C. M. Ketcher, "Effects of Anonymity and Arousal on Aggression," *Journal of Psychology* 102 (1979): 13–19.

53. J. L. Truman, *Criminal Victimization, 2010*, NCJ 235508 (Bureau of Justice Statistics, U.S. Department of Justice, 2011).

54. See, for example, Elijah Anderson, *Code of the Street: Decency, Violence, and the Moral Life of the Inner City* (New York: W. W. Norton, 2000).

55. Raul Caetano, John Schafer, and Carol B. Cunradi, "Alcohol-Related Intimate Partner Violence Among White, Black, and Hispanic Couples in the United States," *Alcohol Research and Health* 25 (2001): 58–65.

56. Darnell F. Hawkins, "What Can We Learn From Data Disaggregation? The Case of Homicide and African Americans," in *Homicide: A Sourcebook of*

Social Research, eds. M. Dwayne Smith and Margaret A. Zahn (Thousand Oaks, CA: Sage, 1999).

57. Arnold S. Linsky, Ronet Bachman, and Murray A. Straus, eds., *Stress, Culture, and Aggression* (New Haven, CT: Yale University Press, 1995).

58. Niehoff, *The Biology of Violence*, 183.

59. Niehoff, *The Biology of Violence*, 185.

60. Niehoff, *The Biology of Violence*.

61. For a summary of this issue, see James Gilligan, *Preventing Violence* (New York: Thames and Hudson, 2001). See also Steven F. Messner and Richard Rosenfeld, "Social Structure and Homicide: Theory and Research," in Smith and Zahn, *Homicide*, 27–41.

62. Ching-Chi Hsieh and M. D. Pugh, "Poverty, Income Inequality, and Violent Crime," *Criminal Justice Review* 18 (1993):182–202.

63. Kirk R. Williams and Robert Flewelling, "The Social Production of Criminal Homicide: A Comparative Study of Disaggregated Rates in American Cities," *American Sociological Review* 54 (1988): 421–431.

64. Gilligan, *Preventing Violence*, 45.

65. Robert K. Merton, *Social Theory and Social Structure* (New York: Free Press, 1968).

66. Steven R. Messner and Richard Rosenfeld, "An Institutional-Anomie Theory of Crime," in *Explaining Criminals and Crime*, eds. Raymond Paternoster and Ronet Bachman (Los Angeles: Roxbury, 2001), 153; Steven F. Messner and Richard Rosenfeld, *Crime and the American Dream*, 4th ed. (Belmont, CA: Wadsworth, 2006).

67. Robert Agnew, "Foundation for a General Strain Theory of Crime and Delinquency," *Criminology* 30 (1992): 47–87.

68. Anderson, *Code of the Street*.

69. Anderson, *Code of the Street*, 92.

70. Albert Bandura, *Aggression: A Social Learning Analysis* (Englewood Cliffs, NJ: Prentice Hall, 1973); K. A. Dodge, J. E. Bates, and G. S. Pettit, "Mechanisms in the Cycle of Violence," *Science* 250 (1990): 1678–1682; L. D. Eron and others, "How Learning Conditions in Early Childhood—Including Mass Media—Relate to Aggression in Late Adolescence," *American Journal of Orthopsychiatry* 44 (1972): 412–413; L. D. Eron and others, "Aggression and Its Correlates Over 22 Years," in *Childhood Aggression and Violence*, eds. D. Crowell, I. Evans, and C. O'Donnell (New York: Plenum, 1987), 249–262; D. Hawkins and Y. Weis, "The Social Development Model: An Integrated Approach to Delinquency Prevention," *Journal of Primary Pediatrics* 6 (1985): 73–97; G. R. Patterson, "Performance Models for Antisocial Boys," *American Psychologist* 41 (1986): 432–444.

71. L. R. Huesmann, "An Information Processing Model for the Development of Aggression," *Aggressive Behavior* 14 (1988): 13–24.

72. Edwin H. Sutherland, *Criminology* (Philadelphia: Lippincott, 1947).

73. Ronald L. Akers and Adam L. Silverman, "Toward a Social Learning Model of Violence and Terrorism," in *Violence: From Theory to Research*, eds. Margaret A. Zahn, Henry H. Brownstein, and Shelly L. Jackson (New York: Lexis/Nexis, 2004), 19–50; Bartol and Bartol, *Criminal Behavior*.

74. Scott H. Decker and Barrik Van Winkle, *Life in the Gang: Family, Friends, and Violence* (New York: Cambridge University Press, 1996).

75. Quoted in Sanyika Shakur, *Monster: The Autobiography of an L.A. Gang Member* (New York: Penguin, 1993), 12.

76. Madeline Levine, *Viewing Violence: How Media Violence Affects Your Child's and Adolescent's Development* (New York: Doubleday, 1996).

77. Dave Grossman and Gloria DeGaetano, *Stop Teaching Our Kids to Kill: A Call to Action Against TV, Movie, and Video Game Violence* (New York: Crown, 1999), 23–24.

78. C. A. Anderson and others, "Violent video game effects on aggression, empathy, and prosocial behavior in Eastern and Western countries," *Psychological Bulletin* 136 (2010): 151–173.

79. Craig A. Anderson and Brad J. Bushman, "Human Aggression," *Annual Review of Psychology* 53 (2002): 27–51; Vincent B. Van Hasselt and Michel Hersen, *Aggression and Violence: An Introductory Text* (Boston: Allyn & Bacon, 2000).

80. L. R. Huesmann, "Psychological Processes Promoting the Relation Between Exposure to Media Violence and Aggressive Behavior by the Viewer," *Journal of Social Issues* 42 (1986): 125–140; L. R. Huesmann, "The Role of Social Information Processing and Cognitive Schema in the Acquisition and Maintenance of Habitual Aggressive Behavior," in *Human Aggression: Theories, Research, and Implications for Policy*, eds. R. G. Green and E. Donnerstein (New York: Academic Press, 1998), 73–109.

81. For a good discussion, see Gregg Barak, *Violence and Nonviolence: Pathways to Understanding* (Thousand Oaks, CA: Sage, 2003).

82. S. L. Smith and E. Donnerstein, "Harmful Effects of Exposure to Media Violence: Learning of Aggression, Emotional Desensitization, and Fear," in *Human Aggression: Theories, Research, and Implications for Policy*, eds. R. G. Green and E. Donnerstein (New York: Academic Press, 1998), 167–202.

83. Denise Kindschi Gosselin, *Heavy Hands: An Introduction to the Crimes of Family Violence*, 3rd ed. (Upper Saddle River, NJ: Pearson/Prentice Hall, 2005); Denise A. Hines and Kathleen Malley-Morrison, *Family Violence in the United States: Defining, Understanding, and Combating Abuse* (Thousand Oaks, CA: Sage, 2005); Kathleen Malley-Morrison

and Denise A. Hines, *Family Violence in a Cultural Perspective: Defining, Understanding, and Combating Abuse* (Thousand Oaks, CA: Sage, 2004).

84. C. S. Widom, "Child Abuse, Neglect, and Violent Criminal Behavior," *Criminology* 27 (1989): 251–271; C. S. Widom, "Does Violence Beget Violence? A Critical Examination of the Literature," *Psychological Bulletin* 106 (1989): 3–28.

85. Michael Gottfredson and Travis Hirschi, *A General Theory of Crime* (Stanford, CA: Stanford University Press, 1990), 97.

86. Robert J. Sampson and John H. Laub, *Crime in the Making: Pathways and Turning Points Through Life* (Cambridge, MA: Harvard University Press, 1993).

87. Solomon Asch, "Effects of Group Pressure Upon the Modification and Distortion of Judgements," in *Readings in Social Psychology*, eds. Guy Swanson, Theodore M. Newcomb, and Eugene L. Hartley (New York: Holt, Rinehart and Winston, 1952).

88. Charles Percy Snow, "Either–Or," *Progressive* (1961): 24.

89. For a good review, see Bartol and Bartol, *Criminal Behavior*.

90. Stanley Milgram, *Obedience to Authority* (New York: Harper Torchbooks, 1969).

91. R. Bachman and R. Schutt, *The Practice of Research in Criminology and Criminal Justice*, 2nd ed. (Thousand Oaks, CA: Sage, 2003).

92. Quoted in David Grossman, *On Killing: The Psychological Cost of Learning to Kill in War and Society* (Boston: Little, Brown, and Company, 1995).

93. Albert Bandura, "Moral Disengagement in the Perpetration of Inhumanities," *Personality and Social Psychology Review* 3 (1999): 193–209.

94. Bandura, "Moral Disengagement," 196.

95. Alex Alvarez, *Governments, Citizens, and Genocide: A Comparative and Interdisciplinary Analysis* (Bloomington: Indiana University Press, 2001).

96. Gustave Le Bon, *The Crowd: A Study of the Popular Mind* (London: Transaction Press, 1995), original work published in 1895.

97. In Tom Postmes, "Deindividuation." Retrieved from website at University of Exeter on February 12, 2006. www.ex.ac.uk/~tpostmes/deindividuation .html.

98. In James Waller, *Becoming Evil: How Ordinary People Commit Genocide and Mass Killing* (New York: Oxford University Press, 2002).

99. Philip G. Zimbardo, "The Human Choice: Individuation, Reason, and Order vs. Deindividuation, Impulse, and Chaos," in Nebraska Symposium on Motivation, eds. W. J. Arnold and D. Levine (Lincoln: University of Nebraska Press, 1969), 237–307.

100. Tom Postmes and Russell Spears, "Deindividuation and Antinormative Behavior: A Meta-Analysis," *Psychological Bulletin* 123 (1998): 238–259.

101. Christopher Browning, *Ordinary Men: Reserve Police Battalion 101 and the Final Solution in Poland* (New York: Aaron Asher, 1992).

102. Richard Holmes, *Acts of War: The Behavior of Men in Battle* (New York: Free Press, 1985).

Chapter 3

1. Richard A. Friedman, "In Gun Debate, a Misguided Focus on Mental Illness," *The New York Times,* December 17, 2012.

2. Craig A. Anderson, Leonard Berkowitz, Edward Donnerstein, L. Rowell Huesmann, James D. Johnson, Daniel Linz, Neil M. Malamuth, and Ellen Wartella, "The Influence of Media Violence on Youth," *Psychological Science in the Public Interest* 4, no. 3 (2003): 81–110, at 81.

3. Jennifer L. Truman, *Criminal Victimization, 2010,* NCJ 235508 (Washington, DC: U.S. Department of Justice, Bureau of Justice Statistics, 2011).

4. Craig Perkins, *Weapon Use and Violent Crime,* NCJ 194820 (Washington, DC: U.S. Department of Justice, Bureau of Justice Statistics, 2003).

5. Perkins, *Weapon Use and Violent Crime.*

6. The Associate Press, "Man Stabs 22 Children in China," *The New York Times,* December 14, 2012.

7. James Barron, "Children Were All Shot Multiple Times With Semiautomatic, Officials Say," *The New York Times,* December 15, 2012.

8. Franklin E. Zimring and Gordon Hawkins, *Crime Is Not the Problem: Lethal Violence in America* (New York: Oxford University Press, 1997).

9. Linda Saltzman, "Weapon Involvement and Injury Outcomes in Family and Intimate Assaults," *Journal of the American Medical Association* 267, no. 22 (1992): 3043–3047.

10. Alison K. Macpherson and Micheal J. Schull, "Penetrating Trauma in Ontario Emergency Departments: A Population Based Study," *Canadian Journal of Emergency Medicine* 9, no. 1 (2007): 16–20.

11. Marianne W. Zawitz, *Guns Used in Crime* (Washington, DC: U.S. Department of Justice, Bureau of Justice Statistics, 1995).

12. D. C. Reedy and C. S. Koper, "Impact of Handgun Types on Gun Assault Outcomes: A Comparison of Gun Assaults Involving Semiautomatic Pistols and Revolvers," *Injury Prevention* 9 (2003): 151–155.

13. Michael A. Bellesiles, *Arming America: The Origins of a National Gun Culture* (New York: Alfred A. Knopf, 2000), 5.

14. Gallup Organization, "Guns," www.galluppoll.com/content/Default.aspx?ci=1645&pg=1&t=dn9bE3n4Vpfqoduzgx-jWy52fOSCRqeHyDNtFzOL02H%2fqLgNEd-J19ppn04Sd4Jynhy3fBQUZQ9JWnhuCSILu55Ug54hwBt.YeP1dMoiGLYKge8cLLK3Tk00JHi8-Jz1YFWGIXE6dR4AnL%2fsvTG5sXAsOj00iWmvu.

15. Lydia Saad, "Self-Reported Gun Ownership in U.S. Is Highest Since 1993," The Gallup Poll, October 26, 2011, http://www.gallup.com/poll/150353/self-reported-gun-ownership-highest-1993.aspx.

16. Gallup Organization, "Americans and Guns: Danger or Defense?" www.galluppoll.com/content/?ci=14509&pg=1.

17. Phillip J. Cook, "Notes on the Availability and Prevalence of Firearms," American Journal of Preventive Medicine 9 (1993), 33–38.

18. The Guardian. DataBlog: Facts are sacred. Gun Homicides and Gun Ownership Listed by Country, http://www.guardian.co.uk/news/datablog/2012/jul/22/gun-homicides-ownership-world-list#data.

19. Joyce Lee Malcolm, "The Origins of an Anglo-American Right," in The Gun Control Debate, ed. Lee Nisbet (Amherst, NY: Prometheus Books, 2001).

20. Philip J. Cook, "The Effect of Gun Availability on Robbery and Robbery Murder: A Cross-Section Study of 50 Large Cities," in Policy Studies Review Annual, eds. Robert H. Haveman and B. Bruce Zellner (Beverly Hills, CA: Sage, 1979).

21. Gallup Organization, "Americans and Guns."

22. See Gary Kleck, Point Blank: Guns and Violence in America (New York: Aldine de Gruyter, 1991); John R. Lott Jr., More Guns, Less Crime (Chicago: University of Chicago Press, 2000).

23. Gary Kleck and Marc Gertz, "Armed Resistance to Crime: The Prevalence and Nature of Self-Defense with a Gun," in The Gun Control Debate: You Decide, 2nd ed., Lee Nisbet (Amherst, NY: Prometheus, 2001).

24. James D. Write and Peter H. Rossi, Armed and Considered Dangerous: A Survey of Felons and Their Firearms, 2nd ed. (Hawthorne, NY: Aldine de Gruyter, 1986).

25. Philip J. Cook and Mark H. Moore, "Guns, Gun Control and Homicide: A Review of Research and Public Policy," in Homicide: A Sourcebook of Social Research, eds. M. Dwayne Smith and Margaret A. Zahn (Thousand Oaks, CA: Sage, 1999).

26. Michael D. Shear, "Obama Vows Fast Action in New Push for Gun Control," The New York Times, December 19, 2012.

27. James B. Jacobs, Can Gun Control Work? (New York: Oxford University Press, 2002).

28. Jacobs, Can Gun Control Work? 24–26.

29. Jacobs, Can Gun Control Work?

30. Jacobs, Can Gun Control Work? 28.

31. Michael Bowling, Gene Lauver, Matthew J. Hickman, and Devon B. Adams, Background Checks for Firearm Transfers, 2004, NCJ 210117 (Washington, DC: U.S. Department of Justice, Bureau of Justice Statistics, 2005).

32. Gallup Organization, "Guns."

33. Jacobs, Can Gun Control Work? 49.

34. MSNBC.com, "Congress Lets Assault Weapons Ban Expire," www.msnbc.msn.com/id/5946127.

35. Jeffrey Jones, "Record-Low 26% in U.S. Favor Handgun Ban," The Gallup Poll, October 26, 2011, http://www.gallup.com/poll/150341/record-low-favor-handgun-ban.aspx.

36. Lydia Saad, "Self-Reported Gun Ownership in U.S. Is Highest Since 1993."

37. Pete Spotts, "Arizona Shooting: Rep. Gabrielle Giffords Hit at Meeting With Constituents," The Christian Science Monitor, January 8, 2001, http://www.csmonitor.com/USA/2011/0108/Arizona-shooting-Rep.-Gabrielle-Giffords-hit-at-meeting-with-constituents.

38. Marc Lacey and David M. Herszenhorn, "In Attack's Wake, Political Repercussions," The New York Times, January 8, 2011, http://www.nytimes.com/2011/01/09/us/politics/09giffords.html?pagewanted=all.

39. Aaron Blake, "Manchin-Toomey Gun Amendment Fails," The Washington Post, April 17, 2013, http://www.washingtonpost.com/blogs/post-politics/wp/2013/04/17/manchin-toomey-gun-amendment-fails/

40. Robert Nash Parker with Linda-Anne Rebhun, Alcohol and Homicide: A Deadly Combination of Two American Traditions (Albany, NY: State University of New York Press, 1995).

41. Marvin Wolfgang, Patterns of Criminal Homicide (Philadelphia: University of Pennsylvania Press, 1958).

42. H. L. Voss and J. R. Hepburn, "Patterns in Criminal Homicide in Chicago," Journal of Criminal Law, Criminology, and Police Science 59, no. 4 (1968): 499–508.

43. Lawrence Greenfeld, Alcohol and Crime, NCJ 168632 (Washington, DC: U.S. Department of Justice, Bureau of Justice Statistics, 1998).

44. Kai Pernanen, Alcohol in Human Violence (New York: Guilford Press, 1991).

45. Gary G. Forrest and Robert H. Gordon, Substance Abuse, Homicide, and Violent Behavior (New York: Gardner Press, 1990).

46. Parker with Rebhun, Alcohol and Homicide.

47. S. P. Taylor, "Aggressive Behavior and Physiological Arousal as a Function of Provocation and the Tendency to Inhibit Aggression," Journal of Personality 35 (1967): 297–310.

48. Brad J. Bushman and Harris M. Cooper, "Effects of Alcohol on Human Aggression: An Integrated Research Review," *Psychological Bulletin* 107, no. 3 (1990): 341–354.

49. Oscar Bukstein, David A. Brent, and Yifrah Kaminer, "Comorbidity of Substance Abuse and Other Psychiatric Disorders in Adolescents," *American Journal of Psychiatry* 146, no. 9 (1989): 1131–1141.

50. Robert Peralta, "Getting Trashed in College: Doing Alcohol, Doing Gender, Doing Violence," *Dissertation Abstracts International, A: The Humanities and Social Sciences* 63, no. 1 (2002): 368–A.

51. Kathryn Graham and Samantha Wells, "Somebody's Gonna Get Their Head Kicked in Tonight!" *British Journal of Criminology* 43 (2003): 546–566.

52. Parker with Rebhun, *Alcohol and Homicide.*

53. Craig MacAndrew and Robert Edgerton, *Drunken Comportment: A Social Explanation* (London: Thomas Nelson, 1969).

54. Jennifer C. Karberg and Doris James, *Substance Dependence Abuse, and Treatment of Jail Inmates, 2002.* NCJ 209588 (Washington, DC: U.S. Department of Justice, Bureau of Justice Statistics, 2002).

55. The percentages are not just for those involved in violent offenses but include all offenses including the sale and use of drugs.

56. Bureau of Justice Statistics, *Drugs and Crime Facts,* NCJ 154043 (Washington, DC: U.S. Department of Justice, 1994).

57. James Inciardi, Hilary Surratt, Dal Chitwood, and Clyde McCoy, "The Origins of Crack," in *The American Pipe Dream,* eds. Dale Chitwood, James Rivers, and James Inciardi (Philadelphia, PA: Harcourt Brace, 1996).

58. Jeffrey Fagan and Ko-lin Chin, "Social Processes of Initiation into Crack," *Journal of Drug Issues* 21 (1991): 313–343.

59. Margaret Leigey and Ronet Bachman, "The Influence of Crack Cocaine on the Likelihood of Incarceration for a Violent Offense: An Examination of a Prison Sample," *Criminal Justice Policy Review* 18 (2007): 1–18.

60. For a review, see Parker with Rebhun, *Alcohol and Homicide.*

61. Henry H. Brownstein, *The Social Reality of Violence and Violent Crime* (Boston: Allyn & Bacon, 2000).

62. Dennis M. Donovan, "Assessment of Addictive Behaviors: Implications of an Emerging Biophysical Model," in *Assessment of Addictive Behaviors,* eds. D. M. Donovan and G. A. Marlatt (New York: Guilford Press, 1988), 6.

63. Bureau of Justice Statistics, *Fact Sheet: Drug-Related Crime,* NCJ 149286 (Washington, DC: U.S. Department of Justice, 1994).

64. R. Barri Flowers, *Drugs, Alcohol, and Criminality in American Society* (Jefferson, NC: McFarland & Company, 1999).

65. Bureau of Justice Statistics, *Drugs and Crime Facts,* NCJ 154043.

66. Hope Corman, Theodore Joyce, and Naci Mocan, "Homicide and Crack in New York City," in *Searching for Alternatives: Drug-Control Policy in the United States,* eds. Melvyn B. Krauss and Edward P. Lazear (Stanford, CA: Hoover Institution Press, 1991).

67. Jim A. Inciardi, *The War on Drugs II* (Mountain View, CA: Mayfield, 1992).

68. United States Archives, *The Constitution of the United States,* Amendments 11–18, www.archives.gov/national-archives-experience/charters/constitution_amendments_ 11–27.html#18.

69. Lana D. Harrison, Michael Backenheimer, and James A. Inciardi, "Cannabis Use in the United States: Implications for Policy," in *Cannabisbeleid in Duitsland, Frankrijk en de Verenigde Staten,* eds. Peter Cohen and Arjan Sas (Amsterdam: Centrum voor Drugsonderzoek, Universiteit van Amsterdam, 1996), 237–247.

70. Richard J. Bonnie and Charles H. Whitebread, "The Forbidden Fruit and the Tree of Knowledge: An Inquiry into the Legal History of American Marijuana Prohibition," *Virginia Law Review* 56, no. 6 (1970), www.druglibrary.org/schaffer/Library/studies/vlr/vlrtoc.htm.

71. Jonathan Eig, "The St. Valentine's Day Massacre—Excerpt from 'Get Capone,' by Jonathan Eig," Chicago Mag.Com, http://www.chicagomag.com/Chicago-Magazine/May-2010/Get-Capone-St-Valentines-Day-Massacre-Jonathan-Eig/.

72. United States Archives, *The Constitution of the United States,* Amendments 11–18.

73. Harrison, Backenheimer, and Inciardi, "Cannabis Use in the United States."

74. Paige Harrison and Allen Beck, *Prisoners in 2004,* NCJ 210677 (U.S. Department of Justice, Bureau of Justice Statistics, 2005).

75. Steven R. Donziger, *The Real War on Crime: The Report of the National Criminal Justice Commission* (New York: Harper Perennial, 1996), 115.

76. John Schwarts, "Drug Terms Reduced, Freeing Prisoners," *The New York Times,* November 1, 2011.

77. The National Institute of Drug Abuse, "Prescription Drugs," www.nida.nih.gov/DrugPages/Prescription.html.

78. Gallup Organization, "Drugs, Smoking, Alcohol Most Important Problem Facing Teens," www.galluppoll.com/content/?ci=21517&pg=1.

79. American Academy of Child and Adolescent Psychiatry, "Children and TV Violence," www.aacap.org/page.ww?section=Facts+for+Families&name=Children+And+TV.

80. T. L. Dietz, "An Examination of Violence and Gender Role Portrayals in Video Games: Implications for Gender Socialization and Aggressive Behavior," *Sex Roles* 38 (1998): 425–442.

81. S. J. Kirsh, *Children, Adolescents, and Media Violence: A Critical Look at the Research*, 2nd ed. (Thousand Oaks, CA.: Sage, 2012).

82. Albert Bandura, *Social Learning Theory* (Englewood Cliffs, NJ: Prentice Hall, 1977).

83. Craig A. Anderson and Rowell L. Huesmann, "Human Aggression: A Social-Cognitive View," in *Handbook of Social Psychology*, eds. M. A. Hogg and J. Cooper (Thousand Oaks, CA: Sage, 2003), 296–323.

84. Dolf Zillmann, "Excitation Transfer in Communication-Mediated Aggressive Behavior," *Journal of Experimental Psychology* 7 (1971): 419–434.

85. Anderson, Berkowitz, Donnerstein, and others, "The Influence of Media Violence on Youth."

86. See for example K. Boyle, *Media and Violence* (London: Sage, 2005), D. Buckinham, *Moving Images: Understanding Children's Emotional Responses to Television* (Manchester: Manchester University Press); A. Hill, *Shocking Entertainment: Viewer Responses to Violent Movies* (Luton: University of Luton Press).

87. Anderson, Berkowitz, Donnerstein, and others, "The Influence of Media Violence on Youth," 86.

88. L. R. Huesmann, J. Moise-Titus, C. L. Podolski, and L. Eron, "Longitudinal Relations Between Children's Exposure to TV Violence and Their Aggressive and Violent Behavior in Young Adulthood, 1977–1992," *Developmental Psychology* 39 (2003): 201–221.

89. Teena Willoughby, Paul J. C. Adachi, and Marie Good, "A Longitudinal Study of the Association Between Violent Video Game Play and Aggression Among Adolescents," *Developmental Psychology* 48, no. 4, 1044–1057.

90. Rene Weber, Klaus Mathiak, and Ute Ritterfeld, "Violent Video Games: Aggressive Thoughts?" (United Press International, 2005), www.physorg.com/printnews.php?newsid= 7168.

91. Jonathan L. Freedman, *Media Violence and Its Effect on Aggression: Assessing the Scientific Evidence* (Toronto: University of Toronto Press, 2002).

92. A. I. Nathanson, "Identifying and Explaining the Relationship Between Parental Mediation and Children's Aggression," *Communication Research* 26, no. 2 (1999): 124–143.

93. David M. Kennedy, Anne M. Piehl, and Anthony A. Braga, "Youth Violence in Boston: Gun Markets, Serious Youth Offenders, and a Use-Reduction Strategy," *Law and Contemporary Problems* 59 (2000): 147–196.

Chapter 4

1. Daniel Webster. Downloaded from http://thinkexist.com/quotation/every_unpunished_murder_ takes_away_something_from/164737.html

2. Terance D. Miethe and Wendy C. Regoeczi, *Rethinking Homicide: Exploring the Structure and Process Underlying Deadly Situations* (New York: Cambridge University Press, 2004), 259.

3. Kim Egger, "Motives for Murder," in *Encyclopedia of Murder and Violent Crime*, ed. Eric Hickey (Thousand Oaks, CA: Sage, 2003), 317.

4. CNN.com, "Teens Accused of Killing Homeless Man 'for Fun.'" Downloaded June 6, 2005, from www.cnn.com/2007/US/03/30/homeless.attack/index.html

5. L. W. Kennedy and D. R. Forde, *When Push Comes to Shove: A Routine Conflict Approach to Violence* (Albany: State University of New York Press, 1999), 7.

6. Bureau of Justice Statistics, *Criminal Victimization in the United States, 2003*, Statistical Tables, Methodology, www.ojp.usdoj.gov/bjs/pub/pdf/cvus03.pdf.

7. Federal Bureau of Investigation (FBI), *Crime in the United States, 2004*, www.fbi.gov/ucr/cius_04/offenses_reported/violent_crime/aggravated_assault.html.

8. J. L. Truman and M. Planty, *Criminal Victimization, 2011* (U.S. Department of Justice: Bureau of Justice Statistics, 2012).

9. J. L. Truman and M. Planty, *Criminal Victimization, 2011.*

10. J. L. Truman, *Criminal Victimization, 2010.* (U.S. Department of Justice: Bureau of Justice Statistics, 2011).

11. NCVS analytic tool calculating percent of simple and aggravated assaults in which offender had weapon.

12. E. Harrell, "Violent Victimization Committed by Strangers, 1993–2010" (U.S. Department of Justice: Bureau of Justice Statistics) , Table 10.

13. J. Lofland, *Deviance and Identity* (Englewood Cliffs, NJ: Prentice Hall, 1969).

14. Miethe and Regoeczi, *Rethinking Homicide*, 273.

15. Monica Davey, "Rate of Killings Rises 38 Percent in Chicago in 2012," *The New York Times*, June 25, 2012.

16. United Nations, *Demographic Yearbook, 1994* (New York: United Nations, 1996).

17. The World Health Organization, "*World Report on Violence and Health*" (Geneva: WHO, 2002).

18. Miethe and Regoeczi, *Rethinking Homicide*, 27.

19. S. H. Decker, "Deviant Homicide: A New Look at the Role of Motives and Victim–Offender Relationships," *Journal of Research in Crime and Delinquency* 333 (1996): 427–449; T. D. Miethe and K. A. Drass, "Exploring the Social Context of Instrumental and Expressive Homicides: An Application of Qualitative Comparative Analysis," *Journal of Quantitative Criminology* 15 (1999): 1–21.

20. D. F. Luckenbill, "Criminal Homicides as Situated Transaction," *Social Problems* 25 (1977): 176–186.

21. M. Wolfgang, *Patterns of Criminal Homicide* (Philadelphia: University of Pennsylvania Press, 1958).

22. K. Polk, *When Men Kill: Scenarios of Masculine Violence* (Cambridge, UK: Cambridge University Press, 1994).

23. M. Wilson and M. Daly, "Competitiveness, Risk-Taking, and Violence: The Young Male Syndrome," *Ethology and Sociobiology* 6 (1985): 59–73.

24. J. Gilligan, *Our Deadly Epidemic and its Causes* (New York: Grosset/Putnam, 1996), 97.

25. K. D. Harries, *Serious Violence* (Springfield, IL: Charles C. Thomas, 1990).

26. J. A. Fox and M. W. Zawitz, "Homicide Trends in the United States. Multiple Victims and Offenders," www.ojp.usdoj.gov/bjs/homicide/tables/multipletab.htm.

27. J. Douglas and M. Olshaker, *The Anatomy of Motive* (New York: Lisa Drew, 1999). Also see A. Alvarez and R. Bachman, *Murder American Style* (New York: McGraw Hill, 2003).

28. Gary Lavergne, *A Sniper in the Tower: The Charles Whitman Murders* (Denton, TX: University of North Texas Press, 1997).

29. Douglas and Olshaker, *The Anatomy of Motive.*

30. Barry Glasner, *The Culture of Fear* (New York: Basic Books, 1999).

31. "Woman Kills 5, Self at Postage Plant," www.usatoday.com/news/ nation/2006–01–31-postal-shooting_x.htm?POE=NEWISVA.

32. "Lockheed Workplace Shootings Targeted Blacks," http://abcnews .go.com/Primetime/story?id=749286&page=1.

33. Quoted in S. Anthony Baron, *Violence in the Workplace: A Prevention and Management Guide for Businesses* (Ventura, CA: Pathfinder Publishing of California, 1993), 12.

34. "Workplace Fatalities," www.bls.gov/news.release/cfoi.t01.htm.

35. G. Warchol, *Workplace Violence, 1992–1996,* NCJ 168634 (Washington, DC: U.S. Department of Justice, Bureau of Justice Statistics, 1998).

36. F. Steel, "Calm Before the Storm: The Littleton School Massacre," www.crimelibrary.com/seria114/littleton/index.htm.

37. "Newtown, Conn., School Shootings (Adam Lanza)," *The New York Times,* Times Topic. Downloaded on January 10, 2012, from http://topics. nytimes.com/top/reference/timestopics/subjects/s/school_shootings/index.html?8qa

38. "School Gunman Stole Police Pistol, Vest," www.cnn.com/2005/US/03/22/school.shooting/index.html.

39. J. A. Fox and J. Levin, *The Will to Kill: Making Sense of Senseless Murder* (Boston: Allyn & Bacon, 2001), 44.

40. National Center for Education Statistics, *Indicators of School Crime and Safety, 2011* (Washington, DC: U.S. Department of Education and U.S. Department of Justice, Bureau of Justice Statistics, 2011).

41. National Center for Education Statistics, *Indicators of School Crime and Safety, 2011.*

42. A series of articles from the *Wichita Eagle* including "BTK Stranger," www.kansas.com/mld/kansas/11000748.htm.

43. Stories from the *Wichita Eagle*, and CNN, including "BTK Took Body to Church," www.cnn .com/2005/LAW/08/18/btk.killings.wed/index.html.

44. "BTK Sentenced to 10 Life Terms," www .cnn.com/2005/LAW/08/ 18/btk.killings/index.html.

45. Douglas and Olshaker, *The Anatomy of Motive,* 190–191.

46. S. Egger, *The Killers Among Us: An Examination of Serial Murder and Its Investigation* (Upper Saddle River, NJ: Prentice Hall, 1990).

47. E. W. Hickey, *Serial Murderers and Their Victims,* 2nd ed., Wadsworth Contemporary Issues in Crime and Justice (Belmont, CA: Wadsworth, 1997).

48. Benjamin Weiser, "Convictions Reinstated in Mob Case," *The New York Times, September 18, 2008.*

49. Egger, *The Killers Among Us,* 180.

50. "The Green River Killer," http://seattle-times.nwsource.com/ html/greenriverkillings.

51. For a review, see Egger, *The Killers Among Us.*

52. R. M. Holmes and S. T. Holmes, *Serial Murder* (Thousand Oaks, CA: Sage, 1998).

53. "All About Genene Jones," www.crimelibrary .com/notorious_ murders/angels/genene_jones/4 .html.

54. Tomas Guillen, *Serial Killers: Issues Explored Through the Green River Murders* (Upper Saddle River, NJ: Pearson/Prentice Hall, 2007), 15.

55. Guillen, *Serial Killers,* 19.

56. J. A. Fox and J. Levin, "Serial Murder: Myths and Empirical Realities," in *Homicide: A Sourcebook of Social Research,* eds. D. M. Smith and M. A. Zahn (Thousand Oaks, CA: Sage, 1999), 168.

57. The terms "psychopath" and "sociopath" were replaced in the third edition of the *Diagnostic and Statistical Manual of Mental Disorders (DSM-III)* with the term "anti-social personality disorder." American Psychiatric Association (APA), *Diagnostic and Statistical Manual of Mental Disorders (DSM-IV)*, 4th ed. (Washington, DC: American Psychiatric Association).

58. R. I. Simon, *Bad Men Do What Good Men Dream: A Forensic Psychiatrist Illuminates the Darker Side of Human Behavior* (Washington, DC: American Psychiatric Press, 1996).

59. "John Wayne Gacy," www.crimelibrary.com/serial/gacy/ gacymain.htm.

60. C. S. Widom, "Does Violence Beget Violence? A Critical Examination of the Literature," *Psychological Bulletin* 106, no. 1 (1989): 3–28.

61. Douglas and Olshaker, *The Anatomy of Motive*, 40.

62. Alvarez and Bachman, *Murder American Style*.

63. Beltway sniper attacks information obtained from a series of articles. Downloaded March 15, 2006, from the *Washington Post* at www.washingtonpost.com/wp-dyn/metro/specials/shootings/2002.

64. Tracy L. Snell, *Capital Punishment, 2010—Statistical Tables* (U.S. Department of Justice: Bureau of Justice Statistics, 2011).

65. There were actually several plaintiffs in the case, including *Gregg v. Georgia, Proffitt v. Florida, Jurek v. Texas, Woodson v. North Carolina*, and *Roberts v. Louisiana*, 428 U.S. 153 (1976).

66. Snell, *Capital Punishment*, 2005.

67. T. Sellin, *The Death Penalty* (Philadelphia: The American Law Institute, 1959).

68. R. D. Peterson and W. C. Bailey, "Is Capital Punishment an Effective Deterrent for Murder? An Examination of Social Science Research," in *America's Experiment With the Death Penalty*, eds. J. R. Acker, R. M. Bohm, and C. S. Lanier (Durham, NC: Carolina Academic Press, 2003), 251–282.

69. R. Berk, "New Claims About Executions and General Deterrence: Déjà Vu All Over Again," *Journal of Empirical Legal Studies* 2 (2005): 303–330 at 330.

70. R. Paternoster, *Capital Punishment in America* (New York: Lexington Books, 1991).

71. R. Paternoster, R. Brame, S. Bacon, and A. Ditchfield, "Justice by Geography and Race: The Administration of the Death Penalty in Maryland, 1978–1999," *Margins* 1 (2004): 1–98.

72. Northwestern University News Release, www.northwestern.edu/univ-relations/media_relations/releases/12_2002/deathrow.html.

73. M. Weisenmiller, "Exonerated, Florida Death Row Inmate Tells His Tale," Common Dreams News Center, www.commondreams.org/headlines06/0804–07.htm

74. CNN.com, "Illinois Suspends Death Penalty: Governor Calls for Review of Flawed System," www.cnn.com/2000/US/01/31/illinois.executions.02/index.html.

75. The Death Penalty Information Center, *The Death Penalty In Flux*, http://www.deathpenaltyinfo.org/death-penalty-flux.

76. Paternoster, *Capital Punishment in America*, 285.

Chapter 5

1. Study from World Health Organization, www.who.int/gender/ violence/multicountry/en.

2. Stories from survivors at the Family Violence Prevention Fund's website at www.endabuse.org/ programs/display.php3?DocID=100120.

3. www.cdc.gov/ncipc/factsheets/ipvoverview.htm.

4. P. Tjaden and N. Thoennes, *Prevalence, Incidence, and Consequences of Violence Against Women: Findings From the National Violence Against Women Survey*, NCJ 172837 (Washington, DC: U.S. Department of Justice, National Institute of Justice and U.S. Department of Health and Human Services, Centers for Disease Control and Prevention, 1998).

5. Neil Websdale, *Understanding Domestic Homicide* (Boston: Northeastern University Press, 1999).

6. The state-level analysis was reported by A. Browne and K. R. Williams, "Exploring the Effect of Resource Availability and the Likelihood of Female-Perpetrated Homicides," *Law and Society Review* 23 (1989): 75–94. The city-level analysis was reported by L. Dugan, D. Nagin, and R. Rosenfeld, "Explaining the Decline in Intimate Partner Homicide: The Effects of Changing Domesticity, Women's Status, and Domestic Violence Resources," *Homicide Studies* 3 (1999): 187–214.

7. S. Catalano, *Intimate Partner Violence, 1993–2010* (Washington, DC: Bureau of Justice Statistics, U.S. Department of Justice, 2012).

8. M. Straus and R. Gelles, *Physical Violence in American Families: Risk Factors and Adaptations to Violence in 8,145 Families* (New Brunswick, NJ: Transaction Press, 1990).

9. W. DeKeseredy and M. Schwartz, "Measuring the Extent of Woman Abuse in Intimate Heterosexual Relationships: A Critique of the Conflict Tactics Scales," U.S. Department of Justice-sponsored VAW.net at www.vaw.umn.edu/Vawnet/ctscritique.htm.

10. Straus and Gelles, *Physical Violence in American Families*.

11. DeKeseredy and Schwartz, "Measuring the Extent of Woman Abuse in Intimate Heterosexual Relationships."

12. If you take 1% of the total female population aged 12 and over as published by the U.S. Census Bureau to be 117,989,375. Estimate obtained at www.census.gov/population/cen2000/phc-t9/tab03.pdf.

13. S. Catalano, *Intimate Partner Violence, 1993–2010.*

14. Tjaden and Thoennes, *Prevalence, Incidence, and Consequences of Violence Against Women.*

15. M. C. Black and others, "The National Intimate Partner and Sexual Violence Survey: 2010 Summary Report," National Center for Injury Prevention and Control of the Centers for Disease Control and Prevention.

16. R. Bachman, "A Comparison of Estimates of Violence Against Women From the NCVS and the NVAWMS," *Violence Against Women* 6 (2000): 839–867.

17. D. K. Gosselin, *Heavy Hands* (Upper Saddle River, NJ: Prentice Hall, 2005).

18. S. Brownmiller, *Against Our Will: Men, Women, and Rape* (New York: Simon and Schuster, 1975); D. Russell, *The Politics of Rape: The Victim's Perspective* (New York: Stein and Day, 1975).

19. R. E. Dobash and R. P. Dobash, "Violent Men and Violent Contexts," in *Rethinking Violence Against Women,* eds. R. E. Dobash and R. P. Dobash (Thousand Oaks, CA: Sage, 1998), 141–168 at 153.

20. Janice Ristock, *No More Secrets: Violence in Lesbian Relationships* (New York: Routledge, 2002).

21. C. S. Greenblat, "Don't Hit Your Wife . . . Unless: Preliminary Findings on Normative Support for the Use of Physical Force by Husbands," *Victimology* 10 (1985): 221–241.

22. C. S. Widom, "Child Abuse, Neglect, and Violent Criminal Behavior," *Criminology* 27 (1989): 251–271; C. S. Widom, "Does Violence Beget Violence? A Critical Examination of the Literature," *Psychological Bulletin* 106 (1989): 3–28.

23. Callie Marie Rennison and Sarah Welchans, *Intimate Partner Violence*, Special Report, NCJ 197838 (Washington, DC: U.S. Department of Justice, Office of Justice Programs, Bureau of Justice Statistics, 2000), www.ojp.usdoj.gov/bjs/abstract/ipv.htm.

24. Denise A. Hines and Kathleen Malley-Morrison, *Family Violence in the United States: Defining, Understanding, and Combating Abuse* (Thousand Oaks, CA: Sage, 2005).

25. L. Coker and others, "Physical and Mental Health Effects of Intimate Violence for Men and Women," *American Journal of Preventive Medicine* 223 (2002): 260–268.

26. Raul Caetano, John Schafer, and Carol B. Cunradi, "Alcohol-Related Intimate Partner Violence Among White, Black, and Hispanic Couples in the United States," *Alcohol Research and Health* 25 (2001): 58–65.

27. N. A. Crowell and A. W. Burgess, *Understanding Violence Against Women* (Washington, DC: National Academy Press, 1996).

28. G. K. Kantor, "Refining the Brushstrokes in Portraits on Alcohol and Wife Assaults," in *Alcohol and Interpersonal Violence: Fostering Multidisciplinary Perspectives*, NIAA Monograph 24, NIH Publication No. 93–3496 (Rockville, MD: National Institute on Alcohol Abuse and Alcoholism, 1993), 281–290.

29. E. S. Buzawa and C. G. Buzawa, *Domestic Violence: The Criminal Justice Response* (Thousand Oaks, CA: Sage, 2003).

30. The Violence Against Women and Department of Justice Reauthorization Act of 2005, H. R. 3402.

31. Statement by Attorney General Eric Holder on the House passage of the Reauthorization of the Violence Against Women Act, http://www.justice.gov/opa/pr/2013/February/13-ag-253.html.

32. L. W. Sherman and R. A. Berk, "The Specific Deterrent Effects of Arrest for Domestic Assault," *American Sociological Review* 49 (1984): 261–272.

33. J. Zorza, "Symposium on Domestic Violence: Criminal Law: The Criminal Law of Misdemeanor Domestic Violence, 1970–1990," *Journal of Criminal Law and Criminology* 83 (1992): 46–72.

34. L. G. Mills, "Mandatory Arrest and Prosecution Policies for Domestic Violence: A Critical Literature Review and the Call for More Research to Test Victim Empowerment Approaches," *Criminal Justice and Behavior* 25 (1998): 306–318.

35. J. Garner, J. Fagan, and C. Maxwell, "Published Findings from the Spousal Assault Replication Program: A Critical Review," *Journal of Quantitative Criminology* 11 (1995): 3–28.

36. R. Paternoster and others, "Do Fair Procedures Matter? The Deterrent Effect of Procedural Justice on Spouse Assault," *Law and Society Review* 31, no. 1 (1997): 163–204.

37. D. A. Ford and M. J. Regoli, "The Criminal Prosecution of Wife Assaulters: Process, Problems, and Effects," in *Legal Responses to Wife Assault: Current Trends and Evaluation,* ed. N. Zoe Hilton (Newbury Park, CA: Sage, 1993), 127–164.

38. Mills, "Mandatory Arrest and Prosecution Policies for Domestic Violence," 317.

39. Ford and Regoli, "The Criminal Prosecution of Wife Assaulters."

40. D. G. Saunders, "The Tendency to Arrest Victims of Domestic Violence: A Preliminary Analysis of Officer Characteristics," *Journal of Interpersonal Violence* 10 (1995): 147–158.

41. L. K. Hamberger and R. Potente, "Counseling Heterosexual Women Arrested for Domestic

Violence: Implications for Theory and Practice," *Violence and Victims* 9 (1994): 125–137.

42. Saunders, "The Tendency to Arrest Victims of Domestic Violence," 148.

43. S. I. Mignon and W. M. Holmes, "Police Response to Mandatory Arrest Laws," *Crime and Delinquency* 41 (1995): 430–442.

44. Mills, "Mandatory Arrest and Prosecution Policies for Domestic Violence," 316.

45. K. Kinports and K. Fischer, "Orders of Protection in Domestic Violence Cases: An Empirical Assessment of the Impact of the Reform Statutes," *Texas Journal of Women and the Law* 2 (1993): 163–275.

46. A. Harrell, B. Smith and L. Newmark, *Court Processing and the Effects of Restraining Orders for Domestic Violence Victims* (Washington, DC: The Urban Institute, 1993).

47. Harrell, Smith, and Newmark, *Court Processing and the Effects of Restraining Orders for Domestic Violence Victims*.

48. Harrell, Smith, and Newmark, *Court Processing and the Effects of Restraining Orders for Domestic Violence Victims*.

49. Kinports and Fischer, "Orders of Protection in Domestic Violence Cases," 172.

50. Harrell, Smith, and Newmark, *Court Processing and the Effects of Restraining Orders for Domestic Violence Victims*; Kinports & Fischer, "Orders of Protection in Domestic Violence Cases"; see also M. Chaudhuri and J. Daly, "Do Restraining Orders Help? Battered Women's Experience With Male Violence and the Legal Process," in *Domestic Violence: The Changing Criminal Justice Response*, eds. E. S. Buzawa and C. G. Buzawa (Westport, CT: Auburn House, 1992).

51. For further information see the National Domestic Violence Fatality Review Initiative website at ndvfri.org.

52. J. C. McClennen, A. B. Summers, and J. G. Daley, "The Lesbian Partner Abuse Scale," *Research on Social Work Practice* 12 (2002): 277–292; S. C. Turell, "A Descriptive Analysis of Same-Sex Relationship Violence for a Diverse Sample," *Journal of Family Violence* 15 (2000): 281–293.

53. C. M. Renzetti, *Violent Betrayal: Partner Abuse in Lesbian Relationships* (Thousand Oaks, CA: Sage, 1992).

54. Tjaden and Thoennes, *Stalking in America*.

55. M. C. Black and others, *The National Intimate Partner and Sexual Violence Survey: 2010, Summary Report* (Washington, DC: National Center for Injury Prevention and Control of the Centers for Disease Control and Prevention, 2011).

56. W. R. Cupach and B. H. Spitzberg, *The Dark Side of Relationship Pursuit: From Attraction to Obsession to Stalking* (Mahwah, NJ: Lawrence Erlebaum, 2004).

57. Tjaden and Thoennes, *Stalking in America*.

58. See for example K. Baum, S. Catalano, M. Rand, and K. Rose, *Stalking Victimization in the United States* (Washington, DC: Bureau of Justice Programs, U.S. Department of Justice, 2009); B. F. Fisher, F. T. Cullen, and M. G. Turner, *The Sexual Victimization of College Women* (Washington, DC: National Institute of Justice, NIJ number 182369).

59. S. Catalano, *Stalking Victims in the United States—Revised* (Washington, DC: The Bureau of Justice Statistics, U.S. Department of Justice, 2012).

60. J. R. Meloy and C. Boyd. "Female Stalkers and Their Victims," *Journal of the American Academy of Psychiatry and the Law* 31 (2003): 211–219; M. P. Brewster, "Trauma Symptoms of Former Intimate Stalking Victims," *Women and Criminal Justice* 13 (2002): 141–161.

61. M. P. Brewster, "Power and Control Dynamics in Prestalking and Stalking Situations," *Journal of Family Violence* 18, no. 4 (2003): 207–217.

62. Quoted in M. P. Brewster, "Power and Control Dynamics," 214.

63. See California Penal Code, section 646.9 (West Supp. 1996).

64. E. Goode, "Suburb's Veneer Cracks: Mother is Held in Deaths," *The New York Times,* March 2011.

65. The exact code states, "A child may not be subjected to physical punishment or other injurious or humiliating treatment," Parenthood and Guardianship Code, Sweden, 1979. From S. L. Bloom and M. Reichert, eds. *Bearing Witness: Violence and Collective Responsibility,* (New York: Haworth Press, 1998).

66. Bureau of Justice Statistics, *Homicide Trends in the U.S.: Infanticide,* www.ojp.usdoj.gov/bjs/homicide/tables/kidsratestab.htm.

67. B. A. Wauchope and M. A. Straus, "Physical Punishment and Physical Abuse of American Children: Incidence Rates by Age, Gender, and Occupational Class," in *Physical Violence in American Families*, eds. M. A. Straus and R. J. Gelles (New Brunswick, NJ: Transaction Press, 1990).

68. Wauchope and Straus, "Physical Punishment and Physical Abuse of American Children," 137.

69. U.S. Department of Health and Human Services, National Center on Child Abuse and Neglect, *Child Maltreatment 2001: Reports from the States to the National Center on Child Abuse and Neglect* (Washington, DC: U.S. Government Printing Office, 2003).

70. C. Crosson-Tower, *Understanding Child Abuse and Neglect*, 6th ed. (Boston: Allyn & Bacon, 2005).

71. Crosson-Tower, *Understanding Child Abuse and Neglect*.

72. Public Law 96–272.

73. M. S. Lachs and K. Pillemer, "Elder Abuse," *The Lancet* 364 (2004): 1263–1267.

74. R. Bonnie and R. Wallace, eds., *Elder Abuse: Abuse, Neglect, and Exploitation in an Aging America* (Washington, DC: National Academy of Sciences Press, 2000).

75. Lachs and Pillemer, "Elder Abuse."

76. www.elderabusecenter.org/default.cfm?p=elderjustice.cfm.

77. See the Center for Elder Abuse and Neglect website at www.elderabuse.org.

Chapter 6

1. The President's Commission on Law Enforcement and Administration of Justice, *The Challenge of Crime in a Free Society* (Washington, DC: U.S. Government Printing Office, 1967), 51.

2. Dina Temple-Raston, *A Death in Texas* (New York: Henry Holt and Company, 2002), 18.

3. R. T. Wright and S. H. Decker, *Armed Robbers in Action: Stickups and Street Culture* (Boston: Northeastern University Press, 1997), 43.

4. M. Wolfgang, *Patterns of Criminal Homicide* (Philadelphia: University of Pennsylvania Press, 1958).

5. Erika Harrell, "Violent Victimization Committed by Strangers, 1993–2010 (Washington DC: BJS, U.S. Department of Justice, 2012).

6. "Robin Hood," www.en.wikipedia.org/wiki/Robin_Hood.

7. M. J. Valencia, "Local News," *The Telegram & Gazette*, February 2, 2006, B1.

8. Charles Wilson, "Police: 7 Killed in Indianapolis Home," The Associated Press, www.washingtonpost.com/wp-dyn/content/article/2006/06/06/AR2006060200176_pf

9. A. Cooper and Erica Smith, *Homicide Trends in the United States, 1980–2008; Annual Rates for 2009 and 2010* (Washington, DC: Bureau of Justice Statistics, U.S. Department of Justice, 2011).

10. John E. Conklin, *Robbery and the Criminal Justice System* (Philadelphia, PA: J. B. Lippincott, 1972), 5.

11. Bureau of Justice Statistics, *Sourcebook of Criminal Justice Statistics, 2003* (Washington, DC: U.S. Department of Justice, 2004).

12. Jennifer Truman and Michael Planty, *Criminal Victimization, 2011* (Washington, DC: Bureau of Justice Statistics, U.S. Department of Justice, 2012).

13. Robbery rates for these conclusions were based on NCVS statistical tables for the NCVS, 2008, NCJ 227669 (Bureau of Justice Statistics, U.S. Department of Justice, 2010).

14. Ronet Bachman, Mark Lachs, and Michelle Meloy, "Reducing Injury Through Self-Protection by Elderly Victims of Violence: The Interaction Effects of Gender of Victim and the Victim/Offender Relationship," *Journal of Elder Abuse and Neglect* 16, no. 4 (2005): 1–24.

15. S. M. Catalano, *Criminal Victimization, 2005* (Washington, DC: Bureau of Justice Statistics, U.S. Department of Justice, 2006).

16. Robbery rates for these conclusions were based on NCVS statistical tables for the NCVS, 2008, NCJ 227669.

17. Robbery data for these conclusions were based on NCVS statistical tables for the NCVS, 2008, NCJ 227669.

18. Robbery data for these conclusions were based on NCVS statistical tables for the NCVS, 2008, NCJ 227669.

19. Roger Matthews, *Armed Robbery* (Cullompton, Devon, UK: Willan, 2002).

20. Wright and Decker employed a snowball sampling procedure, first making contact with four active robbers from another study, having them introduce the researchers to other robbers, who in turn were asked to refer others, and so on. For more details on the methodology, see Wright and Decker, *Armed Robbers in Action*.

21. Elijah Anderson, "The Code of the Streets," *Atlantic Monthly*, 273 (1994), 81–94.

22. Wright and Decker, *Armed Robbers in Action*, 35.

23. J. Katz, *Seductions of Crime: Moral and Sensual Attractions to Doing Evil* (New York: Basic Books, 1988).

24. N. Shover and D. Honaker, "The Socially-Bounded Decision Making of Persistent Property Offenders," *Howard Journal of Criminal Justice* 31 (1992): 276–293 at 283.

25. Shover and Honaker, "The Socially-Bounded Decision Making of Persistent Property Offenders."

26. Wright and Decker, *Armed Robbers in Action*, 48.

27. B. Jacobs, *Robbing Drug Dealers* (New York: Aldine de Gruyter, 2000).

28. Wright and Decker, *Armed Robbers in Action*, 81–82.

29. Wright and Decker, *Armed Robbers in Action*, 86.

30. D. Luckenbill, "Generating Compliance: The Case of Robbery," *Urban Life* 10 (1981): 25–46.

31. Wright and Decker, *Armed Robbers in Action*, 104.

32. Wright and Decker, *Armed Robbers in Action*, 113.

33. J. Miller, "Feminist Theories of Women's Crime: Robbery as a Case Study," in *Of Crime and*

Criminality: The Use of Theory in Everyday Life, ed. S. Simpson (Thousand Oaks, CA: Pine Forge Press, 2000).

34. S. Hallsworth, *Street Crime* (Portland, OR: Willan, 2005), 165.

35. Wright and Decker, *Armed Robbers in Action,* 123.

36. T. H. Cohen and T. Kyckelhahn, *Felony Defendants in Large Urban Counties, 2006* (Washington, DC: Bureau of Justice Statistics, U.S. Department of Justice, 2010).

37. R. Clarke, "Situational Crime Prevention: Theory and Practice," *British Journal of Criminology* 20, no. 2 (1980): 136–147.

38. Hallsworth, *Street Crime.*

39. Wright and Decker, *Armed Robbers in Action,* 138.

40. FBI, *Bank Robbery, 2011 Report,* http://www.fbi.gov/stats-services/publications/bank-crime-statistics-2011/bank-crime-statistics-2011.

41. Gordon Dillow and William Rehder, *Where the Money Is: True Tales From the Bank Robbery Capital of the World* (New York: Norton, 2003).

42. FBI, *Name That Bank Robber: Catchy Monikers Help Nab Culprits,* http://www.fbi.gov/news/stories/2007/june/bandits_062507.

43. FBI, "Wanted Bank Robbers," http://bankrobbers.fbi.gov/bank-robbers-nationwide/#grid/6.

44. FBI, *Bank Robbery,* http://www.fbi.gov/about-us/investigate/vc_majorthefts/bankrobbery.

45. Duane Swierczynski, *This Here's a Stick-Up: The Big, Bad Book of American Bank Robbery* (Indianapolis, IN: Alpha Books, 2002); Michael Newton, *The Encyclopedia of Robberies, Heists, and Capers* (New York: Checkmark, 2002).

46. Newton, *The Encyclopedia of Robberies, Heists, and Capers;* Rehder and Dillow, *Where the Money Is;* Swierczynski, *This Here's a Stick-Up.*

47. Bureau of Labor Statistics, U.S. Department of Labor, "National Census of Fatal Occupational Injuries in 2011 (Preliminary Results)," http://www.bls.gov/news.release/pdf/cfoi.pdf.

48. Bureau of Labor Statistics, U.S. Department of Labor, "National Census of Fatal Occupational Injuries in 2011."

49. Hope M. Tiesman and others, "Workplace Homicides Among U.S. Women: The Role of Intimate Partner Violence," *Annals of Epidemiology* 22 (2012): 277–284.

50. Erika Harrell, *Workplace Violence, 1993–2009* (Washington, DC: Bureau of Justice Statistics, U.S. Department of Justice, 2011).

51. Jessica L. Taylor and Lynn Rew, "A Systematic Review of the Literature: Workplace Violence in the Emergency Department," *Journal of Clinical Nursing* 20 (2010): 1072–1085.

52. D. T. Duhart, *National Crime Victimization Survey: Violence in the Workplace, 1993–1999,* Special Report (Washington, DC: Bureau of Justice Statistics, 2001), http://bjs.ojp.usdoj.gov/content/pub/pdf/vw99.pdf. Accessed on February 2, 2013.

53. E. F. Sygnatur and G. A. Toscano, "Work-related Homicides: The Facts," *Compensation and Working Conditions* (Spring 2000); E. L. Jenkins, "Workplace Violence, United States," in *Encyclopedia of Victimology and Crime Prevention,* vol. 2, eds. B. S. Fishers and S. P. Lab (Thousand Oaks, CA: Sage, 2010), 1078–1084.

54. Dina Temple-Raston, *A Death in Texas.*

55. Temple-Raston, *A Death in Texas,* 134.

56. "Matthew Shepard," http://en.wikipedia.org/wiki/Matthew_ Shepard.

57. Definition found at the FBI's website, www.fbi.gov/ucr/cius_04/ offenses_reported/hate_crime/index.html.

58. *The Huffington Post,* March, 18, 2010, http://www.huffingtonpost.com/2009/10/28/hate-crimes-bill-to-be-si_n_336883.html.

59. FBI, *Hate Crime Statistics, 2011,* http://www.fbi.gov/about-us/cjis/ucr/hate-crime/2011/tables/table-1.

60. Caroline Wolf Harlow, *Hate Crime Reported by Victims and Police,* NCJ 209911 (Washington, DC: U.S. Department of Justice, Bureau of Justice Statistics, 2005). This is the most recent data that has been published by BJS. Hate-motivated incidents are not published in the annual estimates of victimization from the NCVS.

61. Wolf Harlow, *Hate Crime Reported by Victims and Police.*

62. Wolf Harlow, *Hate Crime Reported by Victims and Police,* Table 9.

63. Erik Eckholm, "Amish Sect Leader and Followers Guilty of Hate Crimes," *The New York Times,* September 20, 2012.

64. Michael T. Costelloe and others, "The Social Correlates of Punitiveness Toward Criminals: A Comparison of the Czech Republic and Florida," *The Justice System Journal* 23, no. 2 (2002): 191–220; Michael T. Costelloe, Ted Chiricos, and Marc Gertz, "Punitive Attitudes Toward Criminals: Exploring the Relevance of Crime Salience and Economic Insecurity," *Punishment and Society* 11, no. 1 (2007): 25–29; Devon Johnson, "Anger About Crime and Support for Punitive Criminal Justice Policies," *Punishment and Society* 11, no. 1 (2007): 51–66.

65. J. Levin and G. Rabrenovic, *Why We Hate* (Amherst, NY: Prometheus, 2004).

66. Barbara Perry, *In the Name of Hate: Understanding Hate Crimes* (New York: Routledge, 2001).

67. R. S. Wistrich, *Antisemitism: The Longest Hatred* (New York: Schocken Books, 1991).

68. Anti-Defamation League press release, "Mainstream Web Sites Flooded with Anti-Semitic Comments in Wake of Madoff Scandal," December 19, 2008, http://archive.adl.org/PresRele/ASUS_12/5422_12.htm.

69. Anti-Defamation League press release, "Mainstream Web Sites Flooded with Anti-Semitic Comments in Wake of Madoff Scandal."

70. Anti-Defamation League, "Conspiracy Theorists Blame Jews For Sandy Hook Massacre," December 18, 2012, http://blog.adl.org/anti-semitism/conspiracy-theorists-blame-jews-for-sandy-hook-massacre.

71. Levin and Rabrenovic, *Why We Hate*, 64.

72. Levin and Rabrenovic, *Why We Hate*, 68.

73. D. Altschiller, *Hate Crimes* (Santa Barbara, CA: ABC-CLIO, 1999).

Chapter 7

1. Martin D. Schwartz, *Researching Sexual Violence Against Women: Methodological and Personal Perspectives* (Thousand Oaks, CA: Sage, 1997), xii.

2. Excerpt from an anonymous Florida prisoner who chronicled his ordeal with rape and abuse in prison in a letter to Human Rights Watch, quoted in the Human Rights Watch publication *No Escape: Male Rape in U.S. Prisons*, www.hrw.org/reports/2001/prison/report1.html.

3. Juliet Macur and Nate Schweber, "Rape Case Unfolds on Web and Splits City," *The New York Times*, December 16, 2012.

4. Jim Yardley, "A Village Rape Shatters a Family, and India's Traditional Silence," *The New York Times*, October 27, 2012.

5. While the definition of rape varies across all states and many have replaced the term with a variety of sexual assault codes, for ease of discussion we will use these terms interchangeably throughout the chapter.

6. Howard Swindle, *Trespasses: Portrait of a Serial Rapist* (New York: Penguin, 1996), 58.

7. M. C. Black and others, *The National Intimate Partner and Sexual Violence Survey (NISVS): 2010 Summary Report* (Atlanta, GA: National Center for Injury Prevention and Control, Centers for Disease Control and Prevention, 2011).

8. Ronald M. Holmes and Stephen T. Holmes, *Profiling Violent Crimes: An Investigative Tool* (Thousand Oaks, CA: Sage, 2002).

9. British Home Office, "An Overview of Sexual Offending in England and Wales," http://www.homeoffice.gov.uk/publications/science-research-statistics/research-statistics/crime-research/mojoverview/?view=Standard&pubID=1146199.

10. US Code, Title 18, Chapter 10: #2251, *Sexual exploitation of children.*

11. M. Sheinberg and P. Fraenkel, *The Relational Trauma of Incest: A Family Based Approach to Treatment* (New York: Guilford Press, 2001).

12. The National Center for Victims of Crime, "Statistics on Perpetrators of Child Sexual Abuse," http://www.victimsofcrime.org/news-center/reporter-resources/child-sexual-abuse/statistics-on-perpetrators-of-csa.

13. United States Code 1092(f)(1).

14. Pub. L. 105–244.

15. The survey was funded by the National Institute of Justice and the Bureau of Justice Statistics. For a detailed discussion of the methodology and results, see B. S. Fisher, F. T. Cullen, and M. G. Turner, *The Sexual Victimization of College Women*, NCJ Publication Number 182369 (Washington, DC: U.S. Department of Justice, Office of Justice Programs, 2000).

16. See The National Women's Health Information Center at www.4woman.gov for a detailed discussion of these drugs.

17. Adam Liptak, "Ex-Inmate's Suit Offers View into Sexual Slavery in Prisons," *New York Times*, October 16, 2004, http://query.nytimes.com/search/restricted/articles?res=FAOD13F63F5E0C758DDDA90994

18. Liptak, "Ex-Inmate's Suit Offers View into Sexual Slavery in Prisons."

19. For a classic study of this issue, see Gresham Sykes and Sheldon Messinger, "The Inmate Social Code," in *The Sociology of Punishment and Corrections*, eds. Norman Johnston and others (New York: Wiley, 1970), 401–408.

20. Human Rights Watch, "No Escape: Male Rape in U.S. Prisons" (Human Rights Watch, 2001), 3, http://www.hrw.org/reports/2001/prison/report7.html.

21. Human Rights Watch, "No Escape."

22. Cindy Struckman-Johnson, David Struckman-Johnson, L. Rucker, K. Bumby, and S. Donaldson, "Sexual Coercion Reported by Men and Women in Prison," *Journal of Sex Research* 33, no. 1 (1996): 67–76.

23. Cindy Struckman-Johnson and David Struckman-Johnson, "Sexual Coercion Rates in Seven Midwestern Prison Facilities for Men," *The Prison Journal* 80, no. 4 (2000): 379–390.

24. Bureau of Justice Statistics, *Data Collections for the Prison Rape Elimination Act of 2003, June 30, 2004* (Washington, DC: U.S. Department of Justice, 2004).

25. Bureau of Justice Statistics, *Prison Rape Elimination Act of 2003: PREA Data Collection Activities* (Washington, DC: BJS, 2012).

26. Allen J. Beck and others, *Sexual Victimization in Prisons and Jails Reported by Inmates, 2008–2009* (Washington DC: Bureau of Justice Statistics, U.S. Department of Justice, 2010).

27. Susan Brownmiller, "Making Female Bodies the Battlefield," in *Rape and Society*, eds. P. Searles and R. J. Berger (Boulder, CO: Westview, 1995).

28. Alison Des Forges, *Leave None to Tell the Story: Genocide in Rwanda* (New York: Human Rights Watch, 1999).

29. Carol Rittner, "Using Rape as a Weapon of Genocide," in *Will Genocide Ever End?* eds. Carol Rittner, John K. Roth, and James M. Smith (St. Paul, MN: Paragon House, 2002), 91–97.

30. Bill Berkeley, *The Graves Are Not Yet Full: Race, Tribe, and Power in the Heart of Africa* (New York: Basic Books, 2001).

31. See, for example, Beverley Allen, *Rape Warfare: The Hidden Genocide in Bosnia-Herzegovina and Croatia* (Minneapolis: University of Minnesota Press, 1996); Ed Vulliamy, *Seasons in Hell: Understanding Bosnia's War* (New York: St. Martins Press, 1994).

32. Roy Gutman and David Rieff, *Crimes of War: What the Public Should Know* (New York: W. W. Norton & Co. 1999).

33. United Nations, "Rwanda International Criminal Tribunal Pronounces Guilty Verdict in Historic Genocide Trial," Press Release, September 2, 1998.

34. Human Rights Watch, "Bosnia: Landmark Verdicts for Rape, Torture, and Sexual Enslavement," http://hrw.org/english/docs/2001/02/22/bosher256_tst.htm.

35. See, for example, *USA Today*, "GIs Eyed in Alleged Rape, Murders in Iraq," www.usatoday.com/news/world/iraq/2006-06-30-us-probe_x.htm.

36. J. A. Allison and L. S. Wrightsman, *Rape: The Misunderstood Crime* (Thousand Oaks, CA: Sage, 1993).

37. D. Scully and J. Marolla, "Riding the Bull at Gilley's: Convicted Rapists Describe the Rewards of Rape," in *Rape & Society*, eds. P. Searles and R. J. Berger (Boulder, CO: Westview, 1995).

38. Cited in Swindle, *Trespasses*, 153.

39. Nicholas Groth, *Men Who Rape: The Psychology of the Offender* (New York: Basic Books, 1979), 2.

40. Quoted in Swindle, *Trespasses*, 52–53.

41. R. Knight and R. Prentky, "The Developmental Antecedents and Adult Adaptations of Rapist Subtypes," *Criminal Justice and Behavior* 14 (1987): 403–426. For a good discussion, see Ronald M. Holmes and Stephen T. Holmes, *Profiling Violent Crimes: An Investigative Tool*, 3rd ed. (Thousand Oaks, CA: Sage, 2002).

42. R. R. Hazelwood and A. W. Burgess, *Practical Aspects of Rape Investigation: A Multidisciplinary Approach*, 3rd ed. (Boca Raton, FL: CRC Press, 2008).

43. A. S. Chancellor, *Investigating Sexual Assault Cases* (Burlington, MA: Jones & Bartlett, 2004).

44. A. S. Chancellor, *Investigating Sexual Assault Cases*.

45. Holmes and Holmes, *Profiling Violent Crimes*.

46. S. Brownmiller, *Against Our Will: Men, Women, and Rape* (New York: Simon and Schuster, 1975); D. Russell, *The Politics of Rape: The Victim's Perspective* (New York: Stein and Day, 1975).

47. P. R. Sanday, "The Socio-Cultural Context of Rape: A Cross-Cultural Study," *Journal of Social Issues* 37 (1981): 5–27.

48. L. Baron and M. A. Straus, *Four Theories of Rape in American Society: A State-Level Analysis* (New Haven, CT: Yale University Press, 1989).

49. Scully and Marolla, "Riding the Bull at Gilley's."

50. M. Burt, "Cultural Myths and Supports for Rape," *Journal of Personality and Social Psychology* 38 (1980): 217–230.

51. B. R. Burkhart and M. E. Fromuth, "Individual and Social Psychological Understanding of Sexual Coercion," in *Sexual Coercion: A Sourcebook on Its Nature, Causes, and Prevention*, eds. E. Gruerholdz and M. A. Koralewski (Lexington, MA: Lexington, 1991), 75–89; N. M. Malamuth, "Rape Proclivity Among Males," *Journal of Social Issues* 37 (1981): 138–157; C. L. Muehlenhard and M. A. Linton, "Date Rape and Sexual Aggression in Dating Situations: Incidence and Risk Factors," *Journal of Counseling and Psychology* 34 (1987): 186–196.

52. N. Jane McCandless, "Rape—Definitions," in *Encyclopedia of Murder and Violent Crime*, ed. Eric Hickey (Thousand Oaks, CA: Sage, 2003), 391–392.

53. R. M. Sapolsky, *A Primate's Memoir: A Neuroscientist's Unconventional Life Among the Baboons* (New York: Scribner, 2001).

54. R. Bachman, "Factors Related to Rape Reporting Behavior and Arrest: New Evidence from the National Crime Victimization Survey," *Criminal Justice and Behavior* 25, no. 1 (1998): 8–29; R. Bachman and R. Paternoster, "A Contemporary Look at the Effects of Rape Law Reform: How Far Have We Really Come?" *Journal of Criminal Law and Criminology* 84, no. 3 (1994): 554–574; J. Horney and C. Spohn, "Rape Law Reform and Instrumental Change in Six Urban Jurisdictions," *Law and Society Review* 25 (1991): 117–153; W. A. Kerstetter and B. Van Winkle, "Who Decides? A Study of Complainants' Decision to Prosecute in Rape Cases," *Criminal Justice and Behavior* 17, no. 3 (1990): 268–283.

55. V. R. Wiehe and A. L. Richards, *Intimate Betrayal: Understanding and Responding to the Trauma of Acquaintance Rape* (Thousand Oaks, CA: Sage, 1995), 30.

56. National Victim Center, *Rape in America* (Alexandria, VA: National Victim Centre, 1999).

57. J. C. Marsh, A. Geist, and N. Caplan, *Rape and the Limits of Law Reform* (Boston: Auburn House, 1982).

58. K. Polk, "Rape Reform and Criminal Justice Processing," *Crime and Delinquency* 31 (1985): 191–205.

59. Horney and Spohn, "Rape Law Reform and Instrumental Change in Six Urban Jurisdictions."

60. R. Bachman and P. Smith, "The Adjudication of Rape Since Reforms: Examining the Probability of Conviction and Incarceration at the National and Three State Levels," *Criminal Justice Policy Review* 6 (1994): 342–358.

61. P. Langan and C. Wolf-Harlow, *Child Rape Victims: 1992*, NCJ 147001 (Washington, DC: U.S. Department of Justice, Bureau of Justice Statistics, 1994).

62. L. Greenfeld, *Sex Offenses and Offenders*, NCJ 163392 (Washington, DC: U.S. Department of Justice, Bureau of Justice Statistics, 1997).

63. Bureau of Justice Statistics, "Recidivism Rates Calculated for all Males on February 17, 2013," http://bjs.ojp.usdoj.gov/index.cfm?ty=datool&surl=/recidivism/index.cfm#.

64. The Wetterling Act was part of Public Law 104–145, 110 Statute 1345.

65. Pub. L. 104–236, 110 Stat. 3093.

66. SMART, *Legislative History of Federal Sex Offender Legislation*, http://www.ojp.usdoj.gov/smart/legislation.htm.

67. G. Duwe, W. Donnay, and R. Tewksbury, "Does Residential Proximity Matter? A Geographical Analysis of Sex Offense Recidivism," *Criminal Justice and Behavior* 35 (2008): 484–505.

68. Chrysanthi S. Leon, *Sex Fiends, Perverts, and Pedophiles: Understanding Sex Crime Policy in America* (New York, New York University Press, 2011).

Chapter 8

1. Quoted in Richard Maxwell Brown, *Strain of Violence: Historical Studies of American Violence and Vigilantism* (New York: Oxford University Press, 1975), 3.

2. F. Bartlett, *Remembering* (Cambridge: Cambridge University Press, 1932), 24.

3. *Memoirs of Extraordinary Popular Delusions and the Madness of Crowds*, 1852.

4. BBC News, "French Violence Hits Fresh Peak," http://newsvote.bbc.co.uk/mpapps/pagetools/print/news.bbc.co.uk/2/hi/europe/4413250.stm.

5. *Christian Science Monitor*, "Deep Roots of Paris Riots," www.csmonitor.com/2005/p06s02-woeu.htm.

6. BBC News, "French Violence Hits Fresh Peak."

7. Dan Horn, "The Trigger: Shooting 'Ignites Furious Response,'" *The Cincinnati Enquirer*, http://www.enquirer.com/unrest2001/race2.html.

8. Dan Horn, "The Riots Explode: A City's Dark Week," *The Cincinnati Enquirer*, http://www.enquirer.com/unrest2001/race3.html.

9. Euripides, "Orestes," trans. William Arrowsmith (Chicago: University of Chicago Press, 1959).

10. Julius R. Ruff, *Violence in Early Modern Europe, 1500–1800* (New York: Cambridge University Press, 2001).

11. Ruff, *Violence in Early Modern Europe, 1500–1800*.

12. J. Paul de Castro, *The Gordon Riots* (Oxford: Oxford University Press, 1926); Christopher Hibbert, *King Mob: The Story of Lord George Gordon and the Riots of 1780* (New York: Longmans, 1959); Christopher Hibbert, *The Roots of Evil: A Social History of Crime and Punishment* (Stroud, UK: Sutton, 1963).

13. Cited in Ruff, *Violence in Early Modern Europe, 1500–1800*.

14. Richard J. Gelles and Ann Levine, *Sociology: An Introduction*, 6th ed. (Boston: McGraw Hill, 1999).

15. Peter Hayes, *The People and the Mob: The Ideology of Civil Conflict in Modern Europe* (Westport, CT: Praeger, 1992).

16. Ruff, *Violence in Early Modern Europe, 1500–1800*.

17. Sid Heal, "Crowds, Mobs and Nonlethal Weapons," *Military Review*, March/April 2000, 45–50.

18. R. A. Berk, *Collective Behavior* (New York: Brown 1974), 20.

19. Everett Dean Martin, *The Behavior of Crowds: A Psychological Study* (New York: Harper & Brothers, 1920).

20. Gustave Le Bon, *The Crowd* (London: Ernest Benn, 1952), 32.

21. H. Blumer, "Collective Behavior," in *An Outline of the Principles of Sociology*, ed. R. E. Park (New York: Barnes and Noble, 1939).

22. Clark McPhail, *The Myth of the Madding Crowd* (New York: Aldine De Gruyter, 1991), 225.

23. Paul A. Gilje, *Rioting in America* (Bloomington: Indiana University Press, 1996).

24. David Kirkpatrick and Mayy El Sheikh, "Soccer Fan Riots in Egypt Leave 30 Dead," *The Sydney Morning Herald*, January 28, 2013, http://www.smh.com.au/world/soccer-fan-riots-in-egypt-leave-30-dead-20130127-2dewj.html.

25. Reza Sayah and Amir Ahmed, "30 Dead After Egyptians Angry About Riot Verdicts Try to Storm Prison," CNN.Com, January 27, 2013, http://www.cnn.com/2013/01/26/world/africa/egypt-unrest/index.html.

26. Nancy A Youssef and Amina Ismail, "Riots in Egypt Over Soccer Verdict Have Broader Meaning,"

Seattle Times, January 27, 2013, http://seattletimes.com/html/nationworld/2020229855_egyptbackgrounderxml.html.

27. Heal, "Crowds, Mobs and Nonlethal Weapons."

28. Gilje, Rioting in America.

29. Taken from the Office of the Law Revision Council, which prepares and publishes the United States Code, which is a consolidation and codification by subject matter of the general and permanent laws of the United States. The website is at http://uscode.house.gov/download/pls/18C102.txt.

30. A.R.S. 13–2903, www.azprosecution.org/statutes/title13/ch29/ 13–2903.html.

31. Gilje, Rioting in America, 4.

32. Charles Tilly, The Politics of Collective Violence (New York: Cambridge University Press, 2003), 18.

33. Gilje, Rioting in America, 1.

34. Rodney F. Allen and Charles H. Adair, Violence and Riots in Urban America (Worthington, OH: Charles A. Jones, 1969).

35. James S. Hirsch, Riot and Remembrance: America's Worst Race Riot and Its Legacy (Boston: Houghton Mifflin, 2002); Tim Madigan, The Burning: Massacre, Destruction, and the Tulsa Race Riot of 1921 (New York: Thomas Dunne Books, 2001).

36. Madigan, The Burning.

37. Madigan, The Burning, 70.

38. Hirsch, Riot and Remembrance, 6.

39. Leon Freidman, ed., Violence in America: Final Report of the National Commission on the Causes and Prevention of Violence (New York: The Commission, 1969).

40. Brown, Strain of Violence, 219.

41. Lou Cannon, Official Negligence: How Rodney King and the Riots Changed Los Angeles and the LAPD (New York: Times Books, 1997).

42. Cannon, Official Negligence.

43. Cannon, Official Negligence; Robert M. Fogelson, Violence as Protest: A Study of Riots and Ghettos (Garden City, NY: Doubleday, 1971); Peter Iadicola and Anson Shupe, Violence, Inequality, and Human Freedom (Lanham, MD: Rowman & Littlefield, 2003); Neil Websdale, Policing the Poor: From Slave Plantation to Public Housing (Boston: Northeastern University Press, 2001).

44. Homer Hawkins and Richard Thomas, "White Policing of Black Populations: A History of Race and Social Control in America," in Out of Order: Policing Black People, eds. Ellis Cashmore and Eugene McLaughlin (London: Routledge, 1991), 65–86.

45. Christopher Waldrep, The Many Faces of Judge Lynch: Extralegal Violence and Punishment in America (New York: Palgrave Macmillan, 2002).

46. Quoted in Waldrep, The Many Faces of Judge Lynch, 15.

47. W. Fitzhugh Brundage, Lynching in the New South: Georgia and Virginia, 1880–1930 (Urbana: University of Illinois Press, 1993), 6.

48. Stewart E. Tolnay and E. M. Beck, A Festival of Violence: An Analysis of Southern Lynchings, 1882–1930 (Urbana: University of Illinois Press, 1995).

49. Tolnay and Beck, A Festival of Violence, 17–54.

50. Tolnay and Beck, A Festival of Violence.

51. Tolnay and Beck, A Festival of Violence.

52. Tolnay and Beck, A Festival of Violence, 148–149.

53. For a discussion, see Brundage, Lynching in the New South.

54. Quoted in Tolnay and Beck, A Festival of Violence, 87–88.

55. Quoted in James W. Marquart, Sheldon Ekland-Olson, and Jonathan R. Sorensen, The Rope, The Chair, and the Needle: Capital Punishment in Texas, 1923–1990 (Austin: University of Texas Press, 1994), 7.

56. Tolnay and Beck, A Festival of Violence.

57. See for example, William D. Carrigan, The Making of a Lynching Culture: Violence and Vigilantism in Central Texas, 1836–1916 (Urbana: University of Illinois Press, 2004); Robert P. Ingalls, Urban Vigilantes in the New South, Tampa, 1882–1936 (Gainesville: University Press of Florida, 1988); Waldrep, The Many Faces of Judge Lynch.

58. You can find information about Michael Donald's case on several sites, including the Southern Poverty Law Center's at http://www.splcenter.org/legal/docket/files.jsp?cdrID=10, and Sparticus Educational Services at www.spartacus.schoolnet.co.uk.

59. Brown, Strain of Violence.

60. Brown, Strain of Violence.

61. Jay Monaghan, ed., The Book of the American West (New York: Simon and Schuster, 1963).

62. H. Jon Rosenbaum and Peter C. Sederberg, "Vigilantism: An Analysis of Establishment Violence," in Vigilante Politics, eds. H. Jon Rosenbaum and Peter C. Sederberg (Pittsburgh: University of Pennsylvania Press, 1976), 3–29.

63. Rosenbaum and Sederberg, "Vigilantism."

Chapter 9

1. Quoted in Paul L. Williams, Al Qaeda: Brotherhood of Terror (New York: Alpha, 2002), 49.

2. Irving Louis Horowitz, Taking Lives: Genocide and State Power, 4th ed. (New Brunswick, NJ: Transaction, 1997), 88.

3. P. Schmid, Political Terrorism: A Research Guide to Concepts, Theories, Data Bases and Literature (Amsterdam: North Holland, 1983).

4. Philip Herbst, Talking Terrorism: A Dictionary of the Loaded Language of Political Violence (Westport, CT: Greenwood Press, 2003), 163.

5. Walter Laqueur, *No End to War: Terrorism in the Twenty-First Century* (New York: Continuum, 2004).

6. Laqueur, *No End to War*.

7. David Tucker, "What Is New About the New Terrorism and How Dangerous Is It?" *Terrorism and Political Violence* 13, no. 3 (2001): 1–14.

8. John George and Laird Wilcox, *American Extremists: Militias, Supremacists, Klansmen, Communists, & Others* (Amherst, NY: Prometheus, 1996), 16.

9. Bruce Hoffman, *Inside Terrorism* (New York: Columbia University Press, 1998).

10. Christoph Reuter, *My Life Is a Weapon: A Modern History of Suicide Bombing* (Princeton, NJ: Princeton University Press, 2004).

11. Quoted in Cindy C. Combs, *Terrorism in the Twenty-First Century*, 3rd ed. (Upper Saddle River, NJ: Prentice Hall, 2003), 1.

12. Jane Corbin, *Al-Qaeda* (New York: Thunder's Mouth Press, 2003).

13. Hoffman, *Inside Terrorism*, 30–31.

14. Herbst, *Talking Terrorism*, 166.

15. Samuel P. Huntington, *The Clash of Civilizations and the Remaking of World Order* (New York: Simon and Schuster, 1996).

16. Thomas J. Badey, "Defining International Terrorism: A Pragmatic Approach," *Terrorism and Political Violence* 10 (1998): 90–107.

17. Badey, "Defining International Terrorism," 95.

18. See Combs, *Terrorism in the Twenty-First Century*.

19. Patricia Marchak, *God's Assassins: State Terrorism in Argentina in the 1970s* (Montreal: McGill-Queen's University Press, 1999).

20. The name of the general is Iberico Saint-Jean and he is quoted in Marchak, *God's Assassins*.

21. Marguerite Feitlowitz, *A Lexicon of Terror: Argentina and the Legacies of Torture* (New York: Oxford University Press, 1998); Horacio Verbitsky, *The Flight: Confessions of an Argentine Dirty Warrior* (New York: The New Press, 1996).

22. Frederick H. Gareau, *State Terrorism and the United States: From Counterinsurgency to the War on Terrorism* (Atlanta: Clarity Press, 2004).

23. P. Schmid and J. De Graaf, *Violence as Communication* (London: Sage, 1982).

24. Hoffman, *Inside Terrorism*.

25. See for example, Benjamin A. Valentino, *Final Solutions: Mass Killing and Genocide in the 20th Century* (Ithaca, NY: Cornell University Press, 2004); Gareau, *State Terrorism and the United States*.

26. Herbst, *Talking Terrorism*.

27. James M. Poland, *Understanding Terrorism* (Englewood Cliffs, NJ: Prentice Hall, 1988); Harold J. Vetter and Gary R. Perlstein, *Perspectives on Terrorism* (Pacific Grove, CA: Brooks/Cole, 1991).

28. The term "Zealot" is derived from the Greek word *Zelos* for strong spirit. See Gus Martin, *Understanding Terrorism: Challenges, Perspectives, and Issues* (Thousand Oaks, CA: Sage, 2003); Pamala Griset and Sue Mahan, eds., *Terrorism in Perspective* (Thousand Oaks, CA: Sage, 2003).

29. Rupert Matthews, *The Age of the Gladiators: Savagery & Spectacle in Ancient Rome* (Edison, NJ: Chartwell, 2004); Michael Grant, *The World of Rome* (New York: Meridian, 1960).

30. Matthews, *The Age of the Gladiators*.

31. Bernard Lewis, *The Assassins: A Radical Sect in Islam* (New York: Basic Books, 1967); Andrew Sinclair, *An Anatomy of Terror: A History of Terrorism* (London: Pan, 2003).

32. Robert Payne, *The Dream and the Tomb: A History of the Crusades* (New York: Dorset Press, 1984); David C. Rapoport, "Fear and Trembling: Terrorism in Three Religious Traditions," in *Terrorism in Perspective*, 15–37.

33. Lewis, *The Assassins*.

34. Quoted in Lewis, *The Assassins*, 47–48.

35. Sinclair, *An Anatomy of Terror*.

36. Poland, *Understanding Terrorism*.

37. Lewis, *The Assassins*, 140.

38. John S. C. Abbott, *The French Revolution* (New York: Harper & Brothers, 1859); Simon Schama, *Citizens: A Chronicle of the French Revolution* (New York: Vintage, 1989).

39. The line about the rotten door is from the famous American economist John Kenneth Galbraith, who wrote, "All successful revolutions are the kicking in of a rotten door. The violence of revolutions is the violence of men who charge into a vacuum."

40. Abbott, *The French Revolution*, 329.

41. George Shaw, "Man and Superman," quoted in The Editors of Merriam-Webster, *Webster's New Explorer Dictionary of Quotations* (Springfield, MA: Federal Street Press, 2000).

42. Griset and Mahan, *Terrorism in Perspective*.

43. Maximilien Robespierre, "Justification of the Use of Terror," *Modern History Sourcebook: Robespierre: Terror and Virtue, 1794*, www.fordham.edu/halsall/mod/robespierre-terror.html.

44. Martha Crenshaw and John Pimlott, eds., *Encyclopedia of World Terrorism* (Armonk, NY: M.E. Sharpe, 1997); Hoffman, *Inside Terrorism*.

45. Martin, *Understanding Terrorism*.

46. Sergey Nechayev, "Catechism of the Revolutionist (1869)," in *Voices of Terror: Manifestos, Writings and Manuals of Al Qaeda, Hamas, and Other Terrorists From Around the World and Throughout the Ages*, ed. W. Laqueur (New York: Reed, 2004), 71–75.

47. Nechayev, "Catechism of the Revolutionist."

48. Jeffrey Kluger, "Why We Worry About the Things We Shouldn't and Ignore the Things We Should," *Time* magazine, December 4, 2006, 66.

49. Marc Gerstein, *Flirting With Disaster: Why Accidents Are Rarely Accidental* (New York: Union Square Press, 2008).

50. Federal Bureau of Investigation, *Terrorism, 2000/2001*, Vol. 0308, Edi. by U.S. Department of Justice (Washington, DC: U.S. Government Printing Office, 2004).

51. Institute for Economics and Peace, *2012 Global Terrorism Index: Capturing the Impact of Terrorism for the Last Decade*, http://www.vision-ofhumanity.org/wp-content/uploads/2012/12/2012-Global-Terrorism-Index-Report1.pdf.

52. Harvey W. Kushner, *Terrorism in America: A Structured Approach to Understanding the Terrorist Threat* (Springfield, IL: Charles C. Thomas, 1998).

53. Jerrold M. Post, *Leaders and Their Followers in a Dangerous World: The Psychology of Political Behavior* (Ithaca, NY: Cornell University Press, 2004).

54. Mark Bowden, *Killing Pablo: The Hunt for the World's Greatest Outlaw* (New York: Penguin, 2001).

55. Bowden, *Killing Pablo*.

56. P. Grabosky and M. Stohl, *Crime and Terrorism* (Los Angeles: Sage, 2010).

57. Pumla Gobodo-Madikizela, *A Human Being Died That Night: A South African Story of Forgiveness* (Boston: Houghton Mifflin, 2003); Antjie Krog, *Country of My Skull: Guilt, Sorrow, and the Limits of Forgiveness in the New South Africa* (New York: Three Rivers Press, 1998); Martin Meredith, *Coming to Terms: South Africa's Search for Truth* (New York: Public Affairs, 1999).

58. Gobodo-Madikizela, *A Human Being Died That Night*, 53.

59. Martin, *Understanding Terrorism*.

60. Kushner, *Encyclopedia of Terrorism*.

61. Post, *Leaders and Their Followers in a Dangerous World*.

62. Jay Robert Nash, *Terrorism in the 20th Century* (New York: M. Evans and Company, 1998).

63. Carpetbaggers were usually Northerners and Reconstruction officials who gained a reputation for seizing property and valuables from Southerners and carting off some of the goods in cloth suitcases. See Nash, *Terrorism in the 20th Century*.

64. Andrew Meier, *Chechnya: To the Heart of a Conflict* (New York: W. W. Norton & Co., 2005).

65. Paul Murphy, *The Wolves of Islam: Russia and the Faces of Chechen Terrorism* (Washington, DC: Brassey's Inc., 2004).

66. Kushner, *Encyclopedia of Terrorism*.

67. Robert Jay Lifton, *Destroying the World to Save It: Aum Shinrikyo, Apocalyptic Violence, and the New Global Terrorism* (New York: Henry Holt and Company, 1999).

68. Lifton, *Destroying the World to Save It*.

69. Charles Selengut, *Sacred Fury: Understanding Religious Violence* (Walnut Creek, CA: AltaMira Press, 2003).

70. Post, *Leaders and Their Followers in a Dangerous World*.

71. Charles Kimball, *When Religion Becomes Evil* (New York: HarperCollins, 2002).

72. Selengut, *Sacred Fury*.

73. Quoted in Selengut, *Sacred Fury*, 37.

74. Mark Juergensmeyer, *Terror in the Mind of God: The Global Rise of Religious Violence* (Berkeley: University of California Press, 2000).

75. Quoted in Post, *Leaders and Their Followers in a Dangerous World*, 144.

76. See Post, *Leaders and Their Followers in a Dangerous World*.

77. Marc Sageman, *Understanding Terror Networks* (Philadelphia: University of Pennsylvania Press, 2004).

78. Daniel Benjamin and Steven Simon, *The Age of Sacred Terror: Radical Islam's War Against America* (New York: Random House, 2002).

79. Selengut, *Sacred Fury*.

80. Selengut, *Sacred Fury*.

81. Sageman, *Understanding Terror Networks*.

82. Jerrold M. Post, "Terrorist Psycho-Logic: Terrorist Behavior as a Product of Psychological Forces," in *Origins of Terrorism: Psychologies, Ideologies, Theologies, States of Mind*, ed. W. Reich (New York: Cambridge University Press, 1990); Sageman, *Understanding Terror Networks*.

83. Post, *Leaders and Their Followers in a Dangerous World*.

84. See, for example, Laqueur, *No End to War*.

85. John W. Crayton, "Terrorism and the Psychology of the Self," in *Perspectives on Terrorism*, eds. L. Z. Freedman and Y. Alexander (Wilmington, DE: Scholarly Resources, 1983), 33–41; Richard M. Pearlstein, *The Mind of the Political Terrorist* (Wilmington, DE: Scholarly Resources, 1991).

86. Post, "Terrorist Psycho-Logic."

87. Jeanne N. Knutson, "Social and Psychodynamic Pressures Toward Negative Identity," in *Behavioral and Quantitative Perspectives on Terrorism*, eds. Y. Alexander and J. M. Gleason (New York: Pergamon, 1981), 105–152.

88. Sageman, *Understanding Terror Networks*, 74.

89. Terry McDermott, *Perfect Soldiers, The Hijackers: Who They Were, Why They Did It* (New York: HarperCollins, 2005).

90. Jessica Stern, *Terror in the Name of God: Why Religious Militants Kill* (New York: HarperCollins, 2003).

91. Stern, *Terror in the Name of God*, 38.

92. Joyce M. Davis, *Martyrs: Innocence, Vengeance and Despair in the Middle East* (New York: Palgrave Macmillan, 2003).

93. Assaf Moghadam, "Shifting Trends in Suicide Attacks," *CTC Sentinel*, Combating Terrorism Center at West Point, http://www.ctc.usma.edu/posts/shifting-trends-in-suicide-attacks.

94. Robert A. Pape, *Dying to Win: The Strategic Logic of Suicide Terrorism* (New York: Random House, 2005).

95. Raymond Lamont-Brown, *Kamikaze: Japan's Suicide Samurai* (London: Cassell, 1997).

96. Hala Jaber, *Hezbollah: Born with a Vengeance* (New York: Columbia University Press, 1997).

97. Pape, *Dying to Win*.

98. Kushner, *Encyclopedia of Terrorism*.

99. Pape, *Dying to Win*.

100. Jessica Stern, *The Ultimate Terrorists* (Cambridge, MA: Harvard University Press, 1999).

101. Stern, *The Ultimate Terrorists*, 2.

102. Stern, *The Ultimate Terrorists*.

103. Andrew Nikiforuk, *The Fourth Horseman: A Short History of Epidemics, Plagues, Famines, and Other Scourges* (New York: M. Evans & Company, 1991).

104. John Ellis, *Eye Deep in Hell: Trench Warfare in World War I* (Baltimore: Johns Hopkins Press, 1976); John Keegan, *The First World War* (New York: Vintage, 1998).

105. Michael L. Moodie, "The Chemical Weapons Threat," in *Terrorism and Counterterrorism: Understanding the New Security Environment*, eds. R. D. Howard and R. L. Sawyer (Guilford, CT: McGraw Hill/Dushkin, 2003), 184–203; Cliff Mariani, *Terrorism Prevention and Response: The Definitive Law Enforcement Guide to Prepare for Terrorist Activity* (Flushing, NY: Looseleaf Law Publications, 2003).

106. Lifton, *Destroying the World to Save It*.

Chapter 10

1. Eric Markusen and David Kopf, *The Holocaust and Strategic Bombing: Genocide and Total War in the Twentieth Century* (Boulder, CO: Westview, 1995), 243.

2. Eric D. Weitz, *A Century of Genocide: Utopias of Race and Nation* (Princeton, NJ: Princeton University Press, 2003).

3. R. J. Rummel, *Death by Government* (New Brunswick, NJ: Transaction, 1994).

4. Timothy Longman, "Zaire: Forced to Flee—Violence Against the Tutsis in Zaire," *Human Rights Watch* 8, no. 2 (1996), http://hrw.org/reports/1996/Zaire.htm.

5. William Shawcross, *Deliver Us From Evil: Peacekeepers, Warlords and a World of Endless Conflict* (New York: Simon and Schuster, 2000); Longman, "Zaire."

6. Roger W. Smith, "Human Destructiveness and Politics: the Twentieth Century As an Age of Genocide," in *Genocide and the Modern Age: Etiology and Case Studies of Mass Death*, eds. Isidor Wallimann and Michael N. Dobkowski (Syracuse: Syracuse University Press, 1998).

7. See, for example, footnote in Alex Alvarez, *Governments, Citizens, and Genocide: A Comparative and Interdisciplinary Approach* (Bloomington: Indiana University Press, 2001).

8. Mary Craig, *Tears of Blood: A Cry for Tibet* (Washington, DC: Counterpoint Press, 1999).

9. Craig, *Tears of Blood*.

10. James Dunn, "Genocide in East Timor," in *Century of Genocide: Eyewitness Accounts and Critical Views*, eds. Samuel Totten, William S. Parsons, and Israel W. Charny (New York: Garland Publishing, 1997), 264–290; Matthew Jardine, *East Timor: Genocide in Paradise* (Tucson, AZ: Odion Press, 1995).

11. Dunn, "Genocide in East Timor"; Jardine, *East Timor*; Ben Kiernan, "The Demography of Genocide in Southeast Asia: The Death Tolls in Cambodia, 1975–79, and East Timor, 1975–80," *Critical Asian Studies* 35, no. 4 (2003): 585–597.

12. Jardine, *East Timor*.

13. Dunn, "Genocide in East Timor."

14. See for example Michael Barnett, *Eyewitness to Genocide: The United Nations and Rwanda* (Ithaca, NY: Cornell University Press, 2002); and Linda Melvern, *A People Betrayed: The Role of the West in Rwanda's Genocide* (London: Zed Books, 2000).

15. Samantha Power, *A Problem From Hell: America and the Age of Genocide* (New York: Basic Books, 2002).

16. Steven L. Jacobs, "The UN Convention," in *Will Genocide Ever End?* eds. Carol Rittner, John K. Roth, and James M. Smith (St. Paul, MN: Paragon House, 2002), 35–38.

17. W. Michael Reisman and Chris T. Antoniou, eds., *The Laws of War: A Comprehensive Collection of Primary Documents on International Law Governing Armed Conflict* (New York: Vintage, 1994).

18. Edwin Black, *War Against the Weak: Eugenics and America's Campaign to Create a Master Race* (New York: Four Walls Eight Windows, 2003); Daniel J. Kevles, *In the Name of Eugenics: Genetics and the Uses of Human Heredity* (Cambridge, MA: Harvard University Press, 1995).

19. Brenda J. Child, *Boarding School Seasons: American Indian Families, 1900–1940* (Lincoln, NE: University of Nebraska Press, 1998); Michael C. Coleman,

American Indian Children at School, 1850–1930 (Jackson, MS: University Press of Mississippi, 1993); Jon Reyhner and Jeanne Eder, *American Indian Education: A History* (Norman: University of Oklahoma Press, 2004); Scott Riney, *The Rapid City Indian School, 1898–1933* (Norman: University of Oklahoma Press, 1999); Robert A. Trennert Jr., *The Phoenix Indian School: Forced Assimilation in Arizona, 1891–1935* (Norman: University of Oklahoma Press, 1988).

20. See, for example, Israel W. Charny, "Toward a Generic Definition of Genocide," in *Genocide: Conceptual and Historical Dimensions*, ed. George J. Andreopoulos (Philadelphia: University of Pennsylvania Press, 1994), 64–94.

21. Quoted in David Wallace Adams, *Education for Extinction: American Indians and the Boarding School Experience, 1875–1928* (Kansas, MS: University Press of Kansas, 1995), 21.

22. For a thorough discussion of the intent element of genocide, see William A. Schabas, *Genocide in International Law: The Crimes of Crimes* (New York: Cambridge University Press, 2000); and Lawrence J. LeBlanc, *The United States and the Genocide Convention* (Durham, NC: Duke University Press, 1991).

23. William A. Schabas, *Genocide in International Law* (Cambridge: Cambridge University Press, 2000); The International Criminal Tribunal for Rwanda, "Prosecutor v. Jean-Paul Akayesu" Case no. ICTR-96-4-T. 2 Dec. 1998.

24. Herb Hirsch puts it this way: "If one adheres to a strict interpretation of the language of intent, then the Serbs are, for example, able to argue that their intent is not to commit genocide but to acquire territory, or as perpetrators often argue, to protect themselves from the threat raised by the Bosnian Muslims or Croatians. The concept of 'intent' is ambiguous." Herb Hirsch, *Genocide and the Politics of Memory* (Chapel Hill: University of North Carolina Press, 1995), 202.

25. See, for example, Ward Churchill, *A Little Matter of Genocide: Holocaust and Denial in the Americas 1492 to the Present* (San Francisco: City Light Books, 1997).

26. LeBlanc, *The United States and the Genocide Convention*.

27. Robert Cribb, "The Indonesian Massacres," in *Century of Genocide: Eyewitness Accounts and Critical Views*, eds. Samuel Totten, William S. Parsons, and Israel W. Charny (New York: Garland, 1997), 236–263; Robert Cribb, "Genocide in Indonesia, 1965–1966," *Journal of Genocide Research 3*, no. 2 (2001): 219–239.

28. Leslie Dwyer and Degung Santikarma, "When the World Turned to Chaos: 1965 and Its Aftermath in Bali, Indonesia," in *The Specter of Genocide: Mass Murder in Historical Perspective*, eds. Robert Gellately and Ben Kiernan (Cambridge: Cambridge University Press, 2003), 289–306.

29. William Blum, *Killing Hope: U.S. Military and CIA Interventions Since World War II* (Monroe, ME: Common Courage Press, 1995).

30. Human Rights Watch/Middle East, *Iraq's Crime of Genocide: The Anfal Campaign Against the Kurds* (New Haven, CT: Yale University Press, 1995).

31. Jon Bridgman and Leslie J. Worley, "Genocide of the Hereros," in *Century of Genocide*, eds. Totten, Parsons, and Charny (New York: Routledge, 1997), 3–40.

32. Vahakn Dadrian, *The History of the Armenian Genocide: Ethnic Conflict from the Balkans to Anatolia to the Caucasus*, 3rd ed. (Providence, RI: Bergahn Books, 1995).

33. G. S. Graber, *Caravans to Oblivion: The Armenian Genocide, 1915* (New York: John Wiley & Sons, 1996).

34. Peter Balakian, *The Burning Tigris: The Armenian Genocide and America's Response* (New York: Harper Collins, 2003); Donald E. Miller and Lorna Touryan Miller, *Survivors: An Oral History of the Armenian Genocide* (Berkeley: University of California Press, 1993).

35. Benjamin A. Valentino, *Final Solutions: Mass Killing and Genocide in the 20th Century* (Ithaca, NY: Cornell University Press, 2004).

36. Eric Markusen and David Kopf, *The Holocaust and Strategic Bombing: Genocide and Total War in the Twentieth Century*.

37. See, for example, Walter Laquer, *The Holocaust Encyclopedia* (New Haven, CT: Yale University Press, 2001).

38. Christopher Browning, *Ordinary Men: Reserve Police Battalion 101 and the Final Solution in Poland* (New York: Aaron Asher Books, 1992); Andrew Pollinger, *Death Dealer: The Memoirs of the SS Kommandant at Auschwitz*, ed. Rudolph Höss, trans. Steven Palusky (Buffalo, NY: Prometheus, 1992); Richard L. Rubenstein and J. K. Roth, *Approaches to Auschwitz* (Atlanta: John Knox, 1987).

39. Christopher R. Browning, *The Origins of the Final Solution: The Evolution of Nazi Jewish Policy, September 1939–March 1942* (Lincoln, NE: University of Nebraska Press, 2004); Michael Burleigh, *The Third Reich: A New History* (New York: Hill and Wang, 2000); Deborah Dwork and Robert Jan Van Pelt, *Holocaust: A History* (New York: W. W. Norton and Co., 2002); Richard J. Evans, *The Coming of the Third Reich* (New York: Penguin, 2003).

40. R. J. Rummel, *Death by Government* (New Brunswick, NJ: Transaction, 1994), 111.

41. R. J. Rummel, *Democide: Nazi Genocide and Mass Murder* (New Brunswick, NJ: Transaction, 1992), 13.

42. Rummel, *Democide*.

43. Ben Kiernan, *The Pol Pot Regime: Race, Power, and Genocide in Cambodia Under the Khmer Rouge, 1975–79* (New Haven, CT: Yale University Press, 1996).

44. Ben Kiernan, "The Cambodian Genocide—1975–1979," in *Century of Genocide*, eds. Totten, Parsons, and Charny (New York: Routledge, 1997), 334–371.

45. Rene Lemarchand, "The Rwanda Genocide," in Totten, Parsons, and Charny, *Century of Genocide*, 408–423

46. Philip Gourevitch, *We Wish to Inform You That Tomorrow We Will Be Killed With Our Families* (New York: Farrar Straus and Giroux, 1998); Gerard Prunier, *The Rwanda Crisis: History of a Genocide* (New York: Columbia University Press, 1995); Linda Melvern, *Leave None to Tell the Story: Genocide in Rwanda* (New York: Human Rights Watch, 1999); Linda Melvern, *Conspiracy to Murder: The Rwandan Genocide* (London: Verso, 2004).

47. Melvern, *Conspiracy to Murder.*

48. Churchill, *A Little Matter of Genocide*; Lotte Hughes, *The No-Nonsense Guide to Indigenous Peoples* (London: Verso, 2003); Joe Kane, *Savages* (New York: Vintage, 1996); Marianne Schmink and Charles H. Wood, *Contested Frontiers in Amazonia* (New York: Columbia University Press, 1992); Samuel Totten, William S. Parsons, and Robert K. Hitchcock, "Confronting Genocide and Ethnocide of Indigenous Peoples: An Interdisciplinary Approach to Definition, Intervention, Prevention, and Advocacy," in *Annihilating Difference: The Anthropology of Genocide*, ed. Alexander Laban Hinton (Berkeley: University of California Press, 2002), 54–91.

49. See, for example, Frank Chalk and Kurt Jonassohn, *The History and Sociology of Genocide: Analyses and Case Studies* (New Haven, CT: Yale University Press, 1990); William D. Rubinstein, *Genocide* (Harlow, UK: Pearson/Longman, 2004).

50. Gerhard Herm, *The Celts: The People Who Came Out of the Darkness* (New York: Barnes and Noble, 1975).

51. Cited in Rummel, *Death by Government.*

52. Cited in Rummel, *Death by Government*, 50.

53. Zoe Oldenbourg, *Massacre at Montsegur: A History of the Albigensian Crusade* (Sheffield, UK: Phoenix Press, 2001); John H. Mundy, *The High Middle Ages, 1150–1309* (London: The Folio Society, 1999).

54. Clifford E. Trafzer and Joel R. Hyer, eds., *Exterminate Them!: Written Accounts of the Murder, Rape, and Enslavement of Native Americans During the California Gold Rush* (East Lansing, MI: Michigan State University Press, 1999).

55. See, for example, Churchill, *A Little Matter of Genocide*; Adam Jones, *Genocide: A Comprehensive Introduction* (New York: Routledge, 2006).

56. Quoted in Michael C. Coleman, *American Indian Children at School, 1850–1930*, 46.

57. Helen Fein, *Genocide: A Sociological Perspective* (Thousand Oaks, CA: Sage, 1993).

58. Eric D. Weitz, *A Century of Genocide: Utopias of Race and Nation*, 8.

59. Zygmunt Bauman, *Modernity and the Holocaust* (Ithaca, NY: Cornell University Press, 1991).

60. Rubinstein, *Genocide.*

61. Rubinstein, *Genocide*, 312.

62. Norbert Elias, *The Civilizing Process: The History of Manners* (New York: Urizen, 1978).

63. Steven Pinker, *The Better Angels of Our Nature: Why Violence Has Declined* (New York: Viking Press, 2011).

64. For a review of the major definitions of genocide see Alex Alvarez, *Governments, Citizens, and Genocide: A Comparative and Interdisciplinary Approach.*

65. See Alvarez, *Governments, Citizens, and Genocide.*

66. The first quote comes from Lawrence Eagleburger, cited in Peter Maas, *Love Thy Neighbor: A Story of War* (New York: Vintage, 1996), 205. The second quote was from Secretary of State Warren Christopher, cited in Roger Cohen, *Hearts Grown Brutal: Sagas of Sarajevo* (New York: Random House, 1998), 242–243.

67. Churchill, *A Little Matter of Genocide.*

68. Alexander Dallin and George W. Breslauer, *Political Terror in Communist Systems* (Stanford, CA: Stanford University Press, 1970); Valentino, *Final Solutions.*

69. See for example Jerrold Post, *Leaders and Their Followers in a Dangerous World: The Psychology of Political Behavior* (Ithaca, NY: Cornell University Press, 2004).

70. Helen Fein, "Option Paper: The Roots of Genocidal Violence," in the report of the Stockholm International Forum 2004, 26–28 January, Proceedings: *Preventing Genocide: Threats and Responsibilities* (Danagards, 2004), 149–50.

71. Rummel, *Death by Government*, 17.

72. Rummel, *Death by Government.*

73. Michael Mann, *The Dark Side of Democracy: Explaining Ethnic Cleansing* (New York: Cambridge University Press, 2005).

74. Fein, "Option Paper."

75. Gerard Prunier, *The Rwanda Crisis: History of a Genocide.*

76. Alvarez, *Governments, Citizens, and Genocide.*

77. Alvarez, *Governments, Citizens, and Genocide.*

78. Michael P. Scharf, *Balkan Justice: The Story Behind the First International War Crimes Trial and Nuremberg* (Durham, NC: Carolina Academic Press, 1997), 134.

79. Gourevitch, *We Wish to Inform You,* 309.

80. See Alvarez, *Governments, Citizens, and Genocide.*

81. Mann, *The Dark Side of Democracy.*

82. Quoted in William B. Secrest, *When the Great Spirit Died: The Destruction of the California Indians, 1850–1860* (Sanger, CA: Word Dancer Press, 2003), xiii.

83. Gourevitch, *We Wish to Inform You,* 279.

84. We use the term "he" because all the participants in Milgram's experiment were males. James Waller, *Becoming Evil: How Ordinary People Commit Genocide and Mass Killing* (New York: Oxford University Press, 2002), 106.

85. Neil J. Kressel, *Mass Hate: The Global Rise of Genocide and Terror* (New York: Plenum Press, 1996), 113.

86. Samuel P. Oliner and Pearl M. Oliner, *The Altruistic Personality: Rescuers of Jews in Nazi Europe* (New York: Free Press, 1988).

87. Michael Burleigh, *Death and Deliverance: "Euthanasia in Germany, 1900–1945* (Cambridge, UK: Cambridge University Press, 1994).

88. Olivier Degomme, "Mortality in Darfur: Lessons for Humanitarian Policy," Microcon Policy Briefing, January 2011.

89. Steven L. Burg and Paul S. Shoup, *The War in Bosnia-Herzegovina: Ethnic Conflict and International Intervention* (Armonk, NY: M. E. Sharpe, 1999); Louis Sell, *Slobodan Milosevic and the Destruction of Yugoslavia* (Durham, NH: Duke University Press, 2002); Laura Silber and Allan Little, *Yugoslavia: Death of a Nation* (New York: TV Books, 1996); Susan L. Woodward, *Balkan Tragedy: Chaos and Dissolution After the Cold War* (Washington, DC: The Brookings Institution, 1995).

90. Jan Willem Honig and Norbert Both, *Srebrenica: Record of a War Crime* (New York: Penguin, 1996); David Rohde, *Endgame, The Betrayal and Fall of Srebrenica: Europe's Worst Massacre Since World War II* (New York: Farrar, Straus, and Giroux, 1997).

91. Eric Stover and Gilles Peress, *The Graves: Srebrenica and Vukovar* (Zurich: Scalo, 1998).

92. Norman Cigar and Paul Williams, *Indictment at the Hague: The Milosevic Regime and Crimes of the Balkan Wars* (New York: New York University Press, 2002); Michael P. Scharf and William A. Schabas, *Slobodan Milosevic on Trial: A Companion* (New York: Continuum, 2002).

93. Aryeh Neier, *War Crimes: Brutality, Genocide, Terror, and the Struggle for Justice* (New York: Times Books, 1998).

94. Marguerite Feitlowitz, *A Lexicon of Terror: Argentina and the Legacies of Torture* (New York: Oxford University Press, 1998); Carlos Santiago Nino, *Radical Evil on Trial* (New Haven, CT: Yale University Press, 1996).

Chapter 11

1. Peter Iadicola and Anson Shupe, *Violence, Inequality, and Human Freedom* (Lanham, MD: Rowman & Littlefield), 391.

2. George Palermo, *The Faces of Violence* (Springfield, IL: Charles C Thomas, 1994), 236.

3. James Gilligan, *Violence: Our Deadly Epidemic and Its Causes* (New York: Grosset/Putnam, 1996), 5.

4. President's Commission on Law Enforcement and Administration of Justice, *The Challenge of Crime in a Free Society* (New York: Avon, 1968), 642.

5. Robert N. Anderson and Betty L. Smith, *Deaths: Leading Causes for 2002,* National Vital Statistics Reports (Washington, DC: Center for Disease Control and Prevention, U.S. Department of Health and Human Services, 2005).

6. R. B. Shapiro and K. A. Hassett, *The Economic Benefits of Reducing Violent Crime: A Case Study of 8 American Cities* (Washington, DC: Center for American Progress, June 2012).

7. R. B. Shapiro and K. A. Hassett, *The Economic Benefits of Reducing Violent Crime: A Case Study of 8 American Cities.*

8. Ted R. Miller, Mark A. Cohen, and Shelli B. Rossman, "Victim Costs of Violent Crime and Resulting Injuries," *Health Affairs* 12, no. 4 (1993): 186–197; Ted R. Miller, Mark A. Cohen, and Brian Wiersema, *Victim Costs and Consequences: A New Look* (Washington, DC: U. S. Department of Justice, 1996).

9. Population Information Program, *Population Reports: Ending Violence Against Women* (Baltimore, MD: Population Information Program, Center for Communication Programs, The Johns Hopkins School of Public Health and Center for Health and Gender Equity, 2000).

10. American Psychiatric Association, *Diagnostic and Statistical Manual of Mental Disorders,* 4th ed. (Washington, DC: American Psychiatric Association), 424.

11. Curt R. Bartol and Anne M. Bartol, *Criminal Behavior: A Psychosocial Approach* (Upper Saddle River, NJ: Pearson/Prentice Hall, 2005).

12. R. F. Hanson and others, "Violent Crime and Mental Health," in *Traumatic Stress: From Theory to Practice,* eds. J. R. Freedy and S. E. Hobfoll (New York: Plenum Press, 1995), 129–162; D. G. Kilpatrick and others, "Criminal Victimization: Lifetime Prevalence, Reporting to Police, and Psychological Impact," *Crime and Delinquency* 33, no. 4 (1987): 479–489; H. S. Resnick and others, "Prevalence of Civilian Trauma and PTSD in a Representative National Sample of

Women," *Journal of Clinical and Consulting Psychology* 61 (1993): 6.

13. Miller, Cohen, and Wiersema, *Victim Costs and Consequences.*

14. Albert R. Roberts and Diane Green, "Crisis Intervention With Victims of Violent Crime," in *Crisis Intervention and Time-Limited Cognitive Treatment,* eds. Albert R. Roberts and Diane Green, 2nd ed. (Thousand Oaks, CA: Sage, 2007).

15. Erika Harrell, *Violent Victimization Committed by Strangers, 1993–2010* (Washington, DC: Bureau of Justice Statistics, 2012).

16. D. G. Kilpatrick, A. Seymour, and J. Boyle, *America Speaks Out: Citizens' Attitudes about Victims' Rights and Violence* (Arlington, VA: National Center for Victims of Crime, 1991).

17. Kilpatrick, Seymour, and Boyle, *America Speaks Out.*

18. See, for example, Katherine S. Newman, *Rampage: The Social Roots of School Shootings* (New York: Basic Books, 2004); Kelly A. Zinna, *After Columbine: A Schoolplace Violence Prevention Manual* (Silverthorne, CO: Spectra Publishing, 1999).

19. Keith Sullivan, Mark Cleary, and Ginny Sullivan, *Bullying in Secondary Schools: What It Looks Like and How to Manage It* (Thousand Oaks, CA: Corwin Press, 2004); J. David Hawkins, David P. Farrington, and Richard F. Catalano, "Reducing Violence Through the Schools," in *Violence in American Schools,* eds. Delbert S. Elliott, Beatrix A. Hamburg, and Kirk R. Williams (New York: Cambridge University Press, 1998), 188–216; Faith Samples and Larry Aber, "Evaluation of School-Based Violence Prevention Programs," in *Violence in American Schools,* 217–252; Joan N. Burstyn and Rebecca Stevens, "Involving the Whole School in Violence Prevention," in *Preventing Violence in Schools: A Challenge to American Democracy,* eds. Joan N. Burstyn and others (Mahwah, NJ: Lawrence Erlbaum, 2001), 139–158; Dorothy L. Espelage and Susan M. Swearer, eds., *Bullying in American Schools: A Social-Ecological Perspective on Prevention and Intervention* (Mahwah, NJ: Lawrence Erlbaum, 2004); SuEllen Fried and Paula Fried, *Bullies, Targets, and Witnesses: Helping Children Break the Pain Chain* (New York: M. Evans and Company, 2003).

20. See, for example, Sullivan, Cleary, and Sullivan, *Bullying in Secondary Schools.*

21. Lawrence Sherman and Richard Berk, *The Minneapolis Domestic Violence Experiment* (Washington, DC: Police Foundation Reports 1, 1984); Lawrence Sherman and Richard Berk, "The Specific Deterrent Effects of Arrest for Domestic Assaults," *American Sociological Review* 49 (1984): 261–272.

22. For a summary of this research, see Denise Kindschi Gosselin, *Heavy Hands: An Introduction to the Crimes of Family Violence,* 3rd ed. (Upper Saddle River, NJ: Pearson/Prentice Hall, 2005).

23. See, for example, Eve Buzawa and Carl Buzawa, *Domestic Violence: The Criminal Justice Response,* 2nd ed. (Thousand Oaks, CA: Sage, 1996).

24. Larry K. Gaines and Roger LeRoy Miller, *Criminal Justice in Action,* 2nd ed. (Belmont, CA: Wadsworth/Thomson Learning, 2003).

25. Samuel Walker and Charles M. Katz, *Police in America: An Introduction,* 4th ed. (Boston: McGraw Hill, 2002).

26. James Q. Wilson and George L. Kelling, "Broken Windows," *Atlantic Monthly,* March 1982, 29–38.

27. James Gilligan, *Preventing Violence* (New York: Thames & Hudson, 2001), 7.

28. J. Medina, "California Sheds Prisoners but Grapples with the Courts," *The New York Times,* January 13, 2013.

29. P. K. Lattimore and C. A. Visher, *The multisite evaluation of SVORI: Summary and Synthesis.* (Washington, DC: U.S. Department of Justice, 2009).

30. Commission for the Prevention of Youth Violence, *Youth and Violence, Medicine, Nursing, and Public Health: Connecting the Dots to Prevent Violence* (Washington, DC: American Medical Association, 2000), 2.

31. Commission for the Prevention of Youth Violence, *Youth and Violence, Medicine.*

32. Gilligan, *Preventing Violence.*

33. Marc Riedel and Wayne Welsh, *Criminal Violence: Patterns, Causes, and Prevention* (Los Angeles: Roxbury, 2002).

34. Gilligan, *Preventing Violence.*

35. See, for example, Dennis Sullivan and Larry Tifft, *Restorative Justice: Healing the Foundations of Our Everyday Lives,* 2nd ed. (Monsey, NY: Willow Tree Press, 2005); Howard Zehr and Barb Toews, eds., *Critical Issues in Restorative Justice* (New York: Criminal Justice Press, 2004).

36. Center for Disease Control website, www .colorado.edu/cspv/blueprints/model/overview.html.

37. Gilligan, *Preventing Violence.*

38. See, for example, Iadicola and Shupe, *Violence, Inequality, and Human Freedom;* Gilligan, *Preventing Violence.*

39. Iadicola and Shupe, *Violence, Inequality, and Human Freedom,* 371.

40. Iadicola and Shupe, *Violence, Inequality, and Human Freedom.*

41. Elijah Anderson, *Code of the Street: Decency, Violence, and the Moral Life of the Inner City* (New York: W. W. Norton and Co. 1999), 32.

42. Gilligan, *Preventing Violence,* 82.

43. Jeffrey H. Goldstein, *Aggression and Crimes of Violence,* 2nd ed. (New York: Oxford University Press, 1986).

44. Daniel Ari Kapner, *Alcohol and Other Drugs on Campus: The Scope of the Problem* (Newton,

MA: Higher Education Center for Alcohol and Other Drug Abuse and Violence Prevention, 2006), http://higheredcenter.org/pubs/factsheets/scope.html.

45. Kapner, *Alcohol and Other Drugs on Campus.*

46. William DeJong and others, *Environmental Management: A Comprehensive Strategy for Reducing Alcohol and Other Drug Use on College Campuses* (Washington, DC: U.S. Department of Education, Higher Education Center for Alcohol and Other Drug Prevention, 1998).

47. Shelly Jackson and others, *Batterer Intervention Programs: Where Do We Go From Here?* NCJ 195079 (Washington, DC: U.S. Department of Justice, Office of Justice Programs, 2003).

48. Kerry Healey, Christine Smith, and Chris O'Sullivan, *Batterer Intervention: Program Approaches and Criminal Justice Strategies*, NCJ 168638 (Washington, DC: U.S. Department of Justice Office of Justice Programs, 1998).

49. Healey, Smith, and O'Sullivan, *Batterer Intervention.*

50. A. A. Braga and C. Winship, "What Can Cities Do to Prevent Serious Youth Violence?" *Criminal Justice Matters* 75, no. 1 (2009): 35–37.

Photo Credits

Photo 1.1 © Getty Images.
Photo 1.2 © Getty Images.
Photo 2.1 © Getty Images.
Photo 2.2 © Corbis.
Photo 3.1 © Getty Images News/Chris
    Livingston.
Photo 3.2 © Corbis.
Photo 3.3 © Corbis.
Photo 4.1 © Getty Images.
Photo 5.1 © Corbis.
Photo 5.2 © Corbis.
Photo 6.2 © Corbis.

Photo 7.2 © Corbis.
Photo 7.3 © Corbis.
Photo 7.4 © Getty Images News/Ziyah Gafic.
Photo 8.1 © Corbis.
Photo 8.2 © Getty/ Hulton Archive.
Photo 9.1 © www.rewardsforjustice.net.
Photo 9.2 © Federal Emergency Management
    Agency, www.FEMA.gov.
Photo 9.3 © FBI.
Photo 10.1 © Getty Images.
Photo 10.2 © Getty/ Hulton Archive.
Photo 10.3 © Getty Images.

Glossary

acquisitive mob Mob that is motivated by greed and a desire to acquire goods.

Adam Walsh Child Protection and Safety Act Mandated expanding the definition of "jurisdiction" to include federally-recognized American Indian tribes, expanding the number of sex offenses that must be captured by registrations, and established a new office within the U.S. Justice Department to administer the standards for sex offender notification and registration called the Office of Sex Offender Sentencing, Monitoring, Apprehending, Registering and Tracking (SMART).

addiction Turns a desire or craving for something into an urgent need. When someone is addicted to a drug, they must continue taking it in order to prevent their body from going into withdrawal.

Adoption Assistance and Child Welfare Act of 1980 Intended to prevent unwarranted removal of children from their families by making "reasonable efforts" to keep families together or to unify families in a timely manner if placement could not be avoided.

Adult Protective Services Division of each state's government that is responsible for investigating reports of elder abuse and for the provision of social services to help victims and ameliorate abuse. In most jurisdictions, these services also pertain to abused adults who have a disability, vulnerability, or other impairment as defined by state law, not just to older persons.

aggravated assault An attack or attempted attack with a weapon, regardless of whether or not an injury occurred, and an attack without a weapon when serious injury results.

aggression Behavior that is physical and/or psychologically harmful.

aggressive crowd Members share a common sense of purpose and are impulsive and emotional.

aggressive mob Mob that is motivated by emotion and targets both property and people.

Albigensian Crusade Named after the city of Albi, a Cathar stronghold. The crusade was led by nobles from the north of France who saw an opportunity for land and enrichment in addition to serving their faith and the church. Characterized by numerous massacres, this crusade saw the virtual depopulation of Southern France as entire communities were annihilated.

Alfred P. Murrah Federal Building Oklahoma City federal building that was blown up by Timothy McVeigh and Terry Nichols on April 19, 1995, killing 168 people and injuring 850.

Al Qaeda Islamic terrorist organization founded by Osama bin Laden. This group was responsible for the September 11 attacks on the World Trade Center and the Pentagon.

anger retaliation rapist Someone who feels a tremendous amount of hostility toward women and consequently uses rape as a vehicle of revenge.

anomie A theory which argues that people living in impoverished circumstances have limited access to conventional and legitimate means of success and so turn to violence as a means to achieve success.

Anti-Catholic Gordon Riots Took place in and around London in June of 1780. In less than a week, mobs burned, pillaged, and looted, leaving around 500 people dead. The army was finally called in to quell the disorder.

Anti-Drug Abuse Act of 1988 Called for mandatory minimum sentences for the possession and distribution of drugs by their type and weight.

antisocial personality disorder Individual characterized as being very narcissistic, reckless, and emotionally shallow. People with this disorder are unable to empathize or feel compassion for others.

apartheid A legal system developed in South Africa to keep the races apart and maintain white privilege in a country in which white Africans were outnumbered four to one by black Africans.

Arkan's Tigers Bosnian Serb paramilitary group that rampaged through Muslim-dominated towns, such as Bijeljina, Brčko, and Zvornik, killing, torturing, and raping. They attacked and took Srebrenica on April 18, 1992.

Armed Career Criminal Act of 1984 Imposed a mandatory minimum 15-year prison term on a convicted felon who had three previous convictions for robbery or burglary and who possessed or received a firearm.

Armenian genocide Genocide beginning in 1914 in Turkey in which over a million Armenians were killed.

Army of God A group that has been implicated in the bombing of abortion clinics and the murder of doctors who perform abortions.

Assassins Eleventh century radical Shiite Islamic sect known as the Nizari Isma'ilis. The term has become more broadly used in contemporary times.

Assault Weapons Ban of 1994 Congressional act that banned 19 weapons that looked like military weapons including AK-47s and Uzis. The act was largely symbolic because the banned weapons were rarely used in crimes.

atavisms Evolutionary throwbacks. The idea that individuals are born to be violent and criminal, and they are identifiable through a number of distinguishing physical characteristics, including the following: a small head with a large facial area; a sloping forehead; large, protruding ears; bushy eyebrows that met over the nose; abnormally large teeth; and tattoos.

Aum Shinrikyo Japanese, new religions terrorist organization led by Shoko Asahara, a former yoga teacher who preached that the end of world was coming. This group came to believe that it needed to purify humanity for the coming apocalypse by killing those who were sinful and impure. The name mean "Supreme Truth."

Auschwitz World War II Nazi death camp.

authorized terror Terrorism by governments in order to suppress dissent, quash a social or political movement, or intimidate a population.

Baader-Meinhof Gang Modern German terrorist organization.

banality of evil Hannah Arendt's famous characterization of Adolf Eichmann, the Nazi official who was responsible for much of the logistical organization and planning of the Holocaust genocide. The comment recognizes the perpetrators of genocide tend to be ordinary folks and leads to the understanding that anyone has the potential to participate in this horrible crime.

bank robberies Still relatively common. Today, California has the highest number of bank robberies compared to other states. For example, in 2011, California had 697 bank robberies compared to the state of New York, which had only 339 robberies.

Battered-Child Syndrome A collection of injuries sustained by a child as a result of repeated mistreatment or beating.

Batterer Intervention Programs (BIPs) Alternative to traditional criminal justice responses to mandatory arrest policies for battering.

behaviorally specific questions Questions on surveys that rely on specific behaviors (e.g., forced to have sex against your will) compared to questions that rely on terms (e.g., raped).

bias crime A criminal offense committed against a person, property, or society that is motivated, in whole or in part, by the offender's bias against a race, religion, disability, sexual orientation, or ethnicity/national origin.

bigoted perpetrators Those who have prejudices against the populations being targeted for destruction. Often these hatreds and stereotypes are long standing and ancient, being rooted in history.

blistering agents Blister agents, such as mustard gas, kill by burning whatever parts of the body come into contact with them—such as the skin, eyes, and lungs.

blood agents Kill by affecting the blood after being inhaled. Specifically, these chemicals—such as hydrogen cyanide and cyanogen chloride—prevent the body from utilizing the oxygen in the blood.

Blueprints for Violence Prevention Project Established in 1996 by the University of Colorado at Boulder's Center for the Study and Prevention of Violence (CSPV). This project created a national program intended to identify violence prevention programs that were effective.

Boston Gun Project An interagency, deterrence-based project that includes the Boston Police Department; the Bureau of Alcohol, Tobacco, and Firearms; the Massachusetts Department of Parole; the Boston school police; and a research team from Harvard University. All program participants communicate with one another to share intelligence on a regular basis in order to try to meet the project's goal of preventing violence in inner-city neighborhoods through heightened surveillance, rapid identification of violence and violent groups, and swift sanctions, such as arrest and conviction.

Brady Handgun Violence Prevention Act (Brady Bill) of 1993 Mandated criminal history background checks on persons applying to purchase firearms from federally licensed firearm dealers.

brain dysfunctions Abnormalities in the brain that may predispose a person to become violent. For example, one study using electroencephalographic (EEG) brain scans found that those who showed a long-term pattern of violent behavior were three times more likely (65%) to have abnormalities in their EEG readings than those who were rarely violent.

"Broken Windows" strategy A community policing strategy that emphasizes a crackdown on what are sometimes termed quality-of-life crimes, such as panhandling, public intoxication, loitering, and graffiti. By focusing on these types of relatively minor crimes, police departments have tried to prevent the perpetration of more serious crimes that they felt were encouraged by the urban decay so characteristic of many crime-ridden communities.

brutalization hypothesis The argument that capital punishment may actually serve to increase murder rates rather than cause them to decrease.

BTK killer Stands for "bind, torture, kill." Denise Rader was a serial killer in Wichita, Kansas. He was convicted of killing ten people over the course of 30 years beginning in 1974.

bullying Has emerged as an important area of concern, especially in light of the spate of school shootings that have happened in recent years, since many of the perpetrators have had a history of being bullied by other students.

bureaucratic perpetrators Those who participate in genocide because they work in organizations that are called upon to take part in the apparatus of killing. Their participation may be fairly small, mundane, and appear fairly harmless—such as scheduling trains or compiling lists—but it is nonetheless ultimately lethal.

Bureau of Alcohol, Tobacco, and Firearms Federal law enforcement agency authorized to grant licenses to dealers and manufacturers and to enforce the other requirements of gun control legislation.

burglary When an offender(s) breaks into a residence and steals a homeowner's belongings. This is a property crime because there is no force or threat of force to a person.

careerist perpetrators Those who become perpetrators because they can advance their careers and get promotions and choice assignments through participation. For these individuals, assisting in the persecution of the victims is simply a way to get ahead professionally.

casual crowd Members have no common purpose and still define themselves as individuals.

Cathars One of the best-known historical examples of genocide. This prevalent and popular Christian sect in Southern France during the early 13th century believed that the world was evil and that people should live a frugal and ascetic life in order to avoid being corrupted by the world. They also believed in reincarnation so treated men and women equally.

Centers for Disease Control and Prevention A federal agency of the U.S. government under the Department of Health and Human Services. Its main goal is to protect public health and safety through the control and prevention of disease, injury, and disability. All violence is considered intentional injuries.

character contest A series of interactions in which at least one actor—but usually both—will attempt to establish or "save face."

Chechnya Declared independence when the Soviet Union was disintegrating. Has been wracked by an ever more vicious campaign of state terror perpetuated by the Russians and countered by the Chechens.

chemical and biological weapons Relatively easy for terrorists to obtain and covey to targets. Biological weapons have been around since the Middle Ages.

child abuse When physical violence is used on a child.

Child Abuse Prevention and Treatment Act of 1974 Established the National Center on Child Abuse and Neglect under the U.S. Department of Health, Education, and Welfare.

Child Protection Services Division Each state has a division mandated to protect and remove children from abusive situations.

choking agents Kill by damaging the lungs and causing them to fill with mucus. Examples include phosgene gas and chlorine gas, which were used in World War I.

Church Arson Prevention Act of 1996 Mandated the FBI's Uniform Crime Reporting (UCR) program begin collecting statistics on offenses motivated by bias against physical and mental disabilities, in January 1997.

civil protection order Generally offers victims a temporary judicial injunction that directs an assailant to stop battering, threatening, or harming their victim.

code of the streets Code of behavior that involves protecting one's honor and reputation against acts of disrespect, even with violence if necessary.

cohesive crowd Members gather for a common purpose but still define themselves as individuals.

collective political violence Any violence that is carried out by a state or government, including genocide.

comfort killers Murder for creature comforts, such as financial gain.

Committee of Public Safety and the Revolutionary Tribunal Comprising 12 men, the Committee of Public Safety was invested with more and more dictatorial powers after the beginning of the French Revolution. Its most influential member was a man named Maximilien Robespierre, known to all as "the Incorruptible." Robespierre unleashed a reign of terror that took thousands of lives and destroyed the brief flowering of democratic values that had begun.

communal violence Crowds erupting into uncontrolled and destructive violence in countless places and at numerous times for many different reasons. From ancient times to the present, many societies have confronted the problem of group violence—wracking cities, communities, and entire regions.

Community Mental Health Centers Act of 1963 Provide states and other jurisdictions with federal assistance for treatment programs.

comradely perpetrators Take part in the killing because they don't want to let down their comrades and friends. This kind of killer participates because his bonds to the other members of the group or unit are stronger than any prohibitions he may have against participation.

Conflict Tactics Scale An instrument to measure violence, spans a range of behaviors, including reasoning, verbal aggression, and physical aggression or violence.

conformity When individuals have a natural tendency to conform to the demands of a group.

conformity to peer pressure Related to social learning theory, recognizes the strong rewards that peer groups can provide to their individual members.

confrontational homicide Characterized by altercations that typically evolve from verbal exchanges of insults into physical contests.

Controlled Substance Act of 1970 Consolidated all previous drug laws into one law designed to control prescription drugs *and* illicit drugs.

Convention on the Prevention and Punishment of the Crime of Genocide The event in which the United Nations officially defined genocide and recognized it as a crime under International Law.

convict culture Prison culture which attaches a terrible stigma to "snitches" or "rats" who report on incidents of rape. The "snitches" are the lowest members of the inmate hierarchy.

coordinated community responses Response to violence across the domains of criminal justice, social services, and victim advocacy groups.

crack cocaine A version of its powder derivative.

crime-control vigilantism Collective violence targeted with the elimination of a crime.

criminal homicide Includes murder and manslaughter.

criminal terrorism Refers to terrorism committed to achieve some illicit goal or to protect an illegal operation.

crowd A collection of individuals who may or may not share a common purpose.

cultural genocide Group violence of which genocide has been the most lethal as far as killing during the 20th century.

cycle of violence The idea that those who experience and/or witness violence as a child are more likely to become violent in adulthood, compared with children who do not experience or witness violence.

date-rape drugs Drugs often with no color, smell, or taste that are easily added to flavored drinks without the victim's knowledge. The drugs can affect a victim quickly and serve to render them helpless and unable to refuse sex. Importantly, they also hinder victims' memories so they are unable to recall the victimization or adequately testify on their own behalf.

defensive gun use Self-protective behavior involving guns.

dehumanization It is easier to remove ethical restrictions against violence when we perceive the victims to be less than us or perhaps even less than human.

deindividuation Refers to the long-noted phenomenon of individuals who lose their sense of self and individuality when in a group. This loss of a personal identity means that individuals are more capable of acting outside of the boundaries of their normal behavior.

deliberation Implies that the killing was planned and thought about rather than committed on impulse.

Desaparecidos "The Disappeared Ones." Estimates of the number of victims range from a low of 10,000 to a high of 30,000 who were "disappeared" during the *junta* that ruled Argentina during the 1970s.

despotic genocides Involve situations in which a government uses genocide as a weapon against rivals for political power.

developmental genocides Those in which the targeted groups are seen as an impediment to the colonization and/or exploitation of a given geographic area. This happens most often against indigenous peoples who may be perceived as being in the way of progress.

differential association theory Sociological variant of social learning theory, asserts that if you associate with individuals and groups who use violence and who have attitudes supporting and justifying violence, then you are more likely to engage in violent behavior yourself.

dirty bomb Conventional type of explosive that is laced with radioactive elements.

dirty war During the 1970s, the military *junta* that ruled Argentina engaged in a war against its own citizens. Originally focused on suppressing leftist revolutionaries, the government soon began to attack journalists, writers, intellectuals, students, union organizers, and supporters—in short, anyone who was even suspected of being a leftist sympathizer or of not supporting the state.

disciplined perpetrators Those who participate in a genocide because of the need to conform within certain institutional settings where obeying orders is the norm and disobedience is punished. This is perhaps most applicable to police officers, military personnel, and militia members—all organizations in which obedience is very important.

disinhibitor Substance, such as alcohol, that has the effect of loosening self-restraint on behavior.

dominance A higher rank or status in relationship to others, most common among males. To achieve status, males will commonly resort to violence. Once status is achieved, violence falls dramatically.

drug-facilitated sexual assault Rapes in which the victim is under the influence of "date-rape drugs," which can render them helpless and unable to refuse sex.

Duluth Program The model for most of the BIPs across the country. Based on a feminist perspective on battering, these programs work to teach men about the nature and impact of patriarchy and resocialize them into adopting more equal and nonviolent intimate relationships.

economic deprivation Poverty.

Eighteenth Amendment Outlawed the manufacture, sale, and distribution of alcohol.

Einsatzgruppen Special extermination squads that followed behind the German army in World War II and were tasked with rounding up all Soviet political figures and Jews and then executing them en masse.

elder abuse One of most recent types of family violence to be acknowledged as a social problem and includes physical abuse, psychological abuse, material or financial exploitation, and neglect.

emotional desensitization Reduction in distress-related physiological reactivity to observations or thoughts of violence.

enforcement terror Terrorism in order to suppress dissent, quash a social or political movement, or intimidate a population.

escape mob Characterized by panicked behavior; it is very dangerous and can be instantly aroused into mindless violence.

ethnic cleansing The process or policy of eliminating unwanted ethnic or religious groups by many means, including deportation, forcible displacement, mass murder, or by threats of such acts, with the intent of creating a territory inhabited by people of a homogeneous ethnicity, religion, culture, and/or history.

ethological and biological explanations of violence Theories that state there is an evolutionary benefit to violence. In the past, violent behavior has often proved necessary for survival because it allows for a range of responses to the problem of staying alive, for example to kill and eat prey or as a response to a perceived threat when there is no escape.

Eugenics movement Attempts to improve the human race through selective breeding practices, forced sterilization programs, and similar kinds of policies. These ideas formed the philosophical justification for many discriminatory laws, beliefs, and policies.

excusable homicide Accidental or unintentional killings that did not occur because of negligence or recklessness.

expressive crowd Members share a common purpose and collective sense of anger and/or frustration.

expressive mob Members see violence as a means to express anger, resentment, and frustration.

expressive violence Motivations for violence are emotional, such as jealousy or anger.

extralegal means of social control Controlling an individual or group with measures that are illegal and/or the legality of the measures is ambivalent.

facilitating hardware The weapon used to kill.

Fair Sentencing Act of 2010 Reduced the disparity in sentencing between those using powder versus crack cocaine.

Family Preservation and Support Services Act of 1993 Mandated to expand the services available to strengthen families as well as to provide additional supports for children who must be placed outside the home.

family violence Umbrella term that includes a wide range of behaviors, including physical, sexual, financial, and verbal or other emotional abuse between a number of dyadic relationships: intimates (e.g., spouses and ex-spouses, boy/girlfriends and exes); parents and children; siblings; and the elderly and their caregivers, including their children.

fatality review team Brings together a variety of members from various groups that have an interest in preventing intimate partner violence and may include law enforcement officers, judges, defense and prosecuting attorneys, victim advocates, mental health workers, county coroners, and survivors among others.

fearful perpetrators Lend their help to the killing during a genocide because they genuinely fear that they will be hurt or killed if they don't participate.

Federal Firearms Act of 1938 Intended to decrease gang-related violence and also to control the illegal distribution of alcohol by taxing it heavily.

felony murder Statutes for murders that occur during the commission of another felony, such as a robbery.

Firearms Owners' Protection Act of 1968 Passed with backing of NRA to prohibit the federal government from centralizing the records of firearms owners or firearms transactions and allowed federal firearms licensees to sell arms at temporary locations, such as gun shows.

First Amendment Protects a citizen's right to free speech, including hate speech.

first-degree murder Generally committed with both premeditation and deliberation.

forced assimilation The policy of taking children away from their families and educating them as a way to destroy their native cultures.

frustration-aggression hypothesis Contends that violence is one possible response for individuals who feel frustrated and thwarted in achieving something.

fundamentalist terrorism Terrorism that typically involves attempts to return a faith to its founding beliefs and principles. Fundamentalism divides the world into two easily understood camps: good and evil; right and wrong; light and dark. To the true believer, violence in pursuit of fundamentalist goals is perpetrated in defense of God's word and so is not wrongful. Those who do not share the same vision of their faith are by definition spiritually and morally inferior, and are therefore legitimate victims of righteous violence.

general deterrence argument Someone who is thinking about committing a murder refrains from doing so because they fear the death penalty.

general strain theory Anomie theory refined by Robert Agnew to include strains other than economic conditions. Agnew argues that there are three main sources of the strain: An individual is stopped from achieving a goal; something they possess or value is removed and/or threatened; and something negative or unwanted is imposed. When somebody experiences one of these three situations, and when that occurrence is accompanied by difficulty in coping and a sense of anger, then violence may result as that person lashes out to resolve the situation through force and aggression.

general theory of crime Individual criminality is the result of low self-control. Low self-control is a product of early socialization and *not* a trait innate within individuals.

genocide First coined in 1944 by the Polish lawyer Raphael Lemkin, in his book *Axis Rule in Occupied Europe.* The word was originally meant to bring attention to the atrocities being perpetrated by the Nazis. From the Greek *genos,* which means race or tribe and the Latin *cide,* which translates as killing. The term refers to the killing of a race or tribe or population.

genocide in the Darfur region Darfur is a region in Sudan that is home to about 6 million people from almost 100 tribes, but all are Muslims. After people in this region took up arms against the government, the Sudanese government unleashed Arab militias known as the Janjaweed, who killed over 400,000 people and displaced over 2,500,000 more.

GHB Gamma hydroxybutyric acid. One of the three most common "date-rape drugs."

Guardian Angels Labeled vigilantes by police, this group was founded in 1979 in the Bronx and is still active in a number of communities. Its members patrol the subways, streets, and neighborhoods in order to prevent crime. They can be identified by their red berets.

guerrilla warfare The term means "little war" and originated in the Napoleonic wars after the French army invaded Spain as part of Napoleon's attempt to conquer Europe.

Gun Control Act of 1968 Passed in the wake of urban rioting and the assassination of Martin Luther King Jr. Its five objectives included prohibiting interstate firearm sales, prohibiting sales to the expanded list of "dangerous peoples," added other "dangerous devices" to the prohibited weapons list, prohibited "Saturday Night Specials," and prohibited the importation of military surplus weapons.

gun control legislation Occurs at federal, state, and local levels.

handgun homicides Homicides with handguns. The increase in gun violence in the late 1980s through mid-1990s is attributable to handguns.

hard targets Protected targets.

Harrison Act of 1914 Made nonmedical use of cocaine and heroin illegal.

hate crimes When offenders select a victim because of some characteristic, such as their race or religion.

Hate Crime Statistics Act of 1990 Directed the attorney general to collect data "about crimes that manifest evidence of prejudice based on race, religion, sexual orientation, or ethnicity."

hedonistic lust killers Distinguished by their effort to obtain sexual pleasure from killing. The lust killer derives direct sexual satisfaction from murdering his victims or by having sex with the corpse or by mutilating or cutting off sex organs.

Hereros German South-West Africa in what is present-day Namibia. The first genocide of the 20th century was in this region.

Hezbollah Contemporary Lebanon-based organization. Believe themselves to be *Mujahideen* [holy warriors], who fight a Holy War for the people.

Holocaust Preeminent example of genocide, in which the Nazis killed 21 million people.

homicidal triad Histories of serial killers frequently include these three behaviors: bed-wetting past an appropriate age, cruelty to animals, and fire setting.

human rights violation Any act that violates the inalienable fundamental rights to which a person is entitled.

Hutu Population that controlled the government in Rwanda that instigated the genocide in the 1990s.

ideological genocide The attempted destruction of a population because of a belief system.

ideological perpetrators True believers who find their justification for participation in a genocide in a belief system that demands the destruction of a group. This kind of killer is most typically drawn from among the social elites.

incapacitation Someone who has committed murder is put to death and therefore is prevented from committing another murder in the future.

Inequality Generally described as the economic, social, and political inequality between the rich and the poor.

informal social control Attachments to family, peers and conventional activities, such as school.

institutional-anomie theory of crime Links crime to the existing social structure. Suggest that the high rates of crime and violence found in U.S. society can, in part, be explained with reference to the notion of the "American Dream," which suggests that economic success can be achieved by anyone who works hard, plays by the rules, and is willing to engage in competition with others for jobs, income, and status. Our culture pressures people to strive relentlessly for success—primarily monetary success. Relentless pressure for financial success causes some to turn to crime.

institutional violence Violent behaviors perpetuated in an organizational setting, such as in the family, a workplace, the military, or through a religious organization.

instrumental violence Violence is a means to an end, such as acts committed during a robbery.

insurgency warfare Different from terrorism in that it involves larger, military-style forces that tend to attack the military forces of their enemy and often seek to hold and control territory.

intergenerational transmission of violence theory Sometimes referred to as the cycle of violence. Contends that those who experience and/or witness violence as a child are more likely to become violent in adulthood, compared with children who do not experience or witness violence.

intermale aggression Young men competing for status by being the toughest and strongest.

International Criminal Tribunal at The Hague Sometimes called the International Criminal Court (ICC), it is a permanent tribunal to prosecute individuals for genocide, crimes against humanity, and war crimes.

International Criminal Tribunal for Rwanda First international court to convict someone for the crime of genocide. This international court convicted Jean Paul Akayesu. In this verdict, the court underscored the fact that rape and sexual violence also constitute genocide in the same way as any other act, as long as they are committed with the intent to destroy a particular group. The court defined rape as "the physical invasion of a sexual nature, committed on a person under circumstances which are coercive."

interpersonal violence Assaults, rapes, robberies, and murders.

intimate partner violence Intentional use of physical force against an intimate partner (boy/girlfriend, spouse, or ex). It has been around forever but has only been acknowledged for around the past 30 years.

Islamic *Salafi Jihad* A fundamentalist movement inspired by visions of a holy war in the name of Islam.

Jacobins Extremists led by Robespierre during the French Revolution. They executed a large number of their fellow revolutionaries who had been calling for more moderation.

Jacob Wetterling Act Required persons convicted of a criminal offense against a minor or sexually violent offense and persons deemed to be "sexually violent predators" to register a current address with state law enforcement.

Japanese Red Army Modern Japanese terrorist organization.

Jeanne Clery Disclosure of Campus Security Policy and Campus Crime Statistics Act of 1998 This act requires institutions to publish more specific policies regarding the awareness and prevention of sexual assault and also requires basic rights to be given to sexual assault victims.

jumping in Ritualized violence, often part of initiation into gangs. Proves the toughness of the new member but also symbolizes the centrality of violence to the life of the gang.

justifiable homicide Killings judged to be legally acceptable because they occurred in defense of life or property.

Kenosha Domestic Abuse Intervention Project A mandatory arrest law in Wisconsin. Data from the project indicates that after the laws went into affect, women experienced a 12-fold increase in arrests while the number of men arrested doubled during the same time period.

Ketamine Ketamine hydrochloride. One of the three most common "date-rape drugs."

Khmer Rouge Also called the Red Khmers. This was a Cambodian communist group who overthrew the government in 1975 and established Democratic Kampuchea, which was anything but democratic. The Khmer Rouge had decided it wanted to create a utopian communist Khmer nation, free from what they saw as corrupting and foreign influences. Over a four-year period, the Khmer Rouge systematically starved, beat, worked to death, tortured, and murdered between one and two million of its own citizens.

Kristallnacht or Night of Broken Glass November 9, 1938. After a young Jewish man shot and killed a Nazi diplomatic aide in Paris, the Nazis orchestrated a series of attacks over the next few days that resulted in an estimated 7,500 Jewish businesses being looted, over 1,000 synagogues destroyed, just under 100 murders, and some 30,000 Jews being sent to concentration camps.

Ku Klux Klan (KKK) White supremacist group founded in 1866. Its main purpose was to fight Reconstruction efforts. The KKK is still around today.

Los Angeles City Riot of 1992 Immediate precipitants included the shooting of Latasha Harlins, a 15-year-old African American teenager who had been shot in the back of the head by a Korean owner of a deli store after a dispute. The suspended sentence received by the deli owner was perceived as lenient by the African American community and served to reinforce a belief that African Americans were subject to different standards of justice compared with others.

low-intensity warfare Different from terrorism in that it involves larger, military-style forces that tend to attack the military forces of their enemy and often seek to hold and control territory.

lynch mobs An extralegal execution by a mob.

M19 A Columbian guerrilla movement paid by Pablo Escobar's Medellin drug cartels to blow an airliner out of the sky because he believed a presidential candidate was on board.

mandatory arrest Require police to detain a perpetrator when there is probable cause that an assault or battery has occurred or if a restraining order is violated, regardless of a victim's consent or protestations.

manslaughter Criminal homicides in which the degree of responsibility is considered much less than murder, not only because premeditation and deliberation are absent, but also because the offender did not act with malice.

Marijuana Tax Act of 1937 Tax on the sale of marijuana.

mass murder Generally understood to have taken place when someone kills four or more victims in one location at one general point in time. The killings may stretch over a period of hours, but they are all part of the same emotional experience.

materialist perpetrators Those who try to profit from the genocide.

Matthew Shepard & James Byrd, Jr. Hate Crimes Prevention Act Signed into law by President Obama in March of 2010. The law expanded already existing federal hate crime legislation to include violence based on gender, sexual orientation, gender identity, and disability in addition to the already existing criteria based on race and religion.

megamurderers Totalitarian regimes of the last century have been the most lethal in recent history. Stalin's Soviet Union, Mao's China, Pol Pot's Cambodia, and Hitler's Germany were some of the worst 20th century human rights offenders.

Megan's Law Legislation that allowed the release of offender information "for any purpose permitted under the laws of the state." This gives states the power to determine what kind and how much of the information about offenders is disclosed to whom and for what purpose.

middleman minority groups Serve as intermediaries between producers and consumers in a society. Their role alienates them from the mainstream society.

militia Term in the Second Amendment that is a source of confusion. It's not clear whether the amendment refers to a select group of citizens who serve as soldiers who have the right to bear arms or if all citizens have that right.

Minneapolis Domestic Violence Experiment The first large-scale experiment to test the deterrent effects of arrest on batterers, began 1981.

mission killers On a mission to rid the world of a group of people they perceive as unworthy or inferior in some way.

mob A crowd that is seen as being out of control.

mob violence Large groups of people engaging in what we perceive as mindless and excessive brutality.

muggings Typical street robberies involving individuals, also called *stickups*.

Mujahideen "Holy Warriors" who fight a Holy War for the people.

multicide The killing of more than one person in mass murder, spree murder, or a serial murder.

Muslim Brotherhood A radical Islamic fundamentalist organization.

Narodnaya Volya Also known as the People's Will. The organization employed terror and violence in the cause of anarchy and nationalism in its attempts to destroy the Russian monarchy and Tsar.

National College Women Sexual Assault Victimization Study Carried out by Bonnie Fisher and her colleagues in 1997. The survey involved telephone interviews of 4,446 randomly selected women who were attending a two- or four-year college or university. In addition to rape, the NCWSV asked a series of behaviorally specific questions that sought to assess whether respondents had experienced a range of sexually assaultive victimizations.

National Corrections Reporting Program Administered by the BJS, the program collects data so we can examine what happens when rape offenders are adjudicated.

National Crime Victimization Survey (NCVS) Designed by the U.S. Department of Justice Bureau of Justice Statistics to measure crime victimization.

National Family Violence Survey (NFVS) One of three, large nationally representative surveys that have estimated the annual rates of intimate partner violence.

National Firearms Act of 1934 Intended to decrease gang-related violence and also to control the illegal distribution of alcohol by taxing them heavily.

National Incident Based Reporting System (NIBRS) FBIs national database of crime implemented to include more characteristics of the incident than previous reporting systems. NIBRS data is more specific than the UCR and includes many more offenses that local agencies have to report information on. It includes detailed information on crime incidents, including the characteristics of the victim, such as age, gender, race, ethnicity, and resident status. In all, NIBRS categorizes each incident and arrest in one of 22 basic crime categories that span 46 separate offenses. A total of 53 data elements about the victim, property, and offender are collected under NIBRS.

National Instant Criminal Background Check System Required a background check by the FBI or a state point of contact on all persons applying to receive firearms from a registered firearms dealer.

National Intimate Partner and Sexual Violence Survey (NISVS) Conducted by the Centers for Disease Control and Prevention, not only asked respondents about victimizations that happened to them in the past 12 months but also about victimizations they had experienced in their lifetimes. The survey measured a representative sample of the adult men and women 18 years of age and older.

nationalist-separatist terrorism Exemplified by groups that attempt to create a nation or achieve political autonomy and independence for their people.

National Prohibition Act or Volstead Act Gave federal agencies the power to enforce the 18th Amendment.

National Rifle Association (NRA) Perhaps the most powerful lobbying organization in Washington, D.C., claim that any legislation aimed at controlling the possession of guns by citizens infringes upon their rights.

National Violence Against Women and Men Survey One of three large nationally representative surveys that have estimated the annual rates of intimate partner violence. This survey was introduced to respondents as a survey on personal safety, so, unlike the NCVS, it did not communicate to respondents that interviewers are interested in crimes.

National Youth Survey (NYS) Survey designed to measure offending behavior of adolescents.

Nazis Adolf Hitler's government responsible for the Holocaust in World War II.

negative stereotypes Stereotypes that characterize any group in a negative way. These stereotypes have been shown to increase against immigrant populations during times of economic depression.

nerve agents Kill by inhibiting the functioning of an important enzyme that regulates nerve functioning. These tend to be the most dangerous form of chemical weapons because they are lethal, even in extremely small doses. Examples include tabun and VX.

Netherlands Institute of War Documentation Commissioned by the Dutch government in

1996 in response to a public outcry to investigate the Srebrenica massacre.

new religions terrorism A form of religious extremist terrorism.

New York City Draft Riots of 1863 Began with a preplanned and organized protest of the draft and then spontaneously evolved into a race and class riot.

Older Americans Act of 1965 The first piece of national legislation that expressed society's commitment to protect vulnerable older Americans at risk.

Operation Ceasefire A program launched in Boston, Massachusetts, in the early 1990s that uses rewards and incentives for reducing violence to balance the punishments meted out by the criminal justice system.

Pam Lychner Sexual Offender Tracking and Identification Act of 1996 Named in memory of a victims' rights activist who died in the TWA Flight 800 crash off the coast of Long Island, New York. This act mandated the creation of a national database of convicted sex offenders designed to track offenders as they moved from state to state and cover for states not in compliance with the Wetterling Act.

patriarchy Refers to the inequity of power held by males over females. The term comes from the Greek word for patriarch or "father as ruler." This idea proposes that the subjugation of women by men is built into the organization of society.

phencyclidine or PCP Known as angel dust, ozone, whack, or rocket fuel. This drug can be ingested in many forms and can result in feelings of invulnerability, paranoia, and extreme unease—all of which can lead to aggression.

phrenology Study of the shape of the skull.

political terrorism Terrorism that has as its primary aim some type of political goal, whether it is overthrowing a government, maintaining political power, or changing government policy.

popular justice Has been used as an argument for lynching—the mob is making sure that justice is served in cases where a crime had been committed.

postpartum psychosis Covers a group of mental illnesses with sudden onset of psychotic symptoms following childbirth.

post-traumatic stress disorder (PTSD) Individuals who experience an extreme and distressing event can develop a set of symptoms that include recurrent dreams and nightmares, flashbacks, avoidance behaviors, psychological numbing, outbursts of anger, difficulty concentrating, a heightened startle response, and various other problems that can dramatically affect their ability to function and maintain relationships and jobs.

power assertive rapist Power and dominance are the primary motivating forces. This type of individual is usually very concerned with their physical appearance and tends to be very well dressed and groomed. Violence is often an intrinsic part of the rape, since it visibly confirms their absolute control over the victim.

power/control killers Murder to obtain a sense of domination and total control over their victims. Although sex is sometimes involved, the pleasure is primarily derived from the complete control the killer has over his victim.

power reassurance rapist Generally considered to be the most common type of sexual assaulter and is someone who suffers from low self-esteem and feelings of being inadequate. This may be reflected in their personal appearance since they often tend to have bad personal hygiene and wear dirty clothes. They don't typically have a large friendship network, and their interpersonal skills are fairly minimal, which also means that they often find menial jobs without much responsibility and where they don't interact with the public.

premeditation Knowledge and intention to kill or harm.

prevention versus intervention A preventive philosophy attempts to prevent injury and/or violence from occurring in the first place while intervention relies on "after the fact" mobilization after an event has already occurred.

primary aggressor Allows officers to distinguish between a person who is a victim, largely using violence to defend themselves, and the abuser.

primary homicides Involve intimates, friends, and acquaintances.

primary prevention Involves reaching out to the population at large. This level of prevention concerns the implementation of society- or community-wide preventative measures regardless of individual risk factors.

prison rape Rape and sexual assaults against inmates that occurs inside correctional facilities and can be perpetrated by other inmates or by correctional staff.

Prison Rape Elimination Act of 2003 Requires the Bureau of Justice Statistics to develop a new data collection on the incidence and prevalence of sexual assault within correctional facilities.

procedural justice Contends that conformity to group rules is as much or more because of fair procedures in delivering sanctions as it is to fair or favorable outcomes.

psychoactive effects of drugs Studies attempting to find a link between various drugs and violence have been inconsistent. In addition, all of these studies are correlational and not experimental, which means that no causal relationship has been established.

psychopathy Antisocial personality disorder. Individual is characterized as being very narcissistic, reckless, emotionally shallow, and unable to empathize or feel compassion for others.

public health perspective Examines the factors that are related to the prevalence of violence and tries to prevent them.

race riot Exploded into the U.S. consciousness during the 1960s and yet again in the 1990s. Riots involving race are also ultimately about class.

rape The specific definition of rape varies by state but it generally includes having oral, anal, or vaginal sex with a person against their will; includes both male and female victims and both known and unknown offenders.

rape law reforms By 1980, most states had passed some form of rape reform legislation. Although the nature and scope of rape law reforms vary significantly across jurisdictions, there are common reform themes such as replacing the single crime code of rape with a series of offenses graded by seriousness with commensurate penalties, changing consent standards, eliminating corroboration requirements, and enacting rape shield laws.

Reconstruction Term for the post–Civil War period. Southern whites began relying on violent and repressive tactics, of which lynching was the most lethal manifestation, in order to protect their privileged way of life relative to blacks.

regime-control vigilantism Concerns groups that engage in violence in an effort to control the government if it strays from an acceptable course of action and policy.

regime or state terrorism Refers to the actions of a government in using terror to intimidate and suppress dissent.

relative deprivation A type of inequality; being poor and living within a relatively affluent community.

religious extremist terrorism A form of substate terrorism.

repressive terror Terrorism in order to suppress dissent, quash a social or political movement, or intimidate a population.

restorative justice Largely concerned with repairing the harm and damage caused by violence and criminality. This approach generally relies on cooperative rather than punitive and judgmental processes and often involves mediation, restitution, and similar forms of healing.

retribution The argument that murderers should be executed because they deserve to be.

retributive genocides Perpetrated by one group against another engaged in a struggle for political and social power.

righteous slaughter Perpetrators perceive that their violence is in defense of some important value or principle and that the victims are not innocent but, on the contrary, have brought violence upon themselves.

right-wing terrorism Refers to conservative organizations that seek to preserve a political system or to return society to some past or mythic time of greatness.

riots Group violence that occurs in particular political and social contexts that influence how they are perceived and defined.

robbery Incorporates two threatening elements, the use of force and the theft of property.

Rohyphol Flunitrazepam. One of the three most common "date-rape drugs."

routine activities theory There are three elements that are generally necessary for the commission of a crime to occur: a motivated offender; a suitable target; and lack of capable guardianship.

Rwandan genocide Retributive genocide in which the Hutu government instigated a genocide against the Tutsi population, partially because the Hutus were trying to maintain power during a civil war.

sadism People who derive pleasure from harming others.

sadistic rapist Also known as the anger excitation rapist. This is someone who displays extreme violence and cruelty in his attacks.

same-sex unions Marriage outside of heterosexual relationships.

San Francisco Vigilance Committee A vigilance committee formed by businessmen in the spring of 1851 to protect the lives and property of San Franciscans. The men created a constitution and bylaws and notified the community via the local newspaper that they would punish criminals.

Schedule I drugs Drugs that have no accepted medical utility and a high potential for abuse.

Schedule II drugs Substances having a high abuse risk but also some accepted medical purpose.

Second Amendment Amendment inextricably linked to our current gun culture debate. States "A well regulated Militia, being necessary to the security of a free State, the right of the people to keep and bear Arms, shall not be infringed."

secondary homicides Involve strangers. Also called *stranger crime*.

secondary prevention Focuses on intervention strategies for those who are at an elevated risk of engaging in violence.

second-degree murder Considered a little less serious because they do not involve premeditation and deliberation.

self-protection argument When private citizens have weapons in their homes or are able to carry concealed weapons, they are less likely to be successfully targeted by criminals.

self-protective action About two out of three victims engage in such things as appealing or reasoning with the offender, which seems to help their situation in some way, possibly helping them to avoid injury or protect their property.

semiautomatic weapons Fire more rounds than regular handguns and now account for 80% of all handgun wounds. Allow offenders to inflict multiple wounds.

serial murder The murderer kills on at least three occasions, with an emotional cooling-off period between the incidents. This cooling-off period can last days, weeks, months, or years.

serotonin A substance that helps relay messages over the gap (the synapse) between nerve cells and allows the messages to proceed. Low levels of serotonin are linked to a variety of issues, including depression, suicide, and anxiety as well as impulsive acts of aggression.

sex offender registries Regulations vary by state, but all states have some form of registry in which offenders convicted of various sexual assault statutes must register their location of residence.

sexual assault Sexual victimization.

sexual assault nurse examiners Provide expert testimony for the prosecution in sexual assault cases.

sexual assault response teams Specialized units that respond to rape cases and include a coordinated response to the victimization, including victim assistance workers along with special prosecutors and investigators.

shame The painful feeling arising from the consciousness of something improper or dishonorable done by oneself or another.

Shari'a Islamic law.

Sicarii A radical Jewish group that derived their name from a short, curved knife known as a Sica. The Sicarii were known for bold attacks against the Romans and anyone sympathetic to the Romans when the Romans had control of Palestine.

simple assault attack without a weapon resulting either in no injury, minor injury (for example, bruises, black eyes, cuts, scratches, or swelling) or an undetermined injury requiring less than 2 days of hospitalization. Simple assaults also include cases of attempted assault without a weapon.

single-issue terrorism Groups that are focused on only one particular topic. Earth First!, the Earth Liberation Front, and the Evan Mecham Eco-Terrorist International Conspiracy (EMETIC) are considered single-issue terrorism organizations.

situational crime prevention Seeks to understand technical and structural solutions to crime and in response designs environments or products in ways that minimize the risk of victimization.

social group-control vigilantism Groups whose goal is to keep some population group in their place, usually within the lower levels of class structure.

social learning theory Combines various sociological and psychological insights in trying to make sense of human behavior. We learn from the things we experience, the things we see, and the people with whom we associate. We learn from our surroundings, experiences, acquaintances, friends, and family. Contends that we learn aggression like any other behavior—by watching others and imitating their behavior.

social revolutionary terrorism The type of terrorism most people envision when they think about terrorism. It invariably involves groups trying to overthrow an established order.

sociopathy Also known as psychopathy or antisocial personality disorder. Individuals characterized as being very narcissistic, reckless, emotionally shallow as well as unable to empathize or feel compassion for others. For these individuals, the suffering of others does not touch them emotionally, so they have no compunction about hurting others.

soft targets Defenseless.

Southern Poverty Law Center Has published methods that have been successfully used by communities to combat hate groups.

spillover theory The theory that violence overlaps into different parts of someone's life. For example, some suggest the more society legitimates some kinds of violence, such as in war, capital punishment, and justifiable homicide, the more illegitimate violence, such as robbery and murder, there will be.

spoils of war Something seen as a soldier's right and privilege, such as looting and pillaging and rape.

Spouse Abuse Abatement Programs (SAAPs) An alternative to traditional criminal justice responses that were exclusively punitive.

Spouse Assault Replication Program Published findings of replications of the Minneapolis Domestic Violence Experiment study in six cities funded by the National Institute of Justice. Interestingly, the findings did not uniformly find that arrest was an effective deterrent in spouse assault cases.

spree murder Involves multiple victims at multiple locations with no emotional cooling-off period between the murders.

Srebrenica A town in Bosnia and Herzegovina where more than 8,000 Bosnia Muslims, mainly men and boys, were murdered in July 1995.

stalking According to the National Institute of Justice is a course of conduct directed at a specific person that involves repeated visual or physical proximity, nonconsensual communication, or verbal, written or implied threats, or a combination thereof, that would cause a reasonable person fear, with repeated meaning on two or more occasions.

state-supported terrorism Terrorism that is assisted by a government.

status Place in an hierarchy. Men may act out violently when competing with other men for the higher status or rank in a group.

stickups Name for typical street robberies involving individuals, also called *muggings*.

strain theories Theories that contend that blocked or frustrated needs and desires may result in criminality and violence.

stranger crime People dread most victimization by a stranger, though, with the exception of robbery, most violent crimes occur between people known to one another.

stress and violence Stress, such as that caused by economic deprivation, is related to behavior outcomes including violence.

structural violence Discriminatory social arrangements that can be construed as violent, such as societal inequalities. Examples might be a minority's access to education, health care, an adequate diet, and other necessities for survival and human development.

Student Right-to-Know and Campus Security Act of 1990 Legislation mandating that colleges and universities participating in federal student aid programs "prepare, publish, and distribute, through appropriate publications and mailings, to all current students and employees, and to any applicant for enrollment upon request, an annual security report."

subcultures of violence The idea that members of particular groups or subgroups are prone to violence because of values and beliefs imbedded in their cultures.

substate terrorism Designation Jerrold Post uses to indicate terrorism perpetrated by nongovernmental groups.

suicide bombing The weapon of choice for many modern terrorist organizations. All it takes is a willingness to die for a cause on the part of a young man or woman. There really is no technical training required. Often, explosives are placed in a backpack or satchel with a hand-operated detonator. Other times, they wear a special harness or vest that can easily be concealed under clothing and which distributes the explosives around the body. In either case, the terrorist simply needs to go to a public area, such as a park, restaurant, or bus, and detonate the device.

superpredators A type of violent offender popularized by criminologist John DiIulio. Radically impulsive, brutally remorseless youngsters, including preteenage boys, who murder, assault, rape, rob, burglarize, deal deadly drugs, join gun-toting gangs, and create serious communal disorder.

Supplementary Homicide Reports (SHR) Information about homicide victims and offenders, such as race, gender, and relationship, compiled by the FBI.

symbolic interactionism The idea that human behavior—including assaults and homicides—occurs in social situations, and that the meanings people attach to their behavior is an important element in understanding what takes place in a given circumstance.

Tamil Tigers Otherwise known as Tigers of Tamil Eelam. A Marxist separatist organization in Sri Lanka.

Taylor paradigm Measures aggression by the extent to which subjects give electric shocks to planted confederates (individuals pretending to be subjects themselves but who are really part of the experiment) for some incorrect answer on a given test or task.

territorial aggression Concerns animals that fight to control a piece of land they have marked or defined as their own.

terrorism Encompasses many different types of behavior perpetrated for many different reasons. It can include intimidation, assassinations, bombings, hijackings, theft, military-style attacks, kidnappings, and any number of other violent or threatening acts. May be the intersection of violence with political, racial, ethnic, racial and/or ideological purposes.

tertiary prevention Geared toward intervening in the lives of those who have been impacted by violence.

testosterone High levels of this hormone linked to aggression.

theory of moral disengagement When a person selectively disengages moral prohibitions against negative or destructive behavior in order to avoid seeing themselves as bad people.

thrill killers They derive pleasure from torturing, dominating, terrorizing, and humiliating their victims.

Tulsa Race Riot of 1921 Began after a young African American man named Diamond Dick Rowland stumbled into a white lady as he was entering an elevator and unwittingly grabbed her arm. The young lady assumed the worst and quickly claimed that he had assaulted her. Events escalated into some of the ugliest and most destructive racial violence this country has ever seen.

Tupac Amaru Revolutionary Movement A Peruvian terrorist organization.

Tutsi Rwandan minority. Nearly one million were murdered during the genocide in 1994.

Unabomber Ted Kaczynski, who sent homemade explosive devices to a variety of executives and scientists in his misguided campaign against technology. Before being captured by the FBI, he killed three individuals and wounded 29 others. His behavior was in all likelihood the result of mental illness.

Uniform Crime Reporting Program (UCR) The most widely used source of statistical information about violent crime in the United States.

United Nations An international organization founded in 1945 after WWII by 51 countries committed to maintaining international peace and security, developing friendly relations among nations, and promoting social progress, better living standards and human rights.

unity of human aggression All violence is connected by a web of actions and behaviors, ideas, perceptions, and justifications. While the individual dynamics of specific violent behavior may vary somewhat, violent acts share a number of essential characteristics that bind them together.

universe of obligation Feelings of segregation and marginalization that are heightened during wartime, when a government and population may feel under threat and therefore more inclined to scapegoat a group that can be blamed for the problems and misfortunes of the larger community.

U.S. Department of Education's Higher Education Center for Alocohol, Drug Abuse, and Violence Prevention A national resource center for institutions of higher education concerned with reducing alcohol, other drug use, and violence.

utopia Any vision of a perfect and unattainable society.

victim empowerment Means that victims' rights and wishes are factored into the process of administering justice.

victim precipitation The idea that victims start the conflict that ends in their own death.

vigilante groups Often planned and organized, one of three types of mob violence.

violence Aggressive and/or harmful physical behavior.

Violence Against Women Act Intended to improve criminal justice and community-based responses to intimate partner violence, dating violence, sexual assault, and stalking.

violence prevention suggests that schools adopt specific initiatives to reduce binge drinking on campuses, such as offer and promote social, recreation, extracurricular, and public service options that do not include alcohol and other drugs; create a social, academic, and residential environment that supports health-promoting norms; limit alcohol availability both on and off campus; restrict marketing and promotion of alcoholic beverages both on and off campus; and develop and enforce campus policies and local, state, and federal laws.

Violent Crime Control and Law Enforcement Act of 1994 Amended the Hate Crime Statistics Act to include both physical and mental disabilities.

violent perpetrators Those individuals who enjoy perpetrating violence. While clearly in the minority, some who participate in genocide can clearly be classified as sadistic or psychopathic.

visionary killers Perceive voices or images that command them to kill. This type of killer is rare because they suffer from some sort of psychosis.

Vulnerable Elder Rights Protection Act of 1992 Expanded the Older Americans Act to include mandates for the prevention of elder abuse, neglect, and exploitation.

Wahhabism A form of Islamic fundamentalist revivalist movement named after Muhammad ibn Abd al-Wahhab, an 18th century Arabian who preached a puritanical vision of Islam and influenced many generations of Muslims, including Osama bin Laden.

war crimes Defined by international law, it is often difficult to determine the classification of crimes because of overlap, but generally torture and medical experimentation are considered war crimes.

War on Drugs The primary strategy of this war has been to amplify the legal penalties for trafficking and possession of illicit drugs; consequently, our nation has taken many prisoners of war.

weapons of mass destruction Include nuclear, chemical, biological agents, and nuclear weapons.

whole-school approach A strategy that involves simultaneously working with families, bystanders, and the larger community as well as those perpetuating bullying.

Zealots A group of Jewish rebels who used assassination and terror to fight the Roman occupation.

xenophobia The tendency to have contempt for foreigners or other strangers.

About the Authors

Alex Alvarez earned his PhD in Sociology from the University of New Hampshire in 1991 and is a Professor in the Department of Criminal Justice at Northern Arizona University. From 2001 until 2003 he was the founding Director of the Martin-Springer Institute for Teaching the Holocaust, Tolerance, and Humanitarian Values. His main areas of study have been in the areas of minorities, crime, and criminal justice, and the areas of collective and interpersonal violence. He has published on Native Americans, Latinos, and African Americans, fear of crime, sentencing, as well as on justifiable and criminal homicide, and genocide. His scholarship has appeared in edited volumes and in a range of journals including *Social Science History, The Journal of Criminal Justice,* and *Sociological Imagination.* His first book, *Governments, Citizens, and Genocide* was published by Indiana University Press in 2001 and was a nominee for the Academy of Criminal Justice Sciences book of the year award in 2002, as well as a Raphael Lemkin book award nominee from the International Association of Genocide Scholars in 2003. His second book, *Murder American Style* was released in the summer of 2002. He has also served as an editor for the journal *Violence and Victims,* and is an editorial board member for the journals *War Crimes, Genocide, Crimes Against Humanity: An International Journal,* and *Idea: A Journal of Social Issues.* He has been invited to present his research in various countries such as Austria, Bosnia, Canada, Germany, and Sweden.

Ronet Bachman, PhD, is Professor in the Department of Sociology and Criminal Justice at the University of Delaware. She is coauthor of *Statistical Methods for Crime and Criminal Justice* (3rd ed.), and co-editor of *Explaining Crime and Criminology: Essays in Contemporary Criminal Theory.* In addition, she is author of *Death and Violence on the Reservation;* coauthor of *Stress, Culture, and Aggression in the United States;* and coauthor of *Murder American Style* as well as numerous articles and papers that examine the epidemiology and etiology of violence, with a particular emphasis on women, the elderly, and minority populations. She is currently the Co-PI of a National Institute of Justice–funded study to examine the trajectories of drug-involved offenders 10 years after release from prison using a mixed-method design.

Index

⑤SAGE research**methods**

The essential online tool for researchers from the world's leading methods publisher

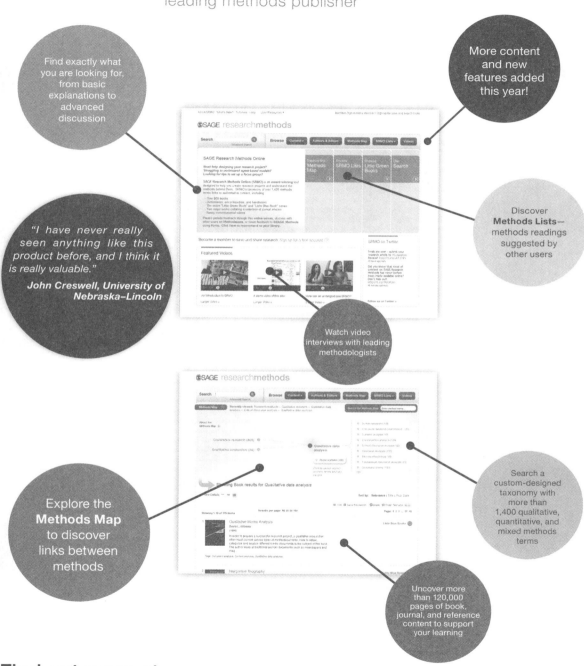

Find exactly what you are looking for, from basic explanations to advanced discussion

More content and new features added this year!

"I have never really seen anything like this product before, and I think it is really valuable."

John Creswell, University of Nebraska–Lincoln

Discover **Methods Lists**— methods readings suggested by other users

Watch video interviews with leading methodologists

Explore the **Methods Map** to discover links between methods

Search a custom-designed taxonomy with more than 1,400 qualitative, quantitative, and mixed methods terms

Uncover more than 120,000 pages of book, journal, and reference content to support your learning

Find out more at
www.sageresearchmethods.com